FIFTH EDITION

AMERICAN POLITICS AND THE AFRICAN AMERICAN QUEST FOR UNIVERSAL FREEDOM

Hanes Walton Jr.
University of Michigan

Robert C. Smith
San Francisco State University

Longman

New York • San Francisco • Boston
London • Toronto • Sydney • Tokyo • Singapore • Madrid
Mexico City • Munich • Paris • Cape Town • Hong Kong • Montreal

We are grateful to our families—Alice, Brandon and Brent and Scottie,
Blanch, Jessica and Scottus-Charles—for their endurance
and support during our years of work on this project.

Editor-in-Chief: Eric Stano
Executive Marketing Manager: Ann Stypuloski
Production Manager: Renata Butera
Project Coordination, Text Design, and Electronic Page Makeup: Shiji Sashi/Integra Software Services, Ltd.
Creative Director: Jayne Conte
Cover Designer: Margaret Kenselaar
Cover Illustration/Photo: President Barack Obama, courtesy of GurganusImages / Shutterstock, Inc; Rosa Parks, courtesy of Library of Congress; Martin Luther King, Jr. courtesy of Library of Congress; Malcolm X, courtesy of Library of Congress
Visual Researcher: Rona Tuccillo
Manufacturing Buyer: Renata Butera
Printer and Binder: R.R. Donnelley/Harrisonburg
Cover Printer: R.R. Donnelley/Harrisonburg
Manager, Rights and Permissions: Zina Arabia
Manager, Visual Research: Beth Brenzel
Manager, Cover Visual Research & Permissions: Karen Sanatar
Image Permission Coordinator: Nancy Seise

For permission to use copyrighted material, grateful acknowledgment is made to the copyright holders on pp. xvii, which are hereby made part of this copyright page.

Library of Congress Cataloging-in-Publication Data

Walton, Hanes
   American politics and the African American quest for universal freedom / Hanes Walton Jr.,
Robert C. Smith.—5th ed.
     p. cm.
Includes bibliographical references and index.
ISBN-13: 978-0-205-63836-9 (alk. paper)
ISBN-10: 0-205-63836-8 (alk. paper)
  1. African Americans—Politics and government. 2. United States—Politics and government.
3. United States—Race relations. I. Smith, Robert Charles, 1947– II. Title.
E185.615.W317 2010
323.1196'073—dc22

                                          2008052841

Visit us at www.pearsonhighered.com

  3 4 5 6 7 8 9 10—DOH—12 11

Longman
is an imprint of

PEARSON

www.pearsonhighered.com

ISBN-13: 978-0-205-63836-9
ISBN-10:   0-205-63836-8

Why Do You Need the New Edition of This Book?

Here are five reasons why the fifth edition of *American Politics and the African American Quest for Universal Freedom* will help you succeed in your course.

New focus on the Obama campaign. With the election of the first African-American president, no text on black politics would be complete without analysis of the historic presidential campaign and its effects on the country and the quest for universal freedom.

Revised and expanded chapters. Using the Obama primary and general election campaigns as case studies, this fifth edition includes a completely rewritten chapter on political parties and a substantially expanded chapter on voting behavior and elections.

A fresh look at race-gender relations. The 2008 Democratic primary race between Senators Hillary Clinton and Barack Obama brought race-gender tensions to the forefront of American politics, and this new edition discusses the issue in the context of the quest for universal freedom.

Updated examples. This new edition uses current examples that keep you up-to-date on the newest developments related to race in American politics, such as the Jena 6 protests and enforcement of civil rights laws.

New analysis of minority relations. Examine how the Obama campaign affected relationships between blacks, Latinos and Asian Americans in their quest for a rainbow coalition for universal freedom.

PEARSON

CONTENTS

PART II   POLITICAL BEHAVIORISM

Part IV   Institutions

APPENDIX

Overview of the Text

This book examines the institutions and processes of American government and politics from the perspective of the African American presence and influence. We want to show how the presence of Africans in the United States affected the founding of the Republic and its political institutions and processes from the colonial era to the present. Blacks, for example, took no part in the drafting of the Declaration of Independence or the design of the Constitution; however, their presence exerted a profound influence on the shaping of both these seminal documents. So it has been throughout American history.

In structure the book follows that of standard works in political science on American government and politics. It is unique, however, in three respects.

First, it is organized around two interrelated themes: the idea of universal freedom and the concept of minority–majority coalitions. In their quest for their own freedom in the United States, blacks have sought to universalize the idea of freedom. In their attack on slavery and racial subordination, black Americans and their leaders have embraced doctrines of universal freedom and equality. In doing so they have had an important influence on the shaping of democratic, constitutional government and on expanding or universalizing the idea of freedom not only for themselves but for all Americans.

But blacks have not acted alone. Indeed, given their status as a subordinate racial minority they could not act alone. Rather, in their quest for freedom blacks have sought to forge coalitions with whites—*minority-inspired majority coalitions.* Historically, however, because of the nation's ambivalence about race, these coalitions tend to be unstable and temporary, requiring that they be constantly rebuilt in what is an ongoing quest. These two themes, the quest for universal freedom and minority–majority coalitions, are pursued throughout much of the book.

The second distinctive aspect of this study is that it is historically informed. In each chapter we trace developments historically. Relevant historical background is critical to understanding the evolution of race and the American democracy. Such material also brings contemporary events into a sharper focus.

Third, in the political behavior chapters (3–6, 9–10), we try to provide students not only with the most current knowledge on the topics but also with information on how the discipline of political science has approached the study of the topics in general and with respect to blacks specifically. In several of these chapters we focus on Gunnar Myrdal and the powerful influence his *American Dilemma* has had on the study of black political behavior.

We first talked about writing this book more than a decade ago. Our principal rationale for writing it is that we saw a void in the available literature. We believe that race is the most important cleavage in American life, with enormous impact on the nation's society, culture, and politics. Indeed, as we show throughout this book, race has always been the enduring fault line in American society and politics—thus the need for a volume that treats this important topic with the seriousness it deserves. This is what we seek to accomplish in a study that has historical sweep and depth and is comprehensive in its coverage of the subject. Although this book is written so as to be readable and interesting to undergraduate students, we have sought to maintain the highest intellectual standards. We believe the study of the rich, varied, and critical presence of African Americans in *all* areas of the political system demands nothing less.

Before closing, we would like to say a word about the intellectual tradition on which this book is based. The scholars who are the founders and innovators in the study of African American politics created this scholarly subfield out of nothing. Working in small African American colleges, without major financial support or grants and with large numbers of classes and students, these scholars launched in small steps and limited ways a new area of academic study. They published in obscure and poorly diffused journals and little-known presses, which resulted, in many instances, in their work being overlooked and undervalued. Racism's manifestations in academia allowed much valuable work to remain unseen. Not only was the result of their research made invisible, but these scholars themselves became invisible in the profession. Of this unseen tradition it has been written:

> The second research tradition in America's life is the unheralded, the unsung, unrecorded but not unnoticed one. Scholars belonging to this tradition literally make something out of nothing and typically produce scholarship at the less recognized institutions of higher learning. These are the places, to use Professor Aaron Wildavsky's apt phrase, where the schools "habitually run out of stamps" and where other sources of support are nonexistent. . . . [Yet] here . . . scholars . . . nevertheless scaled the heights, and produced stellar scholarship.[1]

They persisted and persevered. And while their work is scattered and sometimes difficult to locate, it formed the basis for a new vision and perspective in political science. Beginning in 1885, the discipline of political science emerged during an era of concern about race relations and developed its study of race politics from this perspective. In essence, this race relations perspective on the study of African American politics focused on the concern of whites about stability and social peace rather than the concerns of blacks about freedom and social justice.[2]

By the 1960s this perspective had become the major consensus in the discipline on the study of race. It offered a different perspective on political reality from that of blacks, who during this period were trying to empower themselves in American politics. Thus African American political scientists offered a different perspective, a challenge to the consensus.[3] Instead of focusing on how the African American quest for freedom might distress whites and disrupt stability and social peace, this new perspective focused on how an oppressed group might achieve power so as to provide solutions to long-standing social and economic problems. This perspective deals with freedom and power rather than stability and social peace.

Our book is a part of this intellectual tradition. The purveyors of this tradition include Professors Robert Brisbane and Tobe Johnson of Morehouse College, the ever-erudite Samuel DuBois Cook at Atlanta University, and Professors Emmett Dorsey, Bernard Fall, Harold Gosnell, Ronald Walters, Robert Martin, Vincent Browne, Nathaniel Tillman, Brian Wienstein, Morris Levitt, and Charles Harris at Howard University. Their insightful ideas, cogent theories, and brilliant teaching made this book possible. When we sat down at the Holiday Inn in Jackson, Mississippi, in March 1991 (at the annual meeting of the National Conference of Black Political Scientists), to develop the theme for this book and lay out its goals and structure, we were standing on the shoulders of these pioneering political scientists. They built the intellectual foundation. We hope this work makes them proud. We hope it will do the same for our children.

Finally, a note on style. We use the terms *black* and *African American* interchangeably, having no preference for either and viewing each as a legitimate and accurate name for persons of African descent in the United States.[4]

Changes to the Fifth Edition

The basic purpose of a new edition of a textbook is to keep students current or up to date with developments in the area of study and to incorporate the latest research. The obvious major focus for this new edition is the Obama campaign for the presidency. Obvious because of its historical significance and because it is a wonderful case study in the major themes of this text: minority–majority coalitions in pursuit of universal freedom.

There are already dozens of theses, dissertations, articles, and books being written on the Obama campaign and in the years ahead there will be hundreds. But as we prepare this fifth edition, we are in the midst of the campaign and there are hardly any systematic, scientific studies available. In future editions we will draw on these studies as they become available. At this point we can only analyze the available data, mainly the exit polls and the election results.

Not only are there little systematic, scientific studies available, but the existing theories to explain the Obama phenomenon are likely inadequate. The major theoretical approach political scientists have used to explain the election of blacks in majority white constituencies is the deracialization theory developed by African American political scientists in 1989 to explain mainly the election of Douglass Wilder as the first African American governor of one of the American states (Virginia). While we will draw on this theory, a second explanatory framework is the theory of minority–majority coalitions and universal freedom, which we lay out in Chapter 8 and revisit in Chapters 9 and 10.

Chapter 9 on political parties has been completely rewritten and Chapter 10 on voting behavior and elections has been substantially expanded for this edition. These chapters were reworked in order to provide students with comprehensive, in-depth treatment of the Obama campaigns (primary and general) in the context of the text's historical and systemic understanding of the role of race in the American Party system.

In order to provide for continuity in study, Chapters 9 and 10 will incorporate material on all aspects of the Obama campaign. That is, rather than putting material on the media, political socialization, and political culture in separate chapters, they are interwoven in Chapters 9 and 10. This allows for a seamless narrative and a more complete understanding.

The 2008 presidential campaign was historic not just because an African American man won the Democratic nomination but also because a white woman was his leading competitor. Since its first edition, this text has focused on the unstable character of the coalition between feminists and blacks in the struggle for universal freedom, and the dilemmas confronting black women given their dual struggles against racism and sexism (see Chapters 6 and 7). We discuss race–gender tensions in the 2008 campaign in the context of our historical understanding of race–gender, minority–majority coalitions and universal freedom.

In a similar fashion, we look at what the Obama campaign reveals about the relationship between blacks, Latinos, and Asian Americans in their quest for a rainbow coalition for universal freedom.

The Obama campaign revealed tensions within the black community and its leadership, revolving around questions of racial identity and loyalties. Was Obama, the son of a Kenyan father and white Kansas mother and thus a real *African* American, black enough? Did African American leaders who supported Senator Clinton betray their "blackness"? In other words, were they black enough?

All of these issues and others are explored in Chapters 9 and 10 in an in-depth study of the Obama campaign as a case study in the historic effort of African Americans to build minority–majority coalitions in their long quest for universal freedom in the United States.

Although the Obama campaign is the main focus of this edition, there were other important developments related to race in American politics since the publication of the last edition. The "Jena 6" incident brought about a revival of 1960s-style protests, the Supreme Court continued its retreat in enforcement of civil rights law, and more states relaxed their laws disenfranchising felons.

As always, our aim in this new edition is to provide students with a comprehensive, rigorous, and accessible understanding of how the presence of Africans in the United States has profoundly influenced and influences American politics.

Acknowledgments

We are once again grateful to the anonymous reviewers of the previous editions for their criticisms and comments that led to improvements in this edition. Eric Stano at Longman was his usual steady hand, and Donna Garnier provided expert and timely assistance from the beginning to the completion of this edition, Suijan Guo, Smith's good colleague and friend at San Francisco State, went beyond the boundaries of collegiality and friendship in preparation of the website. We should also like to thank Shiji Sashi for her good and timely copy editing of the manuscript. Finally, kudos to Scottie.

In addition to our colleagues selected by Longman Publishers—Marion Orr, Brown University; Jeanette Mendez, University of Houston; and Sherri L. Wallace, University of Louisville—to read and comment on the manuscript, we are also grateful to Mack Jones of Clark-Atlanta University's political science department, Wilbur Rich of Wellesley's political science department, and Charles Henry of the African American studies department at the University of California, Berkeley, for reading the manuscript and their suggestions that led to its improvement. We are especially grateful to Professor Jones for his detailed chapter-by-chapter critique. Sekou Franklin provided research assistance for Professor Smith.

Margaret Mitchell Ilugbo typed several of the draft chapters for Walton, and Greta Blake designed the tables and figures for the book. We appreciate their fine work.

Scottie Smith's help was indispensable in the preparation of the manuscript. Her discerning and untiring work is deeply appreciated.

HANES WALTON JR.

ROBERT C. SMITH

Notes

1. Hanes Walton Jr., "The Preeminent African American Legal Scholar: J. Clay Smith," *National Political Science Review* 6 (1997): 289.
2. Hanes Walton Jr., Cheryl Miller, and Joseph P. McCormick, "Race and Political Science: The Dual Traditions of Race Relations Politics and African American Politics," in John Dryzek et al., eds., *Political Science and Its History: Research Programs and Political Traditions* (New York: Cambridge University Press, 1994): 145–74; and Hanes Walton, Jr., and Joseph P. McCormick, "The Study of African American Politics as Social Danger: Clues from the Disciplinary Journals," *National Political Science Review* 6 (1997): 229–44.
3. For an intellectually critical collection of essays by African American political scientists on race and the study of politics in the US see Wilbur Rich (ed.) *African American Perspectives on Political Science* (Philadelphia: Temple University Press, 2007).
4. For discussion of the various controversies about names in African American history—that is, what persons of African origins in the United States should call themselves—see W. E. B. Du Bois, "The Name Negro," *The Crisis* 35 (March 1928): 96–101; Lerone Bennett, "What's in a Name?" *Ebony,* November 1967; Ben L. Martin, "From Negro to Black to African-American: The Power of Names and Naming," *Political Science Quarterly* 106 (1991): 83–107; Robert C. Smith, "Remaining Old Realities," *San Francisco Review of Books* 25 (Summer 1990): 16–19; Ruth Grant and Marion Orr, "Language, Race and Politics: From 'Black' to 'African American,'" *Politics & Society* 24 (1996): 137–52; and Sterling Stuckey, *Slave Culture: Foundations of Nationalist Theory* (New York: Oxford University Press, 1987): chap. 4, "Identity and Ideology: The Names Controversy."

Credits

Photo Credits

Page 8: The White House Historical Association; page 23: Elliot Erwitt/Magnum Photos; page 35: AP Images; page 39: Bettmann/Corbis; page 51: Bettmann/Corbis; page 57: Bettmann/Corbis; page 59: The White House Press Office; page 79: Photograph by Isabel Wolseley from The Black Press, USA, 2nd edition by Roland E. Wolseley, 1990. Ames: Iowa State University Press/Blackwell Publishing. ISBN: 9780813804941; page 84: The Granger Collection; page 92 left: Getty Images; page 92 right: Frederick Douglass, 1818-1895. Unidentified photographer, after c. 1847. Daguerreotype, 8 x 6.9 cm. National Portrait Gallery, Smithsonian Institution. NPG.80.21/Art Resource, NY; page 100: The Schomburg Center/Art Resource, NY; page 106: The San Francisco Examiner/AP Images; page 119: AP Images; page 125: Eve Arnold/Magnum Photos; page 136: Bettmann/Corbis; page 137: Bettmann/Corbis; page 143: Landov Media; page 145: Getty Images; page 171: Landov Media; page 176: Landov Media; page 185: Pablo Martinez Monsivais/AP Images; page 197: Ric Feld/AP Images; page 207: Missouri Historical Society, Photographs and Prints Collection; page 214: Cecil Stoughton/LBJ Library Collection; page 231: Bettmann/Corbis; page 243: Collection of the Supreme Court of the United States; page 252: Gordon Parks/Getty Images; page 261: Michael Bryant/MCT/Newscom; page 269: Stephen Ferry/Getty Images; page 293: Scott Applewhite/AP Images; page 294: Jacques M. Chenet/Corbis; page 296: AP Images.

Text Credits

Page 307: Reprinted by arrangement with The Heirs to the Estate of Martin Luther King Jr., c/o Writer's House, Inc. as agent for the proprietor. Copyright © 1963 by Martin Luther King Jr. Copyright renewed 1991 by Coretta Scott King.

Universal Freedom Declared, Universal Freedom Denied

Racism, Slavery, and the Ideology of White Supremacy in the Founding of the Republic

So, what is this thing called freedom? In 1865 General Oliver O. Howard, commissioner of the Freedmen's Bureau, asked an audience of newly freed slaves, "But what did freedom mean? It is necessary to define it for it is apt to be misunderstood."[1] William Riker writes, "The word 'freedom' must be defined. And volumes have been written on this subject without conspicuous success on reaching agreement."[2] Orlando Patterson begins his book *Freedom in the Making of Western Culture* with the observation that "Freedom, like love and beauty, is one of those values better experienced than defined."[3] Finally, John Hope Franklin, in *From Slavery to Freedom: A History of Negro Americans*, writes,

> It must never be overlooked that the concept of freedom that emerged in the modern world bordered on licentiousness and created a situation that approached anarchy. As W. E. B. Du Bois has pointed out, it was the freedom to destroy freedom, the freedom of some to exploit the rights of others. It was, indeed, a concept of freedom with little or no social responsibility. If, then, a man was determined to be free, who was there to tell him that he was not entitled to enslave others.[4]

The idea of freedom is therefore a contested idea, with many often conflicting and contradictory meanings. Since the idea of freedom—universal freedom—is central to this book, in this first chapter we must attempt to define it because, as General Howard said, it is apt to be misunderstood.

In the last two decades an important body of scholarship has emerged on how the idea and practice of freedom began in Europe and the United States. These historical and philosophical studies suggest that the idea of freedom—paradoxically—is inextricably linked to the idea and institution of slavery.[5] With respect to Europe, "it now can be said with some confidence," according to Patterson, "that the idea and value of freedom was the direct product of the institution of slavery. Where there has been no slavery there has never been any trace of freedom even as a minor value."[6] And in the United States, "without the institution of slavery America in all likelihood would have had no democratic tradition and would not have come to enshrine freedom at the very top of the pantheon of values."[7] In other words, the very idea of freedom in the Western world has its origins in the struggles of the slave to become free.

While there is much of value in Patterson's studies, we are not persuaded by his argument that freedom in its origins is a uniquely Western value. On the contrary, we believe freedom is a fundamental, driving force of the human condition. And while slavery was undoubtedly important in the genesis of the idea of freedom in the Western world, it is also likely that the idea in the West stems from other sources such as the desire of people to be free of harsh rule, treatment, or prohibitions that fall short of slavery (freedom of religion, for example).

Freedom: A Typological Analysis

The word *freedom* is difficult to define. Indeed, a number of writers on the subject have concluded that the effort to construct an objective or universal definition may be futile. Increasingly, therefore, students of the subject have sought not to define the term in one all-encompassing definition but rather, given the rich, varied, and conflicting meanings of the word, have sought instead to develop typologies of freedom that are broad and varied enough to cover the diverse shades of meaning held by scholars as well as ordinary women and men.

Table 1.1 displays three typologies of freedom. These typologies are drawn from the most recent scholarship on the subject. Again, these writers do not attempt to develop one universal definition of the term but see freedom as having multiple shades of meaning. Patterson identifies three types of freedom. *Personal freedom* is defined as giving a person the sense that, on the one hand, he or she is not coerced or restrained by another person in doing something desired, and, on the other hand, that one can do as one pleases within the limits of that other person's desire to do the same. *Sovereignal* or *organic* freedom is simply the power to act as one pleases, without regard for others, or simply the ability to impose one's will on another. *Civic freedom* is defined as the capacity of adult members of a community to participate in its life and governance.[8]

Table 1.1 Typologies of Freedom

PATTERSON	FONER	KING
Personal	Natural[a]	Liberal
Sovereignal[b]	Civil	Autonomy
Civic	Political	Participatory
	Social	Collective Deliverance

[a]Foner uses the term *rights* rather than *freedoms*.

[b]In his article Patterson uses the term *organic* instead of *sovereignal* to refer to this type of freedom.

Sources: Orlando Patterson, *Freedom in the Making of Western Culture* (New York: Basic Books, 1991): 3–5; Orlando Patterson, "The Unholy Trinity: Freedom, Slavery and the American Constitution," *Social Research* 54 (Autumn 1987): 556–59; Eric Foner, *Reconstruction: America's Unfinished Revolution, 1863–1877* (New York: Harper & Row, 1988): 231; Richard King, *Civil Rights and the Idea of Freedom* (New York: Oxford University Press, 1992): 26–28.

Eric Foner discusses four notions of freedom—he prefers the term *rights*—that were part of the political vocabulary of the nation's leaders on the eve of the Civil War. *Natural rights*, those rights or freedoms inherent in one's humanity, are what Jefferson in the Declaration of Independence referred to as life, liberty, and the pursuit of happiness. *Civil rights* can be defined as equality of treatment under law, which is seen as essential to the protection of natural rights. *Political rights* involve the right to vote and participate fully in governing the community. *Social rights* involve the right to freely choose personal and business associates.[9]

King identifies "four meanings of freedom within American/western thought that link up with the language of freedom and the goals of the civil rights movement."[10] *Liberal freedom* is the absence of arbitrary legal or institutional restrictions on the individual, including the idea that all citizens are to be treated equally. *Freedom as autonomy* involves an internalized individual state of autonomy, self-determination, pride, and self-respect. *Participatory freedom* involves the right of the individual to participate fully in the political process. *Collective deliverance* is understood as the liberation of a group from external control—from captivity, slavery, or oppression.[11]

Clearly, there is considerable overlap among the types of freedom addressed by Patterson, Foner, and King, especially in the realm of politics or the right of citizens to equal treatment under law and the right to vote and participate in the governance of the community. However, two of the types identified have special relevance to the African American experience and to this book's theme of universal freedom. First, throughout their history in the United States, African Americans have consistently rejected the idea of organic or sovereignal freedom, the notion that one person or group should have the freedom to impose their will on another without regard to the rights of others. This is the freedom of might makes right, of the strong to oppress the weak, of the powerful to dominate the powerless, of the slavemaster to enslave. From its beginning, African American political thought and behavior has been centrally concerned with the abolition of this type of freedom, and in doing so African Americans developed the idea of universal freedom—a freedom that encompasses natural rights, civil rights, and social rights. In rejecting the Patterson notion of sovereignal freedom, blacks in the United States fully embraced King's idea of freedom as collective deliverance. As part of a captive, oppressed, enslaved people, one could expect nothing less. However, in fighting for their own liberation, for their freedom, blacks have had to fight for universal freedom, for the freedom of all people. As Aptheker puts it, "The Negro people have fought like tigers for their freedom, and in doing so have enhanced the freedom struggles of all people."[12]

Freedom, Power, and Politics

All the typologies of freedom listed in Table 1.1 are related in one way or another to power or the lack of power, and power is central to politics and political science. As Lasswell and Kaplan write in their classic study *Power and Society*, "The concept of power is perhaps the most fundamental in the whole of political science: The political process is the shaping, distribution and exercise of power."[13] The definition of power, like freedom, however, also has an ambiguous, elusive quality.[14] At a minimum, scholars agree that A has power over B to the extent that A can affect B's behavior or get B to do something

B otherwise would not do. Max Weber, one of the founders of modern sociology and political science, writes, "In general, we understand by 'power' the chance of a man or a number of men to realize their own will in a communal action against the resistance of others who are participating in the action."[15] Political scientists generally analyze power in terms of (1) its bases, (2) its exercise, and (3) the skill of its exercise in particular circumstances, situations, or contexts. With respect to African American politics, Jones writes that it is "essentially a power struggle between blacks and whites, with the latter trying to maintain their superordinate position vis-à-vis the former."[16] In analyzing African American politics as a quest for universal freedom we need to think in terms of blacks seeking to alter their subordinate status vis-à-vis whites in American society, and the bases of power they have and may choose to use, skillfully or not, in the power struggle, during any given time, place, and context.

Thomas Jefferson and the Writing of the Declaration

After voting to declare independence, the Continental Congress appointed a committee to draft a document setting forth the reasons for the revolution. The committee was composed of Robert Livingston, Roger Sherman, Benjamin Franklin, John Adams, and Thomas Jefferson. The other members turned the task of drafting to Adams and Jefferson, and according to Adams, Jefferson was asked to actually write the document because his writings were characterized by a "peculiar felicitousness of expression."[17] The Declaration, however, is not the creation of one man. Rather, "eighty-six substantive revisions were made in Jefferson's draft, most of them by members of the Continental Congress who also excised about one fourth of the original text."[18] Jefferson was said to be extremely displeased by the changes in his draft and for the remaining 50 years of his life was angry, arguing that the Congress had "mangled" his manuscript.[19]

The majority of the substantive changes or deletions in Jefferson's draft—including the most famous—focused on the long list of charges against King George III. Most historians say that the charges against the King as listed in the Declaration are exaggerated, and in any event they are misplaced since many of the actions complained of were decisions of the Parliament rather than the King. The King, however, made a more convenient target than the anonymous, amorphous Parliament.

The most famous of the changes deleted from Jefferson's draft was the condemnation of the King for engaging in the African slave trade. Jefferson had written:

> He has waged cruel war against human nature itself, violating the most sacred rights of life and liberty in the persons of a distant people who never offended him, captivating and carrying them into slavery in another hemisphere, or to incur miserable death in their transportation thither. This piratical warfare, the opprobrium of infidel powers, is the warfare of the Christian King of Great Britain. Determined to keep open a market when MEN should be bought and sold, he has prostituted his negative for suppressing every legislative attempt to prohibit or restrain this execrable commerce; and this assemblage of horrors might want no fact of distinguished die, he is now exciting these very people to rise among us, and to purchase that liberty of which he deprived them, by murdering the people upon whom he also obtruded them, thus paying off former crimes committed against the liberties of one people, with crimes which he urges them to commit against the lives of others.[20]

This passage, which was to be the climax of the charges against the King, was obviously an exaggeration and an especially disingenuous one; the colonists themselves (including Jefferson) had enthusiastically engaged in slave trading and, as was made clear to Jefferson, had no intention of abandoning it after independence. Jefferson recalls that "the clause too, reprobating the enslaving of the inhabitants of Africa, was struck out in compliance to South Carolina and Georgia, who had never attempted to restrain the importation of slaves and who still wished to continue it."[21] Not only was there opposition to the passage from the southern slave owners, but more tellingly, as Jefferson went on to say, "our northern brethren also I believe felt a little tender under these censures; for tho' their people have few slaves themselves yet they have been pretty considerable carriers of them."[22] In other words, virtually all the leading white men in America, Northerner and Southerner, slave owner and non-slave owner, had economic interests in the perpetuation of slavery. A good part of the new nation's wealth and prosperity was based on the plantation economy. To be consistent, one might have thought that the Continental Congress would also have deleted the phrase on the equality of men and their inherent right to liberty. They did not, apparently seeing no inconsistency since the words did not mean what they said (see Box 1.1 on p. x).

The magnificent words of the Declaration of Independence declaring freedom and equality as universal rights of all "men" were, however, fatally flawed, compromised in that the men who wrote them denied freedom to almost one-fourth of the men in America. To understand how the idea of universal freedom was fundamentally compromised, one needs to see Thomas Jefferson as the paradigmatic figure: author of the Declaration, preeminent intellectual, acquaintance through correspondence of eminent African American intellectual Benjamin Banneker—and also a racist, a white supremacist, and a slave owner.[23]

Racism and White Supremacy Defined

We have described Jefferson—one of the great men of American history and one of the most enlightened men of his day—as a racist and white supremacist; therefore, we should define these terms since they are key distinguishing features of the African American experience in the United States.[24] They are also central to the analysis presented throughout this book. Racism and the ideology of white supremacy are fundamental to an understanding of certain crucial features in the development of the American democracy as well as the different treatment of black and white Americans.

Racism as a scientific concept is not an easy one for the social scientist. It is difficult to define with precision and objectivity; also, the word is often used indiscriminately and in an inflammatory way. We start by distinguishing between racism and the set of ideas used in the United States to justify it. The latter we refer to as the ideology of white supremacy or black inferiority. In the United States, racism was and to some extent still is justified on the basis of the institutionalized belief that Africans are inherently an inferior people. We refer to an individual who holds such beliefs as a *white supremacist*.

By racism we mean, following the definition of Carmichael and Hamilton in *Black Power*, "the predication of decisions and policies on considerations of race for the purpose of subordinating a racial group and maintaining control over it."[25] The definition says nothing about why this is done, about racism's purposes or rationales; thus it does not imply anything about superiority or inferiority of the groups involved. It does not say,

BOX 1.1 LIKE HUMPTY DUMPTY TOLD ALICE, "WHEN I USE A WORD IT MEANS WHAT I SAY IT MEANS"

Before the ink was dry on Jefferson's Declaration, there was controversy about what was meant by the words "all men are created equal." Rufus Choate, speaking in 1776 for Southerners embarrassed by Jefferson's words, said Jefferson did not mean what he said. Rather, the word *men* referred only to nobles and Englishmen who were no better than ordinary American freemen. "If he meant more," Choate said, it was because Jefferson was "unduly influenced by the French school of thought."[a] (Jefferson was frequently accused of being influenced by Jean Jacques Rousseau's writings, a charge that he denied.) On the eve of the Civil War, Chief Justice Roger B. Taney, in his opinion in the *Dred Scott* (1857) case, said that on the surface the words "all men are created equal" applied to blacks. Yet he concluded, "It is too clear for dispute that the enslaved African race were not intended to be included, and formed no part of the people who framed and adopted the Declaration." Similarly, during his famous debates with Abraham Lincoln, Stephen Douglas argued that the phrase simply meant that Americans were not inferior to Englishmen as citizens. It was Lincoln's genius at Gettysburg in his famous address to fundamentally repudiate Choate, Taney, and Douglas in what Garry Wills calls an "audacious" and "clever assault." Lincoln accomplished this by claiming that the Civil War had given rise to a "new birth of freedom" that had been conceived by Jefferson "four score and seven years ago" when he wrote the Declaration.[b] Conservative scholars have long attacked Lincoln's "radical" redefinition of the meaning of the Declaration. Wilmore Kendal, writing a century after Gettysburg, argued that the word *men* in the Declaration referred to property holders or to the nations of the world but not men as such, writing blatantly that "the Declaration of Independence does not commit us to equality as a national goal."[c] As Daniel Boorstin, the former librarian of Congress and author of the celebrated *The Americans: The Democratic Experience* (New York: Vintage Books, 1974), writes, "We have repeated that 'all men are created equal' without daring to discover what it meant and without realizing that probably to none of the men who spoke it did it mean what we would like it to mean."[d]

[a]Quoted in Carl Becker, *The Declaration of Independence: A Study in the History of an Idea* (New York: Vintage Books, 1922, 1970): 27.

[b]Garry Wills, *Lincoln at Gettysburg: The Words That Remade America* (New York: Touchstone, 1992).

[c]Wilmore Kendal, *Basic Symbols of the American Political Tradition* (Baton Rouge: Louisiana State University Press, 1970), as cited in M. E. Bradford, "How to Read the Declaration of Independence: Reconsidering the Kendal Thesis," *The Intercollegiate Review* (Fall 1992): 47.

[d]Ibid., p. 46.

as many definitions and concepts of racism do, that racism involves the belief in the superiority, inherent or otherwise, of a particular group and that on this basis policies are implemented to subordinate and control it. Rather, the definition simply indicates that whenever one observes policies that have the intent or effect of subordinating a racial group, the phenomenon is properly identified as *racism*, whatever, if any, the justificatory ideology may be.

Carmichael and Hamilton's definition is particularly useful to political scientists because it focuses on power as an integral aspect of the phenomenon. For racism to exist, one racial group (or individual) must have the relative power—the capacity to impose its will in terms of policies—over another relatively less powerful group or individual. Without this relative power relationship, racism is a mere sentiment: Although group A may wish to subordinate group B, if it lacks the effective power to do so, the desire remains simply a wish.

Carmichael and Hamilton also write that racism may take two forms: individual and institutional.[26] Individual racism occurs when one person takes into consideration the race of another to subordinate, control, or otherwise discriminate against an individual; institutional racism exists when the normal and accepted patterns and practices of a society's institutions have the *effect* or *consequence* of subordinating or discriminating against an individual or group on the basis of race.[27]

It is in this sense that we refer to Thomas Jefferson as a white supremacist and a racist. He believed that blacks were inherently inferior to whites, stating in his *Notes on Virginia* that they were "inferior by nature, not condition" (see Box 1.2). He was also a racist, individually and institutionally, in that he took the race of individual blacks into consideration so as to discriminate against them, and he supported, although ambivalently, the institution of slavery that subordinated blacks as a group.

Philosophy, Politics, and Interest in Constitution Formation

The framers of the Constitution were influenced in their work by their readings in philosophy and history. But the framers were also practical politicians and men of affairs, and, as in all politics, they were men with distinct interests. In what is generally a sympathetic portrayal of the framers, historian William Freehling writes, "If the Founding Fathers unquestionably dreamed of universal freedom, their ideological posture was weighed down equally with conceptions of priorities, profits, and prejudices that would long make the dream utopian."[28] The first or principal priority of the framers was the formation and preservation of the union of the United States. This priority was thought indispensable to the priority of profit—that is, to the economic and commercial success of the nation. And as Freehling notes, their concern with profits grew out of their preoccupation with property, and slaves as property were crucial; thus, "it made the slaves' right to freedom no more 'natural' than the master's right to property."[29] It was this crucial nexus between profits, property, and slavery that led the men at Philadelphia to turn the idea of universal freedom into a utopian dream.

African Americans in the Constitution

As far as we can tell from the records of the federal convention, slavery was not the subject of much debate at that gathering. Certainly its morality was never at issue, although there were several passionate opponents of slavery present, including the venerable Benjamin Franklin, president of the Pennsylvania Society for Promoting the Abolition of Slavery. But neither Franklin nor any other delegate proposed abolition at Philadelphia, knowing that to do so would destroy any possibility of union. Hence, slavery was simply just another of the issues (such as how the small and large states were to be represented in the Congress) that had to be compromised to accomplish the objective of forming the union.

BOX 1.2   THOMAS JEFFERSON'S *NOTES ON VIRGINIA* AND THE IDEA OF THE INFERIORITY OF THE AFRICAN PEOPLE

In the Declaration of Independence, Jefferson engaged in a kind of moral reasoning to reach his conclusions as to the self-evident equality of men. In his *Notes on Virginia* written several years later, he engaged in a more scientific approach to the analysis of the problem of racial inequality.[a] In doing so, Jefferson the slave-holder made an eloquent condemnation of slavery, proposing his view of a just and equitable way to end slavery in the United States while simultaneously offering what he took to be scientific proof of the inferiority of the African people. Understanding Jefferson's views on race is therefore critical to an appreciation of how racism fundamentally compromised the idea of universal freedom at the very creation of the American Republic.[b]

Thomas Jefferson is the embodiment of the contradiction in the American democracy between its declaration of universal freedom and equality and its practice of slavery. *Source:* The White House Historical Association

In 1780 Francois Barbe-Marbois, the secretary of the French delegation in Philadelphia, sent a letter to each of the state governors requesting that they answer questions on particular customs and conditions in their states. Jefferson delayed his response until after he left the governor's office. Although Jefferson offered a general assessment of conditions in the state, his *Notes* are best known for what he said about slavery, the African people, and Virginia society.

While defending the institution of slavery Jefferson nevertheless saw it as evil and unjust, writing, "There must doubtless be an unhappy influence on the manners of our people produced by the existence of slavery among us. The whole commerce between master and slave is perpetual exercise of the most boisterous passions, the most unremitting despotism on the one part, and degrading submission on the other."[c] In a famous passage that would be echoed by Abraham Lincoln during the Civil War, Jefferson suggested that God would surely punish America: "Indeed, I tremble for my country when I reflect that God is just; that his justice cannot sleep forever. . . . The almighty has no attribute which can take side with us in such a contest."[d]

Since slavery was an evil, but a necessary one given the need for labor in the plantation economy, Jefferson proposed a revision in Virginia law that would gradually free the slaves;

(continued)

BOX 1.2 *continued*

train them; provide tools, seeds, and animals; and then transport them to a new land as a "free and independent people" while simultaneously sending ships "to other parts of the world for an equal number of white inhabitants" to replace them.[e]

Jefferson anticipated that the inevitable question would be why not simply free the slaves and integrate them into Virginia society, thereby saving the money involved in colonialization of the slaves and the transportation of the whites. His response was first that "deep rooted prejudices entertained by whites, ten thousand recollections by the blacks of injuries they have sustained, the real distinctions which nature has made and many other circumstances" made impossible the integration of the black and white populations on the basis of freedom and equality.[f] Indeed, Jefferson believed that if the races were not separated, "convulsions" would occur, probably ending in the "extermination of one or the other race."[g]

Jefferson was not satisfied to base his argument for racial separation on these essentially practical arguments. Rather, he wanted to be "scientific," to base his conclusions on the "facts," on his "empirical observations." Thus, in the *Notes* he advocated what was one of the first of many "scientific proofs" of black inferiority as justification for black subordination. First, he argued that blacks compared to whites were less beautiful, had a "strong and disagreeable odor," and were more "ardent after their female." Ultimately, however, for Jefferson the basis of black inferiority was his "suspicion" that blacks were "inferior in faculties of reason and imagination."[h] Noting that the differences he observed between blacks and whites might be explained by the different conditions under which they lived, Jefferson rejected this explanation, concluding it was not their "condition" but their "nature" that produced the difference.[i]

[a] This distinction between Jefferson's moral reasoning in the Declaration and his scientific approach in the *Notes* is the central theme of Jean Yarbrough, "Race and the Moral Foundation of the American Republic: Another Look at the Declaration and the Notes on Virginia," *Journal of Politics* 53 (February 1991): 90–105. Yarbrough argues that "the self-evident truths of the Declaration rest on a kind of moral reasoning which is morally superior to and incompatible with the so called scientific approach Jefferson adopts in the *Notes*" (p. 90).

[b] A comprehensive treatment of Jefferson's views on race is in Winthrop Jordan, *White over Black: American Attitudes Toward the Negro, 1550–1812* (Baltimore: Penguin Books, 1969): chap. 12, "Thomas Jefferson: Self and Society."

[c] Thomas Jefferson, *Notes on the State of Virginia*, edited by William Peden (Chapel Hill: University of North Carolina Press, 1954): 162–63.

[d] Ibid.

[e] Ibid., pp. 138–39.

[f] Ibid., p. 138. This was also the view of Abraham Lincoln (see chap. 14). In *Democracy in America* (New York: Knopf, 1945)—probably the single most important and influential book ever written on the subject—Alexis de Tocqueville also reached the same pessimistic conclusion that blacks and whites could not live together on the basis of freedom and equality. Tocqueville thought that whites would either subjugate the blacks or exterminate them. See *Democracy in America*, vol. 1, edited by Phillips Bradley (New York: Vintage Books, 1945): chap. 18.

[g] *Notes on the State of Virginia*, pp. 138–39.

[h] Ibid.

[i] Ibid.

Slavery is dealt with explicitly in four places in the Constitution, although the words *slave* and *slavery* are never used. It was James Madison, generally considered the "Father of the Constitution," who insisted that all explicit references to slavery be excluded.[30] It is worth noting, as Joe R. Feagin does, that while the Constitution's racist provisions relating to slavery have been overridden by amendments, they have not been deleted. This is because, as Feagin writes, "At no point has a new Constitutional Convention been held to replace this document with one created by representatives of all the people, including the great majority of the population not represented at the 1787 Convention."[31]

The Three-Fifths Clause, the Slave Power, and the Degradation of the American Democracy

Before the Sixteenth Amendment was adopted (permitting Congress to tax income directly), Congress could impose and collect taxes only on the basis of a state's population. The larger a state's population, the greater its tax burden. For this reason the southern states insisted that the slaves not be counted, as, like horses and cows, they were property. However, for purposes of representation in the House (where each state is allocated seats on the basis of the size of its population), the South wished to count the slaves as persons, although they of course could not vote. This would enhance the South's power not only in the House but also in choosing the president, since the number of votes a state may cast for president in the electoral college is equal to the total of its representation in the House and Senate. The northern states, on the other hand, wished to count the slaves for purposes of taxation but not representation. Hence, the great compromise—the Three-Fifths Clause. In Article I, Section 2, paragraph 3:

> Representatives and direct taxes shall be apportioned among the several states that may be included within this union, according to their respective numbers which shall be determined by adding to the whole number of free persons, including those bound to service for a Term of years and excluding Indians not taxed, three fifths of all other persons.

In attempting to justify or explain this compromise, Madison (in *The Federalist Papers No. 54*) disingenuously puts his words in the mouth of a fictional Southerner:

> The Federal Constitution, therefore, decides with great propriety on the case of our slaves, when it views them in the mixed character of persons and property. . . . Let the slaves be considered, as it is in truth a peculiar one. Let the compromising expedient of the Constitution be mutually adopted which regards them as inhabitants, but as debased by servitude below the equal level of free inhabitants; which regards the slave as divested as of two fifths of the man.[32]

But as Professor Donald Robinson so astutely observes,

> It bears repeating . . . that Madison's formula did not make blacks three-fifths of a human being. It was much worse than that. It gave slave owners a bonus in representation for their human property, while doing nothing for the status of blacks as nonpersons under the law.[33]

For the first time in this textbook we are able to precisely and comprehensively document the extent of this bonus overtime with the specific number and percentage

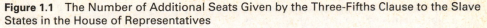

Figure 1.1 The Number of Additional Seats Given by the Three-Fifths Clause to the Slave States in the House of Representatives

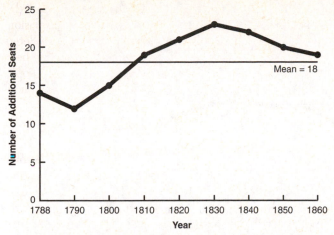

Sources: The population estimates used by the 1787 Constitutional Convention to apportion the first House of Representatives were taken from Merrill Jensen and Robert Becker, eds., *The Documentary History of the First Federal Elections 1788–1790* (Madison: University of Wisconsin Press, 1976): xxiv. The apportionment ratio and seats for each decade from 1790 to 1860 were taken from Department of Commerce, *Congressional District Data Book* 93rd Congress (Washington, DC: Government Printing Office, 1973): Appendix A, 548. Data on the African American slave and free population for 1790–1915 were taken from Department of Commerce, *Negro Population 1790–1915* (Washington, DC: Government Printing Office, 1918): 57. Data on the African American and white populations in each state from 1790 to 1860 were taken from Department of Commerce, *Negroes in the United States 1920–1932* (Washington, DC: Government Printing Office, 1935): 10–11. Calculations for each seat or fraction of a seat for each decade were done by the authors.

of House seats provided by the Three-Fifths Clause to the slaveholding states. In Figures 1.1 and 1.2 we see the number and percentage of additional House seats gained by southern and border states as a consequence of the clause. In the first congressional election in 1788, five states (Georgia, Maryland, North Carolina, South Carolina, and Virginia) gained 14 seats or a bonus of 48 percent, allowing them to reach near parity in the number of House seats (47–53) with the eight larger northern states. This bonus in numbers increased until 1830 and in percentages until 1860, when the numbers began to decline somewhat. Over the nine censuses and reapportionments of House seats from 1778 until 1860 (the Clause was abolished during the 1860s as a result of the Civil War), the mean or average bonus percentage of seats was 25.

Similarly, Figure 1.3 shows the percentage of additional electoral votes going to the slave states as a result of the Three-Fifths Clause, ranging from a low of 8 percent in 1792 to a high of 19 percent in most presidential elections between 1788 and 1860 (the mean over these 19 elections was a 17 percent bonus). This helped the southern states to elect four of the first five presidents.

This is the essence of the slave power and how it degraded the American democracy even among white men. It gave, for example, a white man in Virginia who owned a hundred slaves the equivalent of 60 votes compared to a Pennsylvania white man who owned no slaves having 1 vote.

The slave power was so pervasive and corrupting that Timothy Pickering, George Washington, and John Adams's secretary of state coined the term "Negro President"

Figure 1.2   The Percentage of Additional Seats Given by the Three-Fifths Clause to the Slave States in the House of Representatives

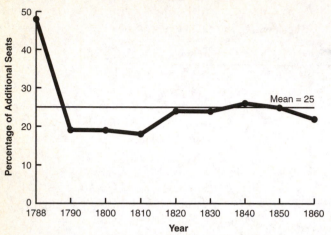

Sources: The population estimates used by the 1787 Constitutional Convention to apportion the first House of Representatives were taken from Merrill Jensen and Robert Becker, eds., *The Documentary History of the First Federal Elections 1788–1790* (Madison: University of Wisconsin Press, 1976): xxiv. The apportionment ratio and seats for each decade from 1790 to 1860 were taken from Department of Commerce, *Congressional District Data Book* 93rd Congress (Washington, DC: Government Printing Office, 1973): Appendix A, 548. Data on the African American slave and free population for 1790 to 1915 were taken from Department of Commerce, *Negro Population 1790–1915* (Washington, DC: Government Printing Office, 1918): 57. Data on the African American and white populations in each state from 1790 to 1860 were taken from Department of Commerce, *Negroes in the United States 1920–1932* (Washington, DC: Government Printing Office, 1935): 10–11. Calculations for each seat or fraction of a seat for each decade were done by the authors.

Figure 1.3   The Percentage of Additional Electoral Votes Given by the Three-Fifths Clause to the Slave States in Presidential Elections

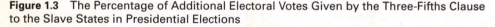

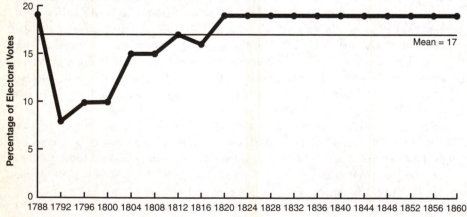

Sources: The total number of additional House of Representatives seats for each state in the slave bloc were taken from the analyses derived to develop the summary for Figure 1.1 and treated as additional electoral votes for that state. The total number of electoral votes for each state that were advantaged by the Three-Fifths Clause were taken from Congressional Quarterly's *Guide to U.S. Elections*, 4th ed., vol. 1 (Washington, DC: Congressional Quarterly, 2001): 817–36. Calculations were prepared by the authors.

and "Negro Congressmen" to refer to those presidents and members of Congress elected on the basis of the three-fifths bonus.[34] Not only did this slave power elect "Negro Presidents" and "Negro Congressmen," it also resulted in "Negros" serving as speakers of the House, and chairs of the Ways and Means Committee (79 and 92 percent of the time, respectively, until 1824), then and now the most powerful House committee.[35]

The Three-Fifths Clause was effectively repealed with the adoption of the Thirteenth Amendment. Ironically, however, this resulted in an increase in the power of southern racists and white supremacists. This is because the emancipated slaves were now counted as whole persons, but from the 1870s to the 1970s most of these whole black persons were denied the right to vote. The authors of the Fourteenth Amendment had anticipated that the former slave owners would attempt to deny the vote to blacks. Therefore, they included in it a provision (Section 2) providing that those states that deprived blacks (actually black men) of the right to vote would be deprived of the proportionate number of seats in the House. But this provision was never enforced.[36] So, in effect the slave power of the seventeenth and eighteenth centuries became the segregation power of the nineteenth and twentieth centuries. Whether slave power or segregation, however, it continued to degrade the democracy and deny African Americans universal freedom.

BOX 1.3   SLAVERY AND THE ELECTORAL COLLEGE

The electoral college is the mechanism used to elect the president of the United States. In the American democracy a person is elected president not on the basis of winning a majority of the votes of the people, but rather on the basis of winning a majority of votes in the electoral college. The electoral college is actually 51 electoral colleges representing the states and the District of Columbia. Each state is granted as many electoral college votes as it has members of Congress, which means that each state and the District of Columbia has at least three electors (based on two senators and a minimum of one member of the House). In all states except Maine and Nebraska the electoral college votes are based on the principle of winner take all. The candidate who wins most of the votes of the people (even if this is less than a majority in a multicandidate race) receives all the state's electoral votes. Thus, a hypothetical candidate running in California who receives 39 percent of the vote in a four-person race would receive 100 percent of the state's 55 electoral votes. This system of choosing the president means that a loser can become the winner. That is—as in the 2000 election of George W. Bush—a person can lose a majority of the votes of the people but nevertheless become president by winning a majority of the electoral votes. This undemocratic system of choosing the president is rooted partly in slavery and was part of several compromises the framers of the Constitution made to accommodate the interests of slaveholders, which undermined the interests of blacks and compromised the principle of democracy.

The framers of the Constitution confronted three alternatives in considering how the president might be elected. The first was election by the Congress. This alternative was rejected

(continued)

BOX 1.3 *continued*

because it violates the principle of the separation of powers. The second alternative was election by the legislatures of the states. It was rejected because it would have violated the principle of an independent federal government. The last—and most obvious and most democratic—method was election by the people. This alternative was rejected because some of the framers said the people would not be educated or informed enough to make a good choice. However, election by the people would also have disadvantaged the slaveholding southern states. James Madison, who at first favored election by the people, changed his mind in favor of the electoral college because he said election by the people would disadvantage the South since their slaves could not vote. The electoral college compromise did not disadvantage the southern states; it gave them a bonus by allowing them to count their slaves in determining electoral votes on the basis of the Three-Fifths Clause used to allocate seats in the House of Representatives. In its earliest years of operation the electoral college did work to the advantage of the South, as four of the first five presidents elected in the first 30 years were slave owners from Virginia.

The electoral college also represented other compromises that undermined democratic principles. While it gave the states with the largest population the larger share of electoral votes, it gave the smaller states a two-seat bonus based on their senators. It left the manner of choosing the electors up to the states except that they were prohibited from holding any federal office (including being members of Congress) and from meeting together as a group (the electors meet separately on the same day in each state's capital). The electors may be chosen in any manner a state's legislature determines—by the legislature itself, by appointment of the governor, or by the voters. (It was not until the 1840s that all states allowed the people to choose the electors in direct elections.) Once selected, the electors are free to vote for anyone they wish (as long as the person meets the constitutional qualifications of age, native-born citizenship, and residency), even if the person did not run in the first place. The states are also free to determine the allocation of the electoral votes—whether winner take all on a statewide basis or proportionally by congressional districts.

Four times the electoral college has resulted in a loser becoming the winner. In 1828 Andrew Jackson won most of the votes of the people and most (but not a majority) of the electoral college votes in a four-man race, but lost the presidency to John Q. Adams. In 1876 Samuel J. Tilden won the popular vote majority but in the so-called "Compromise of 1877" Rutherford B. Hayes won by a one-vote margin in the electoral college. In 1888 Grover Cleveland narrowly won the popular vote but Benjamin Harrison won the electoral college by a large margin. In 2000, Albert Gore won the election by a margin of a half million votes but lost the electoral college by a one-vote margin to George W. Bush. As three ironies of history, the elections of 1876, 1888, and 2000 all involved allegations of suppression of the black vote in Florida and other southern states.

Although the electoral college is partly rooted in slavery, it is unclear whether its abolition in favor of choice by direct vote of the people would advantage or disadvantage African Americans in presidential elections. Although the small states where few blacks live have a bonus in the electoral college, it is the large states of the Northeast and Midwest that decide presidential elections. African Americans are disproportionately represented in these states. Therefore, in close elections African Americans can sometimes constitute the balance of power in determining the winner.

The other clauses dealing explicitly with slavery include Article I, Section 9, paragraph 1, prohibiting Congress from stopping the slave trade before 1808 and limiting any tax on imported slaves to ten dollars; Article V prohibiting any amendment to the Constitution that would alter the 1808 date or rate of taxation on imported slaves; and Article IV, Section 2, paragraph 2, requiring the northern states to return slaves who escaped to freedom back to their bondage in the South. As far as we know, none of these provisions caused much controversy at the convention, although the fugitive slave clause in Article IV initially would have required that escaped slaves be "delivered up as criminals"; this, however, was modified to relieve states of the obligation.[37]

The framers, while committed to freedom, had a limited, nonuniversal vision of it. Freedom was for some—the some who were white men with property, including property in other men, women, and children. Professor Robinson cautions us, "One wants to be fair to the framers, and above all to avoid blaming them as individuals for the sins of the culture, in which we all share. We must be careful not to imply that they should have done better unless we are prepared to show how better provisions might have been achieved politically." Fair enough. But Robinson continues, "At the same time, we must be lucid in recognizing the terrible mistakes made at the founding. In the end the framers failed on their own terms."[38] Or as Thurgood Marshall, the first African American justice of the Supreme Court, said in a speech in 1987 marking the 200th anniversary of the Constitution, ". . . nor do I find the wisdom, foresight, and sense of justice exhibited by the framers particularly profound. To the contrary, the government they devised was defective from the start, requiring several amendments, a civil war, and momentous social transformations to attain the system of constitutional government, and its respect for the individual freedoms and human rights, we hold as fundamental today. When contemporary Americans cite 'The Constitution,' they invoke a concept that is vastly different from what the framers began to construct two centuries ago."[39]

Constitutional Principles and Design

In designing the Constitution the framers were guided by two overarching and interrelated principles. First, the primary object of government was the protection of private property, and second, the power of government had to be limited to avoid tyranny. These two principles are interrelated because a government of unlimited powers could itself become a threat to private property, thereby undermining one of its core purposes. These two principles gave rise to what are the two most important contributions of the framers to the art and practice of government: the idea of the separation of powers of the government into distinct parts or branches, and federalism.

In *The Federalist Papers No. 10*, James Madison, a man of little property himself, wrote, "The diversities in the faculties of men from which the rights of property originates is not less an insuperable obstacle to uniformity of interests. *The protection of these faculties is the first object of government*" (emphasis added).[40] How does government carry out its first object in a democratic society? The problem confronting the framers, stated simply, was this: In a democratic, capitalist society where only a minority has property but a majority has the right to vote, it is likely the majority will use its voting rights to threaten the property rights of the minority. To avoid this danger while preserving what

Madison called the "spirit and form" of democracy was the principal objective of the framers in designing the Constitution.

How is this objective attained? The principal means is through the separation of powers. Again, we quote Madison. Writing in *The Federalist Papers No. 47* he argued, "No political truth is certainly of greater intrinsic value or stamped with the authority of more enlightened patrons of liberty than that . . . the accumulation of all powers, legislative, executive and judiciary, in the same hands . . . may justly be pronounced the very definition of tyranny."[41] It was not, however, the mere separation of powers of the government into four distinct parts (including the two parts of the Congress); in addition, the Constitution allowed the people—the voters—to elect directly only one of the four parts: the House of Representatives, arguably the least powerful of the four.

The second major principle of constitutional design was federalism, a system of government in which powers are shared between a national (federal) government and the governments of the several states. The last of the Bill of Rights, the Tenth Amendment, establishes this federal system by *delegating* some powers to the federal government, *prohibiting* both the states and the federal government from exercising certain powers, and *reserving* all others to the states. The major powers of the federal government were limited to regulating commerce and the currency, conducting diplomacy, and waging war. Everything else done by the government was to be done by the states.

As Robinson writes, when this system of government was being devised, "tensions about slavery were prominent among the forces that maintained the resolve to develop the country without strong direction from Washington."[42] In limiting the power of the federal government in Washington, the framers simultaneously limited the possibility of universal freedom. Again, to quote from Robinson's *Slavery in the Structure of American Politics:*

> Therefore, in the United States a political system "exquisitely" sensitive to elements of which it was composed and whose structure, both formal and informal, was geared to frustrate and facilitate public action at the national level could not be expected to produce action to end slavery, particularly when the group with the most immediate interest in overthrowing slavery was itself completely unrepresented.[43]

African Americans, however, given their status first as slaves and subsequently as a poor, oppressed minority, have always found the status quo unacceptable. They favored—and favor today—rapid, indeed radical, change in the status quo. They have also favored action by the federal government rather than by the states. Historically, African Americans and their allies have made an important contribution to universalizing freedom through their support for a powerful federal government. The power of the federal government has increased markedly during three periods in American history: the Reconstruction Era in the 1860s, the New Deal Era in the 1930s, and the civil rights–Great Society Era of the 1960s. In two of these periods the black quest for freedom was central to the expansion of federal power (see Chapter 2 for more detailed discussion of these three periods of expanding federal power). As we show in the chapter on public opinion, Chapter 5, African Americans remain the most distinctive and persistently liberal of all the various groups of the American population, strongly supporting an activist, interventionist federal government.

FACES AND VOICES IN THE STRUGGLE FOR UNIVERSAL FREEDOM

JAMES FORTEN (1766–1842)

James Forten contributed to universal freedom by working to make the principles of equality expressed by Jefferson in the Declaration of Independence real for all persons. Forten was part of the founding generation of Americans. Born in Philadelphia to a family of free black persons, as a boy he fought in the American Revolution and by the time of his death in 1842 he was among the wealthiest men in the United States. A master sailmaker, Forten employed an integrated workforce and used his wealth to organize and finance the abolitionist movement. In 1813 he published *A Series of Letters by a Man of Color*. In this pamphlet Forten argued that freedom was universal. Anticipating Frederick Douglass's famous 1852 "Fourth of July Address" and Martin Luther King Jr.'s famous 1963 "I Have a Dream" speech, Forten wrote:

> We hold these truths to be self-evident, that God creates all men equal, is one of the most prominent features in the Declaration of Independence, and in the glorious fabric of collected wisdom, our noble Constitution. This idea embraces the Indian and the European, the savage and the saint, the Peruvian and the Laplander, the white man and the African, and whatever measures are adopted subversive of this inestimable privilege, are in direct violation of the letter and sprit of our Constitution, and become subject to the animadversion of all.

> Forten defied the odds, and his life, work, and writings demonstrated that African Americans were equal to the white men of his generation who founded the Republic.[*]

---

[*]Julie Winch, *A Gentleman of Color: The Life of James Forten* (New York: Oxford University Press, 2002).

Summary

Freedom is a major value in Western and American culture. Yet freedom as a value in the West and in the United States has its origins partly in the struggles of slaves for freedom. While espousing the value of freedom, many Western philosophers and many of the founders of the American republic embraced racism and the ideology of white supremacy, which gave them the freedom to deprive others of their freedom. Thus, in writing the social contract—the Constitution—that established the United States, African Americans were left out, thereby setting in motion the centuries—long African American freedom struggle. Power—the central concept in politics and political science—is intimately related to freedom. Whites with power used it to fashion a notion of their freedom that allowed them to destroy freedom for Africans and African Americans. African Americans, on the other hand, with relatively little power, developed the idea of universal freedom as part of their ongoing struggles to reclaim their own freedom.

The American Constitution is a remarkable document, widely admired around the world as one of freedom's great charters. However, from the outset it was a terribly flawed document that compromised the Declaration of Independence's promise of universal freedom and equality. From Thomas Jefferson's Declaration to the writing of the Constitution at Philadelphia, the founders of America compromised the idea of universal freedom in pursuit of a union based on property, profits, slavery, and the ideology of white supremacy. As a result, they created a government of limited powers, one that would act cautiously and slowly. The African American freedom struggle, however, has always required a government that could act decisively—whether to abolish slavery and segregation or to secure social and economic justice. The Constitution itself therefore is one of the factors that has limited and continues to limit their quest for universal freedom.

Selected Bibliography

Beard, Charles. *An Economic Interpretation of the Constitution.* New York: Free Press, 1913, 1965. The classic, controversial book suggesting that the framers of the Constitution wrote an undemocratic document in order to protect their economic interests.

Becker, Carl. *The Declaration of Independence: A Study in the History of an Idea.* New York: Vintage Books, 1922, 1970. The classic study of the writing of the Declaration.

Brown, Robert. *Charles Beard and the Constitution: A Critical Analysis of an Economic Interpretation of the Constitution.* New York: Norton, 1965. A comprehensive critique of Beard's controversial book.

Davis, David Brion. *The Problem of Slavery in Western Culture.* Ithaca, NY: Cornell University Press, 1966. An early, groundbreaking study of the interrelationship between slavery and the emergence of freedom as a value in the Western world.

Farrand, Max. *The Framing of the Constitution of the United States.* New Haven, CT: Yale University Press, 1913. A short, readable account of the writing of the Constitution by the scholar who prepared the four-volume documentary record of the proceedings of the Philadelphia convention.

Fehrenbacher, Don, and Ward McAfree. *The Slaveholding Republic: An Account of the United States Government's Relations to Slavery.* New York: Oxford University Press, 2001. The most recent and the most detailed study of the subject.

Freehling, William. "The Founding Fathers and Slavery." *American Historical Review* 77 (1972): 81–93. A generally sympathetic account of how slavery influenced the framers' work on the Constitution.

Harding, Vincent. *There Is a River: The Black Struggle for Freedom in America.* New York: Harcourt Brace Jovanovich, 1981. A lyrical, poetic, inspiring narrative.

Jordan, Winthrop. *White over Black: American Attitudes Toward the Negro, 1550–1812.* Baltimore: Penguin, 1968. A monumental study tracing the origin and development of white attitudes toward Africans and African Americans from the sixteenth century through the early history of the United States.

Patterson, Orlando. *Freedom in the Making of Western Culture.* New York: Basic Books, 1991. The most recent study of how freedom in the West emerges out of the experience of slavery.

Robinson, Donald. *Slavery in the Structure of American Politics.* New York: Harcourt Brace Jovanovich, 1971. The best book on the role slavery played in the debates and compromises that shaped the writing of the Constitution.

The Federalist Papers. Introduction by Clinton Rossiter. New York: New American Library, 1961. The authoritative interpretation of the Constitution written during the debate on ratification by James Madison, Alexander Hamilton, and John Jay. It is also a classic in American political thought.

Notes

1. Eric Foner, *Reconstruction: America's Unfinished Revolution, 1863–1877* (New York: Harper & Row, 1988): 77.
2. William Riker, *Federalism: Origins, Operation and Significance* (Boston: Little, Brown, 1964): 140.
3. Orlando Patterson, *Freedom in the Making of Western Culture* (New York: Basic Books, 1991): 1.
4. John Hope Franklin, *From Slavery to Freedom: A History of Negro Americans* (New York: Knopf, 1980): 31.
5. See Patterson, *Freedom in the Making of Western Culture* and his "The Unholy Trinity: Freedom, Slavery and the American Constitution," *Social Problems* 54 (Autumn 1987): 543–77. See also Edmund Morgan, *American Slavery, American Freedom: The Ordeal of Colonial Virginia* (New York: Norton, 1975); David Brion Davis, *The Problem of Slavery in Western Culture* (Ithaca, NY: Cornell University Press, 1966), and his *The Problem of Slavery in the Age of Revolution* (Ithaca, NY: Cornell University Press, 1975).
6. Patterson, "The Unholy Trinity," pp. 559–60. Patterson, in *Freedom in the Making of Western Culture*, contends that freedom is a uniquely Western value and that "almost never outside the context of western culture and its influence, has it [non-Western culture] included freedom. Indeed, non-Western peoples have thought so little about freedom that most human languages did not even possess a word for the concept until contact with the West" (p. x).
7. Patterson, "The Unholy Trinity," p. 545.
8. Patterson, *Freedom in the Making of Western Culture*, pp. 3–5.
9. Foner, *Reconstruction*, p. 231.
10. Richard King, *Civil Rights and the Idea of Freedom* (New York: Oxford University Press, 1992): 26.
11. Ibid., pp. 26–28.
12. Herbert Aptheker, *A Documentary History of the Negro People in the United States*, vol. 1 (New York: Citadel Press, 1967): 1.
13. Harold Lasswell and Abraham Kaplan, *Power and Society: A Framework for Political Inquiry* (New Haven, CT: Yale University Press, 1950): 26.
14. Robert Dahl, "The Concept of Power," *Behavioral Science* 2 (July 1957): 201–15.
15. Max Weber, "Class, Status and Party," in H. H. Gerth and C. Wright Mills, eds., *From Max Weber* (New York: Oxford, 1958): 180.
16. Mack Jones, "A Frame of Reference for Black Politics," in Lenneal Henderson, ed., *Black Political Life in the United States* (New York: Chandler Publishing, 1972): 9.
17. Carl Becker, *The Declaration of Independence: A Study in the History of an Idea* (New York: Vintage Books, 1922, 1970): 320.
18. Joseph Ellis, "Editing the Declaration," *Civilization* (July/August 1995): 60. See Becker's *The Declaration of Independence* for a detailed analysis of the various changes made in Jefferson's original draft.
19. Ellis, "Editing the Declaration."
20. Becker, *The Declaration of Independence*, pp. 212–13.
21. From *The Writings of Thomas Jefferson*, p. 324, as cited in Becker, *The Declaration of Independence*, p. 25.

22. Ibid.

23. A comprehensive treatment of Jefferson's views on race is in Winthrop Jordan, *White over Black: American Attitudes Toward the Negro, 1550–1812* (Baltimore: Penguin Books, 1969): chap. 12, "Thomas Jefferson: Self and Society."

24. Jones, "A Frame of Reference for Black Politics," pp. 7–20.

25. Stokely Carmichael and Charles Hamilton, *Black Power: The Politics of Black Liberation* (New York: Vintage Books, 1967): 3–4.

26. Ibid.

27. Jenny Williams, "Redefining Institutional Racism," *Ethnic and Racial Studies* 8 (1985): 323–75; Louis Knowles and Kenneth Prewitt, *Institutional Racism in America* (New York: Prentice Hall, 1969); Robert C. Smith, *Racism in the Post-Civil Rights Era: Now You See It, Now You Don't* (Albany: SUNY Press, 1995): 54–75.

28. William Freehling, "The Founding Fathers and Slavery," *American Historical Review* 77 (1972): 83.

29. Ibid.

30. Ibid.

31. See Joe R. Feagin, *Racist America: Roots, Current Realities and Future Reparations* (New York: Routledge, 2000): 16.

32. *The Federalist Papers.* Introduction by Clinton Rossiter (New York: New American Library, 1961): 337.

33. Donald Robinson, "The Constitutional Legacy of Slavery," *National Political Science Review* 4 (1994): 11.

34. For a provocative discussion of Thomas Jefferson as the first "Negro President," see Garry Wills, *Negro President: Jefferson and Slave Power* (Boston: Houghton Mifflin Co., 2003).

35. See Leonard Richards, *Slave Power* (Baton Rouge: Louisiana State University Press, 2000): 42.

36. For discussion of the last effort to enforce Section 2 organized by the Student Nonviolent Coordinating Committee (SNCC), see Carmichael and Hamilton, *Black Power*, chap. 4.

37. Robinson, "The Constitutional Legacy of Slavery," p. 12.

38. Ibid.

39. Address by Justice Thurgood Marshall at the Annual Seminar of the San Francisco Patent and Trademark Association, May 6, 1987. Reprinted as "Racial Justice and the Constitution: A View from the Bench," in John Hope Franklin and Genna Rae MacNeil, eds., *African Americans and the Living Constitution* (Washington, DC: Smithsonian Institution Press, 1995): 315.

40. *The Federalist Papers*, p. 78. In a way, whether Madison or any of the other framers were themselves men of property is irrelevant since, as Donald Robinson writes, "Every one of them had made a pile of money, married a wealthy woman or committed his professional life to the service of wealthy clients." Donald Robinson, *To the Best of My Ability: The Presidency and the Constitution* (New York: Norton, 1987): 65.

41. Ibid., p. 301.

42. Donald Robinson, Donald, *Slavery in the Structure of American Politics* (New York: Harcourt Brace Jovanovich, 1971): 435.

43. Ibid. In his more recent book on the American political system, Robinson calls for major modifications in the separation of powers so that the federal government may act more coherently and rapidly. See his *To the Best of My Ability*, chap. 12.

CHAPTER 2

Federalism and the Limits of Universal Freedom

Robert Bork, nominated in 1987 by President Reagan for a seat on the Supreme Court, argues that federalism is an important means to protect individual liberty and freedom. Bork argues that indeed federalism is the Constitution's most important protector of an individual's freedom and that it has been of special value to African Americans in their quest for freedom. With respect to African Americans, Bork writes,

> People who found state regulations oppressive could vote with their feet and in massive numbers they did. Blacks engaged in the great migration at a time when southern states blatantly discriminated. . . . [O]f course this freedom to escape came at a price. But if another state allows you the liberty you value, you can move there and the choice is yours alone, not dependent on those who made the Constitution.[1]

In his classic study *Federalism: Origins, Operation and Significance*, William Riker rejects Bork's arguments about the relationship between federalism and freedom, stating flatly that "federalism may have more to do with destroying freedom than encouraging it."[2] With respect to federalism and the African American quest for freedom, Riker is equally harsh in his condemnation: "The main beneficiaries throughout American history have been southern whites, who have been given the freedom to oppress Negroes, first as slaves and later as a depressed caste."[3] Thus, for Riker, "if in the United States one disapproves of racism, one should disapprove of federalism."[4]

For African Americans, at least until the 1960s civil rights revolution, federalism has had an ambivalent, contradictory effect on their quest for universal freedom. The Civil Rights Act of 1964 universalized freedom throughout the United States with respect to race discrimination. Prior to the 1960s, however, federalism operated in an ambivalent way with respect to race, since each state was free to make any laws it wished regarding the oppression of blacks. So, for example, in 1640 Virginia was the first state to pass laws legally enslaving blacks, but in the 1780s Massachusetts was the first state to legally abolish slavery. In the Antebellum Era, antislavery abolitionists used the power of northern state governments to undermine slavery in the South by refusing to return escaped slaves as required by the Constitution and the Fugitive Slave Act—thus, the idea of north to freedom, of following the north star, of north to freedom's promised land. In this sense, until the abolition of slavery in the 1860s, federalism allowed some space, although limited, for African American freedom in the United States.

Figure 2.1 The Percentage of the African American Population in the Rigid (South) and Flexible (Non-South) Segregated States: 1870–1970

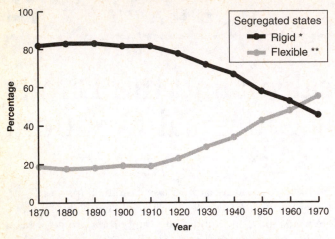

*Rigid segregated states are the 11 states of the Old Confederacy.
**Flexible segregated states are the other states of the Union.

Sources: Adapted from U.S. Bureau of Census, *Negro Population in the United States: 1790–1915* (Washington, DC: Government Printing Office, 1918): 43–44, for the data from 1870 to 1910. U.S. Bureau of Census, *Negro Population in the United States: 1920–1932* (Washington, DC: Government Printing Office, 1935): 9–11, for the data from 1920 to 1930. U.S. Bureau of Census, *Census for Population: 1050 Vol. II: Characteristics of the Population: Part I United States Summary* (Washington, DC: Government Printing Office, 1951): Table 59, 1–106, for the 1950 data. U.S. Bureau of Census, *Historical Statistics of the United States: Colonial Times to 1970* (Washington, DC: Government Printing Office, 1975): 24–37, for data for 1940, 1960, and 1970. All calculations were prepared by the authors.

Similarly, once a system of rigid segregation was imposed in the South beginning in the 1870s, blacks, as the Bork quote points out, began once again to look to the North for freedom, to vote with their feet in the great migration from the South. In Figure 2.1, data are displayed on the percentage of African Americans living in the "rigidly segregated" southern states (see Box 2.1), compared to the more "flexibly segregated" northern states. In 1870, 81 percent of the African American population lived in the rigidly segregated South. Then, starting in the 1920s, a slow, steady migration of African Americans began to the more flexibly segregated North so that by 1970 only 55 percent of African Americans still lived in the South.[5] The Civil Rights Act of 1964, the Voting Rights Act of 1965, and the Fair Housing Act of 1968 universalized freedom insofar as they made racial discrimination illegal throughout the United States, North and South. Therefore, one should probably qualify Riker's blanket condemnation of federalism because during the eras of slavery and segregation, it did provide some opportunity in the North for the exercise of limited forms of freedom.

Federalism: Origins and Operations in the United States

Federalism—the sharing of the powers of government between the national (federal) government and the governments of the states—along with the separation of powers, is one of the major contributions of the framers of the Constitution to the art and practice of government. In Western political thought, the *sovereign power* of the government (its

BOX 2.1   THE "ABSURD" CAREER OF JIM CROW[a]

As most Americans are aware, with the end of Reconstruction and the adoption of the doctrine of "separate but equal" by the Supreme Court in *Plessy v. Ferguson*, the southern states required or permitted the separation of blacks and whites in virtually all areas of life, public and private. Schools, playgrounds, swimming pools, beaches, parks, hotels, hospitals, libraries, restaurants, cemeteries, water fountains, toilets, and buses and streetcars were all segregated. Interracial sex, marriage, and love were also outlawed. Jim Crow's strange career, however, in some places bordered on the absurd. Alabama prohibited blacks and whites from playing checkers together; in some states schoolchildren of different races could not use the same books; Louisiana established separate districts for black and white prostitutes; in Oklahoma blacks and whites could not use the same public telephone. In North Carolina young children could be arrested for interracial kissing. Finally, in Georgia and several other states blacks were required to use separate polling places, separate courthouse doors, separate record rooms, separate record books, separate pens and ink, and separate color-coded tax receipts—white for white taxpayers and pink for blacks.

Source: Elliot Erwitt/Magnum Photos

[a]C. Vann Woodward, *The Strange Career of Jim Crow* (New York: Oxford University Press, 1966). Woodward writes that the origin of the term *Jim Crow* to refer to racial segregation is "lost in obscurity"; however, it is probably related to minstrel songs done by whites in blackface.

supreme, absolute, unrestrained authority over its citizens) could not be divided. Jean Bodin, the leading Western philosopher on the idea of sovereignty, argued that sovereignty could not be divided, that it was indivisible and must reside in a single person (a monarch) or institution (parliament).[6] The framers of the American Constitution rejected Bodin's idea of the indivisibility of the sovereign power of government on the theory that since the people of the United States were sovereign, they, if they wished, could divide sovereignty in order to create a well-ordered government that would secure their liberties.

The idea that ultimate sovereignty or power of the government rests with the people is the underlying philosophical principle of the American government that shapes both federalism and the separation of powers. However, there is a practical reason that the framers felt compelled to adopt the federal system: Without federalism it is unlikely that there could have been a union of all the 13 states. Some of the framers favored a unitary rather than a federal government. The Virginia delegation at Philadelphia proposed in its

Virginia Plan essentially a unitary government. The people as a whole would elect the House and the House in turn would elect the Senate, the president, and the judiciary. Under the plan, the Congress would have unlimited powers to "legislate in all cases to which the separate states are incompetent . . . [and] to negative all laws passed by the several states, contravening in the opinion of the national legislature under the Articles of the union."[7] In other words, the Congress was to have unlimited powers, including the power to "negative" or veto acts of the state legislatures.

The Virginia Plan was rejected by the convention on several grounds. A major reason, however, was that the southern slaveholding states feared that a unitary government with the power to "negative all laws passed by the states" might interfere with their wish to maintain slavery. Thus, philosophical principles aside, federalism was necessary in the United States for wholly practical reasons: to establish the Union.[8]

Who Is Sovereign: The People or the States? An Old Debate Renewed

It is generally accepted today that the whole people of the United States are sovereign and that acting collectively created the U.S. government. This, however, was not always the accepted view. Thomas Jefferson, for example, apparently believed that the United States was created by the states rather than the people and consequently each state had the right to act independently of the federal government by nullifying (vetoing) federal laws with which it disagreed.[9] This view was firmly rejected by Lincoln and in a sense was settled by the Civil War. However, in a 1995 case, Supreme Court Justice Clarence Thomas in a dissenting opinion (joined by the Chief Justice, Justice O'Connor, and Justice Scalia) renewed this 200-year-old debate.

The case is *U.S. Term Limits Inc. et al.* v. *Thornton et al.*, a case dealing with whether a state (in this case Arkansas) could on its own authority impose term limits on its members of Congress.[10] The Court, in a five-to-four decision, said no, holding that only all the people of the United States by amending the Constitution could limit the terms of members of Congress. (On term limits and their probable impact on African Americans in the Congress, see Chapter 11.) In a long dissenting opinion, Justice Thomas, again writing for himself and three of his colleagues, argued that each state could limit congressional terms because *"the ultimate source of the Constitution's authority is the consent of the people of each state, not the consent of the undifferentiated people of the nation as a whole"* (emphasis added).[11] Noting that the "United States" is consistently a plural noun and that the original preamble to the Constitution reads "We the People of the States of New Hampshire, Massachusetts, etc.," Justice Thomas concluded, "The Constitution simply does not recognize any mechanism for action by the undifferentiated people of the nation."[12]

In his opinion for the majority, Justice John Paul Stevens rejected Thomas's analysis. He argued that the states under the Articles of Confederation retained their sovereignty as independent states, but with the adoption of the Constitution, *"the framers envisioned a uniform national system, rejecting the notion that the nation was a collection of states and instead creating a direct link between the national government and the people"* (emphasis added).[13] In a separate concurring opinion, Justice Anthony Kennedy wrote, "In my view, however, it is well settled that the whole people of the United States asserted their political identity and unity of purpose when they created the federal system."[14]

This debate between Justice Thomas and his colleagues on whether the people of the United States or the people of the various states established the Constitution may seem like an arcane, theoretical, academic debate with no practical consequences. It is not. Rather, it is a debate central to the thesis of this book: whether the United States is a nation of uniform, universal rights and freedom, or whether it is one of freedom limited by states' rights. It is also part of an ongoing effort by conservatives on the Court and in the Congress to radically reshape the federal system, by taking power from the federal government and returning it to the states (see the section, "The Rehnquist Court and the Revival of State-Centered Federalism," later in this chapter).

Federalism: Advantages and Disadvantages

Perhaps the most frequently stated advantage of the federal system is that it allows the states to serve as "laboratories" for public policy innovation and experimentation. In other words, each of the 50 states is free to "experiment" with the best ways to deliver education, health, and welfare services, and to provide for the punishment of crime (see Box 2.2). Through the "diffusion of innovation," each state can learn from the successes and failures of the others and change its policies according to what works best.[15] Related to this, federalism grants to citizens "choice," the freedom to move from one state to another in search of a better life.

Another advantage of federalism is that it provides opportunities for minority groups in the country as a whole to be majorities (the Mormons in Utah) or larger, more politically significant minorities (Jews in New York, Latinos in California, or blacks in Louisiana) at the state and local levels. This provision enhances the opportunities for minority groups to participate in politics and to be elected to office, again a situation that would not be possible in a unitary system. This is especially true in the United States because there are not just 51 governments (the 50 states and the federal government) but more than 80,000 units of government including county, city, and town governments; school boards; and other special districts. This enormous diversity of governments is particularly important for African Americans; although they are a national minority, they can become a local majority and control the governments in localities, including many of the nation's larger and more important cities.

There are clear advantages to a federal system, but there are clear disadvantages as well, especially to blacks in their quest for universal rights and freedoms. First, in its essence, federalism is an impediment to universal freedom because it allows the different states to define rights and freedoms for their citizens. Historically, this power has allowed a minority of southern whites to limit the freedom of African Americans, even against the wishes of a majority of the American people. Second, federalism, as a number of political scientists have shown, tends to lead to irresponsible government.[16] Woodrow Wilson, political scientist and 28th president of the United States, eloquently stated the case for the irresponsibility of divided power in his 1898 book *Congressional Government*. Wilson observed that "the more power is divided the more irresponsible it becomes. A mighty baron who can call half the country to arms is watched with great jealousy, and, therefore restrained with more vigilant care than is ever vouchsafed the feeble master of a single and solitary castle."[17] In other words, citizens are more likely to be aware of and exercise restraint on or greater control of one powerful central government

BOX 2.2   FEDERALISM, FELONIES, AND THE RIGHT TO VOTE[a]

Under federalism, each state is free to set its own qualifications for voting, except the vote may not be denied on account of race, religion, gender, age (18), or the person's failure to pay a poll tax. But under what conditions might citizens lose and then regain the right to vote? As part of the voter registration efforts of the 1995 Million Man March, the National Coalition on Black Voter Participation surveyed each of the states in order to learn whether citizens lost their right to vote as a consequence of conviction for a felony and if so, how they could have the right restored. Thirty-five of the 50 states responded to the survey. Three states (Maine, Utah, and Vermont) with small black populations do not deprive convicted felons of the right to vote. Arkansas and West Virginia have no clearly stated procedures for restoration, three states require action by the governor, and most of the rest require action of the state pardon and parole boards or local election commissions. Mississippi (which at 37 percent has the largest percentage black population of any state) is different. Its constitution states, "The legislature, *may* by a two-thirds vote of both houses, of all members elected, restore the right of suffrage to any person disqualified by reason of crime, but the reason therefore shall be spread upon the journal and the vote shall be by yeas and nays." Thus, in Mississippi it is more difficult for a citizen who has committed a crime to regain the right to vote than it is to impeach the president of the United States. In Mississippi, African Americans are more than three times as likely to be convicted of felonies as whites. Thus, they are three times as likely to lose the right to vote, and once lost, it is very difficult to regain. Perhaps these are mere coincidences, but it is striking that in Mississippi—the state with the worst history of race oppression and the largest black population—citizens find it more difficult than in any other of the 35 responding states to regain their voting rights once lost. It is striking because the effect of the Mississippi procedure is to deny the vote to a large number of its black citizens.

In the 2004 election, 4,686,539 Americans were denied the right to vote because they had been convicted of a crime. A recent study using data from the U.S. Census's Current Population Survey estimates the net effect of felony disenfranchisement laws on the probability of voting by blacks and whites. It found that overall voter turnout is lower in states with the most restrictive felony disenfranchisement laws.[b] In terms of blacks, specifically the probability of blacks in those states voting in the 1996 presidential election declined by 10 percent and in 2000 by 7 percent.[c] The authors also looked specifically at Florida, the site of the closely contested Bush–Gore 2000 presidential race. They found that "in 1996 an estimated 204,600 African American men were disenfranchised because of criminal convictions in the state. If disenfranchisement figures were similar (or greater) in 2000 it is possible that the election results might have been different if Florida had a less restrictive criminal disenfranchisement law."[d] In 2007 Florida's newly elected Republican Governor, Charlie Crist, persuaded the state's Executive Clemency Board to immediately restore voting rights to most felons who have served their sentences.

Congressman John Conyers, the senior African American member of Congress, introduced legislation in 2000 that would restore voting rights in federal elections to former

(continued)

BOX 2.2 *continued*

prisoners nationwide (although their right to vote in state and local elections would still be left to the states). This legislation, however, has been blocked in committee as critics contend it is unconstitutional because it extends the power of the federal government into an area reserved to the states. However, in 2005 two states took actions to restore voting rights to felons. In Iowa, Governor Tom Vilsack issued an executive order restoring voting rights to all felons who had completed their sentences, and in Nebraska the legislature overrode the governor's veto and voted to overturn its ban on felony voting and automatically restore voting rights to felons after they complete their sentences and a two-year waiting period.[e]

In 2007, the Maryland General Assembly adopted legislation allowing all felons to vote immediately after they complete their sentences, including parole or probation, and Rhode Island adopted an even more liberal law allowing felons on parole or probation to vote.

[a]Hanes Walton, Jr. and Simone Green, "Voting Rights and the Million Man March: The Problem of Restoration of Voting Rights for Ex-Convicts/Felons," *African American Research Perspectives* 3 (Winter 1997): 68–74. It is estimated that 13 percent of black men compared to less than 2 percent of white men have lost the right to vote as a result of felony convictions, including 32 percent of the African American men in Alabama, 31 percent in Florida, and 29 percent in Mississippi.

[b]Aman McLeod, Ismail White, and Amelia Gavin, "The Locked Ballot Box: The Impact of State Criminal Disenfranchisement Laws on African American Voting Behavior and Implications for Reform," *The Virginia Journal of Social Policy and Law* 11 (2003): 66–88.

[c]Ibid., p. 79.

[d]Ibid., p. 83.

[e]The most comprehensive study of the history, nature, and social and political implications of denying ex-felons the right to vote is Elizabeth Hull, *The Disenfranchisement of Ex-Felons* (Philadelphia: Temple University Press, 2006).

than they are of scores of state and local governments. This situation is even more the case today than when Wilson was writing in 1898, given the development of a national news media (particularly television) that focuses its attention on events in Washington. Average citizens living in Detroit or San Francisco are more likely to be aware of what the president and the Congress are doing in Washington than they are of what the governor and legislature are doing in Lansing and Sacramento.

E. E. Schattsneider has argued that widening or nationalizing the scope of government decision making tends to enhance the power of minority groups.[18] That is, a minority such as African Americans is more likely to be able to influence decision makers in Washington than in any of the 50 state capitals. This is because decisions at the national level tend to be more visible, and minority interest groups tend to be better organized in national than state politics. For this reason, for example, African American leaders opposed the efforts of the Republican congressional majority in 1995 to transfer responsibility for social welfare programs (welfare, Medicaid, food stamps, etc.) to the states. Another reason African Americans oppose the transfer of social programs to the states is that instead of one uniform, universal standard for welfare or Medicaid, there would be 51. Again, this is part of the essence of federalism. As Riker writes, "The grant of autonomy to local majorities to create confused policies has resulted in a cost to the whole society that is probably greater than the cost of uniformity."[19] To relate Riker's point to the theme of this book, uniformity in national policies, as opposed to multiple state policies, is more likely to result in universal rights and freedoms.

Reconstruction, the New Deal, and the Civil Rights Movement: The Triumph of National-Centered Power

Throughout American history there has been debate and conflict between those who favor *national-centered power* and those who favor *state-centered power.* Generally, the American political tradition tends to favor state-centered power, and advocates of national-centered power have tended to prevail only in times of national crisis. Even then, the advocates of state-centered power reassert themselves in calls for a return of power to the states. Frederick Douglass during Reconstruction—the first triumph of national-centered power—observed that "no political idea is more deeply rooted in the minds of the country [than] the right of each state to control its own affairs."[20] Thus, it is not surprising that after each period of expanding national power, there were subsequent calls for a return of power to the states.

Reconstruction

National-centered power—greater authority and responsibility to the federal government—has triumphed only during periods of crisis. The first such crisis, the gravest in the nation's history, was the Civil War and the effort to reconstruct the South in its aftermath. As Reconstruction historian Eric Foner shows, an activist federal government as an instrument of reform emerges in the Reconstruction Era of the Civil War.[21]

During this period, the power of the president—particularly his commander-in-chief powers—expanded enormously under Lincoln. Then under President Andrew Johnson, the powers of Congress also expanded as that body passed several civil rights laws requiring the states to accord the newly freed slaves universal freedom and equal rights. For a time during this period, the U.S. Army was maintained in the southern states to enforce these rights. The federal government also established its first social welfare agency—the Freedmen's Bureau—to provide assistance first to the newly freed slaves and subsequently to poor whites displaced by the war. Finally, three amendments were added to the Constitution: the Thirteenth abolishing slavery, the Fourteenth establishing universal citizenship and equality and fairness under law for all persons, and the Fifteenth guaranteeing voting rights to all men regardless of race. The Fourteenth Amendment eventually was to become one of the most important mechanisms for expanding the power of the federal government in relationship to the states.

The New Deal

National-centered power expanded for a second time during Franklin Roosevelt's New Deal.[22] In the midst of the Great Depression the federal government took on a wide array of responsibilities previously left to the states or market forces, including universal access of the elderly to retirement income, welfare for fatherless children, and government-supported public works jobs for the unemployed. In addition to the beginnings of the modern welfare state, the New Deal also expanded the power of the regulatory state with respect to banking, agriculture, the stock market, and the relationship between workers and their employers. The Supreme Court initially declared many of the New Deal programs unconstitutional because the Court said they exceeded the federal government's Article 1, Section 8 powers. Eventually, however, under pressure from the popular Roosevelt, the Court changed its mind and approved virtually all aspects of the New Deal.

Thus, for the first time in American history, Congress established a series of universal programs designed to assure the employment and social security of *all* its citizens.

During the New Deal the federal government also established a series of grants in aid to the states and localities—funds to assist them in carrying out their responsibilities in such areas as public works, housing, and health. These grants in aid were vastly expanded in the 1960s as part of Lyndon Johnson's Great Society (by the 1970s there were more than 600 such specific grants covering everything from alcohol and drug abuse to youth training programs). These grants usually come with strings attached; that is, they carry uniform or universal conditions that states and localities must comply with.

The Civil Rights Revolution and the Great Society

The civil rights reforms of the 1960s ushered in the last great expansion of federal power. In a sense these reforms were a second reconstruction or a completion of the first. As in the original Reconstruction, Congress passed three new civil rights laws guaranteeing universal access to the ballot, public education, employment, restaurants, hotels and other public places, and the sale and rental of housing. Two new amendments were added to the Constitution granting the right to vote for president to the largely black city of Washington, D.C., and abolishing the poll tax. The Supreme Court, then the president, and finally the Congress began to enforce the Fourteenth and Fifteenth Amendments for the first time in 100 years. And on two occasions (Little Rock in 1957 and the University of Mississippi in 1962), the U.S. Army, again for the first time in a century, was deployed in the South to enforce African American civil rights.

Federal social welfare programs also expanded during this period as a part of Lyndon Johnson's Great Society and "war on poverty." Universal access to health care for the elderly and to nursing homes for the poor elderly were guaranteed, as was health care for the poor. The Great Society also provided federal support for elementary and secondary education and loans and grants for college and postgraduate education. Again, these were universal programs, providing support to persons no matter where they lived in the country.

Yet, as always in American history, there was reaction to this expanding power of the federal government from those favoring state-centered power. During Reconstruction, Foner writes, "A more powerful national state and a growing sense that blacks were entitled to some measure of civil equality produced their own countervailing tendencies as localism, laissez-faire and racism, persistent forces in the nineteenth century American life, reasserted themselves."[23] One hundred years later these same persistent, countervailing tendencies emerged in reaction to the Great Society and civil rights reforms of the 1960s. Beginning in 1968 with the election of Richard Nixon, again in 1980 with the election of Ronald Reagan, and again in 1994 with the election of Republican congressional majorities, these forces of localism, laissez-faire, and racism reasserted themselves, continuing the historic tension and conflict between advocates of national-centered and state-centered power.

The Fourteenth Amendment: The American Charter of Universal Freedom

Of the Fourteenth Amendment, Fred Friendly and Martha Elliot write, "It was as if Congress had held a second constitutional convention and created a federal government of vastly expanded proportions."[24] And of the three Civil War amendments, including the Fourteenth, Justice Samuel Miller in the *Slaughterhouse Cases* wrote,

No one can fail to be impressed with the one prevailing purpose found in them all, lying at the foundation of each, and without which none of them would have been suggested; we mean the freedom of the slave race, the security and firm establishment of that freedom and the protection of the newly made freeman and citizen from the oppression of those who had formerly exercised dominion over him.[25]

Of the Fourteenth specifically, Justice Miller wrote, *"It is so clearly a provision for that race . . . that a strong case would be necessary for its application to any other"* (emphasis added).[26]

Although the Fourteenth Amendment did vastly expand the power of the federal government in relation to the states and establish a basis for the protection of the freedom of African Americans, it took 100 years for this to happen. In the meantime, contrary to Justice Miller's view, the amendment has been applied to persons of other races, including those fictitious persons called corporations. *Indeed, until the 1960s the amendment was more frequently used to protect the freedom of corporations than it was the freedom of blacks.* Thus, to fully appreciate how the amendment became the great charter of universal freedom for all Americans, we need to trace the history of its adoption and implementation from the 1860s to the 1960s.

The Fourteenth Amendment: Origins and Development

The Fourteenth Amendment was approved by the House and Senate in 1866 and ratified by the necessary three-fourths of the states two years later. William Nelson noted that much of the opposition to the amendment, North and South, was "deeply racist" as opponents argued that equality should not be granted to the "inferior races," specifically not just blacks but also Indians and the Chinese on the West Coast.[27] Although racism was the principal basis of opposition, opponents also argued that the amendment violated the principles of federalism as it gave the federal government unprecedented authority to interfere in the affairs of the states.

The Fourteenth Amendment, with five sections, is one of the longest amendments to the Constitution. The most important and controversial part is Section 1, which establishes universal citizenship and declares freedom and equality throughout the United States. As Friendly and Elliot wrote in *The Constitution: That Delicate Balance*, the following 17 words brought about a "quiet revolution" in American government and politics: *No state shall make or enforce any law which shall abridge the privileges of immunities of citizens of the United States, nor shall any state deprive any person of life, liberty or property without due process of law; nor deny to any person within its jurisdiction the equal protection of the law.*[28] The controversy about this important language is whether its authors intended it to "incorporate" the Bill of Rights—that is, whether the "privileges and immunities" of citizens of the United States are those rights spelled out in the first nine amendments to the Constitution.[29]

Although the principal sponsors of the amendment in both the House and the Senate (Representative Jonathan Bingham of New York and Senator Jacob Howard of Michigan) declared during the debates that it would require the states to abide by the Bill of Rights, there is still no agreement even today among scholars who have studied the amendment's history. Some argue that the intent of the Fourteenth Amendment was clearly to incorporate the Bill of Rights.[30] Others are just as certain from their research that this was not the amendment's intent.[31] There is, as Professor William Nelson notes, voluminous research to support both sides of the argument; thus, he concludes there is an "impasse in scholarship."[32] That is, we do not know for sure—and perhaps never will—the intent of the framers of the amendment.

The Supreme Court and the Fourteenth Amendment, 1865–1925: Universal Freedom Denied

The Supreme Court historically has also been divided on the intent of the amendment. Immediately after its adoption, the Court took the view that it did not make the Bill of Rights applicable to the states. The *Slaughterhouse Cases* were the first heard by the Court under the Fourteenth Amendment. In his opinion for the court's majority, Justice Miller rejected the argument that the amendment's privileges and immunities clause incorporated the Bill of Rights, holding that the only rights protected were access to Washington, D.C., and coastal seaports; the right to protection on the high seas; the right to use the navigable waters of the United States; the right of assembly and petition; and the privilege of *habeas corpus*. Three justices dissented in this case; however, what modern legal scholars call Justice Miller's "pernicious" opinion remained the law of the land until the beginning of the twentieth century.[33]

The Supreme Court took a similar view in its reading of the amendment's equal protection clause when it declared the Civil Rights Act of 1875 unconstitutional. This act prohibited racial discrimination in public accommodations such as hotels, theaters, and streetcars. In the *Civil Rights Cases of 1883*, Justice Joseph Bradley declared that the Fourteenth Amendment's equal protection clause only prohibited discrimination by the states, not private businesses or persons. In language reminiscent of that used today by conservative judges and others who oppose affirmative action, Justice Bradley declared,

> When a man has emerged from slavery, and by the aid of beneficent legislation has shaken off the inseparable concomitants of that state, there must be some stage in the progress of his elevation when he takes the rank of a mere citizen, and ceases to be the special favorite of the laws, and when his rights as a citizen, or a man, are to be protected in the ordinary modes by which other men's rights are protected.[34]

In his dissent, Justice John Marshall Harlan argued that the civil rights law did not make blacks "special favorites of the law" and that the clear purpose of both the Thirteenth and the Fourteenth Amendments was to establish and decree "universal freedom throughout the United States." In 1896 in *Plessy* v. *Ferguson*, the Court continued its narrow reading of the amendment when it declared that racial segregation did not violate the equal protection clause. Again Justice Harlan dissented, declaring that the Fourteenth Amendment made the Constitution "color blind"; but his view was not to prevail until the Supreme Court's 1954 *Brown* v. *Board of Education* decision.

Ironically, until the 1960s, the Fourteenth Amendment's great charter of universal freedom was used to protect the freedom of corporations rather than that of African Americans or any other real persons. William Blackstone, in his *Commentaries on the Laws of England* published in 1765, defines corporations as "artificial persons who may maintain a perpetual succession and enjoy a kind of legal immortality."[35] In 1905 in

Lochner v. *New York* the Supreme Court struck down a New York state law that limited the hours of bakery workers to 10 hours a day and 60 hours a week. The Court held that New York's minimum hours law violated "the general rights to make a contract in relation to his business which is part of the liberty of the individual protected by the Fourteenth Amendment of the federal Constitution."[36] New York had passed the law in the exercise of its *police powers*—that is, to protect the health and safety of the workers; however, the Court held that the "liberty of contract" guaranteed by the Fourteenth Amendment's due process of law clause meant that if a business wanted to require its workers to work more than 60 hours a week, the states could not interfere. Using similar reasoning the Court subsequently invalidated other government regulations of business, including child labor laws.[37] The Court's decision in *Lochner* was controversial but it remained the law until the Court changed its mind during the Depression, when government regulation of corporations and the economy became more imperative, not to mention popular.

The Supreme Court and the Fourteenth Amendment, 1925–1968: The Universalization of Freedom

Today the Fourteenth Amendment is largely used to protect civil liberties and civil rights. *Civil liberties* are generally understood as the rights of individuals that are protected from government abridgement. *Civil rights* are generally understood as the right of minorities (blacks, women, homosexuals) to freedom and equality under the law. The Court first began to interpret the Fourteenth Amendment as protecting civil liberties embodied in the Bill of Rights in 1925, and it began to seriously enforce the amendment's guarantee of equality for blacks and other minorities in the 1950s and 1960s.

In 1925 in *Gitlow* v. *New York*, the Supreme Court began the gradual process of incorporating or universalizing the Bill of Rights. In this case, the Court for the first time held that "freedom of speech and of the press . . . are among the fundamental personal rights and 'liberties' protected by the due process clause of the Fourteenth Amendment from impairment by the states."[38] In *Gitlow* the Court overturned more than 50 years of prior decisions on the Fourteenth Amendment. Then, as Table 2.1 shows, the Court began a gradual, year-by-year, amendment-by-amendment process, sometimes called *selective incorporation of the Bill of Rights*. In this process, the Court applied the rest of the First Amendment to the states, and then in the 1960s it applied those provisions of the Bill of Rights dealing with the rights of persons accused of crimes (the Fourth, Fifth, Sixth, and Eighth Amendments). And in 1973 in *Roe* v. *Wade*, the Court interpreted the Fourteenth Amendment as creating a right to privacy (either in the Fourteenth's guarantee of liberty or as a Ninth Amendment unmentioned right) that is broad enough to cover a woman's right to choose an abortion. Thus, by the end of the 1960s virtually all the important provisions of the Bill of Rights had been incorporated or made universal throughout the United States.

With respect to civil rights, in 1954 the Supreme Court declared in *Brown* v. *Board of Education* that, at least in terms of the public schools, racial segregation was a violation of the Fourteenth Amendment's equal protection clause, reversing the half-century precedent set in *Plessy* v. *Ferguson*. Then in the 1960s, Congress, responding to the protests and demonstrations led by Dr. Martin Luther King Jr., passed a series of laws designed to enforce the Fourteenth's guarantee of universal freedom and equality. But in passing the public accommodations section of the 1964 Civil Rights Act (which

Table 2.1 Dates of U.S. Supreme Court Decisions Ensuring Bill of Rights Protections Nationwide

FREEDOM	YEAR OF INCORPORATION/ UNIVERSALIZATION
Free speech (1)[a]	1925
Free press (1)	1931
Freedom of assembly (1)	1937
Freedom of religion (1)	1934
Unreasonable search and seizure (4)	1949
Cruel and unusual punishment (8)	1962
Right to lawyer in criminal cases (6)	1963
No self-incrimination (5)	1964
Remain silent when questioned by police (6)	1966

[a]Number in parentheses refers to the amendment to the Constitution addressing that right or freedom. The Court first incorporated the right to privacy in *Griswold* v. *Connecticut* (381 U.S. 479, 85. S.Ct., 1678), a 1965 case involving the right of married couples to use contraceptives.

Source: Craig Ducat and Harold Chase, *Constitutional Interpretation*, 4th ed. (St. Paul, MN: West, 1988): 845–46.

prohibited discrimination in hotels, motels, and restaurants), Congress relied not on the Fourteenth Amendment but instead on its power to regulate interstate commerce (because hotels and motels received products or served customers who crossed state lines). Since the Supreme Court in 1883 had invalidated a similar civil rights law based on the Fourteenth's Section 5 enforcement power, the Congress, by using the commerce clause, avoided the problem of having the Court overrule yet another of its precedents. (In general, the Court is reluctant to overturn its prior decisions, relying on the principle of *stare decisis*—let the previous decision stand.)[39] This led Justice William O. Douglas in his concurring opinion in the case, *Heart of Atlanta Motel* v. *the United States*, upholding the 1964 law to write:

> I am reluctant to . . . rest solely on the commerce clause. My reluctance is not due to any conviction that Congress lacks the power to regulate commerce in the interests of human rights. It is rather my belief that the right of the people to be free of state action that discriminates against them because of race . . . occupies a more protected place in our constitutional system than does the movement of cattle, fruit, steel and coal across state lines. Hence, I would prefer to rest on the assertion of legislative power contained in section 5 of the Fourteenth Amendment which states "The Congress shall have the power to enforce, by appropriate legislation, the provisions of this article"—a power which the Court concedes was exercised at least in part.[40]

One hundred years after the adoption of the Fourteenth Amendment it became the Constitution's great charter of freedom in fact as well as theory, establishing a new vision of universal freedom, equality, and liberty under law for all Americans. It is a vision of freedom that Abraham Lincoln invoked in 1863 at Gettysburg and that Martin Luther King Jr. invoked a hundred years later at the Lincoln Memorial in Washington (see Box 2.3).

To achieve Lincoln's vision and King's dream required a fundamental transformation in federalism as well as reversal by the Supreme Court of more than 50 years of its decisions on the relationship between federalism and freedom. Unfortunately, for African Americans and others interested in universal freedom, the Supreme Court once more appears to be reversing itself. This time, however, the Court is seeking to limit freedom by reviving old principles of federalism and states' rights.

The Fourteenth Amendment and the Freedom of Homosexuals

As we have seen, as early as 1965 the Supreme Court in the *Griswold* contraceptive case used the Fourteenth Amendment's due process clause (no state shall deprive any person of life, liberty, or property without due process of law) to establish a right of privacy in sexuality as a liberty secured by the amendment. Subsequently, in *Roe* in 1973 the Court held that this liberty encompassed the right of a woman to terminate a pregnancy.[41] However, in 1986 in *Bowers* v. *Hardwick* the Court refused to extend this liberty to adults engaging in consensual homosexual conduct, whether by same-sex or different-sex couples (the Georgia stature in question made anal or oral sex even by married couples a crime). In *Bowers*, Justice Byron White writing for a 5-4 majority held that "there was no such thing as a fundamental right to commit homosexual sodomy . . . [and] to hold that an act of homosexual sodomy is somehow protected as a fundamental right would be to cast aside millenia of moral teaching."[42] Thus, the majority reasoned that a state in the exercise of its police powers could criminalize homosexual conduct.

In 2003 in *Lawrence et al.* v. *Texas* the Court in a 5-4 decision reversed *Bowers*. Justice Anthony Kennedy, writing for the majority, concluded that *Bowers* was so clearly wrongly decided that it could not be allowed to stand. Justice Kennedy wrote "the petitioners are entitled to respect for their private lives. The state cannot demean their existence or control their destiny by making their private sexual conduct a crime. Their right to liberty under the Due Process Clause gives them the full right to engage in their conduct without government intervention."[43] Justice Sandra Day O'Connor, who was a part of the *Bowers*'s majority in 1986, refused to overrule it on Fourteenth Amendment liberty grounds in 2003. Instead, she used the amendment's equal protection clause to declare the Texas statute unconstitutional because it punished homosexual conduct by same-sex couples only. Thus, the law, she argued, deprived homosexuals of the equal protection of the law. Justice Antonin Scalia, also part of the *Bowers*'s majority, writing for himself, the chief justice, and Justice Clarence Thomas, would have reaffirmed *Bowers*, holding that there is no fundamental liberty to engage in homosexual conduct. Therefore, a state has a right to punish what its people and legislature consider immoral conduct. Scalia also argued that *Lawrence* "effectively decrees the end of all morals legislation" and thus leaves on "shaky Constitutional grounds" criminal laws against "bigamy, adultery, incest, beastiality and obscenity, as well as laws limiting marriage to opposite sex couples."

At the time of *Bowers*, 25 states prohibited homosexual conduct in some fashion. By 2003 only 13 did so, of which 4, such as Texas, only punished homosexual couples. Thus, the Fourteenth Amendment, which was once said to be so clearly a provision for the colored race that it would not likely be used for any other group, was used in 2003 to universalize freedom for homosexuals throughout the United States.

BOX 2.3   ABRAHAM LINCOLN AT GETTYSBURG AND MARTIN LUTHER KING JR. AT LINCOLN MEMORIAL: TWO SPEECHES IN THE QUEST FOR UNIVERSAL FREEDOM

In 1863 Abraham Lincoln was asked to deliver "a few appropriate remarks" at the dedication of the cemetery at the Gettysburg battlefield. One hundred years later Martin Luther King Jr. was asked to deliver the closing remarks at the Lincoln Memorial after the March on Washington. Lincoln spoke for three minutes before a crowd of 20,000. King spoke for 17 minutes before a crowd of 250,000. Lincoln spoke on the bloody battlefield at Gettysburg to give meaning to the Civil War. King spoke at the Lincoln's Memorial to give meaning to the civil rights movement's bloody battles then taking place in the South. Of all the American presidents, Abraham Lincoln was the most gifted in the rhetoric of freedom, and of all the leaders of the African American people, Martin Luther King Jr. was the most gifted in the rhetoric of freedom. Each man in his own time and his own way sought to universalize the idea.

Dr. Martin Luther King Jr. delivers the "I Have A Dream" speech from the Lincoln Memorial, August 28, 1963. *Source:* AP Images

Lincoln at Gettysburg invoked the words of Thomas Jefferson written "four score and seven years ago" in order to declare that *all* men are created equal and that the Civil War that would free the slaves had ushered in "a new birth of freedom." At Lincoln's Memorial, King invoked the words of Lincoln's Emancipation Proclamation written, as King said, "five score years ago" to declare that he had a dream of universal freedom, a dream that one day "*all* of God's children, black men and white men, Jews and Gentiles, Protestants and Catholics, will be able to join hands and sing in the words of the old Negro spiritual 'Free at last! Free at last! Thank God Almighty, we are free at last!'"

Abraham Lincoln was murdered on April 15, 1865. Martin Luther King Jr. was murdered on April 4, 1968. Neither man died in vain because by their words and deeds they helped to remake the idea of freedom for America and the world.

[a]On Lincoln's address, see Garry Wills, *Lincoln at Gettysburg: The Words That Remade America* (New York: Touchstone, 1992), and on King's "I Have a Dream Speech," see Drew Hansen, *The Dream: Martin Luther King Jr. and the Speech That Inspired a Nation* (New York: Ecco, 2003).

The Rehnquist Court and the Revival of State-Centered Federalism

The "states are not mere political subdivisions of the United States." So said Justice Sandra Day O'Connor in *New York* v. *United States*, a case invalidating a federal law that required the states either to regulate low-level radioactive waste within their boundaries or to assume legal liability for it.[44] Justice O'Connor's observation in this case and the decision of the Court seem to represent an attempt by the Court's conservative majority to radically alter the existing relationship between the federal government and the states. In doing so the Court is reopening once again the 200-year-old debate between advocates of national-centered versus state-centered power in American politics.

Ever since his appointment to the Court by President Nixon in 1972, the late Chief Justice Rehnquist (he was elevated to the chief justice position by President Reagan in 1986) had been an advocate of state-centered federalism, arguing that much of the Court's federalism jurisprudence since the New Deal was wrong and not supported by a fair reading of the Constitution. Until the 1980s, Rehnquist was a lonely dissenter, as his views on federalism (and civil liberties and civil rights) were not shared by his colleagues on the nine-member Court. However, with the appointments of Justices O'Connor, Scalia, and Anthony Kennedy by President Reagan, and Justice Thomas by President Bush, Rehnquist frequently commanded a narrow five-person majority on many federalism and Fourteenth Amendment cases.

Several recent cases decided by the Court suggest that it may be returning to its Reconstruction Era jurisprudence. Earlier in this chapter we discussed Justice Thomas's extraordinary dissent in the term limits case, in which he argued that the federal government has only those powers expressly granted or necessarily implied in the Constitution. In his opinion for the Court's narrow majority in the term limits case, Justice John Paul Stevens said this of Thomas's dissent:

> It would seem to suggest that if the Constitution is silent about the exercise of a particular power—that is, where the Constitution does not speak either expressly or by necessary implications—the federal government lacks the power and the states enjoy it. . . . Under the dissent's unyielding approach, it would seem *McCulloch* was wrongly decided. Similarly, the dissent's approach would invalidate our dormant commerce clause jurisprudence.[45]

Although Thomas and his colleagues did not prevail in the term limits case (Justice Kennedy, as he occasionally does, voted with the Court's more centrist or liberal justices in this case), in several important cases involving the powers of Congress and federal-state relations, the conservatives have been in the majority. In *United States* v. *Lopez*, the five-person conservative majority declared unconstitutional a federal law that prohibited the possession of guns near a school.[46] This was the first time since the New Deal that the Court invalidated an act of Congress based on its exercise of its commerce clause powers. Similarly, in *Seminole Tribe* v. *Florida*, the Court held (again five to four) that individuals could not sue a state to enforce federal laws or rights passed by Congress pursuant to its authority under the commerce clause. Such suits, Chief Justice Rehnquist said, were an "unconstitutional intrusion on state sovereignty." In deciding this case, the Court overturned its own decision of six years earlier in *Pennsylvania* v. *Union Gas*, in which it explicitly held that Congress could use its commerce clause authority to grant rights to citizens enforceable in the federal courts against the states.[47] In his dissent in *Seminole Tribe*, Justice Stevens used unusually strong language, describing the majority's decision as "a sharp break with the past," "shocking," and "profoundly misguided."[48]

In its 1996–1997 and 1998–1999 terms, the Court continued its "sharp break with the past" in the area of federalism. In the 1996–1997 term, the Court's conservative majority invalidated three federal laws, the Religious Freedom Restoration Act (providing that no state or locality could enforce laws that "substantially burden" religious observances without showing a "compelling need"); a provision of the "Brady" gun control law requiring state law enforcement officials to conduct background checks of prospective gun purchasers; and the Communications Decency Act (prohibiting obscene or indecent material on the Internet). In the 1998–1999 term, the Court also decided three cases that increased the power of the states at the expense of Congress and of private citizens. The first made states immune from suits by state employees for violations of federal labor law. The second made states immune from suits by patent owners for infringement of their patents by state universities or other state agencies, and the third prevented persons from bringing unfair competition cases against the states. Summing up these cases, the *New York Times* legal correspondent concluded that they represented "the most powerful indication yet of a narrow majority's determination to reconfigure the balance between state and Federal authority in favor of the states."[49]

In its 2000–2001 term the Court continued its attack on the idea of universal or national rights by declaring several acts of Congress unconstitutional. In 1994 Congress passed the Violence Against Women's Act. The act provided women with the right to sue individuals in federal court for acts of violence against them. In declaring the act unconstitutional, the Court's five-person majority declared that violence against women did not significantly impact interstate commerce. (The act was based on Congress's commerce clause powers.)[50] In *Kimel* v. *Florida Board of Regents* the Court ruled that Congress exceeded its authority when it allowed federal lawsuits by state employees alleging discrimination on the basis of age. Writing for the majority, Justice O'Connor concluded, "States may discriminate on the basis of age without offending the Fourteenth Amendment if the age classification in question is rationally related to a legitimate state interest."[51] Finally, in *Board of Trustees of the University of Alabama et al.* v. *Garrett et al.* the Court ruled that states were immune from suits under the 1991 Americans with Disabilities Act if the state's discrimination had a "rational basis." Writing for the majority, Chief Justice Rehnquist said, "The Fourteenth Amendment does not require states to make special accommodations for the disabled, so long as their actions toward individuals are rational. They could quite hardheadedly—and perhaps hardheartedly—hold to job requirements which do not make allowance for the disabled."[52] In each of these cases the four more liberal justices who dissented declared that the majority's decisions were a radical curtailment of Congress's authority to regulate the economy and protect civil rights.

The Rehnquist Court's relentless attack on the idea of universal freedom or federally guaranteed rights came to somewhat of a halt in its 2002–2004 terms. Although its decisions since the mid-1990s returning power to the states on the basis of the Tenth and Eleventh Amendments have not been noticed by the public at large, they have excited concern in academic and legal circles and among those concerned with civil liberties and civil rights. A good example of this concern is the 2002 book by John T. Noonan, a judge on the Ninth Circuit Court of Appeals. Noonan is so alarmed by the Rehnquist Court's state-centered federalism that he wrote *Narrowing the Nation's Power: The Supreme Court*

Sides with the States to call the matter to broad public attention.[53] Noonan essentially takes the view of the dissenting justices in the federalism cases since the 1990s; a stance somewhat unusual for a lower court judge who is supposed to follow and implement the decisions of the Supreme Court majority. But Noonan believes so strongly that the Rehnquist majority is wrong (particularly in the way it has interpreted the Eleventh Amendment to deprive individuals of the right to sue the states) that he argues he is obligated as an informed citizen to speak out. And speak out he does, arguing that the Court's recent federalism decisions are hypocritical; without foundation in the history or text of the Constitution; and threaten, if not halted and reversed, to undermine principles of universal freedom and democratic government.

Although it is doubtful that Noonan's book or the many critical articles in the law reviews about the Court's federalism cases have affected its decisions, in 2003 and 2004 it did appear in two important cases to back away, if only slightly, from its state-centered federalism. The two cases involved the Family Leave Act and the Americans with Disabilities Act. However, in one case the Court continued to narrow the power of the federal government in relationship to the states. In a 5-4 decision the Court ruled that the Eleventh Amendment prohibited the federal government from suing the states to enforce its regulations. In this case the Federal Maritime Commission sued the Port of Charleston, South Carolina, in order to enforce provisions of the Federal Shipping Act. Justice Thomas, writing for the majority, said the Eleventh Amendment precluded the suit because the amendment's preeminent purpose was to "accord the states the dignity that is consistent with their status as sovereign entities."[54] Justice Stephen Breyer, writing for the dissenters, rejected the idea that the states were "sovereign" and went on to argue that the majority decision lacked "any firm anchor in the Constitution's text."[55]

This, however, was a rather minor, technical administrative case without great impact on the rights and freedoms of the people (it involved a dispute about a ship that claimed it had been wrongfully denied berth at the Charleston port), although the principle underlying the decision has potential far-reaching implications. In two cases with broad and immediate impact on the lives of ordinary people the Court backed way from its rigid adherence to state-centered federalism. In 2003 in *Nevada Department of Human Resources* v. *Hibbs* the Court upheld the right of persons to sue the states to enforce provisions of the Family Leave Act. In 1993 Congress, using the Fourteenth Amendment's equal protection clause, enacted the Family Leave Act in order to remedy what it viewed as widespread gender discrimination in the workplace (the act allows men and women to take up to 12 weeks of unpaid leave to care for a sick relative). William Hibbs, an employee of Nevada's Department of Human Resources, was fired when he took leave to care for his sick wife. He then sued the state and in a 6-3 decision the Court rejected Nevada's claim of sovereign immunity under the Eleventh Amendment. The Chief Justice wrote that the act was "narrowly targeted" to "protect the right to be free from gender-based discrimination in the workforce by addressing the pervasive sex-role sterotype that caring for family members is women's work."[56]

In 2004 the Court upheld provisions of the Americans with Disabilities Act, allowing individuals to sue states that fail to provide access (ramps or elevators) to their courthouses. Although the Court had previously rejected the right of the disabled to sue states for employment discrimination, in *Tennessee* v. *Lane* a 5-4 majority said access to the courts was such a fundamental right that the states' Eleventh Amendment immunity had to give way to Congress's authority to enforce the equal protection clause of the

Fourteenth Amendment.[57] Justice Stevens's opinion was limited, however, to access to courthouses, and a particularly egregious case of discrimination in which George Lane, a paraplegic, was literally forced to crawl up the stairs of the Courthouse in Benton, Tennessee. (When his case was not heard in the morning session and he refused to crawl up a second time, he was arrested and jailed for failing to appear.)[58] That is, Justice Stevens specifically refused to rule that states could be sued if they denied access to the disabled to other public places such as classrooms, swimming pools, or libraries. It is generally believed that Justice Stevens refused to extend his opinion to cover all public places because Justice O'Connor (who joined his opinion) would have dissented. Thus while the Court in its 2002–2004 terms retreated a bit from state-centered federalism, it still does not have a majority that embraces the Fourteenth Amendment as the great charter of universal freedom for all Americans in all cases.

FACES AND VOICES IN THE STRUGGLE FOR UNIVERSAL FREEDOM

ELEANOR ROOSEVELT (1884–1962)

Eleanor Roosevelt, wife of President Franklin D. Roosevelt, contributed to universal freedom and equality through a passionate commitment to racial equality in the 1930s and 1940s and her work in the drafting and enacting of the United Nations (UN) Declaration of Human Rights. Mrs. Roosevelt, with little success, constantly prodded her husband to take a forthright position in opposition to lynchings and in support of African American freedom and equality. Although she could not "educate" her husband on universal freedom and equality, she did educate the

Source: Bettmann/Corbis

public through her speeches and her "My Day" column, which she wrote daily from 1936 to 1962. Mrs. Roosevelt also championed the cause of women, workers, and the poor and dispossessed.

After her husband's death, President Truman in 1945 appointed her to head the UN Human Rights Commission. Three years later she was the major figure in securing adoption by the international community of the Declaration of Human Rights. The UN Declaration declares that all persons are equal and human rights are universal. In addition to civil rights, the Declaration also declares that all persons are entitled to social and economic rights, including the "right to a standard of living adequate for the health and well being of his family including food, clothing, housing, medical care and social services."[*]

---

[*]Shelia K. Hershan, *The Candles She Lit: The Legacy of Eleanor Roosevelt* (Westport, CT: Praeger, 1993).

Summary

Federalism is an integral part of the American system of government. But from the beginning of the country's history there has been tension and debate between those who favor state-centered power and those who favor national-centered power. For most of American history, advocates of state-centered power have been dominant. However, in three periods of national crisis—two of which were directly related to the African American freedom struggle—advocates of national-centered power triumphed. During the Civil War and Reconstruction, the Depression and the New Deal, and the 1960s civil rights revolution, the powers of the federal government in relationship to the states were enormously expanded. In each of these periods the federal government began to play a more active role in protecting civil liberties and civil rights and in regulating the market economy. The Fourteenth Amendment, adopted after the Civil War to secure the freedom and equality of African Americans, has been central to the expansion of national-centered power, serving as the great charter of universal freedom for all Americans.

Yet after each period of expanding federal power the forces of states' rights and localism reasserted themselves. In the earliest days of the Republic these forces were generally liberal, progressive, antifederalist Democrats, but since the Civil War and especially since the New Deal, conservative Republicans have generally been hostile to expanding the power of the federal government. Since the election of Richard Nixon in 1968, Republican presidents have consistently called for a return of power to the states. The idea of states' rights appears to be the direction of the current conservative majority on the Supreme Court. Thus, the tide in American politics may once again be shifting toward state-centered power and limited rather than universal freedom.

Selected Bibliography

Curtis, Michael. *No State Shall Abridge: The Fourteenth Amendment and the Bill of Rights.* Durham, NC: Duke University Press, 1988. A strong argument for the case that the Fourteenth Amendment was intended to incorporate the Bill of Rights.

Dye, Thomas. *American Federalism.* Lexington, MA: Lexington Books, 1990. One of the better recent studies of the operations of the federal system.

Foner, Eric. *Reconstruction: America's Unfinished Revolution, 1863–1877.* New York: Harper & Row, 1988. The definitive study of the Reconstruction Era and the first major expansion of the power of the federal government.

Grodzins, Morton. *The American System.* Chicago: Rand McNally, 1966. A standard study of the operations of the federal system.

Nelson, William. *The Fourteenth Amendment: From Political Principle to Judicial Doctrine.* Cambridge, MA: Harvard University Press, 1988. A balanced analysis of the debate on the intent of the framers of the Fourteenth Amendment and the Bill of Rights, and the relationship of their intent to federalism.

Noonan, John, T. *Narrowing the Nation's Power: The Supreme Court Sides with the States.* Berkeley: University of California Press, 2002. A federal appeals court judge's critique of the Rehnquist Court's state-centered federalism.

Riker, William. *Federalism, Origin, Operation and Significance.* Boston: Little, Brown, 1964. An important study whose thesis is that federalism in the United States operates to limit freedom and benefit southern racists.

Notes

1. Robert Bork, *The Tempting of America: The Seduction of the Law* (New York: Free Press, 1990): 52–53. Bork's nomination to the Court was defeated 58 to 42.
2. William Riker, *Federalism: Origins, Operation and Significance* (Boston: Little, Brown, 1964): 140.
3. Ibid., pp. 132–33.
4. Ibid., p. 155.
5. On the great black migration from the South to the North between the 1920s and the 1960s, see Neil Flingstein, *Going North: Migration of Blacks and Whites from the South 1900–1950* (New York: Academic Press, 1981), and James Grossman, *Land of Hope: Chicago, Black Southerners and the Great Migration* (Chicago: University of Chicago Press, 1989).
6. Jean Bodin's political theory and idea of sovereignty are discussed in George Sabine, *A History of Political Theory*, 4th ed. (Hinsdale, IL: Dryden Press, 1973): 377–84.
7. Max Farand, *The Records of the Federal Constitutional Convention* (New Haven, CT: Yale University Press, 1937), vol. 1, cited in Riker, *Federalism*, p. 22.
8. Of the 190-plus governments in the world, about 17 are federal—mostly in large nations such as Australia, Canada, India, and Nigeria.
9. The most famous proponent of this view in American history is South Carolina's Senator John C. Calhoun in his doctrine of "concurrent majorities," which argues that on legislation affecting the interests of the states, both congressional and state legislative majorities should be required. In other words, the states should have a veto over federal laws affecting the state's vital interests. See Calhoun's *A Disquisition on Government*, edited by C. G. Post (New York: Liberal Arts Press, 1963).
10. *U.S. Term Limits, Inc. et al.* v. *Thornton et al.* (slip opinion) #93-1456 (1995). A slip opinion is a preliminary draft of a decision issued prior to formal publication.
11. Ibid.
12. Ibid. Justice Thomas contends that the framers deleted the reference to the states in the Preamble because they were not certain that all the states would ratify the Constitution.
13. Ibid.
14. Ibid.
15. See Jack L. Walker's classic article on this topic, "The Diffusion of Innovation Among the American States," *American Political Science Review* 63 (September 1969): 880–99.
16. See E. E. Schattsneider, *The Semi-Sovereign People* (New York: Holt, Rinehart and Winston, 1960); Grant McConnell, *Private Power and American Democracy* (New York: Vintage Books, 1966); and Woodrow Wilson, *Congressional Government: A Study in American Politics* (Gloucester, MA: Peter Smith, 1885, 1973).
17. Wilson, *Congressional Government*, p. 77.
18. Schattsneider, *The Semi-Sovereign People*.
19. Riker, *Federalism*, p. 144.
20. Eric Foner, *Reconstruction: America's Unfinished Revolution, 1863–1877* (New York: Harper & Row, 1988): 251.
21. Ibid.; see especially Chaps. 6–10.
22. On the New Deal, see William Leuchtenburg, *Franklin D. Roosevelt and the New Deal* (New York: Crowell, 1967), and Otis Graham, *An Encore for Reform: The Old Progressives and the New Deal* (New York: Oxford, 1967).
23. Foner, *Reconstruction*, p. 34.
24. Fred Friendly and Martha Elliot, *The Constitution: That Delicate Balance* (New York: McGraw-Hill, 1984): 18.

25. *The Slaughterhouse Cases*, 16 Wall (83 U.S.) 26 (1873) as reprinted in Kermit Hall, William Wiecek, and Paul Finkelman, eds., *American Legal History: Cases and Materials* (New York: Oxford University Press, 1991): 240.

26. Ibid., p. 240. In its 2000–2001 term, the Supreme Court provided striking examples of how the Fourteenth Amendment is applied to protect the rights and freedoms of persons who are not of the black "race." In *Troxel et vir* v. *Granville* (#99-138, 2000) the Court declared unconstitutional a Washington state law that granted grandparents visitation rights to the daughter of their deceased son, over the objections of the girl's mother. In declaring the law unconstitutional the Court held that the Fourteenth Amendment's due process clause provides protection against government interference with certain fundamental rights and liberties of all persons, and that one of those rights is the right of parents to make decisions about rearing their children without government intrusion. In an ironic decision—given the origins and purposes of the amendment—in *Bush* v. *Gore* (#00-949, 2000) the Court used the amendment's equal protection clause to in effect award the presidency to Bush, the candidate opposed by more than 90 percent of the blacks for whom the amendment was originally adopted.

27. William Nelson, *The Fourteenth Amendment: From Political Principle to Judicial Doctrine* (Cambridge, MA: Harvard University Press, 1988): 96.

28. Friendly and Elliot, *That Delicate Balance*, p. 18.

29. In 1833 the Supreme Court in *Barron* v. *Baltimore* held that the Bill of Rights applied only to the federal government.

30. See, for example, Michael Curtis, *No State Shall Abridge: The Fourteenth Amendment and the Bill of Rights* (Durham: Duke University Press, 1988). This is also Foner's view in *Reconstruction*, pp. 251–61.

31. Charles Fairman, "Does the Fourteenth Amendment Incorporate the Bill of Rights: The Original Understanding," *Stanford Law Review* 2 (1949): 5–139.

32. Nelson, *The Fourteenth Amendment*, chap. 1.

33. The term *pernicious* is used by Hall, Wiecek, and Finkelman in *American Legal History* to describe the opinion; p. 241.

34. *The Civil Rights Cases*, 109 U.S. 3 (1883) as reprinted in Hall, Wiecek, and Finkelman, p. 241.

35. Ibid., p. 140.

36. *Lochner* v. *New York*, 198 U.S. 45 (1905).

37. Traditionally, the idea of due process of law as it is found in the Fifth and Fourteenth Amendments was *procedural*—that a person would have a fair trial and hearing. *Lochner* and similar decisions introduced the notion of *substantive* due process—the idea that the substance of a legislative act in and of itself could be unfair and thus a violation of due process.

38. *Gitlow* v. *New York*, 268 U.S. 652 (1952). Benjamin Gitlow was a communist who advocated violent revolution. He was convicted under New York's criminal anarchy law. In deciding the case, however, the Court did not overturn his conviction but simply made the theoretical point that the free speech clause applied to the states.

39. Another reason that the commerce clause rather than the Fourteenth Amendment was used is that it permitted the leaders of the Senate to refer the bill to the Commerce Committee (which was chaired by Senator Warren Magnuson, a pro-civil rights liberal from Washington) rather than the Judiciary Committee, which was chaired by James Eastland, a racist, white supremacist from Mississippi. See Robert Loevy, *Hubert Humphrey and the Civil Rights Act of 1964: First Person Accounts of Congressional Enactment of the Law That Ended Racial Segregation* (Albany: SUNY Press, 1996).

40. *Heart of Atlanta Motel, Inc.* v. *United States*, 379 U.S. 241 85 S.CT., 348 (1964).

41. The history of the Court's right to privacy cases and sexuality (including *Bowers*) is examined in David Garrow, *Liberty and Sexuality: The Right to Privacy and the Making of* Roe v. Wade (New York: Macmillan Publishing, 1994).

42. *Bowers* v. *Hardwick*, 478 U.S. 186 (1986).

43. *Lawrence et al.* v. *Texas* (slip opinion) #02-102 (2003).

44. *New York* v. *United States*, 505 U.S. 144 (1995).

45. Justice Stevens's reference to McCulloch is to *McCulloch* v. *Maryland* (4 Wheaton 316), decided in 1819. This case, along with *Marbury* v. *Madison* (1 Cranch, 137, 1813), in which the Court first asserted its power of judicial review, is one of the landmark cases in the development of constitutional jurisprudence in the United States. In *McCulloch* the Court established two fundamental principles that Thomas's dissent appears to challenge. The first is the doctrine of implied powers, which asserts that Congress has powers beyond those expressly listed in Article 1, Section 8; second is the doctrine of the supremacy of federal laws over those enacted by the states. Justice Stevens's reference to commerce clause jurisprudence refers to Article I's interstate commerce clause, which since the New Deal has been the major constitutional basis for Congress's authority to pass laws regulating the economy as well as social welfare and civil rights legislation.

46. *United States* v. *Lopez* (slip opinion) #93-1260 (1995).

47. *Pennsylvania* v. *Union Gas*, 491 U.S. 1, 24 (1989).

48. *Seminole Tribe of Florida* v. *Florida et al.* (slip opinion) #94-12 (1996).

49. Linda Greenhouse, "States Are Given New Legal Shield by Supreme Court," *New York Times on the Web* (June 24, 1999).

50. *United States* v. *Morrison et al.*, 529, U.S. (2001). In this case a female student at Virginia Polytechnic Institute sued three male students who she alleged raped her.

51. In this case several Florida State University professors sued the state board of regents, contending that younger faculty members were treated more favorably when it came to salaries and promotions. In this case the Court also ruled that the Eleventh Amendment gave the states immunity from most suits by individuals in federal court.

52. In this case, Alabama in one instance demoted an employee after she was treated for breast cancer, and in another refused to make accommodations for an employee who said his health required that he work in an environment free of carbon monoxide and cigarette smoke.

53. John T. Noonan, *Narrowing the Nation's Power: The Supreme Court Sides with the States* (Berkeley: University of California Press, 2002).

54. Linda Greenhouse, "Supreme Court Expands Rights of States in Maritime Suit," *New York Times* (May 28, 2002).

55. Ibid.

56. *Nevada Department of Human Resources* v. *Hibbs* (slip opinion) #01-1368 (2003).

57. *Tennessee* v. *Lane* (slip opinion) #02-1667 (2004).

58. Adam Cohen, "Can Disabled People Be Forced to Crawl up the Courthouse Steps?" *New York Times* (January 11, 2004).

CHAPTER 3

Political Culture

In political science, *political culture* is generally understood in terms of "psychological or subjective orientations towards politics."[1] Specifically, political culture refers to political orientations—attitudes toward the political system and toward the role of the individual in the system. Simply put, the concept refers to the individual's attitudes, beliefs, and values about politics and the political system.

The concept of political culture has been divided into three components: (1) a *cognitive* component—knowledge and beliefs about political reality; (2) an *affective* component—feelings with respect to politics, political leaders, and institutions; and (3) an *evaluative* component—one's commitment to political values and ideas.[2]

The Concept of Political Culture and the Invisibility of African Americans

The concept of political culture in modern political science was first proposed by Gabriel Almond and Sidney Verba in their classic study *The Civic Culture*, a book comparing political cultures across five nations.[3] Blacks were invisible in this original study.[4] Almond writes, "our American sample yielded only under a hundred black respondents, hardly representative of the black population. Hence, we failed to deal with the political attitudes of American Blacks."[5]

In evaluating this pioneering empirical work on the concept, one analyst declares, "One major omission from the description of American politics in *The Civic Culture*, which seems rather glaring in retrospect, is the absence of any separate treatment of the political culture of America's black minority."[6] He concludes with the observation: "The omission of a control variable as important in the American political context as race was a costly sacrifice for the sake of comparability, as the events of the subsequent decade made clear."[7] Thus, in its initial formation and operationalization, the African American political subculture did not appear, and in its second reincarnation or "renaissance" no portrait of the African American political subculture was visible.[8]

But this did not happen simply because political scientists were oblivious to the matter of race. David Easton, between the initial formation of the concept and its subsequent reformulation, offers new insights. His redefinition of the concept acknowledges that various subgroups in the political system distinguished by race, ethnicity, language, religion, and the like may be regulated by different normative and value systems and conceptions of authority, and these are regarded as political subcultures. Thus, a *subculture* or *political subculture* refers to patterns that are dominant within the respective subgroups, but which other members of the system may choose to ignore and reject without remorse, guilt, shame, condemnation, or fear of sanctions. In short, there is not a single homogeneous political culture but a composite of several subculture variations.[9]

The Literature on the African American Political Culture

Not all political scientists have avoided investigating how race and political culture linked and intersected with each other to shape African American political behavior. There is a small but growing body of literature that has (1) defined the concept, (2) explicated some of the essential component parts, and (3) provided a residual empirical testing of some of the component parts of African American political culture. This literature tended to explore the concept by observing conventional African American political behavior. However, a study of the 1992 Los Angeles riots postulated and then demonstrated that the African American political culture influences, informs, and impacts unconventional political behavior as well, and that manifestations of these influences can be found in the political attitudes of individual African Americans.[10]

What is African American political culture? It "is composed of both intrapsychic and external systemic factors that originate from elements both inside and outside of the black community."[11] Professor Charles Henry added to the definitional equation by asserting that this culture places "its emphasis on identity and self-respect and . . . [that it is] coded in a black church tradition that blends a sacred and secular vision."[12]

Earlier, several African American social scientists such as W. E. B. Du Bois and Ralph Bunche had suggested *political consciousness* as one measurable component of African American political culture—that is, supporting African American political candidates, organizing African American political parties, holding state and national political conventions, and forming political caucuses and leagues. Speaking of this self-conscious type of political activity, Bunche said, "The Negro is very much a political animal and . . . his political urges will find expression in other channels whenever he is deprived of participation in the usual political processes."[13]

Charles Hamilton and Matthew Holden delineated additional component parts of the African American political culture, including the importance of the spoken word.[14] African American political rhetoric, or what David Howard-Pitney calls the African American Jeremiad (political sermon), has been demonstrated to be an essential element in the African American political culture and it has a significant and influential impact on African American political behavior.[15]

To the components of (1) political consciousness and (2) political sermons, Holden added the element of political factionalism. This is the force that works against group unity—contending, contentious, and clashing ideologies such as nationalism versus integration.[16] Furthermore, Holden identified political opposition to racism as a central component of the African American political culture. Maulana Karenga has mapped out the specific features of oppositional politics in the community's political culture as they were expressed in the rhetoric of Malcolm X.[17]

Beyond the literature on defining the African American political culture concept and specifying its component parts, there are efforts to measure the concept empirically. Robert C. Smith and Richard Seltzer used a residual measurement technique to show that elements of African American political culture existed in African American mass political attitudes.[18]

Smith and Seltzer found three elements of African American political culture that distinguish it from the culture of whites. First, blacks of all social classes, to a greater degree than whites, were alienated or distrustful of government and societal institutions, as well as suspicious or distrustful of the motives of other individuals. Second, blacks of all social classes were more religious than whites. Third, blacks were distinctively a liberal group, especially on issues of the economy and the welfare state.[19]

Along with the empirical study of Smith and Seltzer, some equally interesting theoretical work is emerging. An exploration of the 1992 Los Angeles riots survey, for example, revealed the possibility of not only a linkage between riot behavior and community values and norms, but also a strong correlation between political attitudes, the resultant behavior, and the African American political culture. This research suggested that the African American political culture shapes both conventional and unconventional community behavior such as riots, protest demonstrations, strikes, marches, and protest theater.[20] When the theoretical and empirical literature is seen in a collective fashion and then synthesized to expose its common denominator, one sees that the African American political culture contains both supportive and opposing values and beliefs in regard to the American political system.

The African American Political Culture: An Empirical Estimation

In modern political science, most concepts must have some empirical estimation of their viability if they are to be useful in explaining political behavior. This means that manifestations of the concept under study will appear in mass political attitudes and behavior. This crucial assumption is built on the existence of culture-bearing and culture-transmitting institutions. The African American community has continually created and generated such institutions of different varieties and successes. Karenga states that Malcolm X was such an institution because he taught African Americans oppositional politics.[21] An earlier work on the African American political culture suggested that men such as L. H. Stanton and Clarence Holte, founders and editors of *National Scene*, a monthly black newspaper magazine supplement, operated as culture-bearing institutions.[22] Others have included Martin Luther King, Jr., as well as his national holiday. In fact, if cultural values are to circulate within the political community, culture-bearing institutions must be present and operative. In addition, these institutions must absorb and reject certain features out of the social milieu from which they emerge and develop their own version of the mix of cultural values for transmission. Finally, these institutions need not be permanent or strong institutions to have an impact; rather, they can be fragile, transient, and inconsistent.

Therefore, if we begin with a search for the initial component of political culture—that is, the *cognitive aspect*—it should be sought through survey questions that seek to tap into and reveal the racial consciousness of the African American community. Three national surveys of the African American community asked questions that probed the nature of racial consciousness in mass attitudes.

The first of these were two National Black Election Studies (NBES) conducted in 1984 and 1988. In Table 3.1, we see African American political culture directly, with racial consciousness being the component. The table shows at least three aspects of this consciousness: (1) as it relates to the African American community itself, (2) as it relates to the

Table 3.1 The Racial Consciousness Component (in Percentages) of the African American Political Culture: The National Black Election Study—1984 and 1988

		YEARS	
ASPECT OF RACIAL CONSCIOUSNESS		1984	1988
Community Consciousness			
Common Fate for Blacks:	Do you think what happens generally to black people in this country will have something to do with what happens in your life?		
Yes		69%	70%
No		25	22
Missing Data		6	9
Political Consciousness			
Black Vote Makes Difference in Presidential Election:	If enough vote, they can make a difference in who gets elected.		
Agree Strongly		71%	65%
Agree Somewhat		18	16
Disagree Somewhat		6	8
Disagree Strongly		5	5
Missing Data		2	7
Electoral Consciousness			
Vote for Black Candidates:	Blacks should always vote for black candidates when they run.		
Strongly Agree		5%	7%
Agree		9	13
Disagree		40	39
Strongly Disagree		20	18
Missing Data		26	22

Source: National Black Election Panel Study, 1984 and 1988. University of Michigan, Institute for Social Research, Ann Arbor.

community's political participation, and (3) as it relates to African American political candidates. Using specific questions that tap these elements, the researchers found substantial empirical support at the individual attitudinal level for this aspect of African American political culture.

In both the 1984 and 1988 elections, the community and political consciousness aspects of the culture remained very high and positive. Individuals revealed in their attitudes that the community had a common fate and that voting in presidential elections could make a major difference. (By the second term of the Reagan presidency, this belief in the impact of presidential voting was somewhat reduced.)

In terms of electoral consciousness, individual attitudes revealed that black candidates come under scrutiny and that voting for them is not considered the only way to express one's voting behavior. The findings here are consistent with the findings about political consciousness. Voting is important to enhance one's community, but the road to empowerment does not rest solely on supporting black candidates.

Overall, the empirical evidence in Table 3.1 strongly suggests support for the cognitive component of the African American political culture. Racial consciousness is a part of the community's political culture through its attitudes, and this consciousness is based more in the community than in the individual.

Another national survey is the 1993 National Black Politics Survey (NBPS). This survey reveals individual attitudes manifesting the cognitive component of the political culture. Table 3.2 reveals that three-fourths (75 percent) of all African Americans see themselves linked by a common fate. This shows a very strong sense of community consciousness.

Two-thirds of the community sees the need for political involvement, especially if it provides black political control. Finally, there is the element of electoral consciousness: One-fourth of the community (26 percent) feels there should be a "racial vote," that blacks should always vote for African American candidates irrespective of ideology, character, issues, and/or past service to the community. Three-fourths of the community disagrees with the idea of a "racial vote."

Table 3.2 The Racial Consciousness Component (in Percentages) of the African American Political Culture: The National Black Politics Survey—1993

ASPECT OF RACIAL CONSCIOUSNESS	YEAR 1993
Community Consciousness	
Common Fate for Blacks:	Do you think what happens generally to black people in this country will have something to do with what happens in your life?
Yes	75%
No	21
Don't Know	3
Not Applicable	1
Political Consciousness	
Black Political Involvement:	Blacks should have control over the government in most black communities.
Strongly Agree	23%
Agree	42
Disagree	26
Strongly Disagree	5
Don't Know/Don't Care	4
Refused/Not Applicable	1
Electoral Consciousness	
Vote for Black Candidates:	Blacks should always vote for black candidates when they run.
Strongly Agree	9%
Agree	17
Disagree	55
Strongly Disagree	18
Don't Care/Don't Know	1
Not Applicable	1

Source: National Black Politics Survey, 1993, University of Chicago.

This absence of a racial vote in black consciousness can be seen by studying the outcomes of the various elections where African Americans sought major party presidential nominations. There was relatively little evidence of this phenomenon in the candidacies of Shirley Chisholm and Al Sharpton, and it was completely absent when the conservative Alan Keyes ran for the Republican nomination. It was strongly evident, however, when Jesse Jackson ran in 1984 and 1988 and when Barack Obama ran in 2008 (see Chapter 9). This suggests that the racial consciousness variable in African American voting depends on the candidate and the political context.

The second component, the affective component of the African American political culture, should appear in individual-level mass attitudes that express feelings, sentiments, and emotions about presidents, Congress, the courts, the bureaucracy, political parties, laws, and public policies. Among questions related to these political entities, items on presidential approval have occurred with the greatest frequency in national polls and surveys. The Gallup organization, which first asked members of the public in 1933 if they approved of the president's performance, included too few African Americans in early samples for reliable estimates.[23] Analysis of these approval data have shown that presidents do not appeal equally to all groups in the public.

> Each of the presidents . . . has experienced a different pattern of public support. There has been a considerable range in both the levels and the volatility of presidential approval and each president has had sources of special strength and weakness in support among particular segments of the public.[24]

In terms of partisan support, this is especially true of African Americans. During the presidency of Republican Dwight Eisenhower in the 1950s, there were moderate differences between blacks and whites in presidential approval, but in the Reagan years during the 1980s there was extreme racial polarization.[25] Since 1964, the Democratic Party and Democratic presidents have usually been able to count on substantial support from the black community, while the Republican Party and Republican presidents have enjoyed relatively little support.[26]

Turning to the third and final component of the political culture concept, the evaluative component, evidence of this should appear in answers to questions about "trust" in government as well as how well government responds to individuals' needs and demands. The National Election Studies (NES) cumulative data (1952–1994), aggregated by decades for presidential and congressional years, provide fairly reliable estimates. In addition, this procedure gives a time dimension to the empirical results. Table 3.3 indicates that the trust of African Americans in the American political system peaked in the sixties, the period of heightened civil rights legislation; it dropped in the Nixon–Ford years; and it reached something of a plateau in the 1980s. Trust in the system was lowest in the Nixon–Ford years, but has stabilized since the 1980s.

Trust during congressional election years reveals a similar but slightly different pattern. As during the presidential years, trust in the system is generally low; however, unlike the presidential years, this low level of trust is consistent in all years observed for congressional elections.

Many in political science stress political alienation as the cause of this declining confidence, claiming that African Americans are the most unstable and volatile group in the polity. As such, they are dangerous to the polity itself. Such reasoning is fallacious

Table 3.3 The Evaluative (Trust) Component (in Percentages) of the African American Political Culture: The National Election Study—1964–2000

	LEVELS OF TRUST				
PRESIDENTIAL YEARS	1964–68	1972–76	1980–84–88	1992–96	2000
Low Trust	19%	71%	61%	58%	68%
Moderate Trust	11	10	12	17	28
High Trust	70	19	27	24	4
CONGRESSIONAL YEARS		1974–78		1994	
Low Trust		65%		67%	
Moderate Trust		13		13	
High Trust		23		21	

Note: Trust is measured by how respondents answered the following question: How much do you think you can trust the government in Washington to do what is right: just about always, most of the time, some of the time, or almost never?

Source: National Election Studies Cumulative File, Presidential and Congressional Years, University of Michigan, Institute for Social Research, Ann Arbor.

because it rests on psychological determinants and not systemic ones such as governmental responsiveness.

As one looks at a systemic determinant such as governmental responsiveness to the African American community, data in Table 3.4 show a clear and significant correlation between low and high responsiveness by government and low and high trust among African Americans. The highest system responsiveness, which took place in the sixties, is also the period of highest trust; the period in which low responsiveness was greatest closely parallels the period of lowest trust. After 1980, the NES dropped the responsiveness question from its survey; consequently, following the two variables over time is impossible. Nevertheless, it is clear that African American trust in government is related to governmental performance as much as it is to alienation or other individual psychological determinants.

Table 3.4 The Evaluative (Responsiveness) Component (in Percentages) of the African American Political Culture: The National Election Study—1964–1980

	LEVELS OF RESPONSIVENESS[a]		
PRESIDENTIAL YEARS	1964–68	1972–76	1980
Low	19%	21%	24%
Moderate	40	60	48
High	52	19	28
CONGRESSIONAL YEARS	1970–74–78		
Low	24%		
Moderate	52		
High	23		

[a]Responsiveness is measured by how respondents answered a question asking whether they thought the government in Washington paid attention to people like themselves.

Source: National Election Studies Cumulative File, Presidential and Congressional Years, University of Michigan, Institute for Social Research, Ann Arbor.

FACES AND VOICES IN THE STRUGGLE FOR UNIVERSAL FREEDOM

HARRY BELAFONTE (1927–)

Harry Belafonte, the singer and actor, used his status as a cultural icon to advance the cause of universal freedom through his support of the civil rights movement, the anti-apartheid movement, and the cause of international human rights. In 1965 Belafonte's "The Banana Boat Song (Day-O)" became an instant classic and made him an international celebrity. In this same year he met Martin Luther King Jr. and became his abiding friend, advisor, and financial supporter. He rallied celebrities to support the movement, financed the freedom rides, and raised funds to bail protesters (including

Belafonte with Dr. King in a 1960s protest march.   *Source:* Bettmann/Corbis

Dr. King) out of jail. After Dr. King's death, Belafonte became active in the anti-apartheid movement and close friend and advisor to Nelson Mandela. In 1987 the United Nations Children Fund named him a general goodwill ambassador.

Conscious of the role that music and art can play in freedom movements, Belafonte was instrumental in bringing to American attention the South African musicians Hugh Masekela and Miriam Makeba. In 1985 he organized an all-star cast to produce "We Are the World," a multicultural recording that raised millions of dollars for famine relief in Africa. And in 2001 he finally released *A Long Road to Freedom*, a historical album on the African American musical tradition.

The son of Jamaican immigrants, Belafonte's music and his music history represent a systematic effort to show that African, African American, and Caribbean music are part of an integral tradition related to the freedom struggles of African people.

We have found empirical evidence for all three component parts of the political culture concept. We know that at the very least, manifestations of the African American political culture tend to surface in the mass attitudes of the community. Second, we can infer from the empirical data that the African American political culture influences and impacts African American political behavior.

Summary

The political culture or subculture of African Americans is characterized by a relatively high degree of racial group consciousness and relatively low levels of trust in the government, although this level of trust varies with the responsiveness of the system. The political culture is also characterized by a mix of oppositional and supportive attitudes with respect to the political system. It also displays a relatively high degree of religiosity and ideological liberalism, attitudes considered in greater detail in Chapter 5.

Selected Bibliography

Almond, Gabriel, and Sidney Verba. *The Civic Culture*. Princeton, NJ: Princeton University Press, 1963. This classic behavioral study compares the political cultures of five nations.

Almond, Gabriel, and Sidney Verba, eds. *The Civic Culture Revisited*. Boston: Little, Brown, 1980. A conceptual and methodological reexamination of the concept by an international group of scholars.

Divine, Donald. *The Political Culture of the United States*. Boston: Little, Brown, 1972. A pioneering behavioralist effort to locate the component parts of the nation's political culture.

Henry, Charles. *Culture and African American Politics*. Bloomington: Indiana University Press, 1990. An examination of the roots and nature of African American culture, focusing on religion and music.

Jones, Leroi. *Blues People: The Negro Experience in White America and the Music That Developed from It*. New York: William Morrow, 1963. An influential study of the centrality of music in African American culture.

Smith, Robert C., and Richard Seltzer. *Race, Class and Culture: A Study in Afro-American Mass Opinion*. Albany: SUNY Press, 1992. An effort to identify empirically certain components of African American political culture.

Walton, Hanes, Jr. "African American Political Culture: The Moral Voice and Perspective in the Recent Urban Riots." In Hanes Walton, Jr., ed., *African American Power and Politics: The Political Context Variable*. New York: Columbia University Press, 1997. Explores and delineates the existence of the African American political culture in nonconventional political behavior.

Notes

1. Glenda Patrick, "Political Culture," in Giovani Sartori, ed., *Social Science Concepts: A Systematic Analysis* (Beverly Hills: Sage, 1984): 266.
2. Ibid., pp. 273–85.
3. Gabriel Almond and Sidney Verba, *The Civic Culture: Political Attitudes in Five Nations* (Princeton, NJ: Princeton University Press, 1963). The five nations were the United States, the United Kingdom, West Germany, Mexico, and Italy.
4. For some of the more interesting studies of political culture in the United States, see Donald Devine, *The Political Culture of the United States* (Boston: Little, Brown, 1972); and Daniel Elazar, *American Federalism: A View from the States* (New York: Crowell, 1972).
5. Gabriel Almond, "The Intellectual History of the Civic Culture Concept," in Gabriel Almond and Sidney Verba, eds., *The Civic Culture Revisited* (Boston: Little, Brown, 1980): 23.
6. Alan Abramowitz, "The United States: Political Culture Under Stress," in Almond and Verba, *The Civic Culture*, pp. 180–81.
7. Ibid.
8. William Reisinger, "The Renaissance of a Rubric: Political Culture as Concept and Theory," *International Journal of Public Opinion Research* 7 (Winter 1995): 348.
9. Quoted in Patrick, "Political Culture," p. 272.

10. Hanes Walton, Jr., "African American Political Culture: The Moral Voice and Perspective in the Recent Urban Riots," in Hanes Walton, Jr., ed., *African American Power and Politics: The Political Context Variable* (New York: Columbia University Press, 1997): 93–108.

11. Hanes Walton, Jr., *Invisible Politics: Black Political Behavior* (Albany: SUNY Press, 1985): 26.

12. Charles Henry, *Culture and African American Politics* (Bloomington: Indiana University Press, 1990): 107.

13. Quoted in Walton, *Invisible Politics*, p. 27.

14. Matthew Holden, Jr., *The Politics of the Black "Nation"* (New York: Chandler, 1973); Charles Hamilton, *The Black Political Experience in America* (New York: Putnam, 1973).

15. David Howard-Pitney, *The Afro-American Jeremiad: Appeals for Justice in America* (Philadelphia: Temple University Press, 1990).

16. Holden, *The Politics of the Black "Nation,"* pp. 43–95.

17. Maulana Karenga, "The Oppositional Logic of Malcolm X: Differentialism, Engagement and Resistance," *Western Journal of Black Studies* 17 (Spring 1993): 6–16.

18. Robert C. Smith and Richard Seltzer, *Race, Class, and Culture: A Study in Afro-American Mass Opinion* (Albany: SUNY Press, 1992). This study used the National Opinion Research Center's 1987 General Social Survey, which included an oversample of 544 blacks.

19. Ibid.

20. Walton, "African American Political Culture," pp. 93–108.

21. Karenga, "The Oppositional Logic of Malcolm X."

22. See Walton, *Invisible Politics*, pp. 36–39; and Hanes Walton, Jr., "The Literary Works of a Black Bibliophile: Clarence L. Holte," *Western Journal of Black Studies* 1 (December 1977): 286–97.

23. Frederick Mosteller et al., *The Pre-Election Polls of 1948* (New York: Social Science Research Council, 1949).

24. George Edwards, III, and Alec Gallup, *Presidential Approval: A Sourcebook* (Baltimore: Johns Hopkins University Press, 1990): 188.

25. Ibid.

26. Michael Dawson, "African American Political Opinion: Volatility in the Reagan–Bush Era," in Walton, *African American Power and Politics*, chap. 8.

CHAPTER 4

Political Socialization

Political culture refers to attitudes, values, and beliefs about politics and the political system. *Political socialization* refers to the ongoing process by which individuals acquire these attitudes, values, and beliefs.[1] In simple terms, political socialization refers to the processes of political learning. For purposes of studying this process, political scientists usually center their attention on what are called *agents of socialization*—those mechanisms by which individuals acquire their attitudes, beliefs, and values.[2] The agents include *family, church, school, peer groups*, the *media*, and *political events*.

Gunnar Myrdal and the Political Socialization of African Americans

In his influential study, *An American Dilemma: The Negro Problem and Modern Democracy*, Gunnar Myrdal suggested that the political socialization process in black America was dysfunctional because it failed to socialize blacks into the white "mainstream" political culture. This is because, Myrdal argued, the agents of socialization were dysfunctional. Of these agents, he wrote,

> The instability of the Negro family, the inadequacy of educational facilities for Negroes, the emotionalism in the Negro church, the insufficiency and unwholesomeness of Negro recreational activity, the plethora of Negro sociable organizations, the narrowness of interests of the average Negro, the provincialism of his political speculation, the high Negro crime rate, the cultivation of the arts to the neglect of other fields, superstition, personality difficulties, and other characteristics are mainly forms of social pathology which, for the most part, are created by caste pressure.[3]

Myrdal's contention that the socialization process in black America was dysfunctional or "pathological" was based on his view that "it is to the advantage of American Negroes as individuals and as a group to become assimilated into American culture, to acquire the traits held in esteem by dominant whites."[4] Although Myrdal noted that certain features of the African American culture and certain agents were positive (mainly the black media), he wrote, "It does not gainsay our assumption that *here in America*, American culture is 'highest' in the pragmatic sense and that adherence to it is practical for any individual or group which is not strong enough to change it" (emphasis by Myrdal).[5]

Since it was clear that blacks were not strong enough to change the dominant culture, they should direct their socialization toward white mainstream culture at the expense of the African American subculture.

The Literature on African American Political Socialization

Myrdal's thesis prevailed and became very influential. Very few of the early socialization studies analyzed African Americans. As a group and as individuals, they were simply omitted.[6] When such studies did appear, the majority of them offered empirical support for the Myrdal thesis. These studies supported Myrdal's assertion by showing that virtually all of the socialization agents in the African American community were dysfunctional.[7]

However, a few of these early studies did find some different realities about African American political socialization that denied the Myrdal thesis. Indeed, in some of these few positive studies one could discern that African American political socialization was different from that of whites, and that "the process has at least three steps, including *resocialization* as well as *counter socialization.*"[8] One of the central agents of socialization in the black community was the church and its religion. Researchers theorized that "in the black community, in sharp contrast to the white, the church plays the dominant role in the socialization process. The family, the school and peer groups in that order are the next significant agents."[9] Among the reasons for the prominence of the church are the oral tradition and moralism of the political culture and the political activism of the church.[10] A third factor is that the church and its religion may provide a source and foundation for oppositional politics. God can be seen as a higher power than the institutions of slavery and segregation.

There are reasons for the existence and use of these different types of socializing agents in the African American community. Myrdal correctly observed that "different" socializing tactics have been and are

> the result of the rising Negro protest that there is in nearly the entire Negro population, a theoretical belief that Negroes are just as highly endowed with inherent capabilities and propensities as are white people. An emphatic assertion of equality of the Negro people's potentialities is a central theory in the propagation of Negro race consciousness and race pride.[11]

With this assertion, Myrdal embraced what he had earlier denied and declared impossible: African Americans socializing themselves toward an oppositional posture to racism, segregation, and discrimination. His embrace continues, "It cannot be doubted that the spirit of American Negroes in all classes . . . [is] the protest motive . . . [and it] is still rising. . . . Its existence, its popular spread, and its content are a testimony of Negro unrest. Its cumulative effect in spurring race consciousness must be tremendous."[12] Thus "defeatism and racial inferiority, cannot be said publicly. The protest motive does not allow it. No Negro leader could ever preach it. No Negro newspaper could print it. It must be denied eagerly and persistently."[13]

Therefore, despite all the alleged weaknesses Myrdal claimed for each of the agents of African American political socialization, the realities are that these "agents" socialized inside the African American community *an oppositional political culture* and new subcultural agents of socialization. Beyond the church and religion, as agents of socialization, there are others—for example, those of civil rights protests. Morris, Brown, and Hatchett write, "The Montgomery bus boycott was a ground-breaking political development. First, it endured for an entire year (381 days) despite the intense opposition of the local white community. The long duration of the boycott maximized its local, regional and national influences and visibility."[14] In a word, it socialized: "From a political standpoint, the black community was never to be the same after the Montgomery bus boycott. Indeed, nonviolent movements against racial segregation began to emerge in other communities such as Tallahassee, Florida and Birmingham, Alabama even while the Montgomery movement was still in process."[15] Thus, scholars have concluded, "The movement itself was a tool of political socialization. Its mass tactics required people to learn and execute new forms of political behavior."[16]

But if the civil rights movement became a different agent of political socialization, so did the black power movement that followed. Morris, Hatchett, and Brown write,

> The black-power ideology signalled a more radical thrust in the movement. First, its propo-
> nents either relaxed or rejected the goal of racial integration. Second, the strategy of non
> violence was rejected in favor of self-defense and the view that change should be achieved
> by "any means necessary." Finally, black-power advocates either relaxed or rejected the
> assumption that the civil rights movement should have an interracial character.[17]

These assumptions differentiated this activity from the older civil rights movement, which was to be expected, given some of the failures and shortcomings of that movement.

After the black power movement,

> the riots became the main mechanism for the resocialization of blacks and the crystal-
> lization of the new nationalist ideology. And . . . the riots themselves were catalytic
> agents in the resocialization of both rioters and blacks as a whole. While a very small
> proportion of blacks . . . took part in the riots, a much larger proportion sympathized
> with the rioters and saw the riots as protest.[18]

This was not only true in the mid- and late sixties, but it was true also in the 1992 Los Angeles riots.[19]

One can add to the different socializing agents not only the civil rights movement, the black power movement, and the riots, but also cultural events and projects.

In the 1960s and 1970s, black artists—visual, literary, and performing—began to focus on political issues and to develop new images of blacks and the black community, stemming from the black power movement [20] (see Box 4.1).

When the black power movement peaked, as the civil rights movement had done before it, a new African American socializing agent appeared—African American Democratic presidential candidates. First came the 1972 presidential campaign of African American congresswoman Shirley Chisholm.[21] Her performance in the Democratic presidential primaries was unique and dramatic. Her effort galvanized thousands of women and African American Democrats.[22] Although the electoral dimension of the Chisholm campaign failed, its socializing influence was important.

In 1984 and 1988, civil rights activist Reverend Jesse Jackson took a page from Chisholm and entered the Democratic presidential primaries. It was a sensation in the African American community,[23] and at the level of political socialization it generated significant grassroots political activities and local candidacies for office.[24] It also enlarged the number of registered voters. Thus, it socialized both masses and elites in the community.

In the aftermath of these presidential candidacies, a different socializing agent came in the form of the dramatic Million Man March in October 1995.[25] Led by the contro-versial black nationalist religious figure Louis Farrakhan, the march brought more African Americans to Washington, D.C., than did King's 1963 March on Washington, and

BOX 4.1   AFRICAN AMERICAN MUSIC AS AN AGENT OF POLITICAL SOCIALIZATION

Many observers of African American culture have pointed to the important role played by music in the socialization process. African Americans have often been heard to say, "You can tell where black people are at any given moment by our music." The novelist James Baldwin once said, "It is only in his music that the Negro in America has been able to tell his story." The political scientist Charles Henry argues that music, especially the blues, is an important socialization agent in African American politics; historian Frank Kofsky has demonstrated a relationship between the revolution in jazz symbolized in the work of John Coltrane and the militant nationalism of Malcolm X; poet and musicologist Leroi Jones points historically to a relationship between black music and black politics; and music critic Nelson George argues that in the 1960s and 1970s rhythm and blues was inspired by and gave inspiration to the civil rights and black power movements.[a]

From "Keep on Pushing" in the 1960s to "A New World Order" in the 1990s, Curtis Mayfield's music consistently involved political messages or "sermons," often dealing with themes of freedom.   *Source:* Bettmann/Corbis

In a comprehensive study of black music as a political agent during the 1960s, Robert Walker carried out a content analysis of all 1,100 songs that appeared on *Billboard's* cumulative annual best-selling black (soul) listings from 1946 to 1972. Walker's hypothesis was that the events of the 1960s produced a distinctive race group consciousness and solidarity that was manifested in an increase in songs with a political message. His data show a steady increase in "message songs" beginning after 1957 and that a sustained increase of "inordinate proportions" occurred between 1966 and 1969, the peak years of the black movement. By comparing black to white music in this same period, Walker was able to show that this increase in message music was peculiar to black music.[b] Among the popular songs with a political message during this period were James Brown's "I'm Black and I'm Proud," the Temptations' "Message to the Black Man," Marvin Gaye's "Inner City Blues," B. B. King's "Why I Sing the Blues," and Curtis Mayfield's "We're a Winner." Mayfield's "We're a Winner" was thought to be so politically inflammatory that some black radio stations were urged not play it for fear it might cause riots in the summer of 1968.

In some ways rap artists embraced the Obama campaign in the same fashion rhythm and blues artists embraced the civil rights and black power movements. Obama rap songs and lyrics and online videos appeared throughout the campaign by such artists as Ludacris, Nas, and Jay-Z. (Will I.AM.'s "Yes We Can" You Tube music video was viewed by nearly ten million

(continued)

BOX 4.1 *continued*

people prior to the Democratic convention.) Obama even used Jay-Z's "dirt-off—my shoulder" gesture to dismiss his critics. A hip-hop fan, Obama, however, at times criticized artists for misogynist lyrics, use of the "N" word, and materialism.

[a]Charles Henry, *Culture and African American Politics* (Bloomington: Indiana University Press, 1990); Frank Kofsky, *Black Nationalism and the Revolution in Music* (New York: Pathfinder Press, 1970); Leroi Jones, *Blues People* (New York: Morrow, 1963); Nelson George, *The Death of Rhythm and Blues* (New York: Dutton, 1989). For a history of black music and its relationship to politics, hear the six-CD collection (108 recordings ranging from gospel to rap), *Say It Loud: A Celebration of Black Music in America*, produced by Patrick Milligan, Shawn Amos, and Quincy Newell (Los Angeles: Rhino Entertainment, 2001); and Harry Belafonte's 5-CD collection, *The Long Road to Freedom: An Anthology of Black Music* (New York: Buddha Records, 2001).

[b]Robert Walker, "Soul and Society," Ph.D. dissertation, Stanford University, 1976.

it sent numerous individuals back to their local communities committed and reinvigorated toward developing grassroots self-help organizations and programs.

The confederate flag protests organized by African Americans in several Southern states were efforts to socialize blacks and whites to embrace the idea that political symbols—such as the confederate flag—should not represent values of racism and white supremacism. While many whites in the South claim that the flag was merely a symbol of their heritage, many blacks view the flag as divisive and insulting, and hence the efforts to have it removed may have been seen as an effort at socialization and resocialization of African Americans and whites in the South and throughout the country.

Overall, not all of the different socializing events that emerge inside the African American community generate the same impact and influence. Yet these different agents of the political resocialization of African Americans are clearly visible and have an impact. The question is whether manifestations of these realities can be empirically identified from surveying mass African American attitudes. Professor Ronald Brown has attempted to do so in his work on religion, the church, and African American socialization.

African American Political Socialization: An Empirical Estimation of Religion and the Church as Agents

Professor Ronald Brown took the theories about the church and religion as African American socializing agents, reduced them to a psychological dimension, and placed them as testable propositions in questionnaire form in two National Black Election Studies and the National Black Politics Survey. Brown undertook these studies with a variety of different colleagues, but he has been the most consistent and persistent analyst of the religious attribute. In his first work, with colleagues Richard Allen and Michael Dawson, Brown stressed that an African American racial belief system existed and that religiosity influenced and socialized that belief system. Writing about this approach, Brown and his colleagues told "how belief systems in general and this belief system in particular help process, constrain, and bias one's interpretations of reality and influence social and political behavior." The article then shows how "religiosity . . . influences the content of individual

African American belief systems."[26] Subsequent studies documented a strong relationship between religiosity, voting, and other forms of political participation, as well as a sense of racial identification, consciousness, and political obligation to the black community.[27]

BOX 4.2   THE AFRICAN AMERICAN CHURCH

Faith in God, the belief that "God will deliver us some day," has been described as the single most common theme in African American culture.[a] Given the central role of religion in black life, the church becomes the central political institution in the black community. Freedom is also central in the African American religious tradition. Lincoln and Mamiya write,

"A major aspect of black Christian belief is found in the importance given to the word 'freedom.' Throughout black history the term 'freedom' has found deep religious resonance in the lives and hopes of African Americans. . . . In song, word and deed freedom has always been the superlative value of the black cosmos."[b]

Bill Clinton speaking at a black church in Baltimore, the Sunday before the 1998 midterm elections. The church is a major agent of political socialization and mobilization in the black community.   *Source:* The White House Press Office

African Americans are more religious than whites (measured by frequency of church attendance and prayer, and subjective identification with God), and religiously inclined blacks are more likely to vote and engage in other forms of political participation, such as lobbying.[c] "The church historically has always been the central arena of the political activities of blacks, the place where the 'struggle for power and the thirst for power could be satisfied.' "[d] In the United States today there are approximately 60,000 black churches, 50,000 clergy, and a membership of more than 17 million. These churches are organized into seven denominations. Although in recent years white evangelical Christians have begun to use the church as a political base (forming the Christian Coalition led by the Reverend Pat Robertson, a 1988 Republican candidate for president), the black church has always been politically conscious and active. During the 1960s the largest black church denomination—the National Baptist Convention—was led by a conservative, anti–civil rights clergyman, the Reverend J. H. Jackson. Jackson's leadership was challenged by Dr. Martin Luther King Jr. and other progressive ministers, and the black church became the principal base of the civil rights movement. Today, it is

(continued)

BOX 4.2 continued

a principal base of political organizing and electoral campaigning. It served as an important source of organizing and fundraising for Jesse Jackson's two presidential campaigns and functions as a platform for white politicians seeking the support and votes of African Americans.

*a*Matthew Holden, Jr., *The Politics of the Black Nation* (New York: Chandler, 1973): 17.

*b*C. Eric Lincoln and Lawrence Mamiya, *The Black Church in the African American Experience* (Durham, NC: Duke University Press, 1990): 3–4.

*c*Robert C. Smith and Richard Seltzer, *Race, Class and Culture: A Study in Afro-American Mass Opinion* (Albany: SUNY Press, 1992): 29–30, 126–28. For a thorough study of the impact of religion on black political participation, see Fredrick Harris, *Something Within: Religion and African American Political Activism* (New York: Oxford University Press, 1999).

*d*E. Franklin Frazier, *The Negro Church in America* (New York: Schocken Books, 1964): 43.

The informal institutions of the community—beauty shops, barbershops, and other places of gathering—act as agents of socialization. Harris-Lacewell shows that these "cultural sites" have significant influences on grassroots public opinion and help shape African American thought and behavior.[28] Studies also show that African American opinion tends to be shaped by "bottom-up" influences from grassroots organizations and local protests instead of "top-down" influences from elites.[29] This runs counter to how public opinion is thought to be shaped in general in America.

Collective Memory: The Transmission Belt of African American Political Socialization

Recently, the fourth wave of the University of Michigan's longitudinal political socialization project (running from 1965 to 1997) was completed. It demonstrates that the dominant political socialization model, which focuses on the transmission process between generations from parents to children, does not completely explain the process.[30] Although our discussion in this chapter is focused on the similar and the unique agents of political socialization within the African American experience, with this recently completed research we can address in another way the question of how the black community transmits values and beliefs from generation to generation. This research indicates that it is done through a process called "collective memory." This collective memory within the black community allows the agents of socialization to not only transmit recent events such as black presidential campaigns or other contemporary political events but to integrate them with the past (slavery, the civil rights movement, etc.) in order to transmit beliefs and values. This collective memory is the intergenerational transmission belt that helps to maintain the value of universal freedom in African American politics.

Research on this collective memory has been based on multiple methodologies that have been invaluable in bringing depth to the understanding of this vital but underexplored process. In addition to surveys by political scientists, this process has been examined using historical and sociological methods.[31] The work of the political scientist Fredrick Harris, centering on religion and the church, shows that they are among the main repositories of this memory and principal agents of its intergenerational transmission.[32] And African

American psychologists, who use the concept of collective identity, are also doing important theoretical and empirical work on collective memory.[33]

Summary

The political socialization process of black Americans is shaped by the same agents that shape the process in the United States generally—family, church, school, peers, the media, and political events. However, to the extent that these institutions are different in the black community, then the outcome of the process—political culture and public opinion—will also be different. The church—because of the religiosity of blacks and the historical role of the black church as a political institution—is a particularly powerful agent of political socialization, and some scholars see music as an important agent. Finally, events from the civil rights movement of the 1960s to the campaign of Barack Obama in 2008 also shape political attitudes, opinion, and behavior and contribute to the development of a "collective memory."

Selected Bibliography

Abramson, Paul. *The Political Socialization of Black Americans: A Critical Evaluation of Research on Efficacy and Trust*. New York: Free Press, 1977. A solid review and assessment of the early literature on black political socialization.

Brown, Ronald, and Monica Wolford. "Religious Resources and African American Political Action." *National Political Science Review* 4 (1994): 30–48. A pathbreaking empirical article charting the effects of religion and the church as agents of political socialization.

Conover, Pamela. "Political Socialization: Where's the Politics?" In William Crotty, ed., *Political Science: Looking to the Future, Political Behavior*, vol. 3. Evanston, IL: Northwestern University Press, 1991. An overview of the origins and evolution of the concept.

Fendrich, James Max. *Ideal Citizens: The Legacy of the Civil Rights Movement*. Albany: SUNY Press, 1993. A study of the long-term socializing effects of the civil rights movement.

George, Nelson. *The Death of Rhythm and Blues*. New York: Dutton, 1989. An analysis of the relationship between black music and the black movements of the 1960s and 1970s.

Harris, Fredrick. *Something Within: Religion in African American Political Activism*. New York: Oxford University Press, 1999. The most comprehensive study of the subject.

Lincoln, Eric C., and Lawrence Mamiya. *The Black Church and the African American Experience*. Durham, NC: Duke University Press, 1990. A comprehensive historical study of the role of the black church.

Morris, Aldon, Shirley Hatchett, and Ronald Brown. "The Civil Rights Movement and Black Political Socialization." In R. Siegel, ed., *Political Learning in Adulthood*. Chicago: University of Chicago Press, 1989. An excellent pioneering article demonstrating the impact and influence of ad hoc and transitory socializing agents in the African American community.

Notes

1. Pamela Johnston Conover, "Political Socialization: Where's the Politics?" in William Crotty, ed., *Political Science: Looking to the Future. Political Behavior*, vol. 3 (Evanston: Northwestern University Press, 1991): 126.
2. Ibid.

3. Gunnar Myrdal, *An American Dilemma: The Negro Problem and Modern Democracy* (New York: Harper & Brothers, 1944): 929.
4. Ibid.
5. Ibid.
6. Hanes Walton, *Invisible Politics* (Albany: SUNY Press, 1985): 45–47.
7. For an edited volume that includes many of these questionable studies, see Charles Bullock and Harrell Rogers, eds., *Black Political Attitudes* (Chicago: Markham, 1972).
8. Walton, *Invisible Politics,* p. 48.
9. Ibid.
10. Ibid.
11. Myrdal, *An American Dilemma,* p. 758.
12. Ibid., p. 744.
13. Ibid., p. 758.
14. Aldon Morris, Shirley Hatchett, and Ronald Brown, "The Civil Rights Movement and Black Political Socialization," in R. S. Siegel, ed., *Political Learning in Adulthood* (Chicago: University of Chicago Press, 1989): 282.
15. Ibid
16. Ibid., p. 284.
17. Ibid., p. 290.
18. Ibid., p. 292.
19. See Lawrence Bobo, Camille Zubrinsky, James Johnson, Jr., and Melvin Oliver, "Public Opinion Before and After a Spring of Discontent," in Mark Baldassare, ed., *The Los Angeles Riots: Lessons for the Urban Future* (Denver: Westview Press, 1994): 103–34.
20. Morris, Hatchett, and Brown, "The Civil Rights Movement," p. 293. See also Michael Schwarz, *Visions of a Liberated Future: Black Arts Movement Writings* (New York: Thunder Mouth Press, 1989).
21. Shirley Chisholm, *The Good Fight* (New York: Harper & Row, 1973).
22. Hanes Walton, Jr., "Black Female Presidential Candidates: Bass, Mitchell, Chisholm, Wright, Reid, Vans and Fulani," in Hanes Walton, Jr., ed., *Black Politics and Black Political Behavior: A Linkage Analysis* (Westport, CT: Praeger, 1994): 251–74.
23. On the Jackson campaigns, see Joseph McCormick and Robert C. Smith, "Through the Prism of Afro-American Culture: An Interpretation of the Jackson Campaign Style," in L. Barker and R. Walters, eds., *Jesse Jackson's Presidential Campaign: Challenge and Change in American Politics* (Urbana: University of Illinois Press, 1988): 96–107; Robert C. Smith, "From Insurgency Toward Inclusion: The Jackson Campaigns of 1984 and 1988," in Lorenzo Morris, ed., *The Social and Political Implications of the 1984 Jesse Jackson Presidential Campaign* (Westport, CT: Praeger, 1990): 215–31; Ronald Walters, *Black Presidential Politics in America: A Strategic Approach* (Albany: SUNY Press, 1988); Lucius Barber, *Our Time Has Come* (Urbana: University of Illinois Press, 1989); Charles P. Henry, *Jesse Jackson: The Search for Common Ground* (Oakland, CA: Black Scholar Press, 1991); Thomas Cavanah and Lorin Foster, *Jesse Jackson's Campaign: The Primaries and Caucuses* (Washington, DC: Joint Center for Political Studies, 1984).
24. Leslie McLemore and Mary Coleman, "The Jesse Jackson Campaign and the Institution-alization of Grass-Roots Politics: A Comparative Perspective," in Hanes Walton, Jr., ed., *Black Politics and Black Political Behavior: A Linkage Analysis* (Westport, CT: Praeger, 1994): 49–60.
25. Hanes Walton, Jr., "Public Policy Responses to the Million Man March," *The Black Scholar* 25 (Fall 1995): 17–23; Hanes Walton, Jr., and Simone Green, "Voting Rights and the Million Man March: The Problem of Restoration of Voting Rights for Ex-Convicts," *African American Perspectives* (Winter 1997): 68–74.

26. Richard Allen, Michael Dawson, and Ronald Brown, "A Schema-Based Approach to Modeling an African American Racial Belief System," *American Political Science Review* 83 (June 1989): 421.

27. Ronald Brown and Monica Wolford, "Religious Resources and African American Political Action," *National Political Science Review* 2 (1990): 25–37; Laura Reese and Ronald Brown, "The Effects of Religious Messages on Racial Identity and System Blame Among African Americans," *Journal of Politics* 57 (1995): 23–35.

28. Melissa Victoria Harris-Lacewell, *Barbershops, Bibles and BET: Everyday Talk and Black Political Thought* (Princeton, NJ: Princeton University Press, 2004).

29. Taeku Lee, *Mobilizing Public Opinion: Black Insurgency and Racial Attitudes in the Civil Rights Era* (Chicago: University of Chicago Press, 2002). This innovative study used, among other methods, analysis of more than 6,000 letters from African Americans to the president, from 1948 to 1965.

30. M. Kent Jennings, "Survey Research and Political Socialization," in James House et al., eds., *A Telescope on Society: Survey Research and Social Science at the University of Michigan and Beyond* (Ann Arbor: University of Michigan Press, 2004): 101–2. Jennings, the principal investigator of this four-wave study who has followed the same members of a 1965 senior class over 32 years, summarizes the latest research on the model from the study's vantage point.

31. See Genevieve Fabre and Robert O'Meally, *History and Memory in African-American Culture* (New York: Oxford University Press, 1994); Howard Shuman and Jacqueline Scott, "Generations and Collective Memories," *American Sociological Review* 54 (1989): 359–81; Maurice Halbwachs, *The Collective Memory* (New York: Harper & Row, 1951); Mary Francis Berry and John Blassingame, *Long Memory: The Black Experience in America* (New York: Oxford University Press, 1982).

32. See Fredrick C. Harris, *Something Within: Religion in African American Political Activism* (New York: Oxford University Press, 1999); and his recent work "'They Kept the Story Before Them': Collective Memory, Micromobilization, and Black Political Activism in the 1960s" (Rochester: University of Rochester, unpublished paper): 1–39.

33. For the best theoretical psychological work, see William E. Cross, Jr., *Shades of Black: Diversity in African American Identity* (Philadelphia: Temple University Press, 1991). For the best empirical work, see Richard Allen, *The Concept of Self: A Study of Black Identity and Self-Esteem* (Detroit: Wayne State University Press, 2001).

CHAPTER 5

Public Opinion

Like many of the terms used by social scientists, *public opinion* has no precise, universally agreed-on definition.[1] Lord Bryce said of public opinion, it is the "aggregate of views men hold . . . that affect the community," whereas V. O. Key in *Public Opinion and American Democracy* specifically links the term to government, writing that public opinion is those "opinions held by private persons which governments find it prudent to heed."[2] Bernard Hennessy, on the other hand, writes that it is simply "the complex of preferences expressed by a significant number of persons on an issue of general importance."[3] Lane and Sears avoid the problem of definition altogether, assuming (presumably) that its meaning is obvious. So they write that "opinions have to be *about* something,"[4] and the "something" they say *public* opinion is about is (1) the political system, (2) the choice of group loyalties and identifications (race, religion, region, and social class), (3) choice of leaders, and (4) public policy preferences.[5]

Gunnar Myrdal and African American Public Opinion

Myrdal dismissed the African American socialization process as dysfunctional and one of its products—black public opinion—as irrelevant. Myrdal saw America's race problem as a "white problem," a problem rooted fundamentally in the prejudiced attitudes of whites. Thus, to understand race in America, one needed to see white attitudes as hegemonic while black attitudes were secondary or inconsequential. Myrdal wrote,

> In the practical and political struggles of effecting changes, the views of white Americans are . . . strategic. The Negro's entire life and, consequently, also his opinions on the Negro problem are in the main to be considered as secondary reactions to more primary pressures from the side of the dominant majority.[6]

In other words, there was no distinct or independent black opinion. Rather, Myrdal believed that "these secondary attitudes, being largely defensive responses to white attitudes and actions, were relatively superficial responses, not deeply rooted in the individual psyche or in cultural memory and could easily be altered."[7]

Until the 1980s, the ghost of Myrdal's paradigm haunted the study of African American mass opinion, resulting in relatively few studies of the phenomenon. Blacks were included in national polls and surveys in numbers reflecting their proportion of the population, but typically these surveys yielded too few respondents to produce valid and reliable findings or to explore opinion differences internal to the black community in terms of such things as gender, class, age, or region (the typical national sample of 1,500 to 2,000 persons would include about 150 to 200 blacks).

The ghost of Myrdal was exorcised through a combination of factors. First, African American studies began to grow and develop as a discipline. Second, interest increased in African American society and politics in the traditional disciplines of political science and sociology. Third, scholars began to recognize the radically erroneous nature of Myrdal's argument that black opinion is a mere derivative, secondary, transitory response to white opinion. Gradually and even grudgingly, the social science community recognized that black opinion was worthy of study in its own right.[8]

As a result of these changes, survey and polling organizations began to conduct surveys specifically designed to study black opinion. They systematically "oversampled" the black population to obtain samples large enough to yield valid and reliable results and to permit the study of intragroup opinion within the black community. Altogether, these changes have led in the last decade to "burgeoning research on race as an issue in American life."[9]

But Myrdal was not just influential in arguing for the primacy of white public opinion. Once the race problem in America was defined as an attitudinal problem, the study of racial attitudes became a necessary and crucial feature of race relations. Myrdal's second influence, then, is that he provided a scholarly justification for the study of racial attitudes in America. Such a study from an empirical perspective could lead to and help improve American society. Here was a central purpose and function for the study of racial attitudes. Myrdal had set the research agenda for the study of race and public opinion.

White Public Opinion on Race and Racism

From the inception of the scientific study of American public opinion more than 40 years ago, countless surveys have found that the American public is in general indifferent and uninformed about politics, political leaders, ideologies, and issues.[10] Very few Americans structure their opinions on politics in ideological terms, and their views on issues tend to be ad hoc, inconsistent, transitory, and often contradictory. These generalizations hold for virtually all issues—foreign and domestic—except for race.

In one of the classic studies documenting the lack of ideological or issue content in white American mass opinion, Phillip Converse wrote, "For the bulk of the mass public the object with the highest centrality is the visible, familiar population grouping (Negroes) rather than abstract relations among parts of government and the like."[11] More than 30 years later Kinder and Sanders concluded, "Compared with opinion on other matters, opinions on race are coherent, more tenaciously held and more difficult to alter. . . . [White] Americans know what they think on matters of race."[12] Thus, *the first thing to note about the race opinion of whites is that it tends to be one of the few consistent anchors in the thinking of white Americans.*

Second, in the last 30 years, surveys have shown a steady and generally consistent decline in overt expressions of racist and white supremacist attitudes among white Americans.[13] For example, in 1963, 31 percent of whites agreed with the statement that blacks were an inferior people; in 1978, 15 percent agreed.[14] Studies also show that white Americans by large margins now embrace the *principle* of racial equality.[15]

However, while white Americans in general are less openly racist in their attitudes toward blacks, hostility toward the race has by no means disappeared or withered away.

Instead, it has become less obvious, more subtle, and more difficult to document. This new, more subtle form of racism has been labeled "symbolic racism," "modern racism," "racial resentment," or "laissez-faire racism."[16] What this research purports to show is that white Americans are not racist in the old-fashioned way; instead, they resent or are hostile to blacks because of the whites' commitment to basic or core American values, particularly individualism.[17] White Americans prize self-sufficiency and individualism, and they believe that black Americans lack these values. Sniderman summarizes the research this way: "White Americans resist equality in the name of self-reliance, achievement, individual initiative, and they do so not merely because the value of individualism provides a socially acceptable pretext but because it provides an integral component of the new racism."[18]

In this modern racism, blacks, according to whites, are not inferior and could get ahead in society except that they lack the initiative or drive to succeed. As a function of individualism, modern or symbolic racism is a product of the "finest and proudest of American values."[19] It is as American as the flag, baseball, the Fourth of July, and apple pie.

Blacks, of course, disagree, viewing racism and racial discrimination as the principal explanation for persistent inequalities between the races.[20] As Kinder and Sanders summarize this racial chasm:

> Whites tend to think that racial discrimination is no longer a problem; that prejudice has withered away, that the real worry these days is reverse discrimination, penalizing innocent whites for the sins of the distant past. Meanwhile, blacks see racial discrimination as ubiquitous; they think of prejudice as a plague; they say that racial discrimination, not affirmative action, is still the rule in American society.[21]

Finally, Hochschild notes that well-off, middle class blacks tend to see more discrimination than poor blacks; see less of a decline in racism; expect less improvements in the future; and claim to have experienced more discrimination in their own lives.[22]

African American Public Opinion: Alienation

A key component of contemporary African American public opinion is a pervasive and deep sense of alienation from or distrust of the government. As we noted in Chapter 3, black trust in the government in general tends to fluctuate with system responsiveness to black concerns. For example, trust in the federal government was very high during the 1960s era of liberal Democratic reforms when Lyndon Johnson was president and very low during the 1980s era of conservative Republican reaction when Ronald Reagan was president. However, surveys conducted during the 1990s show a level of distrust or alienation from the government that is apparently independent of the perception of the responsiveness of government to black concerns or whether Democrats or Republicans occupy the presidency.

For example, multiple surveys conducted throughout the 1990s show that African Americans were far more likely than whites to believe that the "government deliberately makes sure that drugs are easily available in poor black neighborhoods in order to harm black people"—64 percent of blacks compared to 6 percent of whites.

A comparable racial gap also occurs when respondents were asked whether they believed the Central Intelligence Agency (CIA) was involved in importing cocaine into the black community—78 percent of blacks agreed with this statement compared to 16 percent of whites. By a margin of 59 percent to 15 percent, blacks are more likely to agree that "the government does not make a strong effort to combat AIDS in the black community because the government cares less about black people than whites." Perhaps most striking, blacks were less likely than whites to deny the possibility that HIV and AIDS are being used as a plot to deliberately kill African Americans: 79 percent of blacks compared to 38 percent of whites.[23]

Again, these opinions, which cut across lines of age, class, and gender, were observed during the Clinton presidency, which was widely viewed by blacks as the most responsive to their concerns since the 1960s Johnson administration.

Hurricane Katrina and the Racial Divide in Opinion

This pervasive and deep sense of alienation from and distrust of the American government as well as the deep racial divide between blacks and whites was reflected in public opinion on Hurricane Katrina. First, like opinion on the prevalence of AIDS and drugs in the black community, many African Americans embraced conspiracy as an explanation for the flooding of New Orleans' disproportionately black areas (80 percent of the city's black residents lived in flooded areas, compared to 54 percent of the city's whites). In congressional testimony and interviews with the media, many black evacuees from the city indicated they believed the levees near the overwhelmingly black Lower Ninth Ward were deliberately bombed in order to save the wealthy, white areas of the city. Although no polls asked about this possibility, on the basis of what we know about black public opinion we would not be surprised if this as a *possibility* would not have been believed by a majority of black New Orleanians or black Americans generally.

Several polls were conducted to measure black and white opinion about the government's response to Katrina, and they reflected this profound sense of alienation and large racial cleavages. A CNN/USA *Today* poll found that 60 percent of blacks believed that race caused the delayed government response, a view shared by only 12 percent of whites.[24] Similarly, a Pew poll found that 66 percent of blacks thought the government's response would have been faster if most of the victims had been white, a view shared by only 17 percent of whites.[25] The Pew poll also found that 71 percent of blacks thought the hurricane showed that racial inequality was still a major problem in the United States, compared to 32 percent of whites. A poll by University of Chicago political science professor Michael Dawson found similar results, with 84 percent of blacks believing the response of the government would have been faster if the victims had been white (20 percent of whites) and 90 percent agreeing that Katrina showed there was a problem of continued racial inequality in the United States, compared to 38 percent of whites.[26] These data are not surprising given what we know about black and white opinion, but they show how Katrina illuminated and reinforced African American distrust of the government and how deeply Africans Americans are separated in their opinions from their fellow white citizens.

African American Ideology: Liberalism

Although there are a variety of ways of defining ideology, for purposes of our discussion of liberalism in this section we mean the opinions that individuals express about the role of government in society, government spending and taxation, and attitudes toward certain social and moral issues. In general, liberalism tends to favor an active role for government, higher rates of taxation and government spending, and more tolerant attitudes toward such issues as abortion and homosexual rights.

In Table 5.1, data from the 1996 General Social Survey (GSS) are displayed comparing black and white attitudes toward government spending on a variety of problems facing the country. Specifically, the question asks whether the government was spending "too much money on it [the program or problem], too little, or about the right amount." Responses that indicate too little or the right amount are classified as liberal. That is, a liberal here is one who supports government spending either at present levels or with an increase; a conservative is one who thinks the government is spending too much on the problem or program.

With two exceptions, of the ten programs or policy areas designated, blacks indicated that the government was either spending too little or the right amount. The two exceptions are highway spending and space exploration. The differences on highway spending are modest; however, spending on space elicits a substantial difference, with 60 percent of whites indicating that the spending amount is too little or about right, compared to 26 percent of blacks. The 1996 GSS did not ask about the defense budget, but in its previous surveys, similar racial differences have been found on defense spending. These findings show that black Americans tend to favor spending on programs that are devoted to improving the living conditions of people rather than infrastructure, the military, or science and technology.

Table 5.1 Racial Differences in Attitudes Toward Government Spending on Selected Programs (Percentage Saying Spending Is Too Little/Right Amount)

	BLACK	WHITE
Environment	75%	59%
Health	81	66
Cities	77	58
Crime	82	67
Drugs	78	58
Welfare	42	10
Social Security	71	49
Parks, Highways	35	39
Race	85	26
Space	26	60

Note: 1996 survey included a sample of 3,000 persons, including more than 400 blacks.

Source: General Social Survey, 1996, University of Chicago, National Opinion Research Center.

The biggest difference in attitudes toward government spending is, not surprisingly, toward spending to "improve the conditions of blacks": 26 percent of whites say the government is spending too little or the right amount compared to 85 percent of blacks.

The GSS measures the government spending issue by linking support for increased government spending to higher taxes to see whether this alters opinion. It does not. As the data in Table 5.2 indicate, blacks continue to show strong support for government spending on domestic programs, even when told a tax increase might be required to pay for it.

Let us examine two other measures that tap the degree of liberalism among blacks and whites. In Table 5.3 we show opinions on the role of government in assuring the health and well-being of the people—that is, the extent to which respondents embrace programs of *universal rights.* Specifically, the questions ask whether it is the government's responsibility to assure the availability of jobs, health care, a college education, or an overall decent standard of living. On each of these ideas, African American opinion is much more liberal than that of whites.

Table 5.4 shows that among blacks there is even substantial support for moving beyond liberalism toward an embrace of socialist ideas favoring government ownership of electric utilities, banks, and hospitals. Finally, blacks are more likely to agree that it is the government's responsibility to promote an egalitarian society by reducing income differences between the rich and poor: 73 percent of blacks compared to 44 percent of whites.

Although blacks are more liberal on the role of the government in universalizing rights, they are not so liberal on social and moral issues. As Table 5.5 shows, blacks tend

Table 5.2 Racial Differences in Attitudes Toward Government Spending on Selected Programs, Even If Tax Increase Is Required (Percentage Agreeing)

	BLACK	WHITE
Health	87%	64%
Schools	54	25
Retirement Benefits	79	46
Unemployment Benefits	69	21
Culture/Arts	68	51

Source: General Social Survey, 1996, University of Chicago, National Opinion Research Center.

Table 5.3 Racial Differences in Attitudes Toward the Social Welfare Responsibilities of Government (Percentage Saying Welfare Is Government Responsibility)

	BLACK	WHITE
To Provide Jobs	74%	33%
Health Care	69	33
Assure Decent Standard of Living	70	33
Decent Living for Unemployed	77	43
Financial Aid to College Students	62	30
Decent Housing for All	50	14

Source: General Social Survey, 1996, University of Chicago, National Opinion Research Center.

Table 5.4 Racial Differences in Attitudes Toward Government Ownership of Selected Private Enterprises (Percentage Favoring Government Ownership)

	BLACK	WHITE
Electric Utilities	39%	17%
Hospitals	59	20
Banks	47	18
Government Should Reduce Income Inequality Between Rich and Poor	73	44

Source: General Social Survey, 1996, University of Chicago, National Opinion Research Center.

Table 5.5 Racial Differences in Attitudes Toward Selected Social, Moral Issues

	BLACK	WHITE
Approve Supreme Court Decision Denying School Prayer[a]	29%	43%
Consider Homosexuality Wrong[b]	75	64
Approve of Abortion for Any Reason a Woman Chooses[c]	49	59

[a]The question read: The U.S. Supreme Court has ruled that no state or local government may *require* the reading of the Lord's Prayer or Bible verses in public schools. What are your views on this—do you approve or disapprove of the Court's ruling?

[b]The question read: What about sexual relations between two adults of the same sex—do you think it is always wrong, almost always wrong, wrong only sometimes, or not wrong at all?

[c]The question read: Please tell me whether or not you think it should be possible for a pregnant woman to obtain a *legal* abortion: if there is a strong chance of a serious defect in the baby; if she is married and does not want any more children; if the woman's health is seriously endangered by the pregnancy; if the family has a very low income and cannot afford any more children; if she became pregnant as a result of rape; if she is not married and does not want to marry the man; if the woman wants it for any reason.

Source: General Social Survey, 1996, University of Chicago, National Opinion Research Center. The abortion response is from the 1989 survey.

to be somewhat more conservative on issues of homosexuality, abortion, and school prayer. However, conservatism on these issues does not translate into support for conservative candidates. Instead, blacks tend to vote on the basis of material rather than moral issues.

African American Ideology: Black Nationalism

While African Americans embrace most tenets of the liberal ideology, the 1993 National Black Politics Survey suggests they also embrace elements of black nationalism. Table 5.6 clearly demonstrates strong attitudinal support for African American autonomy or nationalism.

Most previous studies have largely treated black nationalism as a singular, uniform ideology. But recent, careful, innovative empirical research has found that like all ideologies, black nationalism is complex, fluid, and hence multidimensional, having at least two dimensions that can be characterized as "community nationalism" and "separatist nationalism." The former category can be said to exist when African Americans "control and support communities and institutions where they predominate," while the

Table 5.6 Percentage of Support for African American Autonomy in Mass Public Opinion

STATEMENTS FROM SURVEY	PERCENTAGE AGREEING
Blacks should rely on themselves and not others.	68
Blacks should control the government in black communities.	89
Blacks should participate in black-only organizations whenever possible.	67
Blacks should shop in black stores whenever possible.	84
Black children should study an African language.	70

Source: Michael Dawson and Ronald Brown, "Black Discontent: The Preliminary Report of the 1993–1994 National Black Politics Study," Report 1, University of Chicago. The results are based on a representative, randomly selected sample of the national black population. Percentages are of respondents agreeing with the statement.

latter category "rejects inclusion within the white-dominated American state and seeks the creation of a new homeland."[27] The recent research also reveals that better-educated, middle-class African Americans support community nationalism, while younger, poorer, less-educated African Americans tend to favor separatist nationalism. However, despite these differences supporters of both dimensions of black nationalism converge around the belief that "whites want to keep blacks down" and that "Africa is a special homeland for blacks." But they diverge around the issue of whether other racial and ethnic groups should be used as allies and coalition partners. Those African Americans who support separatist nationalism see no benefits in forming coalitions and joining alliances with whites, while community nationalists have no problem with such allies and coalitions. The groups are also divided on the outlook for the future. Ironically, separatists see themselves as achieving their goals and objectives and for them the future is bright and promising. The community nationalists doubt that they will be able to achieve their goals and therefore are quite pessimistic about the future.

Also, contrary to the view of many scholars, the black nationalist ideology is not associated with a general mistrust, hatred, or intolerance. A very strong adherence to the nationalist ideology is associated with disaffection from whites but not gays, lesbians, feminists, or middle-class blacks.[28]

African American Ideology: Feminism

Since the 1970s, feminism has emerged as an important ideology in African American politics (see pp. 121–23). Feminism—the ideology of gender equality and freedom—deals with the intersection of race, class, gender, and sexuality. Dawson writes that the "adherents of black feminism exhibit more agreement on what constitutes the political core of their ideology than the adherents of any other ideology" in the black community.[29] However, he also notes that feminism is often in conflict with other ideologies in the black community, especially black nationalism.[30] Harris-Lacewell also notes that feminism, like conservatism, is unpopular among many segments of the black community, partly because it is critical of black sexism and patriarchy.[31] But for most black women race trumps gender. That is, "race remains the dominant screen through which black women view politics, not only because most consider racism a greater evil than sexism, but because gender is simply a weak vehicle for political identification."[32]

In other words, for black women race is a more salient category of identification than gender.

Feminism, however, is not monolithic. There are divisions among black feminists based on ideology, and differences based on class, sexual orientation, age, and marital status. Ideologically, there is a liberal feminism that focuses on things like abortion rights (since *Roe* v. *Wade* the right to an abortion has become widely accepted in the black community, generally supported by the public, and supported by virtually all black organizations and leaders except black nationalists), equal employment and pay, health and child care, violence against women, and the full inclusion of women in the political process. Radical feminists support these liberal objectives but also focus on the perceived interrelationships between racism, sexism, heterosexism, and capitalism. Thus, unlike liberal feminists, they tend to support socialism and gay rights. Liberal feminists tend to be advocates of traditional marriage and the strengthening of the traditional family, while radicals often see marriage and the traditional family as patriarchal structures that inevitably oppress women. These ideological differences within feminism are to some extent rooted in and related to age, sexual orientation, class, and marital status.

African American Opinion: Monolithic and Diverse

African American opinion compared to the opinion of whites is near monolithically liberal; however, there is also considerable diversity. In the most comprehensive study of black opinion, Dawson found that while liberalism was the dominant ideology there was some degree of support in black opinion for a variety of ideologies, including conservatism.[33] Since the Reagan administration, black conservative spokespersons (largely in the media, think tanks, and universities) have argued that liberal black politicians and civil rights leaders have imposed the liberal ideology on the masses of blacks, and, acting as a kind of thought police, have suppressed and marginalized conservative ideas.[34] The available social science research, however, indicates that while African Americans were not immune to the conservative political climate ushered in by the Reagan presidency, there was little increase in black support for the Republican Party and its conservative ideology.[35] While there is a great deal of ideological diversity in black America—Marxism, feminism, black nationalism— conservatism is the weakest of the ideologies among African Americans.

Nor is there any evidence that this ideology is imposed on the black community by politicians and civil rights leaders. Rather, studies show that black opinion is shaped at the mass level by a variety of community institutions, such as barbershops, churches, and the black media.[36] These institutions contribute to the diversity of black opinion by airing multiple ideologies and complex belief systems.

Summary

Since the 1960s, there has been a major decline in racist and white supremacist opinion among white Americans. However, scholars of race opinion have identified what they call modern racism, where whites today do not say blacks are inferior but rather they say blacks lack the initiative or drive to succeed. Meanwhile, African American opinion tends to blame racism for the failure of blacks to get ahead in the United States. African American public opinion also has a strong degree of racial group identification and consciousness, alienation from or distrust of the government, and ideological liberalism. There is also a tendency for strong support of elements of black nationalism.

Selected Bibliography

Converse, Phillip. "The Nature of Belief Systems in Mass Publics." In David Apter, ed., *Ideology and Its Discontent.* New York: Free Press, 1964. A seminal work on the methodology of studying public opinion.

Dawson, Michael. *Behind the Mule: Race and Class in African-American Politics.* Princeton, NJ: Princeton University Press, 1994. A study that analyzes the relationship between racial and class attitudes and their different influences on individual political behavior.

————. *Black Visions: The Roots of Contemporary African-American Political Ideologies.* Chicago: University of Chicago Press, 2001. A comprehensive study of the subject.

Harris-Lacewell, Melissa Victoria. *Barbershops, Bibles and BET: Everyday Talk and Black Political Thought.* Princeton, NJ: Princeton University Press, 2004. An interesting study of opinion formation in black America.

Key, V. O. *Public Opinion and American Democracy.* New York: Alfred Knopf, 1961. The classic study of public opinion and its relationship to government leaders and the policy process.

Kinder, Donald, and Lynn Sanders. *Divided by Color: Racial Politics and Democratic Ideals.* Chicago: University of Chicago Press, 1996. A comprehensive study of black–white opinion differences in the United States.

Rosenstone, Steven J., and John Mark Hensen. *Mobilization, Participation and Democracy in America.* New York: Macmillan, 1993. Covers African American attitudes about political mobilization and participation in America's democratic system.

Sigelman, Lee, and Susan Welch. *Black Americans' Views of Racial Inequality: The Dream Deferred.* Cambridge, MA: Cambridge University Press, 1994. A pathbreaking analysis of black opinion about the sources of blacks' inequality in American society and the appropriate means for achieving equality.

Smith, Robert C., and Richard Seltzer. *Contemporary Controversies and the American Racial Divide.* Laham, MD: Rowman & Littlefield, 2000. A study of the huge differences between blacks and whites on recent controversial issues, such as O. J. Simpson, Rodney King, AIDS-HIV, the Iraq War, and crack cocaine.

Tate, Katherine. *From Protest to Politics: The New Black Voters in American Elections.* Enlarged edition. Cambridge, MA: Harvard University Press, 1994. Analyzes the attitudes of African American voters in the 1984, 1988, and 1992 presidential elections.

Notes

1. Bernard Hennessy, *Public Opinion*, 5th ed. (Belmont, CA: Brooks/Cole, 1985).
2. V. O. Key, *Public Opinion and American Democracy* (New York: Knopf, 1961): 14.
3. Hennessy, *Public Opinion*, p. 8.
4. Robert Lane and David Sears, *Public Opinion* (Englewood Cliffs, NJ: Prentice Hall, 1964): 2.
5. Ibid., pp. 2–3.
6. Gunnar Myrdal, *An American Dilemma: The Negro Problem and Modern Democracy* (New York: Harper & Row, 1944, 1962): 1, 143.
7. Ibid.

8. See Hanes Walton, Jr., *Invisible Politics: Black Political Behavior* (Albany: SUNY Press, 1985): chap. 4.

9. Paul Sniderman, "The New Look in Public Opinion Research," in A. Finifter, ed., *The State of the Discipline, II* (Washington, DC: American Political Science Association, 1993): 231.

10. Donald Kinder, "Diversity and Complexity in Public Opinion," in A. Finifter, ed., *The State of the Discipline, I* (Washington, DC: American Political Science Association, 1983); and Sniderman, "The New Look in Public Opinion."

11. Phillip Converse, "The Nature of Belief Systems in Mass Publics," in D. Apter, ed., *Ideology and Its Discontent* (New York: Free Press, 1964): 238.

12. Donald Kinder and Lynn Sanders, *Divided by Color: Racial Politics and American Democracy* (Chicago: University of Chicago Press, 1996): 14.

13. Howard Schuman, C. Steeth, and L. Bobo, *Racial Attitudes in America: Trends and Interpretations* (Cambridge, MA: Harvard University Press, 1985).

14. Louis Harris, *A Study of Attitudes Toward Racial and Religious Minorities and Women* (New York: National Conference of Christians and Jews, 1978): 16. By the late 1990s, only 10 percent of whites agreed with the statement that blacks were an inferior people.

15. Schuman, Steeth, and Bobo, *Racial Attitudes in America.* See also Paul Sniderman and Michael Hagan, *Race and Inequality: A Study in American Values* (Chatham, NJ: Chatham House, 1985).

16. David Sears, "Symbolic Racism," in P. Katz and D. Taylor, eds., *Eliminating Racism* (New York: Plenum, 1988); Kinder and Sanders, *Divided by Color*, pp. 272–76; and Lawrence Bobo, J. Klugel, and R. Smith, "Laissez-Faire Racism: The Crystallization of a 'Kinder, Gentler' Anti-Black Ideology," in S. Tuch and J. Martin, eds., *Racial Attitudes in the 1990s: Continuity and Change* (Westport, CT: Praeger, 1997).

17. Sniderman and Hagan, *Race and Inequality.*

18. Sinderman, "The New Look in Public Opinion Research", p. 232.

19. Sears, "Symbolic Racism," p. 54.

20. Lee Seligman and Susan Welch, *Black Americans' Views of Inequality* (Cambridge, MA: Cambridge University Press, 1994).

21. Kinder and Sanders, *Divided by Color*, p. 287.

22. Jennifer Hochschild, *Facing Up to the American Dream: Race, Class, and the Soul of the Nation* (Princeton, NJ: Princeton University Press, 1995).

23. These and related data are analyzed in detail in Robert C. Smith and Richard Seltzer, *Contemporary Controversies and the American Racial Divide* (Boulder, CO: Rowman Littlefield, 2000): chap. 5, "Rumors and Conspiracies: Justified Paranoia."

24. "Reaction to Katrina Split on Racial Lines," *USA Today*, September 13, 2005.

25. Pew Poll for the People and the Press, September 13, 2005.

26. Glen Ford and Peter Gamble, "Katrina: A Study, Black Consensus, White Dispute," *The Black Commentator*, January 5, 2006.

27. Robert Brown and Todd Shaw, "Separate Nations: Two Attitudinal Dimensions of Black Nationalism," *Journal of Politics* 64 (2002): 20–44.

28. See Mary Herring, Thomas Jankowski, and Ronald Brown, "Pro-Black Doesn't Mean Anti-White: The Structure of African American Group Identity," *Journal of Politics* 61 (1999): 363–86, and Darren Davis and Robert Brown, "The Antipathy of Black Nationalism: Behavioral and Attitudinal Implications of African American Ideology," *American Journal of Political Science* 46 (2000): 717–32.

29. Michael Dawson, *Black Visions: The Roots of Contemporary African American Political Ideologies* (Chicago: University of Chicago Press, 2001): 153.

30. Ibid, p. 140.

31. Melissa Victoria Harris-Lacewell, *Barbershops, Bibles and BET: Everyday Talk and Black Political Thought* (Princeton, NJ: Princeton University Press, 2004): 115.

32. Claudine Gay and Katherine Tate, "Doubly Bound: The Impact of Gender and Race on the Politics of Black Women," *Political Psychology* 19 (1998): 12.

33. Dawson, *Black Visions: The Roots of Contemporary African-American Political Ideologies.*

34. Shelby Steele, *The Content of Our Character: A New Vision of Race in America* (New York: St. Martin's Press, 1990).

35. Michael Dawson, "African American Opinion: Volatility in the Reagan-Bush Era," in Hanes Walton, Jr., ed., *African American Power and Politics: The Political Context Variable* (New York: Columbia University Press, 1997).

36. See Taeku Lee, Mobilizing Public Opinion: Black Insurgency and Racial Attitudes in the Civil Rights Era (Chicago: University of Chicago Press, 2002); and Harris-Lacewell, Barbershops, Bibles and BET.

CHAPTER 6

African Americans and the Media

"We wish to plead our own cause. Too long have others spoken for us."[1] So said the editorial in the first edition of the first black newspaper, appropriately called *Freedom's Journal*, founded in 1827 by Samuel Cornish and John B. Russwurm. Since 1827, the black press and the black church have been central institutions in the African American freedom struggle.

Gunnar Myrdal and the African American Media

Here is how Myrdal described the African American media:

> Most white people in America are entirely unaware of the bitter and relentless criticism of themselves; of their policies in domestic or international affairs; their legal and political practices; their business enterprises; their churches, schools, and other institutions; their social customs, their opinions and prejudices; and almost everything else in white American civilization. Week in and week out these are presented to the Negro people in their own press. It is a fighting press.[2]

Of all the African American institutions, the press was the most positive, useful, important, and functional in Myrdal's eyes. Throughout his study of it, Myrdal heaped praise and accolades upon the black press. He talked about it not only as an institution but also in terms of media habits and attentiveness. He wrote,

> Practically all Negroes who can read are exposed to the influence of the Negro press at least some of the time. Perhaps a third of the Negro families in cities regularly subscribe to Negro newspapers, but the proportion is much smaller in rural areas. The readers of the Negro press are, however, the most alert and articulate individuals who form Negro opinion. Newspapers are commonly passed from family to family, and they are sometimes read out loud in informal gatherings. They are available in barbershops, passed by word of mouth among those who cannot read. Indirectly, therefore, even aside from circulation figures, this press influences a large proportion of the Negro population.[3]

These insights led him to further assert that "no unifying central agency directs the opinions in the Negro press. . . . By and large, the Negro press provides the news and the opinions which its reading public wants."[4] Here one sees very strong media habits and attentiveness among the African American community.

The question arises as to why. Myrdal is quite clear on this point:

> The more important and open expressions of the Negro protest are to be found in the news coverage of the whole American Negro world and, to an extent, the Negro world outside the United States, and also in the columns and editorials on the status of the Negro people.[5]

For Myrdal, *"The press defines the Negro group to the Negroes themselves* [emphasis by Myrdal]. The individual is invited to share in the sufferings, grievances, and pretensions of the millions of Negroes far outside the narrow local community." Hence, "this creates a feeling of strength and solidarity. The press, more than any other institution, has created the Negro group as a social and psychological reality to the individual Negro."[6] For Myrdal, the African American press is a centralizing protest device. It is the driving and motivating force in African American electoral and nonelectoral political behavior. It is the tool that socializes the African American community and carries the message of struggle to the next generation. Finally, it is home to the centerpiece of the African American political culture: *protest.*

In addition to its role in defining the black community and fostering the tradition of protest, the black press also has been an agent for the creation and maintenance of solidarity. Here is how Myrdal explained this role:

> For this reason the Negro press is far more than a mere expression of the Negro protest. By expressing the protest, the press also magnifies it, acting like a huge sounding board. The press is also the chief agency of group control. It tells the individual how he should think and feel as an American Negro and creates a tremendous power of suggestion by implying that all other Negroes think and feel in this manner. It keeps the Negro spokesman in line. Every public figure knows he will be reported, and he has to weigh his words carefully. Both the leaders and the masses are kept under racial discipline by the press. This promotes unanimity without the aid of central direction.[7]

Another powerful function of the press was to attack and remake the stereotypes and negative characterizations that the white press visited on the community. Myrdal argued, "The display of Negro 'society news' in the Negro press is partly an answer to the social derogation from the whites."[8]

The African American Media and African Americans in the Mass Media

Before turning to the literature on African Americans and the media, we first examine the contemporary African American media and the presence of blacks in the mainstream or mass media.

The African American Media

Like the media in general, the African American media are quite diverse. They include about 200 weekly newspapers, approximately 450 black-oriented radio stations, several national circulation news and special interest magazines, and BET, the cable entertainment and information network. (African Americans own 0.6 percent of full power television stations and 3 percent of radio stations.)[9] In general, the black weeklies serve as the voice for the local African American communities, focusing on local rather than national news.[10] Their focus tends to be on the internal black community's civic, cultural, and religious affairs. The mainstream or white media tend to ignore the internal life of the black community, thus the black media serve as a vehicle for intragroup communication and solidarity. Many, although not all, of the black weeklies serve as watchdogs on local government and continue the tradition of a fighting, protest press discussed by Myrdal. For example, while the *Los Angeles Times* tended to present the O. J. Simpson arrest and trial in an unsympathetic way, the black *Los Angeles Sentinel* in effect became Simpson's champion in the media, apparently reflecting the views of the city's black community as the *Los Angeles Times* reflected the views of the city's whites.[11]

At the national level, there are several general circulation news and information magazines, including *Ebony* and *Jet*. However, *Emerge*, the only serious national black news magazine, was shut down in 2000 by Robert Johnson, the owner of its parent company BET, because it had failed to show a profit in its 15 years of publication (see Box 6.1). There are also specialized magazines such as *Essence* (focusing on women), *The Source* (the hard-news hip-hop magazine), and *Black Enterprises* (focusing on business). Although these magazines occasionally provide critical coverage on race issues and internal black society, culture, and politics (with the exception to some extent of *Jet*), they generally tend to focus on celebrities, consumerism, and showcasing the black middle class. Thus, with the closure of *Emerge* there is not a national circulation magazine providing hard news and critical commentary on issues important to the black community. Perhaps the most powerful voice in black media is Tom Joyner, whose morning radio program is heard by about 10 million listeners in more than 100 cities, giving him an audience size equivalent to Howard Stern and Rush Limbaugh. (During the 2008 election, Joyner's program was a major forum for the mobilization of the black vote.) Joyner also operates a website, TomJoyner.com. XM 169 "The Power," the satellite radio station with the potential to reach a national audience, is a talk channel that deals with social, economic, cultural, and political issues from African American perspectives (the power@xmradio.com).

African Americans and the New Media

As an alternative to the traditional media's limited focus and coverage, there are a substantial number of "new media" outlets that provide much more critical news and analysis of issues from African American perspectives. Among the better of these sites are Africana.com, *The Black World Today* (tbwt.com), diversityinc.com, and Blackelectorate.com. The major civil rights organizations, black members of Congress, and the Congressional Black Caucus also maintain sites, as does the National Newspaper Publishers Association, the trade association of the black newspapers that distributes news exclusively from the black media (BlackPressUSA.com). The racial "digital divide" has also narrowed. In 2000, it was estimated that only 36 percent of black households were online compared to 54 percent of whites, 41 percent of English-speaking Latinos, and 69 percent of Asian Americans. By 2006, it was estimated that 61 percent of blacks were online.[12] Young black online activists and bloggers are also beginning to play larger roles in the predominantly white blogsphere. Color of change, the San Francisco–based online activist organization which calls itself the

BOX 6.1   MEDIA CONGLOMERATES AND THE AFRICAN AMERICAN MEDIA

The mass media in the United States are business corporations that provide news, information, and entertainment in order to make a profit. In recent years in pursuit of profits, many media companies have been purchased by large, multinational corporations. For example, NBC is owned by General Electric, CBS by Viacom, ABC by Walt Disney, and Time-Warner is an enormous media conglomerate that owns *Time* and CNN, and is also the largest magazine publisher, the largest record company, the second largest cable company, and one of the largest book publishers in the world. This trend toward media conglomeration in 2001 affected the African American media when BET, the only black cable company, was purchased by Viacom for $3 billion. Earlier Time-Warner had purchased *Essence*, the black women's magazine, and later Africana.com, a major

Freedom's Journal, the first black newspaper in the United States.   *Source:* Photograph by Isabel Wolseley from *The Black Press,* USA, 2nd edition by Roland E. Wolselely. 1990. Ames: Iowa State University Press/Blackwell Publishing. ISBN: 9780813804941

black online news site. While the acquisition of these black media outlets by large, white-owned conglomerates may provide more resources for news gathering, programming, marketing, and distribution, it may also result in less competition and the loss of independent African American voices in the media. It also may result in undue focus on the corporate bottom line at the expense of independent, critical, and controversial reporting of the news from African American perspectives.

These concerns were raised by many black critics of the Viacom–BET deal, who alleged that it was a "sellout" of the black community. These concerns were heightened when in 2002 BET abruptly stopped publication of *Emerge*—the only serious national black news magazine—and subsequently fired Tavis Smiley, the outspoken host of "BET Tonight," the nightly news and information program.[a] Both *Emerge* and Smiley's program

(continued)

BOX 6.1 continued

were serious and often controversial and provocative venues for the discussion of social, cultural, and political issues in the African American community. The closure of *Emerge* and especially the firing of Smiley led thousands of blacks to send faxes, emails, and letters of protest. (Smiley later went on to have a successful career hosting radio and television talk shows on NPR and PBS.)

Since its inception in 1980, BET was constantly criticized for its steady fare of often sexually suggestive music videos instead of more diversified entertainment and news and information programming. Robert Johnson, BET's founder, indicated that the Viacom deal allowed him to continue to run BET for five years and that during this period he intended to use the conglomerate's resources to diversify and expand programming. What will happen after this five-year period will presumably depend on Viacom's white corporate managers. Whatever happens, there will be concern among some blacks that the authenticity of BET's content will be affected because it will no longer be black owned or controlled.

---

black@moveon.org, for example, was part of a coalition of black bloggers, radio show hosts, and activists that mobilized more than 20,000 people to protest in Jena, Louisiana, in 2007 (on the Jena protest see Chapter 7).

African Americans in the Mass Media

Until the 1960s, relatively few blacks were employed in the mass media. In the aftermath of the riots in the 1960s, many newspapers and radio and television stations for the first time began to hire black reporters, editors, and producers.[13] Yet, even today, their numbers in the mainstream, mass media are relatively small. Table 6.1 displays data on African Americans in the nation's radio, television, and daily newspaper workforces. Blacks constitute 5.3 percent of newspaper, 9.9 percent of television, and 5 percent of

Table 6.1 African Americans in the Mass Media: Television, Radio, and Major Newspapers, 2000

MEDIA	PERCENTAGE OF AFRICAN AMERICANS
Radio	
News Workforce	5
News Directors	1.5
Television	
News Workforce	9.9
News Directors	0.6
Newspapers	
News Workforce	5.3

Source: Data on radio and television personnel are based on a survey of all operating, nonsatellite television stations in the United States and a sample of 1,193 radio stations. The survey was conducted in 2000 by the Radio-Television News Directors Association and Ball State University. Data on newspaper personnel are based on a 2000 survey of the 1,446 daily newspapers conducted by the American Society of Newspaper Editors.

radio workforces. But in the important decision-making position of news director, blacks make up only 1.5 percent in radio and 0.6 percent in television. Blacks and other minorities in the mass media tend to be concentrated in larger cities; one-fourth of minority television journalists work in the 25 largest cities compared to 10 percent in the nation's smallest cities.[14] The same phenomenon is observed with respect to newspapers. Indeed, 44 percent of the nation's daily newspapers (mostly in smaller cities) have no black reporters.[15]

The mainstream or mass media is just that: "mass" media; this designation means that it gathers and reports news of interest to the mass public—in general, middle-class whites. For this reason, news in the newspapers and on radio and television tends to be essentially the same, whether one watches CBS or ABC or reads the *New York Times*, the *Detroit Free Press*, the *Washington Post*, the *San Francisco Chronicle*, or *Time* or *Newsweek*, although the *Washington Post* and the *New York Times* do provide more detailed stories on national and international affairs.

In an important study, sociologist Herbert Gans argues that the primary motive guiding the mass media is the preservation of "social order," the prevailing values and power relationships in the society.[16] The African American community, however, tends to be dissatisfied with the prevailing values and power relationships. This dissatisfaction tends to place in a difficult position the African American journalist who wishes to reflect the perspective of his community. She or he must simultaneously seek to balance the "black perspective" on the news with the mass media's social control perspective. A former *Washington Post* reporter describes this as a "creative tension" between "Uncle Tomming and mau mauing."[17]

Mass Media Coverage of African Americans

Most of the early literature on the media dealt with the creation of stereotypes. Media scholars Dates and Barlow laid out the theory of this dimension as follows:

> Stereotypes are especially effective in conveying ideological messages because they are so laden with ritual and myth, particularly in the case of African Americans, but, invariably these black representations are totally at odds with the reality of African Americans as individual people. . . . The conflict is indicative of a deep cultural schism, which precipitated the ideological struggle, between white and black image makers in the first place.[18]

These scholars continued their insights with these remarks:

> Black media stereotypes are not the natural, much less harmless, products of an idealized popular culture; rather, they are more commonly socially constructual images that are selective, partial, one-dimensional, and distorted in their portrayal of African Americans. Moreover, stereotyped black images most often are frozen, incapable of growth, change, innovation or transformation.[19]

Since the 1950s, content analysis of the mass media has consistently shown that the routine, day-to-day coverage of African Americans is predominantly negative and stereotypical; blacks are portrayed as poor or criminal or they are shown as entertainers and athletes. While this kind of coverage declined somewhat in the 1960s during the civil rights era, it resurfaced in the 1970s and continued to dominate coverage of blacks in the 1990s.[20]

Therefore, with these realities as given, the dominant trend in African American portraiture has been created and nurtured by succeeding generations of white image makers, beginning as far back as the colonial era. Its opposite has been created and maintained by black image makers in response to the omissions and distortions of the former.[21]

One of the first works to address this image presentation problem in political terms was C. Anthony Broh's *A Horse of a Different Color: Television's Treatment of Jesse Jackson's 1984 Presidential Campaign*. This monograph found that "black candidates for the presidency will have to overcome the media's stereotypes. Campaign reporters explain politics with clichés, and a black presidential candidate will have to learn to confront, or to manage, those stereotypes."[22] The media in 1984, Broh argued, refused to treat the Jackson candidacy seriously.

In the 1988 campaign, the same reality pertained. The Jackson candidacy was essentially dismissed.[23] The same was true of L. Douglas Wilder's 1992 campaign, although he was the former governor of Virginia.[24] In his brief campaign, the media used the Wilder candidacy to try to undermine and eliminate another possible Jesse Jackson candidacy.[25] This treatment also occurs at the subpresidential levels.

In their analysis of news coverage of the 1989 New York mayoral contest (David Dinkins versus Rudolph Guiliani) and the Virginia gubernatorial race (Wilder versus J. Marshall Coleman), media analysts revealed "that racial references of one kind or another were a fairly common feature of news about these two campaigns. This daily supply of ethnic and racial references . . . might conceptually have heightened the salience of racial attitudes among white voters and contributed indirectly to the election day surprises."[26] The analysts concluded that these "stimuli in the news stream . . . may activate racial attitudes and stereotypes, crystallizing [white voters'] (perhaps socially undesirable) opinions, helping to shift their candidate preferences, or encouraging them to turn out on election day."[27] In comparison, the mainstream media treated the putative 1996 presidential campaign of Colin Powell with great respect and positive portrayals. Although the media did not treat the campaigns of Carol Mosely Braun and Al Sharpton as serious candidacies for the Democratic presidential nomination in 2004, their campaigns received fairly extensive coverage in both the print and electronic media, and the treatment of both was generally free of racial bias or stereotypes (the media's coverage of Obama's campaign is discussed in Chapters 9 and 10).

A major study of television coverage of the 1992 Los Angeles riots uncovered a similar pattern of stereotypical coverage. First, although the Los Angeles riots were the nation's first "multicultural riots" involving Latinos, blacks, whites, and Asians, the coverage on both local and network television portrayed it stereotypically as a black riot.[28] For example, Latinos were a majority of the people arrested for rioting; but when the three local Los Angeles stations reported arrests, almost 60 percent of the people they showed were black. Latinos made up only 24 percent of the rioters shown on the networks and 33 percent on the local stations.[29] Television news also portrayed the causes of the riots as criminality and lawlessness rather than addressing the underlying problems of racism and poverty or as a protest of the acquittal of the policemen who beat Rodney King. Eighty percent of the local coverage focused on criminality as the primary cause of the riot. Although the three networks did address other causes, 60 percent of their coverage also focused on lawlessness as the principal explanation of the riot.[30]

There is much less literature on the micro-level dimension of the African American media. Using Myrdal's conclusion that the African American press is much more important to blacks than the white press is to whites, in the post–civil rights era, as a result of integration, the black press has declined as both an instrument of protest and of group solidarity and direction. It has declined as an instrument of protest because the withering away of overt white supremacism and racism removes the direct targets of protest that had given purpose to black press since the founding of the first newspaper. It has declined as an instrument of group solidarity and direction as a result of the integration of all blacks, in various ways, into the mainstream of American society. Also because of integration, black newspapers have suffered a decline in the quality of reporting, editing, and production as they are less able to attract talented journalists who find more prestigious and better-paying jobs in the mainstream media. As a result of all these factors, black newspapers are read less and therefore have less impact on black community solidarity and direction. Black newspapers are also read less because the mainstream media does a somewhat better job in the post–civil rights era of covering the internal life of the black community.

Media Coverage of Hurricane Katrina: The Persistence of Stereotypes

In general, the media—particularly television and especially CNN and FOX news—did a thorough job of covering Hurricane Katrina and its aftermath. Reporters in New Orleans from CNN and FOX dramatically displayed the sufferings of the victims and the neglect and incompetence of the bureaucracy's response. The reporters—sometimes angrily—tenaciously attempted to hold those in government responsible for the inaction and ineptitude. For example, Ted Koppel on the ABC News program *Nightline* in an interview with Michael Brown, the head of FEMA (the Federal Emergency Management Agency, the agency responsible for handling the federal government's response), responded indignantly to Brown's seeming lack of knowledge of the suffering of the people "Don't you guys watch television?; don't you guys listen to the radio? Our reporters have been reporting about it for more than today."[31] And in a blistering editorial that likely spurred President Bush to become more visibly engaged in dealing with the disaster, the *New York Times* accused the government of blatant incompetence and Bush of a woeful lack of leadership. The *Times* described the President's first speech after Katrina as "one of the worst of his life" and concluded "nothing about the President's demeanor . . . which seemed casual to the point of carelessness suggested that he understood the depth of the current crisis."[32]

However, along with these profiles in journalistic excellence and courage, there was also the familiar stereotypical media coverage of the African American victims. The most widely commented on example of this phenomenon was two Associated Press photos and accompanying captions. Both photos showed persons taking food from an abandoned grocery store. The caption under the photo of the black man described his behavior as "looting," while the photo of two whites described the same behavior as "finding" food. Television newscasts repeatedly broadcast photos (often the same ones) showing blacks allegedly looting, reinforcing the stereotype of African Americans as criminals.

The media also reported unsubstantiated allegations and rumors—later proven false—of violent and sadistic behavior by black men in the Superdome and other shelters, including robberies, sniper attacks, rape, murder, and mayhem. Although many of these rumors were given credence by the city's African American mayor and police chief, as Dyson writes, "It is safe to say that the media's framework was ready to receive and recycle rumors of vicious black behavior because such rumors seemed to confirm a widely held view about poor blacks."[33]

FACES AND VOICES IN THE STRUGGLE FOR UNIVERSAL FREEDOM

IDA B. WELLS-BARNETT (1862–1931)

Ida B. Wells-Barnett used her pen to pursue the cause of universal freedom. Perhaps the most famous black journalist of her time, she was sometimes referred to as the "princess of the black press." Born during slavery, at age 16 she assumed responsibility for raising her five siblings after her parents died of yellow fever. After attending Fisk University, she edited two newspapers and then began writing a weekly column under the pen name "Iola." This column, which was published in black newspapers throughout the country, made her one of the most prominent African American leaders in the United States.

Wells-Barnett is best known for her campaign against lynching. After three of her friends were lynched, at great personal risk she became the nation's leading crusader against lynching. She conducted detailed investigations and wrote articles and pamphlets and lectured throughout the United States and Europe. Her 1895 *Red Record: Tabulated Statistics and Alleged Causes of Lynching in the United States* is a classic study of the subject. In addition to work in the media, Wells-Barnett was a founding member of the National Association for the Advancement of Colored People (NAACP), a leader of the National Association of Colored Women, and was active in several women's suffrage organizations. She also ran unsuccessfully for the Illinois state senate.*

GR1724 IDA BELL WELLS (1862-1931).
Credit: The Granger Collection, New York.

Barnett on Commemorative US postage stamp.
Source: The Granger collection

---

*Linda O. Murray, *To Keep the Waters Troubled: The Life of Ida B. Wells* (New York: Oxford University Press, 1998).

Summary

Since the 1827 founding of *Freedom's Journal*, the first black newspaper, the media have been a central institution in the African American struggle for freedom and equality and a major agent of political socialization. As a result of the integration of blacks into the mainstream media and the expanded coverage of the black community, the influence of the black media has declined since the 1960s. Yet the black media—print, electronic, and the new online outlets—are still important institutions in black America. This is partly because blacks are not fully or proportionately integrated into the mainstream media and there is still a tendency toward racial stereotyping in mainstream media coverage of the African American community.

Selected Bibliography

Dates, Jannette, and William Barlow, eds. *Split Images: African Americans in the Mass Media*, 2nd ed. Washington, DC: Howard University Press, 1993. The leading work on the macro-level dimension of the media and African Americans.

Gans, Herbert. *Deciding What's News: A Study of the* CBS Evening News, NBC Nightly News, Newsweek *and* Time. New York: Pantheon, 1979. An important sociological analysis of the relationship between social order and conflict in determining what is news.

Graber, Doris. *Mass Media and American Politics*, 4th ed. Washington, DC: Congressional Quarterly, 1992. The standard political science analysis of the role of the media in American politics.

Nelson, Jill. *Volunteer Slavery: My Authentic Negro Experience*. Chicago: Nobel Press, 1993. A humorous and passionate account of the travails of the *Washington Post Magazine*'s first black and first woman reporter, a post from which she resigned because she says she was unable to tolerate the *Post*'s "paternalistic culture."

Wolseley, Roland. *The Black Press, U.S.A.*, 2nd ed. Ames: Iowa State University Press, 1990. A general survey of the black press, covering newspapers and magazines.

Notes

1. See "The First Negro Newspaper's Opening Editorial, 1827," in Herbert Aptheker, ed., *A Documentary History of the Negro People in the United States* (New York: Citadel, 1967): 82.
2. Gunnar Myrdal, *An American Dilemma: The Negro Problem and Modern Democracy* (New York: Harper & Brothers, 1944): 908.
3. Ibid., p. 909.
4. Ibid.
5. Ibid., p. 910.
6. Ibid.
7. Ibid., p. 911.
8. Ibid., p. 909.
9. *Black American Information Directory, 1994–95* (Detroit: Gate, 1994).
10. Roland Wolseley, *The Black Press, U.S.A.* (Ames: Iowa State University Press, 1990).
11. Ronald Jacobs, "Civil Society and Crisis: Culture, Discourse and the Rodney King Beating," *American Journal of Sociology* 101 (1996): 1238–72.
12. Michael Marriott, "Digital Divide Narrows," *West County Times*, March 30, 2006.

13. The National Advisory Commission on Civil Disorders (popularly known as the Kerner Commission) was appointed by President Johnson to investigate the causes of the riots. The Commission's findings pointed to the absence of black reporters and scant coverage of the black community as factors contributing to the discontent that led to the riots. Also, many newspapers and television stations found that without black reporters they could not adequately cover the riots since white reporters were reluctant to go into the black community or did not understand what they saw and heard.
14. See Vernon Johnson, "Minorities and Women in Television News" and "Minorities and Women in Radio News" (University of Missouri, School of Journalism, 1996).
15. American Society of Newspaper Editors, press release on the 1996 Annual Survey on Diversity in the Newsroom, April 16, 1996.
16. See Herbert Gans, *Deciding What's News: A Study of the* CBS Evening News, NBC Nightly News, Newsweek *and* Time (New York: Pantheon, 1979).
17. Jill Nelson, *Volunteer Slavery: My Authentic Negro Experience* (Chicago: Noble Press, 1993).
18. Jannette Dates and William Barlow, eds., "Introduction: A War of Images," *Split Images: African Americans in the Mass Media*, 2nd ed. (Washington, DC: Howard University Press, 1993): 5.
19. Ibid.
20. See Carolyn Martindale, *The White Press and Black America* (Westport, CT: Greenwood Press, 1986); Ted Pease and J. Frazier Smith, *The Newsroom Barometer: Job Satisfaction and the Impact of Racial Diversity* (Columbus, OH: E. W. Scripps School of Journalism, Ohio State University, 1991); and Martin Gilens, "Race and Poverty in America: Public Perceptions and the American News Media," *Public Opinion Quarterly* 60 (1996): 515–41.
21. Dates and Barlow, "Introduction: A War of Images," p. 3.
22. C. Anthony Broh, *A Horse of a Different Color: Television's Treatment of Jesse Jackson's 1984 Presidential Campaign* (Washington, DC: Joint Center for Political and Economic Studies, 1987): 83.
23. Elizabeth Colton, *The Jackson Phenomenon: The Man, the Power, the Message* (New York: Doubleday, 1989).
24. Paula McClain and Steven Tauber, "African American Presidential Candidate: The Failed Campaign of Governor L. Douglas Wilder," in Hanes Walton, Jr., ed., *African American Power and Politics: The Political Context Variable* (New York: Columbia University Press, 1997).
25. See Arnold Gibbons, *Race, Politics and the White Media: The Jesse Jackson Campaigns* (Lanham, MD: University Press of America, 1993).
26. Michael Traogott, Vincent Price, and Edward Czilli, "Polls Apart: Race, Politics and Journalism" (Paper presented at the Annual Conference of the American Association for Public Opinion Research, Pleasant Run Resort, St. Charles, IL, May 20–23, 1993): 12; Michael Traogott and Vincent Price, "The Polls—A Review: Exit Polls in the 1989 Virginia Gubernatorial Race: Where Did They Go Wrong?" *Public Opinion Quarterly* 56 (1992): 245–55.
27. Traogott, Price, and Czilli, "Polls Apart," p. 13.
28. Erna Smith, "Transmitting Race: The Los Angeles Riot in Television News" (Research Paper No. R-11, Joan Shorenstein Barone Center, John F. Kennedy School of Government, Harvard University, Cambridge, MA, 1994).
29. Ibid., p. 9.
30. Ibid., p. 11.
31. ABC News, "Nightline," September 10, 2005, as quoted in Michael Eric Dyson, *Come Hell or High Water: Hurricane Katrina and the Color of Disaster* (New York: Basic Civitas, 2006): 72.
32. "Waiting for a Leader," *New York Times*, September 1, 2005, quoted in ibid., p. 73.
33. Dyson, *Come Hell or High Water*, p. 174.

CHAPTER 7

Social Movements and a Theory of African American Coalition Politics

For much of their history in the United States, African Americans have been excluded from the normal, routine processes of political participation such as lobbying, voting, elections, and political parties. Indeed, in the Republic's more than 200-year history, African Americans have been included as nearly full participants for less than 50 years—the ten-year Reconstruction period from 1867 to 1877 plus the years since the adoption of the Voting Rights Act in 1965. As for much of their history African Americans have been excluded from the interest group, electoral, and party systems, they have had to resort to social movements to challenge the exclusionary system. William Gamson makes this point when he observes that in the United States certain groups have been systematically denied entry into the political process and gain entry only through protest or system crisis—what he calls "the breakdown of the normal operation of the system or through demonstration on the part of challenging groups of a willingness to violate 'rules of the game' by resorting to illegitimate means of carrying on political conflict."[1]

Therefore, before we examine African American interest group, voting, and party behavior, we need to look first at African American participation in social movements. A *social movement* may be understood as a group of persons organized in a sustained, self-conscious challenge to an existing system and its values or power relationships. An *interest group* is typically defined as a group of persons who share a common interest and seek to influence the government to adopt policies favorable to that interest. In other words, movements challenge systems whereas interest groups accept and work within systems. In this chapter we examine the history, development, and contemporary manifestations of African American social movement behavior. Before doing this, however, we develop a theory of African American minority–majority coalition politics.

A Theory of African American Coalition Politics

This book has two major themes. The first is that African Americans in their quest for freedom in the United States have sought to universalize the idea of freedom. The second theme is that African Americans—given their status first as slaves and then as an oppressed racial minority—have had to form coalitions with whites to achieve their freedom. Historically, however, these black–white coalitions have been tenuous and unstable, requiring constant rebuilding in an ongoing quest. To understand the dynamic instability of African American coalition politics, we must know some basic concepts and theoretical propositions.

There are various concepts and definitions of coalitions, including complicated, technical-mathematical ones and social-psychological and economic cost/benefit analyses.[2] But simply, a *coalition* involves two or more persons or groups bringing their resources together to achieve a common objective. When a group can achieve its objectives alone, it is less likely to join a coalition. Historically, as blacks have sought freedom in the United States, this has rarely been the case for them. They have always needed coalition partners to achieve many, if not all, of their objectives. However, blacks frequently have not been able to find coalition partners among whites for their objectives; thus, they have been forced to act alone. Black nationalists in the United States reject in principle the possibility of whites as reliable coalition partners and therefore always embrace the strategy of *intraracial* coalitions among blacks rather than *interracial* coalitions with whites. But even those blacks (the overwhelming majority) who in principle accept the idea of interracial coalitions have also embraced the go-it-alone strategy, when suitable white coalition partners were not available or when independent race group organizations were thought to be preferable or complementary to coalition politics. A final theoretical point is that a coalition, to be viable, must have sufficient resources—money, status, size—to achieve its objectives vis-à-vis opposing groups and coalitions. In summary, a theory of African American coalition politics suggests that blacks will seek to pool their resources with whites, when possible, in order to achieve their objectives. When suitable white partners are not available they will seek to pool their resources among themselves to achieve these objectives.[3]

Historically, as Figure 7.1 shows, African Americans have sought to form or participate in two categories of coalitions. The first type is a *rights-based coalition*, one that seeks to achieve fundamental universal freedom in terms of basic human, constitutional, and legal rights; examples are the abolitionist and civil rights movements. The second is a *material-based coalition*, which seeks access to economic benefits such as land, education, employment, and social security; examples are the populist movement, Franklin Roosevelt's New Deal Coalition, and Jesse Jackson's Rainbow Coalition.[4] Historically, also, the rights-based coalitions have had priority over the material-based ones. For example, before the black slaves could fight for land and education, their first objective had to be the abolition of slavery. Similarly, a major objective of black leaders and organizations during the 1970s was to form a material-based coalition to secure passage of legislation guaranteeing full employment (see the discussion of the Humphrey-Hawkins Act in Chapter 11). Before this material-based issue could become the priority, however, the rights-based objectives of the civil rights movement had to be achieved.

African American minority–majority coalitions tend to be tenuous and unstable because of racism, white supremacist thinking, and the ambivalence of white Americans toward race and universal freedom and equality. Figure 7.2 displays the white and other coalition partners of blacks from the founding of the Republic in the 1770s to the present. It shows that in both rights- and material-based coalitions, blacks have over time formed coalitions

Figure 7.1   The Dual Categories for Coalition Formation of African Americans: Rights- and Material-Based

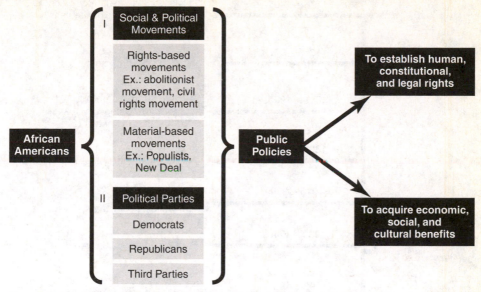

Sources: Adapted from Hanes Walton, Jr., *Black Politics: A Theoretical and Structural Analysis* (Philadelphia: J. B. Lippincott, 1972); and Robert Allen, *The Reluctant Reformers: Reform Movements in the United States* (Washington, DC: Howard University Press, 1993).

with all elements of the white population (and since the 1960s, other racial minority groups)—Quakers and Jews, middle-class professionals and poor white farmers, white liberals and white conservatives, rural whites and urban whites, and white men and white women. Yet, as we show in this chapter and in the following ones on electoral and party coalitions, these varied coalitions have frequently been weak and unstable because of the forces of racism and white supremacy.

In summary, here are the basic elements of this theory of African American coalitions, as we use them to analyze black social movements in this chapter and to examine interest groups, elections, and party behavior in Chapters 8, 9, and 10:

- Coalitions with whites are necessary if blacks are to achieve most, if not all, of their policy goals, whether rights- or material-based.
- Black–white coalitions tend to shift from rights-based to material-based, depending on historical conditions.
- Viable coalitions with whites are sometimes not possible, forcing blacks to act alone in black nationalist or other forms of intragroup coalitions.
- Because of racism and white supremacist thinking, when coalitions with whites are formed they tend to be tenuous, unstable, and frequently short-lived, requiring constant rebuilding.

Given these basic theoretical points, we begin by analyzing the first significant African American coalition: the rights-based abolitionist movement.

Figure 7.2 African American Coalition Partners, 1700s–1990s

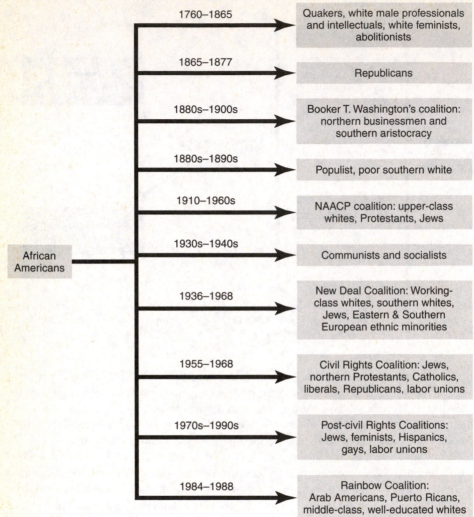

1760–1865	Quakers, white male professionals and intellectuals, white feminists, abolitionists
1865–1877	Republicans
1880s–1900s	Booker T. Washington's coalition: northern businessmen and southern aristocracy
1880s–1890s	Populist, poor southern white
1910–1960s	NAACP coalition: upper-class whites, Protestants, Jews
1930s–1940s	Communists and socialists
1936–1968	New Deal Coalition: Working-class whites, southern whites, Jews, Eastern & Southern European ethnic minorities
1955–1968	Civil Rights Coalition: Jews, northern Protestants, Catholics, liberals, Republicans, labor unions
1970s–1990s	Post-civil Rights Coalitions: Jews, feminists, Hispanics, gays, labor unions
1984–1988	Rainbow Coalition: Arab Americans, Puerto Ricans, middle-class, well-educated whites

Sources: Robert Allen, *The Reluctant Reformers: Reform Movements in the United States* (Washington, DC: Howard University Press, 1973); and Robert Smith, *We Have No Leaders: African Americans in the Post–Civil Rights Era* (Albany: SUNY Press, 1996).

The First Rights-Based Movement: The Abolitionist Coalition

The movement that emerged in the 1830s to abolish slavery was the first rights-based coalition in the United States. It, like the early-twentieth-century civil rights movement, was organized and led by well-educated, middle- to upper-class black and white males, many of whom (especially among the blacks) were ministers.[5] The abolitionist movement anticipates the conflicts and tensions that have characterized all subsequent reform coalitions involving African Americans and whites, whether rights- or material-based.

In *The Reluctant Reformers: Racism and Social Reform Movements in the United States*, Robert Allen analyzes six major social reform movements, beginning with the abolitionist movement and including populism, the progressive movement, feminism, the labor movement, and the socialist and communist movements. African Americans were involved in each of these reform movements in coalitions with whites. These alliances span a hundred years, from the 1830s to the 1930s, and as Allen points out, they cover the whole span of social classes from middle- and upper-class whites in the abolitionist movement to poor and working-class whites in the populist and labor movements. Some of these movements were based in the North; some, like the populist movements, were rural; others, like the progressive and labor movements, were predominantly urban. White men led most of these movements, but white women in the 1860s developed a movement of their own. However, as Allen writes, none of these differences among whites—middle class or poor, urban or rural, North or South, male or female—"correlates with anti-racist thinking."[6] That is, beginning with the abolitionist movement, racism and the ideology of white supremacy have operated to effectively undermine all reform coalitions in the United States.

The principal white leader of the abolitionist movement was William Lloyd Garrison, who in 1833 founded the American Anti-Slavery Society. The leading black abolitionist was Frederick Douglass. Although both Douglass and Garrison were "militant abolitionists," favoring the immediate abolition of slavery, they differed over strategy and tactics. Eventually these differences led to the breakup of the coalition.

Garrison was an uncompromising critic of slavery and the Constitution that ordained it, as may be seen in the following famous quote from the first issue of his newspaper *The Liberator*:

> Let southern oppressors tremble . . . let northern apologists tremble, let all the enemies of the persecuted blacks tremble. . . . Urge me not to use moderation in a cause like the present. I am in earnest—I will not equivocate—I will not excuse—and I will be heard![7]

Despite this militancy, Garrison was committed to "moral suasion," nonviolence, and white leadership of the abolitionist movement. Garrison and his followers were also opposed to the formation of the National Negro Congress. These positions eventually led Douglass and other black abolitionists to break with Garrison and seek their way alone. One hundred years later, similar differences between blacks and whites would lead to a breakup of the civil rights coalition and the emergence of the separatist black power movement.

Although the middle-class whites who led the abolitionist movement were not racists, many were white supremacists and based their opposition to slavery not on a belief in the equality of the races but on moral and religious grounds. That is, although blacks might not be the equal of whites, for one man to enslave another was nevertheless a violation of the principles of the Declaration of Independence and Jesus' doctrine of universal brotherhood.[8] This moral and religious basis of the movement led many whites to insist that nonviolent resistance was the only acceptable way to oppose slavery.

Douglass initially embraced Garrison's moralism and nonviolence, but as time went on and these approaches did not prove successful, he and many other black abolitionists abandoned a sole reliance on moral suasion and embraced political action (support for the antislavery Liberty Party) and violent resistance and revolt. The final reason for the collapse of the abolitionist coalition was the issue of who should lead it—in Douglass's words, who should be part of "the generalship of the movement." Douglass argued that whites in the movement ignored blacks, refusing to recognize or respect their leadership. In words that sound like Stokely Carmichael and the 1960 black power advocates, Douglass said:

> The man who has *suffered* the wrong is the man to demand the redress—the man struck is the man to CRY OUT and he who has endured *the cruel pangs of slavery* is the man to *advocate liberty.* It is evident that we must be our own representatives and advocates, but peculiarly—not distinct from—but in connection with our white friends.[9]

This first rights-based coalition did not directly result in the abolition of slavery but it did, along with the slave revolts and John Brown's raid at Harpers Ferry, contribute to the climate that resulted in the crisis leading up to the Civil War.[10]

Abolitionism and Feminism

Early feminists—advocates of equality of rights for women—supported the abolition of slavery as part of a general moral stance in favor of universal freedom for all persons. Frederick Douglass and many black abolitionists were strong supporters of women's rights, again as part of a general moral stance in favor of universal freedom.[11] Thus, these two rights-based movements formed a coalition on the basis of equality and universal freedom for all persons without regard for race or gender. Yet this coalition, like the abolitionist coalition, was tenuous and unstable; in the end, it collapsed.

William Lloyd Garrison and Frederick Douglass, leaders of the abolitionist movement, the first rights-based coalition for universal freedom.   *Sources:* Getty Images; Frederick Douglass, 1818–1895. Unidentified Photographer, after c. 1847. Daguerrotype, 8 x 6.9 cm. National Portrait Gallery, Smithsonian Institution. NPG.80.21/Art Resource, NY

First, unlike Douglass, many abolitionists, black and white, discriminated against women, refusing, for example, to allow women to sign the Anti-Slavery Society's Declaration of Principles, hold leadership positions in the group, or serve as antislavery lecturers. (Women, black and white, later formed their own National Female Anti-Slavery Society.) Although most white feminists were also middle-class professionals, men nevertheless argued that they were inferior to men in status and therefore should not be allowed to exercise freedom on the same basis as men.

On the other hand, many white feminists were white supremacists who embraced the antislavery coalition only as a means to advance the cause of women's rights. As Allen noted, "With the exception of equal rights, feminists and other female reformers shared the same views as the men of their class."[12]

The key issue, however, in the collapse of the black–feminist coalition was black suffrage—whether black men should be granted the right to vote before white women. This issue first emerged with the adoption of the Fourteenth Amendment, which for the first time included the word *male* in the Constitution. Foner contends that feminist leaders felt a "deep sense of betrayal" by this action and "consequently embarked on a course that severed their historic alliance with abolitionism and created an independent feminist movement, seeking a new constituency outside of the reform milieu."[13]

The decisive break came with the adoption of the Fifteenth Amendment, which granted black men the right to vote but denied it to women. Leading feminists opposed the amendment unless women were included because they said it would permit black men, their "inferiors," more rights than white women. Frederick Douglass, a supporter of women's suffrage and vice president of the Women's Equal Rights League, made an eloquent rebuttal to these arguments:

> I must say that I do not see how any one can pretend that there is the same urgency in giving the ballot to the woman as the Negro. With us the matter is a question of life and death, at least in fifteen states of the union. When women are dragged from their houses and hung up on lamp posts; when their children are torn from their arms and their brains dashed on the pavement; when they are the object of insult and outrage at every turn; when they are in danger of having their homes burnt down over their heads; when their children are not allowed to enter schools; then they will have an urgency to the ballot equal to our own.[14]

Douglass's arguments were not persuasive, and by the end of Reconstruction, the white feminist movement had become "predominantly (although not solely) the fight of white women to be included in the rights and privileges of a racist society."[15] This again illustrates our theoretical point about the tenuousness and instability of black–white coalitions. These tensions and conflicts between the women's-based rights movement and the black-based rights movement continue 100 years later, as reflected in the debate about the inclusion of gender in the Civil Rights Act of 1964 and the debate about affirmative action in the 1990s.

Booker T. Washington's Coalition for Limited Freedom

In many ways the strangest and most paradoxical coalition in African American politics is the one fashioned by Booker T. Washington in the aftermath of Reconstruction. It can be considered strange and paradoxical because it was a coalition for limited rather than universal freedom. For a brief period of time during Reconstruction, African Americans had the freedom to exercise their basic civil rights, including the right to vote, hold office, and have access along with whites to places of public accommodation such as inns, theaters, and restaurants. However, as a result of the so-called Compromise of 1877 that led to the disputed election of President Rutherford B. Hayes, these freedoms were taken away. The essence of the 1877 Compromise was Hayes's promise to withdraw the army from the southern states in exchange for the electoral votes that would allow him to become president. The withdrawal of these soldiers was critical to the end of Reconstruction since they had protected the newly freed slaves in the exercise of their newly won freedoms. Once the soldiers left, white southerners engaged in a campaign of open terror, torture, massacres, and lynchings in order to deprive African Americans of their freedoms. In spite of the Fourteenth and Fifteenth Amendments, blacks were denied the right to vote, denied access to public office, denied access to public places, and denied access to quality education. Finally, in the 1896 case of *Plessy* v. *Ferguson* the Supreme Court codified this denial of freedom by declaring that the Fourteenth Amendment's guarantee of equality did not prevent the states from segregating the races in all public places, from streetcars to schoolrooms.

Frederick Douglass and other African American leaders bitterly protested this denial of freedom as a betrayal not only of the Negro but also of the very idea of freedom for which the war had been fought. While Frederick Douglass and others continued their fight for universal freedom, Booker T. Washington, the head of Tuskegee University in Alabama and probably the single most powerful African American leader in the history of the United States, formed a coalition with the former southern slave owners and northern businessmen that embraced the idea of limited freedom. That is, he argued that the newly freed slaves were not at the time ready for universal freedom because he said they lacked the necessary education, property, and character. Thus, he argued that Reconstruction was a mistake and that blacks, at least temporarily, should give up their quest for universal freedom in terms of social and political rights. In return for giving up social and political freedoms Washington asked the former slave owners to grant blacks personal autonomy or freedom, the freedom to work, and the freedom to develop their own economic, social, and cultural institutions on a separate but equal basis.[16]

Booker Washington's thought is ambivalent and controversial. He is viewed by many African Americans as the quintessential "Uncle Tom"—a man who sold out the interests of the race to rich and powerful whites. Yet, for others he was a pragmatic politician who made the best deal for his people he could, given the concrete conditions and circumstances of the time—circumstances of overwhelming white hostility and antiblack violence. There was also in Washington's thought a powerful strain of black nationalism in terms of racial separatism in economics, education, and community autonomy. (Marcus Garvey, the 1920s black nationalist leader, originally came to the United States to visit Washington, whose thought had tremendously impressed him as a young man in Jamaica.) In any event, Washington's thought is unique in the African American experience since it embraced limited, not universal freedom. However, it should be clear that for Washington this was a temporary accommodation to the conditions of the time. That is, he thought—wrongly as it turned out—that through education, work, and property African Americans would eventually "earn" universal freedom or what he called "full citizenship rights."

Material-Based Coalitions: From Populism to Communism

Populism

The populist movement of the 1890s set the pattern of all future material-based coalitions between whites and African Americans. C. Vann Woodward, historian of the populist movement, writes, "It is altogether probable that during the brief populist upheaval of the nineties Negroes and Native whites achieved a greater comity of mind and harmony of political purpose [than] ever before or since in the south."[17] A reexamination of Woodward's research on the populist movement shows, as one historian says, that he was "much too generous"—that rather than being a grand coalition of poor whites and blacks, populism from the outset was undermined by the racism and white supremacist thinking of its white leaders who sought to manipulate their black coalition partners for their own interests.[18]

The populist movement emerged out of the economic depression of the 1890s as black sharecroppers and poor white farmers were faced with falling wages and prices, high taxes, and heavy debt. As a result of this crisis there was a material basis for a coalition between these two groups, who by pooling their resources (including their votes) could effectively challenge the power of the dominant economic and political elites. Led by Tom Watson of Georgia, the populists formed the Southern Alliance and later the Populist Party, both of which advocated such progressive reforms as debt relief, government ownership or regulation of the railroads, and a graduated income tax. Although some white populists for a time sincerely tried to build a biracial, class-oriented movement, from the outset racism was a major stumbling block. For example, blacks were not allowed to join the Southern Alliance; rather, they were segregated in a separate white-led Colored Farmers Alliance. And while the Populist Party appealed for black voter support and allowed blacks to serve as leaders (although in small numbers), it too was eventually undermined as poor whites were convinced by Democratic Party leaders that a vote for the interracial Populist Party was racial treason.[19] As a result, white populists eventually succumbed to what Richard Hoftstader called the "Negro bogey," and within a decade this first material-based coalition of African Americans and whites had collapsed.[20] Eventually, Tom Watson, the movement's leader, turned from preaching interracial unity and solidarity to an extreme form of racism and white supremacy, supporting lynching and the disenfranchisement of blacks.[21] Thus, within the short span of a decade, populism went from "colored and white in the ditch unite" to "lynch the Negro."[22]

The Progressives

The populist movement was, as Hofstader writes, "the first modern political movement of practical importance in the United States to insist that the federal government has some responsibility for the common weal; indeed it was the first such movement to attack seriously the problems created by industrialism."[23] It was succeeded a generation later by the progressive movement. The progressives, unlike the populists, were largely urban, middle-class professional whites who sought, like the populists, federal regulation of the economy and reforms in the political process, such as the initiative and referendum. It too, however, was affected by the "Negro bogey."[24] The Progressive Party, for example, refused to condemn racial discrimination, lynching, or the denial of black voting rights. One of its principal leaders, President Theodore Roosevelt, was one of the most racist presidents of the twentieth century (see Chapter 12).

The Labor Movement

The African American people are largely a working-class people; therefore, their natural coalition partners should be working-class whites and their trade union organizations. As Carmichael and Hamilton said in their chapter "The Myth of Coalitions" in the book *Black Power*, "It is hoped eventually that there will be a coalition of poor whites and blacks. This is the only coalition which seems acceptable to us and we see such a coalition as the major instrument of change in American society."[25] For much of American history Carmichael and Hamilton's hope for a coalition with the white working class has been just that, a hope, because "the history of the American labor movement is one long and shameful story of exclusion, discrimination, outright treachery and open violence against Black, Mexican, Chinese and other nonwhite workers."[26] With a few exceptions—the Knights of Labor during Reconstruction and the International Workers of the World early in the twentieth century—American trade unions have either excluded blacks or forced them into segregated unions.[27] Even today, although organized labor has abolished racial segregation and was a major partner in the 1960s civil rights coalition, the white working class continues to exhibit more racist, white supremacist thinking than do middle-class, professional whites. In the early 1980s Robert Bostch conducted a series of interviews with white and black working-class men specifically designed to explore the prospects for coalition politics. Bostch concluded that working-class white men

> exhibit enough racial prejudice so that they could be separated from their black working class peers on a number of issues. . . . Blacks are seen as threatening because they wish to use the powers of the national government to change the rules of meritocracy to gain an unfair advantage. This stereotype embitters white workers toward all governmental power and threatens to alienate whites from blacks, who generally feel they are discriminated against.[28]

As is shown in Chapters 9 and 10, blacks and working-class whites were partners, although uneasy ones, in the New Deal Coalition (which enacted many of the reform proposals of the populists and progressives), but this was because President Franklin D. Roosevelt scrupulously avoided taking any stand on race issues, even refusing to support antilynching legislation. Once the Democratic Party in the 1960s embraced the cause of civil rights, the New Deal Coalition of blacks and working-class whites began to collapse. Despite eloquent pleas and constant campaigning on working-class concerns, Jesse Jackson in his two campaigns for president received more support from middle-class white professionals than from poor and working-class whites, as did Barack Obama in 2008.

Socialists and Communists

Even socialists and communists have not been able to avoid the "Negro bogey" of racism and white supremacy. The Socialist Party was organized in 1901, and although it was ostensibly devoted to a broad-based coalition of workers, it initially embraced racism and white supremacy. Jack London, one of the party's founders, said, "I am first a white man and only then socialist," and the party's newspaper, *Appeal to Reason*, declared, "Socialists believe in justice to the Negro, not social equality. Socialism will separate the races."[29] Only when the socialists began to face competition from the Communist Party did they change their racist position, begin to recruit blacks (such as A. Phillip Randolph, the labor leader), and, under the leadership of Norman Thomas in the 1930s, take forthright stands against racial segregation and discrimination.[30]

The Communist Party, according to Robert Allen,

> has left a lasting imprint on the struggle for racial equality. Despite the generally negative image of the party conveyed in popular media and standard history texts, the Communist Party in its heyday probably did more than any other predominantly white political group to promote racial equality in American life.[31]

However, as the African American novelist Richard Wright argued in his eloquent essay in *The God That Failed*, although the Communist Party supported the cause of racial equality sincerely, it was also a part of a strategy dictated from Russia to manipulate African Americans in order to further the objectives of the Soviet Union.[32]

Historically, blacks have been willing to join as partners in material-based reform coalitions with whites; however, whites have been reluctant, unreliable partners, forcing blacks to act alone or seek white partners in rights-based coalitions.

A "Rainbow" Coalition?

In 1984 and 1988 Jesse Jackson ran for the Democratic Party's presidential nomination. In both campaigns he sought to build what he called a "Rainbow Coalition" of blacks and other "peoples of color"—Latinos and Arab and Asian Americans—as well as progressive or liberal whites. The idea of a multiracial coalition of peoples of color is attractive to African American leaders because since the 1960s the United States has become increasingly racially diverse as a result of immigration from Asia, Latin America, and to a somewhat less extent, Africa. Until the 1960s the immigration laws of the United States were based on principles of racism. Enacted in the 1920s, these laws generally excluded persons from eastern and southern Europe and the so-called Third World. Partly as a result of the antiracism reform climate brought about by the civil rights movement, the immigration laws were changed in 1965 to permit immigration from all parts of the world. These changes in the law, the globalization of the economy, and the creation of refugees as a result of wars in Asia, Africa, and Latin America have resulted in a massive influx of immigrants, legal and illegal, since the 1970s. The 2000 U.S. Census indicated that persons from Latin America or "Hispanics" accounted for 12.5 percent of the U.S. population of 281,421,906, Asian Americans 3.6 percent, African Americans 12.5 percent, and non-Hispanic whites 61.4 percent—about half the Hispanics identified themselves as white. (This represents a dramatic change from the 1960s when blacks and whites accounted for approximately 90 percent of the population.) Although it is common for social scientists and journalists to refer to Hispanics and Asian Americans as if they are single, discrete ethnic groups, they obviously are not and to treat them as single, discrete groups conceals the extent of ethnic diversity in the United States. While Latinos share a common language, they do not necessarily share a common culture, and Asian Americans do not share a common language, let alone a culture. Thus, it is important to break down these artificially created groups because they may hold different racial and political attitudes and engage in different political behavior. Among Hispanics the largest ethnic group is Mexican Americans at 58.5 percent, Puerto Ricans are 28.4 percent, Cubans 3.5 percent, and persons from other Latin American countries 21 percent. Among Asian Americans the breakdown is Chinese at 23.7 percent, Filipinos (classified as Asian although many speak Spanish) 18 percent, Korean 9.5 percent, Japanese 7 percent, Asian Indians 16 percent, Vietnamese 11 percent, and persons from other Asian countries 12.5 percent.

Given this ethnic diversity, the idea of a rainbow coalition of people of color is based on the assumption that the new immigrants tend to be poor and may face discrimination or racism from the white majority, and therefore there is an objective basis for a coalition with blacks in terms of support for civil rights and social welfare legislation. Blacks and the leaders of Asian American and Latino communities are part of a broad leadership coalition for civil rights, but it has been marked by tensions and conflicts (see Box 8.2). At the mass level, while majorities of both Latinos and Asian Americans feel they face discrimination from the white majority, they feel they have more in common with whites than they do with blacks.[33] Latinos and Asian Americans in general may tend to embrace the same negative stereotypes about blacks. For example, a recent report shows that 51 percent of Latinos, 53 percent of Asian Americans, and 45 percent of whites said they believed blacks were prone to crime and violence; and 40 percent of whites, 33 percent of Latinos, and 48 percent of Asian Americans said they believed blacks "care less about family." As the authors of the report write, these negative stereotypes regarding blacks constitute a "serious barrier" to cooperation and coalitions between blacks and other people of color.[34] Thus, Jesse Jackson in his two campaigns for president received relatively little support from other groups of color except Puerto Ricans in New York. There is also competition for political offices and resources between blacks and Mexican Americans in California and Texas; between blacks and Cuban Americans in Florida; between blacks and Puerto Ricans in New York and Illinois; and even between blacks and African Americans of West Indian origins in New York. Thus, whether in the twenty-first century the relationship between blacks and the new immigrants will be characterized by cooperation and coalition or competition and conflict is unclear.[35]

African Americans, Immigration, and the Prospects for a New Majority Coalition

In late 2005 the House of Representatives passed a tough immigration bill that would have made illegal immigration a felony, imposed new penalties on illegal immigrants, required groups giving assistance to individuals to check their legal status, and erected fences along large portions of the Mexican border. This action sparked mass protest demonstrations by immigrants (mainly Latino) throughout the United States. In Los Angeles more than a half million protested, and there were massive protests in other cities including Chicago, Denver, and Washington, D.C. While marching in opposition to the House bill, protest leaders endorsed legislation supported by President Bush and passed by the Senate that would establish a guest worker program and provide a "pathway" to possible citizenship for the estimated 12 million illegal immigrants in the United States.

The Congressional Black Caucus, the NAACP, Senator Barack Obama, and most other African American leaders and organizations joined the opposition to the House bill, while supporting some version of the legislation passed by the Senate.[36] While national opinion polls show that African Americans are generally supportive of immigrant rights,[37] there is also a sense of "unease" in the black public about the possibility of losing jobs to immigrants.[38]

Historically, African Americans have been skeptical or hostile to immigration, fearing competition for jobs.[39] As Frederick Douglass said in the 1880s referring to the waves of immigrants from Europe, "The old employment by which we have heretofore gained our livelihood, are gradually and it may seem inevitably, passing into other hands. Every hour sees the black man elbowed out of employment by some newly arrived immigrant whose hunger and color are thought to give him a better title to the place."[40] Yet, the reforms that ended racial discrimination in the nation's immigration laws in 1965 and opened the doors to immigrants from all over the world were partly an outgrowth of the civil rights movement. As Vernon Briggs writes, "It was the passage of the Civil Rights Act of 1964 ... that created the national climate needed to legislatively end the discriminatory national origin system the following year with the adoption of the Immigration Act of 1965."[41] However, in 1977 it was Barbara Jordan, the nationally renowned African American congresswoman from Texas, who chaired a commission that recommended, among other things, substantial reductions in the annual level of legal immigration, limits on the admission of unskilled adults, and a concerted effort to stop illegal immigration.[42]

Although the econometrics literature is mixed on the impact of immigration on the employment and wages of low-income workers in general and African Americans particularly,[43] it is clear that immigration has increased the supply of low-wage labor, which tends to reduce wages and employment opportunities for low-wage American citizens and legal immigrants.[44] Employers may also prefer to hire illegal immigrants, who are viewed as harder working and less complaining than native-born Americans. Yet, immigrants also likely contribute to growth in the overall economy and may do certain kinds of work that native-born Americans are unwilling to do, at least at the prevailing wages.[45] Finally, the new immigrants from Latin America, Asia, and, to a lesser extent, Africa may provide a long-term basis for the expansion of a multicultural rainbow coalition that could increase support for affirmative action, unionization, living wages, and national health insurance.

By 2050 the U.S. Census Bureau estimates that nonwhites will constitute half the U.S. population, bringing an end to the majority status of white or European Americans. (Latinos are projected to constitute 24 percent of the population, blacks 14 percent, Asians 8 percent, and 4 percent Native American, Hawaiian and Pacific Islanders, and mixed race.)[46] This suggests the possibility or prospect in the future that a rainbow coalition could become the electoral majority in the United States. In other words, immigrants could become the basis for a new coalition in the quest for universal freedom.

The Second Rights-Based Coalition: The Civil Rights Movement

The NAACP Coalition

The civil rights movement has its origins in the Niagara Conference called by W. E. B. Du Bois in 1905 (see Box 7.1). Four years after the conference, the National Association for the Advancement of Colored People (NAACP) was founded; until the 1960s it was the principal civil rights protest organization. Until the late 1960s, the NAACP was the

BOX 7.1 WE FACE A CONDITION, NOT A THEORY: W. E. B. DU BOIS AND THE CHANGING AFRICAN AMERICAN QUEST FOR UNIVERSAL FREEDOM

It is often suggested that political philosophy and ideas are the products of the concrete conditions and circumstances of a people. Nowhere is this better demonstrated than in the long life and career of Dr. W. E. B. Du Bois, the greatest scholar and thinker in the history of African American thought. Du Bois was born on February 23, 1868, in Great Barrington, Massachusetts. He died 95 years later in the West African country of Ghana on the eve of the 1963 March on Washington. In these 95 years, Du Bois's life was one of extraordinary scholarship and political leadership, a life that at one point or another embraced every tendency in African American thought—integration, black nationalism, and finally socialism and communism.

Du Bois graduated from Fisk University, a black institution in Nashville, Tennessee, in 1888. In 1895 he became the first African American to receive a Ph.D. from Harvard (he came within a couple of months of earning a second Ph.D. from the University of Berlin). His doctoral dissertation, *The Suppression of the African Slave Trade to the United States, 1638–1870*, was the first volume published in Harvard's Historical Studies series. He later went on to publish 15 other books on politics and race, three historical novels, two autobiographies, and numerous essays and works of fiction and poetry. While a professor at Atlanta University, Du Bois directed the first large-scale social science research project on the problem of race in the United States. Among his more important books are *Black Reconstruction in America*, a massive study showing that Reconstruction was one of the first efforts in American history to achieve democracy for working people; *The Philadelphia Negro: A Social Study*, the first sociological analysis of an urban community; and *The Souls of*

Dr. W. E. B. Du Bois, preeminent African American intellectual, a leader of the civil rights and Pan-African movements, embraced communism in the last years of his life. *Source:* Schomburg Center/Art Resource, NY

(continued)

BOX 7.1 continued

Black Folk, his classic analysis of the psychological, cultural, and sociopolitical underpinnings of the African American experience. Probably no other book has had a greater impact on African American thinking than *The Souls of Black Folk*. In it Du Bois states for the first time the enduring tension in African American thought between integration and nationalism:

> One ever feels his twoness—an American, a Negro, two souls, two thoughts, two unreconciled strivings, two warring ideals in one dark body, whose dogged strength alone keeps it from being torn asunder. . . . He simply wishes to make it possible for a man to be both a Negro and American, without being cursed and spit upon by his fellows, without having the doors of opportunity closed roughly in his face.

In addition to his life of the mind and scholarship, Du Bois was an extraordinary political leader (from the death of Booker T. Washington in 1915 until the mid-1930s, Du Bois was probably the most influential African American leader). Early in his career, Du Bois remarked, "We face a condition, not a theory." Therefore, any philosophy, ideology, or strategy that gave promise of altering the oppressed conditions of the race should be embraced. As the conditions of African Americans changed, so did the thought of Du Bois. Early in his career in his famous "Conservation of Races" essay, Du Bois appears to embrace black nationalism and separate development as a means to conserve the distinctive culture of the group. Later, in the face of Booker Washington's accommodation of the segregation and racial oppression that emerged after the end of Reconstruction, Du Bois embraced integration, organizing in 1905 the Niagara Conference as a forum for militant protest for civil rights and universal freedom in the United States. In organizing the Niagara Conference and authoring its manifesto, Du Bois became the "Father of the Civil Rights Movement." Four years later in 1909, Du Bois was the only black among the founders of the NAACP. Until the 1930s he edited *The Crisis*, the NAACP's magazine, using it as a forum to attack white supremacy and racism and to espouse the cause of equality and universal freedom. Watching the deteriorating conditions of blacks during the Depression, Du Bois once again embraced black nationalism, arguing that blacks should develop a separate "group economy" of producers and cooperative consumers. Charging that the NAACP had become too identified with the concerns of middle-class blacks, in 1934 Du Bois resigned from the association and his editorship of *The Crisis*. Du Bois also expressed his interest in nationalism in terms of Pan-Africanism—the idea that the African people everywhere share a common culture and interest. In 1900 he organized the first Pan-African Conference in London, which brought together African leaders and intellectuals from Africa, the United States, and the Caribbean. He was a principal leader of the four other Pan-African Conferences held between 1912 and 1927. At the end of World War I and again at the end of World War II, Du Bois attended the peace conferences, urging that the European powers should develop plans to free their African colonies. Du Bois briefly joined the Socialist Party in 1912 and continued to flirt with socialist ideas thereafter; however, during the 1950s he apparently came to the conclusion that universal freedom for blacks and working people could not be achieved under capitalism and so in 1956 he joined the Communist Party and shortly thereafter moved to Ghana. The last years of his life were spent editing the *Encyclopedia Africana*, a project funded and supported by the Ghana Academy of Sciences.

(continued)

BOX 7.1 *continued*

In his autobiography, Du Bois wrote,

I think I may say without boasting that in the period 1910 to 1930 I was a main factor in revolutionizing the attitude of the American Negro toward caste. My stinging hammer blows made Negroes aware of themselves, confident of their possibilities and determined self-assertion. So much so that today common slogans among Negro people are taken bodily from the words of my mouth.

Du Bois was not an immodest man; in fact, he was often referred to as an arrogant elitist, but in regard to the observation above, he was not exaggerating.[a]

[a]There are several good book-length studies of Du Bois's life and career. See Francis Broderick, *W. E. B. Du Bois: New Leader in Time of Crisis* (Palo Alto, CA: Stanford University Press, 1959); Elliot Rudwick, *W. E. B. Du Bois: Propagandist of the Negro Protest* (New York: Athenaeum, 1968); Gerald Horne, *Black and Red: W. E. B. Du Bois and the Afro-American Response to the Cold War, 1944–63* (Albany: SUNY Press, 1986); David L. Lewis, *W. E. B. Du Bois: Autobiography of a Race, 1868–1919* (New York: Henry Holt, 1973); and Lewis, *W. E. B. Du Bois: The Fight for Equality and the American Century, 1919–1963* (New York: Henry Holt, 2000).

classic black–white rights-based coalition. It was founded by upper-middle-class white Protestants and Jews on the hundredth anniversary of the birth of Abraham Lincoln. Several of the founders were socialists, including Mary White Ovington and William English Walling. The only black among the leaders was Du Bois.

From the beginning, there was tension between blacks and whites in the organization over its leadership and strategy. William Monroe Trotter and a number of other blacks who were involved in the Niagara Conference refused to join the group, arguing that whites could not be trusted to advance the cause of blacks. These tensions over white leadership continued until the 1960s (the association did not get its first black executive director until James Weldon Johnson was appointed in 1920) when blacks took over all the top leadership positions and the overwhelming majority of seats on the executive board.

The Strategy of the NAACP, 1910–1954: Persuasion, Lobbying, and Litigation

The civil rights movement may be divided into three phases, based on the dominant strategy employed to pursue its goals.[47] From roughly 1910 to the 1930s, the dominant forms of activity were persuasion and lobbying. During these years the NAACP developed a campaign of public education and propaganda under the direction of Du Bois, editor of the NAACP magazine, *The Crisis*.[48] This campaign was designed to combat white supremacist propaganda and shape a favorable climate of public opinion on civil rights for African Americans.

The NAACP also engaged in an unsuccessful lobbying effort to convince Congress to pass a law making lynching a federal crime. Under the federal system, lynching—the ritual murder of blacks by southern racists—was a state crime, but southern states refused to arrest and punish the perpetrators. Thus, there was need for a federal law. Although the antilynching legislation twice passed the House, it was defeated in the Senate as a result of southern filibusters.[49] The NAACP was more successful in other lobbying efforts. It succeeded in blocking passage of immigration legislation that would have prohibited the legal entry into the United States of persons of African descent. And in a coalition with organized labor, it was successful in lobbying the Senate to defeat President Herbert Hoover's nomination of John C. Parker to the Supreme Court because of his alleged antilabor and antiblack views.[50]

From the 1930s to the 1950s, litigation was the dominant strategy of the NAACP. In 1939 the NAACP created a separate organization—the NAACP Legal Defense Fund—and this organization under the leadership of Charles Hamilton Houston and later Thurgood Marshall filed a series of cases in the Supreme Court seeking enforcement of the Fourteenth and Fifteenth Amendments. Several important cases were won during this period, including *Smith* v. *Allwright*, which invalidated the Texas Democratic Party's whites-only primary, and the famous *Brown* v. *Board of Education* decision, which reversed the doctrine of separate but equal established in 1896 in *Plessy* v. *Ferguson*[51] (see Chapter 13).

The Southern Christian Leadership Conference and the Strategy of Protest, 1955–1965

The final phase of the civil rights movement involved mass protests and demonstrations.[52] From the 1900s until the 1950s the civil rights movement was dominated by the middle-class, northern-based NAACP coalition. From 1955 to 1965 the movement was dominated by Dr. Martin Luther King Jr. and the Southern Christian Leadership Conference (SCLC). Unlike the NAACP, the SCLC was an intraracial coalition of black ministers and churches based in the South.[53] Beginning with the Montgomery bus boycott, King and the SCLC led a series of demonstrations in the South protesting segregation in public places and the denial of black voting rights. King and the SCLC were later joined in the southern protest movement by the Student Nonviolent Coordinating Committee (SNCC), an interracial coalition of black and white college students, and the Congress of Racial Equality (CORE), also an interracial coalition of black and white activists.[54]

Although the strategy of King and his colleagues was to hold peaceful, nonviolent demonstrations, these actions were met with widespread violence by racist southern whites (including the police). This violence, televised around the world, forced a reluctant President Kennedy (and later President Lyndon Johnson) to propose comprehensive civil rights and voting rights legislation. After the violent demonstrations in 1963 at Birmingham, Alabama, President Kennedy proposed the Civil Rights Act, which Congress enacted in 1964. After the violent demonstrations in Selma, Alabama, in 1965, President Johnson proposed and Congress passed the Voting Rights Act.

Two points should be emphasized about the passage of these laws in 1964 and 1965. First, the president and Congress responded to the demands of the movement only after the violence at Selma and Birmingham was televised. Second, the strategy of protest developed by Dr. King and his associates was deliberately designed to bring pressure on the president and Congress by activating a broad lobbying coalition: liberals, labor, and northern religious groups.[55] It was this broad coalition—not blacks acting alone—that brought about the ultimate passage of the first comprehensive civil rights legislation since Reconstruction.[56] However—as our theory of African American coalition politics predicts—almost immediately after the passage of the Voting Rights Act, this coalition of blacks and whites began to fall apart, as blacks shifted from a rights-based movement politics to a material-based interest group politics.

The Black Power Movement and the Transformation from Movement to Interest Group Politics

The Origins of the Black Power Movement

The political scientist Sidney Tarrow writes:

> Protest cycles can either end suddenly, through repression, or more slowly, through a combination of features: the institutionalization of the most successful movements, factionalization within them and new groups which rise on the crest of the wave, and the exhaustion of mass political involvement. The combination of institutionalization and factionalization often produce determined minorities, who respond to the decline of popular involvement by turning upon themselves and—in some cases— using organized violence.[57]

This combination of features characterized the end of the civil rights movement.[58]

Two weeks after the signing of the Voting Rights Act, Watts, the black section of Los Angeles, exploded in three days of rioting. The 1965 Watts rebellion was followed by a series of riots in most of the large cities of the North. In 1966, Stokely Carmichael, the newly elected chairman of the SNCC, started the black power movement. The urban riots and black power led to a fundamental transformation of the civil rights movement and the emergence of a new structure of black interest organizations.

The SNCC—the most radical of the civil rights organizations—sparked this transformation by introducing the rhetoric and symbol of black power during the 1966 Meredith March in Mississippi.[59] For several years, the more nationalistic SNCC workers had attempted to bring a greater number of nationalist themes into the civil rights movement, themes drawn from Malcolm X and Algerian writer Frantz Fanon.[60] In 1966 they prepared a position paper that set forth the fundamental themes of black power, including a call for the exclusion of whites from the organization. Although Stokely Carmichael initially joined the majority of the SNCC staff in rejecting these nationalist themes, after he defeated the incumbent SNCC chairman John Lewis (now a congressman from Georgia) in a bitter and divisive election, he changed his position and embraced the principles of black power. He then persuaded the SNCC to join the Meredith March and use it as a forum to articulate and build support for black power. For a week, television coverage of the Meredith March highlighted the divisions within the civil rights movement. In his speeches, Dr. King continued to espouse the philosophy of black–white coalitions, integration, and nonviolence, while Carmichael shouted black power and called for racial separatism and violent resistance to attacks by southern racists. Although the national media presented black power as a radical, revolutionary movement, it actually had a dual impact on African American politics: one radical, one reform.

The Dual Impact of Black Power: Radicalism and Reform

As Figure 7.3 illustrates, the black power movement sparked two separate, distinct, and contradictory developments in black politics. First, it stimulated the development of a wide variety of radical, nationalistic, and revolutionary organizations and leaders, including Huey

Figure 7.3 The Dual Impact of the Black Power Movement on African American Politics, 1960–1990

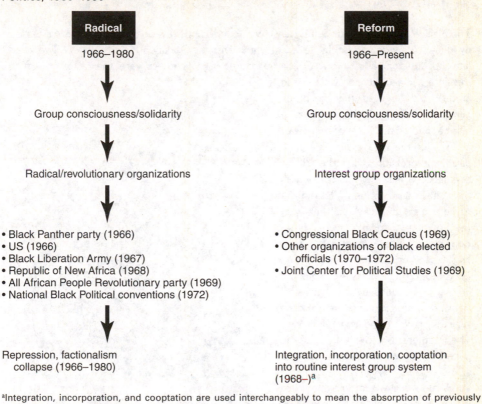

Radical	Reform
1966–1980	1966–Present

Group consciousness/solidarity

Group consciousness/solidarity

Radical/revolutionary organizations

Interest group organizations

• Black Panther party (1966)
• US (1966)
• Black Liberation Army (1967)
• Republic of New Africa (1968)
• All African People Revolutionary party (1969)
• National Black Political conventions (1972)

• Congressional Black Caucus (1969)
• Other organizations of black elected officials (1970–1972)
• Joint Center for Political Studies (1969)

Repression, factionalism collapse (1966–1980)

Integration, incorporation, cooptation into routine interest group system (1968–)[a]

[a]Integration, incorporation, and cooptation are used interchangeably to mean the absorption of previously unrepresented groups into the routine operation of the political system.

Source: Robert C. Smith, *We Have No Leaders: African Americans in the Post–Civil Rights Era* (Albany: SUNY Press, 1996).

Newton and the Black Panther Party (see Box 7.2), Ron Karenga and US (a radical cultural nationalist organization), and Imari Obadele and the Republic of New Africa (discussed in Chapter 8). For a decade the African American freedom struggle took a sharp turn toward radicalism. However, by 1980, as a result of factionalism and infighting within and among the groups, and political repression by the Federal Bureau of Investigation (FBI), the army, and the police, the radical wing of the movement had collapsed.[61]

The second development sparked by black power was the beginning of the integration or incorporation of blacks into the routine interest group structure of conventional American politics. Although radicalism and nationalism characterized the early years of black power, ultimately it came to represent, as Figure 7.3 shows, a mild form of reformist black nationalism appealing to race group consciousness, solidarity, and independent, all-black interest group organizations.[62]

Black Power and Race Group Solidarity

Black power contributed to an increase in black group identification and solidarity. Political scientist Warren Miller observed that, as a result of black power,

BOX 7.2 THE BLACK PANTHER PARTY

The Black Panther Party for Self-Defense was founded in 1966, one year after the Watts riot, by Huey P. Newton and Bobby Seale, student activists at Oakland's Merritt College. Two years later, FBI director J. Edgar Hoover declared that the Black Panthers were "the greatest threat to the internal security of the United States" and targeted the group for elimination.[a] By 1970, the party was in disarray and on the verge of collapse as a result of the FBI's systematic campaign of repression and of the group's own factional infighting and corruption.

The Black Panthers adopted the name and symbol, black panther, from the Lowndes County, Alabama, Freedom Democratic Party, which used a black panther as its symbol. (The Lowndes County party was founded in the early 1960s by southern civil rights workers to encourage blacks to register to vote and run for office.) The Panthers, as the full name of the party implies, was originally founded as a "self-defense" organization. Newton and Seale were aware that the police in the nation's big cities frequently harassed and brutalized blacks. To try to stop this kind of police misconduct, the Panthers (dressed in black leather jackets and berets) organized armed patrols and dispatched them to the

Huey P. Newton and Bobby Seale, founders of the Black Panther Party. *Source:* S.F. Examiner/AP Images

scene of any police incident involving blacks. Their purpose was to observe the behavior of the officers. Their slogan, to "Observe and protect," was derived from the Los Angeles Police Department's motto, "To serve and protect." Although the Panthers did not intervene in the police incidents, the mere presence of armed black men observing their behavior alarmed the police. Soon a series of deadly gun battles occurred between the Panthers and the police in Oakland and San Francisco. Shortly thereafter the California legislature began consideration of legislation to ban carrying loaded weapons in public. To protest this legislation, 30 armed Panthers marched into the state capitol at Sacramento on May 2, 1967. This demonstration received widespread attention and brought the heretofore obscure group to the attention of the nation. The image of armed black men dressed in black captured the imagination of young blacks across the country, and Panther party membership and chapters grew rapidly. By late 1968, the group had a membership estimated at 3,000–5,000 and more than 30 chapters

(continued)

BOX 7.2 *continued*

throughout the United States. Accompanying this rapid growth in membership, the Panthers adopted the ideology of revolutionary black nationalism and Marxist-Leninism, calling for violent revolution to overthrow the government of the United States.

Many of the Black Panthers were brave young men and women, willing to sacrifice their lives for freedom. Despite the paranoia and corruption of some of its top leaders, in the early years the party did good works, including forcefully challenging police brutality and providing a variety of community services such as free medical clinics, breakfast programs for poor kids, and food cooperatives. However, once the party turned from a primarily self-defense and self-help group to violent revolution, its destruction was inevitable, since no government that has the power will long tolerate a violent challenge to its authority.[b]

[a]U.S. Congress, Senate, *Select Committee to Study Government Operations with Respect to Intelligence Activities and the Rights of Americans, Book III, Final Report* (Washington, DC: Government Printing Office, 1976): 187.

[b]For an overview of the rise and decline of the Panthers, see Charles E. Jones, ed., *The Black Panther Party Reconsidered* (Baltimore: Black Classics Press, 1998).

the appropriate dimension for understanding the political behavior of black citizens may have changed. Contemporary black leaders may have helped shape the political meaning of being black in ways black leaders two decades before could not. Certainly, racial identity is now the most useful prescriptive measure of the political choice of many citizens.[63]

Table 7.1 displays data showing the extent to which individuals think in "group benefit" terms—that is, the degree to which an individual evaluates political issues and events in terms of their positive or negative impact on the group or group interests.[64] The data show the progression of black political conceptualization in terms of racial group interest during the 20-year period 1960–1980—from 26 percent in 1960 to 54 percent in 1980; comparable figures for whites are 42 percent in 1960 and 28 percent in 1980. Although the highest level of group benefit responses among blacks is observed in 1968 at the high point of the black power movement, even after black power declined in salience, the group benefit percentages did not return to their earlier low levels. This rise in group-based identification and solidarity is true of all categories of blacks, irrespective of gender, education, age, or partisan affiliation.[65]

Table 7.1 Racial Differences in "Group Benefit" Level of Political Conceptualization: 1960–1980

	1960	1964	1968	1972	1976	1980
Whites	31%	25%	20%	24%	23%	28%
Blacks	26%	47%	60%	51%	48%	54%

Source: Paul R. Hagner and John C. Pierce, "Racial Differences in Political Conceptualization," *Western Political Quarterly* 37 (June 1984): 222. Employing data from the Interuniversity Consortium for Political Research at the University of Michigan, Hagner and Pierce identified four major levels of political conceptualization: ideological, group benefit, nature of the times, and no political content. The "group benefit" category measures the extent to which individuals evaluate political issues in terms of their negative or positive impact on the group or group interests.

Black Power, Black Groups, and System Incorporation

Related to this increase in race group consciousness and solidarity, the black power movement also sparked the creation of a large number of new, racially exclusive (all-black) interest group organizations, including for a time an intraracial black coalition—the National Black Political Convention.[66] From 1966 to 1969—the peak years of black power activism—more than 70 new black interest organizations were formed.[67] These organizations covered a broad range of interests—business and economic, educational and cultural, and professional and political. Also during this period the growing number of black elected officials began to form racially separate caucuses, including the Congressional Black Caucus and caucuses of black mayors, school board members, and state legislators.[68]

At the beginning of this chapter we discussed the argument of William Gamson that some groups are excluded from the routine system of American interest group politics and gain entry only as a result of a crisis in the system or if the excluded group shows a willingness to violate the "rules of the game" by resorting to illegitimate means for carrying on political conflict. The radical, revolutionary rhetoric of black power, the summers of urban riots from 1965 to 1968, and the revolutionary politics of the Black Panthers and other groups created a perception of crisis and showed that some blacks were indeed willing to engage in illegitimate forms of political conflict. Thus, the most enduring consequence of black power was reform, not radicalism—the Congressional Black Caucus rather than the Black Panther Party.

Yet another consequence of the black power and civil rights movements was their impact on other American citizens who felt excluded from the system. These black movements of the 1960s served as models for a wave of social movements and interest groups in the late 1960s and 1970s. Among the groups that patterned their activities after the civil rights and black power movements are women, Indians, Mexican Americans, Puerto Ricans, gays, Chinese Americans, the elderly, and, to an extent, the youth and antiwar protesters.[69]

The "Jena 6" Protests

For a brief moment in the Fall of 2007, the spirit of protest and mass mobilization came to life in the small town of Jena, Louisiana. The protests began a year earlier with a tree and two nooses. At a high school assembly in the poor, racially divided mining town of 3,000, a black student asked if black students could sit under a tree where usually only white students sat. The next day two nooses hung from the tree. Black parents, outraged by this symbolism of lynching, demanded that the white students who hung the noose be expelled. Although the principal recommended expulsion, the school board overruled him and gave the students three-day suspensions. Over the next several days, arsonists burned down part of the school and there were daily fights between black and white students. Ultimately, six black teens were charged as adults with attempted murder for assaulting a white student. Although charges against some of the students were later reduced, Mychall Bell, the first to be tried, was convicted by an all-white jury of aggravated battery and sentenced to 15 years in prison.

Soon a grassroots movement spread across black America to protest what was seen as the unequal treatment of young black men by a racist criminal justice system

FACES AND VOICES IN THE STRUGGLE FOR UNIVERSAL FREEDOM

JOHN BROWN (1800–1859)

John Brown, a deeply religious white man, was so committed to African American freedom and equality that he was willing to do what few black Americans have been willing to do—use revolutionary violence to fight for freedom. In 1859 Brown and an interracial group of 22 men attacked the federal arsenal at Harpers Ferry, Virginia. Their plan was to seize weapons, flee into the mountains, and establish a base of operations to wage guerilla war. Prior to Harpers Ferry, Brown and his men had killed pro-slavery settlers in Kansas, pledging to "purge this land with blood" in order to end slavery and establish democracy for all. Completely free of white supremacist thinking, Brown interacted with African Americans on the basis of complete equality.

Brown's raid at Harpers Ferry failed. He and most of his men were killed or captured and quickly executed. At his sentencing Brown made an eloquent speech in favor of universal freedom. The day of his execution was declared "martyr's day" by black leaders; businesses were closed and churches held memorial services. The song "John Brown's Body" became a Union marching song during the Civil War and is an enduring part of the African American folk tradition.

Although Brown's raid failed, historians agree that it contributed to the intensification of the crisis that resulted in the bloody Civil War that emancipated the slaves.*

*David Reynolds, *John Brown: The Man Who Killed Slavery, Sparked the Civil War and Seeded Civil Rights* (New York: Knopf, 2005).

(see Chapter 15). Civil rights activists Jesse Jackson, Al Sharpton, and Martin Luther King III led the protests, but national attention was initially drawn to the case by a grassroots movement on black college campuses, black radio stations, and websites including *YouTube, Facebook*, and *Color of Change*. This movement ended with a march and rally of more than 20,000 persons in Jena, making it one of the largest protest demonstrations in the South since the 1960s civil rights era. A week before the march, a Louisiana appeals court overturned Bell's conviction, ruling that he should not have been tried as an adult.

Although the Jena protest was limited in scope and duration, it demonstrated to many the potential for a revitalization of movements of protest in the twenty-first century.

Summary

When a group is excluded from participation in the political system, it will often resort to social movements as a means to challenge the system in order to gain entry and inclusion. From the abolitionist movement of the 1830s to the civil rights and black power movements of the 1960s, African Americans engaged in movement politics. Throughout, however, as an oppressed, relatively powerless minority they have had to form coalitions with whites—whites of both genders and all ideologies, regions, and social classes. Because of racism and white supremacy, these coalitions have tended to be tenous, unstable, and short-lived, and have been more effective on rights-based than material-based issues. The black movements of the 1960s served as models and inspiration for similar movements among other Americans.

Selected Bibliography

Alex-Assensoh, Yvette, and Lawrence Hanks, eds. *Black and Multiracial Politics in America.* New York: New York University Press, 2000. A useful collection of papers exploring the relationship between black and multiracial politics.

Allen, Robert. *The Reluctant Reformers: Racism and Social Reform Movements in the United States.* Washington, DC: Howard University Press, 1983. A study of how racism historically has undermined liberal and progressive reform movements in the United States.

Browning, Rufus, D. Marshall, and D. Tabb. *Protest Is Not Enough: The Struggle of Blacks and Hispanics in Urban Politics.* Berkeley: University of California Press, 1984. An influential study of the conditions and policy consequences of multiethnic coalitions in post–civil rights era urban politics.

Carmichael, Stokely, and Charles Hamilton. *Black Power: The Politics of Liberation in America.* New York: Vintage Books, 1967. The influential manifesto of the rationale and strategy for the transformation from civil rights movement politics to black interest group politics.

Freeman, Jo, ed. *Social Movements of the Sixties and Seventies.* New York: Longman, 1983. A collection of papers showing how the African American civil rights and black power movements served as a model for social movement activism of many other groups in American society.

Gomes, Ralph, and Linda Faye Williams. "Coalition Politics: Past, Present and Future." In Ralph Gomes and Linda Williams, eds. *From Exclusion to Inclusion: The Long Struggle for African American Political Power.* Westport, CT: Praeger, 1992. A historical analysis of African American coalition politics and a discussion of future prospects.

Kluger, Richard. *Simple Justice: The History of* Brown v. Board of Education *and Black America's Struggle for Racial Equality.* New York: Vintage Books, 1977. A long but interesting account of the NAACP's litigation strategy from the 1930s to the 1950s, focusing on a detailed study of the famous *Brown* school desegregation case.

Morris, Aldon. *Origins of the Civil Rights Movement.* New York: Free Press, 1984. A study of the development of the final protest phase of the civil rights movement, focusing on the role of indigenous institutions such as black churches and colleges.

Nelson, William, and Jessica Lavariega Moniforti, eds. *Black and Latino/a Politics: Issues in Political Development in the United States.* Miami, FL: Barnhardt & Ashe Publishing, 2005. A wide-ranging collection of essays on black and Latino politics and their interrelationships.

Payne, Charles. *I've Got the Light of Freedom: The Organizing Tradition in Mississippi.* Berkeley: University of California Press, 1995. An alluringly written account of the role of local movements during the civil rights era.

Piven, Frances Fox, and Richard Cloward. *Poor People's Movements: Why They Succeed, Why They Fail.* New York: Vintage Books, 1977. A detailed study of how various reform movements of poor people have been transformed into interest groups and thereby rendered largely ineffective.

Shulman, Steven, ed. *The Impact of Immigration on African Americans.* New Brunswick, NJ: Transaction, 2004. This volume presents research and analysis that reflects and advances the debate about the economic and political consequences of immigration for African Americans.

Smith, Robert C. "Black Power and the Transformation from Protest to Politics." *Political Science Quarterly* 96 (Fall 1981): 431–44. A theoretical and empirical analysis of the important role of the black power movement in shaping contemporary black politics.

Walters, Ronald, and Robert C. Smith. *African American Leadership*. Albany: SUNY Press, 1999. A treatment of the topic historically, theoretically, and in relationship to its practice.

Wilke, H. A. M. *Coalition Politics*. New York: Harcourt, 1985. Although somewhat technical, a useful collection of papers on theory and research on coalition formations in politics.

Zangrando, Robert. *The NAACP Struggle Against Lynching, 1909–1965*. Philadelphia: Temple University Press, 1980. A study of the NAACP's lobbying strategy, focusing on the unsuccessful effort to secure passage of federal antilynching legislation.

Notes

1. William Gamson, "Stable Unrepresentation in American Society," *The American Behavioral Scientist* 12 (November–December 1968): 18.
2. See Aldon Morris and Cedric Herring, "Theory and Research on Social Movements," in Samuel Long, ed., *Annual Review of Political Science*, vol. 2 (Norwood, NJ: Ablex, 1987): 137–98; and H. A. M. Wilkie, ed., *Coalition Formation* (New York: Harcourt, 1985).
3. Ralph Gomes and Linda Williams, eds., "Coalition Politics: Past, Present and Future." *From Exclusion to Inclusion: The Long Struggle for African American Political Power* (New York: Greenwood Press, 1992): 129–60.
4. In drawing a distinction between material- and rights-based issues and coalitions, we do not mean to imply that the right to health care or a job might not be appropriately viewed as a civil or citizenship right. Rather, the point is that in the United States a sharp line is usually drawn between economic and political or civil rights, a distinction African Americans and their leaders, willingly or not, have embraced. See Dana Hamilton and Charles Hamilton, *The Dual Agenda: Social Policies of Civil Rights Organizations, New Deal to Present* (New York: Columbia University Press, 1996).
5. On the abolitionist movement, see Leronne Bennett, *Before the Mayflower* (Baltimore: Penguin Books, 1966): chap. 6; John Hope Franklin, *From Slavery to Freedom* (New York: Knopf, 1980): 180–89; and Robert Allen, *The Reluctant Reformers: Racism and Social Reform Movements in the United States* (Washington, DC: Howard University Press, 1983): chap. 2.
6. Allen, *The Reluctant Reformers*, p. 248.
7. Quoted in Allen, *The Reluctant Reformers*, p. 24.
8. Franklin, *From Slavery to Freedom*, p. 182.
9. Quoted in Bennett, *Before the Mayflower*, p. 149.
10. On the slave revolts, see Herbert Aptheker, *American Negro Slave Revolts* (New York: Columbia University Press, 1948); and Eugene Genovese, *From Rebellion to Revolution: Afro-American Slave Revolts in the Making of the New World* (New York: Vintage Books, 1981).
11. Benjamin Quarles, "Frederick Douglass and the Women's Rights Movement," *Journal of Negro History* 25 (1940), and Phillip Foner, *Frederick Douglass on Women's Rights* (Westport, CT: Greenwood Press, 1976).
12. Allen, *The Reluctant Reformers*, p. 128.
13. Eric Foner, *Reconstruction: America's Unfinished Revolution, 1863–1877* (New York: Harper & Row, 1988): 253–54.
14. Quoted in Allen, *The Reluctant Reformers*, p. 143.
15. Ibid., p. 128.

16. Washington stated his ideas most succinctly in his famous Atlanta Exposition Address delivered in September 1895 at Atlanta's Cotton States Exposition. The address is reprinted in the 2nd edition of August Meier, Elliott Rudwick, and Francis Broderick, eds., *Black Protest Thought in the Twentieth Century* (New York: The Bobbs-Merrill Co., 1971): 3–8. On Washington's leadership of black America, see Louis Harlan, *Booker T. Washington: The Making of a Black Leader* (New York: Oxford University Press, 1972) and his *Booker T. Washington: The Wizard of Tuskegee* (New York: Oxford University Press, 1983).

17. C. Vann Woodward, *The Strange Career of Jim Crow* (New York: Oxford University Press, 1966): 64. See also Woodward's detailed study of populism, *Tom Watson: Agrarian Rebel* (New York: Oxford, 1938, 1963).

18. John Herbert Roper, *C. Vann Woodward, Southerner* (Athens: University of Georgia Press, 1987): 114.

19. On blacks and the populist movement, see Charles Crowe, "Tom Watson, Populists and Blacks Reconsidered," *Journal of Negro History* 40 (April 1970): 99–116; and Gerald Gaither, *Blacks and the Populist Revolt: Ballots and Bigotry* (Tuscaloosa: University of Alabama Press, 1977).

20. Richard Hofstadter, *The Age of Reform* (New York: Vintage Books, 1955): 61.

21. Historians disagree as to whether Watson was always a racist or whether his attitudes changed over time with changing circumstances.

22. This quote is from Roper, *C. Vann Woodward*, p. 121.

23. Hofstadter, *The Age of Reform*, p. 61.

24. On the progressives, see Hofstadter, *The Age of Reform*, chaps. 4–7.

25. Stokely Carmichael and Charles Hamilton, *Black Power* (New York: Vintage Books, 1967): 82.

26. Allen, *The Reluctant Reformers*, p. 166.

27. On the racist, exclusionary history of organized labor, see Phillip Foner, *Organized Labor and the Black Worker, 1619–1981* (New York: Praeger, 1974).

28. Robert Bostch, *We Shall Not Overcome* (Chapel Hill: University of North Carolina Press, 1981): 196.

29. Allen, *The Reluctant Reformers*, p. 213.

30. Ibid., p. 215.

31. Ibid. On the important role the Communist Party played in the African American freedom struggle, see Mark Naison, *Communists in Harlem During the Depression* (Urbana: University of Illinois Press, 1983).

32. Richard Crossman, ed., *The God That Failed* (New York: Harper & Row, 1949). On this point, see also Harold Cruse, *The Crisis of the Negro Intellectual* (New York: William Morrow, 1967): 147–71.

33. National Conference of Christians and Jews, *Taking America's Pulse: The Full Report of the National Conference Survey on Inter-Group Relations* (New York: National Conference of Christians and Jews, 1994): 7. See also Paula McClain, et al., "Racial Distancing in a Southern City: Immigrant Views of Black Americans," *Journal of Politics* 68 (2006): 541–84.

34. Ibid.

35. See Paula McClain and Albert Karnig, "Black and Hispanic Socioeconomic and Political Competition," *American Political Science Review* 84 (1990): 535–45; and Yvette Alex-Assensoh and Lawrence Hanks, eds., *Black and Multiracial Politics in America* (New York: New York University Press, 2000).

36. Michael Cottman, "NAACP, Barack Obama Call for Earned Citizenship for Illegal Immigrants," blackamericaweb.com, April 3, 2006.

37. Adrian Pantoja, "Friends or Foes?: African American Attitudes Toward the Political and Economic Consequences of Immigration," in William Nelson and Jessica Lavarcega Moniforti, eds., *Black and Latino/a Politics: Issues in Political Development in the United States* (Miami, FL: Barnhardt and Ashe Publishing, 2005): 177–88.

38. Rachel Swains, "Growing Unease for Some Blacks on Immigration," *New York Times*, May 4, 2006.

39. Roger Daniels, *Coming to America: A History of Immigration and Ethnicity* (New York: HarperCollins, 1990): 76, 323.

40. Quoted in Steven Shulman and Robert C. Smith, "Immigration and African Americans," in Cecilia Conrad et al., eds., *African Americans in the U.S. Economy* (Boulder: Rowman & Littlefield, 2005): 199.

41. Vernon Briggs, "The Economic Well-Being of Black Americans: The Overarching Influence of U.S. Immigration Policies," in Steven Shulman, ed., *The Impact of Immigration on African Americans* (New Brunswick, NJ: Transaction Publisher, 2004): 12.

42. U.S. Commission on Immigration, *Reform, Legal Immigration: Setting Priorities* (Washington, DC, 1994), cited in ibid, p. 19.

43. See Shulman, *The Impact of Immigration on African Americans*.

44. Ibid.

45. Ibid.

46. *Projected Population Change in the United States, by Race and Hispanic Origin: 2000 to 2050* (Washington, DC: U.S. Bureau of the Census, 2001).

47. See Robert C. Smith, "Politics Is Not Enough: On the Institutionalization of the Afro-American Freedom Struggle," pp. 97–126, in Gomes and Williams, eds., *From Exclusion to Inclusion*; and Robert C. Smith, *We Have No Leaders: African Americans in the Post–Civil Rights Era* (Albany: SUNY Press, 1996): chap. 1.

48. David Lewis, *W. E. B. Du Bois: Biography of a Race, 1868–1919* (New York: Henry Holt, 1993): chap. 15.

49. Robert Zangrando, *The NAACP Crusade Against Lynching, 1909–1950* (Philadelphia: Temple University Press, 1980).

50. Gilbert Ware, "Lobbying as a Means of Protest: The NAACP as an Agent of Equality," *Journal of Negro Education* 33 (Spring 1964): 103–7. On the NAACP's lobbying strategy, see the biography of its long-time chief Washington lobbyist by Denton Watson, *Lion in the Lobby: Clarence Mitchell and the Black Struggle* (New York: William Morrow, 1990).

51. Richard Kluger, *Simple Justice: History of* Brown v. Board of Education *and Black America's Struggle for Racial Equality* (New York: Vintage Books, 1975).

52. Aldon Morris, *The Origins of the Civil Rights Movement* (New York: Free Press, 1984).

53. David Garrow, *Bearing the Cross: Martin Luther King, Jr., and the Southern Christian Leadership Conference* (New York: William Morrow, 1986).

54. Clayborne Carson, *In Struggle: SNCC and the Black Awakening of the 1960s* (Cambridge, MA: Harvard University Press, 1981); and August Meier and Elliot Rudwick, *CORE: A Study in the Civil Rights Movement* (New York: Oxford University Press, 1973). For excellent studies of the heroic role of ordinary people in the civil rights movement, see John Dittmer, *Local People: The Struggle for Civil Rights in Mississippi* (Urbana: University of Illinois Press, 1995); and Charles Payne, *I've Got the Light of Freedom: The Organizing Tradition and the Mississippi Freedom Struggle* (Berkeley: University of California Press, 1995).

55. Michael Lipsky, "Protest as a Political Resource," *American Political Science Review* 62 (1968): 1144–58; and David Garrow, *Protest at Selma* (New Haven, CT: Yale University Press, 1978): chap. 7.

56. The last of the 1960s civil rights acts—the Fair Housing Act of 1968—was enacted shortly after Dr. King's murder, in part as a kind of final memorial tribute to him. Prior to his death the bill appeared to be stalled in Congress.

57. Sidney Tarrow, "Aiming at a Moving Target: Social Science and the Recent Rebellions in Eastern Europe," *Political Science and Politics* 24 (1991): 15.

58. Smith, *We Have No Leaders*, chaps. 1–2.

59. The Meredith March was initially organized by James Meredith, the first known African American to be graduated from the University of Mississippi, as a "march against fear." It was designed to demonstrate to blacks in the state that they need not fear to exercise their newly gained civil rights. On the second day of the march, Meredith was shot and wounded. The civil rights leadership then decided to continue the march in Meredith's honor and as a means to demonstrate to the nation the continuing climate of fear and violence in the state.

60. Carson, *In Struggle*, chap. 14.

61. By political repression, we mean "a process by which those in power try to keep themselves in power by attempting to destroy or render harmless organizations and ideologies that threaten their power"; see Robert Goldstein, *Political Repression in Modern America* (Cambridge, MA: Schenkman Press, 1979): xvi. The FBI's program of political repression was called COINTELPRO (for counterintelligence program). The black groups targeted by the program included the SNCC, the SCLC, the Nation of Islam, and the Black Panther Party. See Nelson Blackstock, *COINTELPRO: The FBI's Secret War on Political Freedom* (New York: Vintage Books, 1975); and Stephen Tompkins, "Army Feared King, Secretly Watched Him, Spying on Blacks Started 75 Years Ago," *Memphis Commercial Appeal*, March 21, 1993, p. A1.

62. See Robert C. Smith, "Black Power and the Transformation from Protest to Politics," *Political Science Quarterly* 96 (Fall 1981): 431–44; and Smith, *We Have No Leaders*, chap. 1.

63. Quoted in Paul Hagner and John Pierce, "Racial Differences in Political Conceptualization," *Western Political Quarterly* 37 (June 1984): 215.

64. Ibid., p. 214.

65. Ibid., p. 215.

66. Smith, *We Have No Leaders*, chap. 2.

67. Smith, "Black Power and the Transformation from Protest to Politics," pp. 436–37.

68. Ibid.

69. See Jo Freeman, ed., *Social Movements of the Sixties and Seventies* (New York: Longman, 1983).

CHAPTER 8

Interest Groups

As late as the late 1960s, with the exception of the NAACP, the Urban League, and, to a lesser extent, the SCLC and the National Council of Negro Women, there was little organized black interest group influence on the Washington policy-making process. Even the NAACP and Urban League were engaged mainly in rights-based civil rights lobbying rather than in broader, material-based public policy concerns.[1] However, since the 1970s blacks have developed a significant presence in the Washington policy-making process, one that focuses on both rights-based and broader, material-based policy interests.

Table 8.1 displays the contemporary structure of black interest groups, illustrating the range of interest and policy concerns of the organized black community. Many of these groups (such as the National Medical Association and the National Association of Black Manufacturers), like their white counterparts, are special interest organizations, generally pursuing their own narrow professional or economic interests. Others, like Trans Africa, have a single policy focus—in its case, American foreign policy toward Africa and the Caribbean. (On Trans Africa's influence on policy in these regions, see Chapter 16.) Still others have broad, multiple-policy agendas (the NAACP, the Congressional Black Caucus), lobbying on the full range of domestic and foreign policy issues.

Black Groups, the "Black Agenda," and the Problem of Resource Constraint

The broad-based policy agenda encompassing both rights- and material-based issues is one of the major problems confronting the African American lobby in Washington. It is agenda-rich but resource-poor. Political scientist Dianne Pinderhughes writes:

> The subordinate, dependent status of the black population limits the capacity of black interests to create well-funded and supported groups capable of the consistent monitoring required in administration and implementation of law. This same status multiplies the number of potential issue areas of importance to black constituencies, but their resource difficulties limit the number of issues they can address, and weaken their likelihood of being taken seriously within any of those areas.[2]

The problem identified by Pinderhughes may be seen by comparing the data in Tables 8.2 and 8.3, which show, respectively, the post–civil rights era black agenda of African Americans and the resources of the three major Washington black interest organizations compared with the resources of selected nonblack Washington-based interest groups.

Table 8.1 The Structure of African American Interest Organizations—Selected Groups

CIVIL RIGHTS	ECONOMIC/PROFESSIONAL
NAACP (1909)[a]	National Medical Association (1885)
Urban League (1910)	National Bar Association (1925)
Southern Christian Leadership Conference (1957)	National Business League (1900)
NAACP Legal Defense Fund (1939)	National Conference of Black Lawyers (1969)
National Council of Negro Women (1937)	National Association of Black Manufacturers (1970)
	Coalition of Black Trade Unionists (1972)
PUBLIC POLICY	**CAUCUSES OF BLACK ELECTED OFFICIALS**
Trans Africa (1977)	Congressional Black Caucus (1969)
Children's Defense Fund (1973)[b]	National Caucus of Black Elected Officials (1970)
National Association of Black Social Workers (1969)	Southern Conference of Black Mayors (1972) National Black Caucus of State Legislators (1977) National Caucus of Black School Board Members (1971)
RELIGIOUS	
National Baptist Convention (1882)	
Nation of Islam (1930)	

[a]Year in parentheses refers to the year the group was organized. For a fairly comprehensive list of black organizations, their purposes, and their memberships, see *A Guide to Black Organizations* (New York: Philip Morris, 1984) .

[b]Strictly speaking, the Children's Defense Fund is an interracial advocacy organization; however, it was founded and is led by a black woman—Marion Wright Edelman—and much of its advocacy is for poor and disadvantaged minority children.

The Joint Center for Political and Economic Studies is a Washington-based think tank devoted to research on African American affairs (Box 8.1). In 1976 it called a bipartisan (Democrats and Republicans) conference of more than 1,000 black elected officials as well as appointed officials then serving in the Carter administration. At the conference's conclusion, the group issued a document, the "Seven Point Mandate," that it said represented a leadership consensus on the post–civil rights era black agenda. The items on that agenda are displayed in Table 8.2.

Table 8.2 The Post–Civil Rights Era Black Agenda

Full employment

Welfare reform to include a guaranteed income

Comprehensive national health insurance

Increased federal funding for elementary, secondary, and higher education

Busing for purposes of integrated education

Minority business set-asides

International sanctions on South Africa and repeal of the Byrd Amendment[a]

[a]The Byrd Amendment was an act of Congress permitting the import of chrome from the then-apartheid regime of Rhodesia (now Zimbabwe) in violation of sanctions imposed by the United Nations. It was repealed in 1977.

Source: "Seven Point Mandate," *Focus* 14 (1976): 8. *Focus* is the monthly newsletter of the Joint Center for Political and Economic Studies.

Table 8.3 A Comparison of the Resources of the Three Major African American Interest Organizations with selected Nonblack Organizations

AFRICAN AMERICAN ORGANIZATION	ESTIMATED MEMBERSHIP	ANNUAL BUDGET
NAACP	150–250,000; 2,000 local chapters[a]	$45[b]
Urban League	118 local affiliates	49
Congressional Black Caucus[c]	39 members of Congress	5.5[a]
NON-AFRICAN AMERICAN ORGANIZATIONS		
American Association of Retired Persons	33 million	450
Mothers Against Drunk Driving	3.2 million	45
National Rifle Association	3 million	98
Sierra Club	550,000	43
Anti-Defamation League	30 Affiliate Offices	24
Christian Coalition	1.5 million; 1,500 chapters	15
Human Rights Campaign	250,000	15

[a]In previous editions of the text we reported NAACP membership at 500,000. However, in 2006 new NAACP President Bruce Gordon admitted that the organization had for decades inflated its membership, and that the actual membership varied in any given year from 150,000 to 250,000. See Hazel Trice Edney, "NAACP Launches Membership Drive; Confirms Numbers Inflated," *Amsterdam News*, June 19, 2006.

[b]Unless otherwise noted, the budget figure is in millions of dollars for the year 2000.

[c]The budget for the Congressional Black Caucus is for the Congressional Black Caucus Foundation, a separate, tax-exempt organization formed in 1982 to raise funds to support the group. Until 1995, the Caucus itself raised $4,000 from each of its members to support its operations. The Republican congressional majority under Speaker Newt Gingrich discontinued this form of member support.

Sources: Immanuel Ness, *Encyclopedia of Interest Groups and Lobbyists in the United States* (Armonk, NY: M. E. Sharpe, 2000); and various annual reports.

The agenda includes *rights-based items* (busing for purposes of school desegregation and contract set-asides for minority businesses), but its main items are *material-based, nonracial issues,* such as universal health insurance and full employment. In this sense, the "black" agenda is not really black but is rather a broad-based liberal reform agenda. It is also a consensus agenda. With minor changes in emphasis and specifics, the original items remain the principal issues on the black agenda today. (The minor changes involve less concern with busing and more with affirmative action; the Byrd Amendment has been repealed, and abolition of apartheid has removed the need for sanctions on South Africa.)

Blacks therefore have a broad-based material and rights agenda; yet when compared to other lobby groups in Washington—many with narrow, single-issue agendas—black groups have relatively few resources. Table 8.3 displays data on the membership and financial resources of selected Washington interest groups, including the three most important black groups. Although the African American groups are not competitive in membership or budgets with such giants of the lobbying world as the American Association of Retired Persons (with its 33 million members and $450 million annual budget, no group can be competitive with this Association that seeks membership from and claims to represent everybody over the age of 50), or even the National Rifle Association (NRA).

The NRA has three million members and a budget of almost $100 million, compared to the NAACP's 200,000 members and $45 million budget. The budgets of the three black groups are reasonably competitive in resources with groups such as Mothers Against Drunk Driving and the Christian Coalition (except for its membership), the Sierra Club, the Jewish Anti-Defamation League, and the Human Rights Campaign, the principal

BOX 8.1   THE JOINT CENTER FOR POLITICAL AND ECONOMIC STUDIES

Think tanks—organizations of scholars and former government officials who do research and planning on domestic and foreign policy issues—are an important part of the policy-making process in the United States.[a] They develop ideas that shape the public policy debate, and unlike university-based scholars, they tend to be directly linked to Washington policy makers, frequently serving in the government for periods of time and then returning to the think tank to do research on policy-related issues. For example, many of the ideas that shaped the Reagan administration's early policy agenda came directly from the Heritage Foundation, a conservative think tank. Other important Washington think tanks include the Brookings Institution, the American Enterprise Institute, and the Urban Institute.

As the civil rights era drew to a close and black politics began its shift from movement-style protests to routine interest group policies, it was recognized early that African Americans needed their own think tank. The Joint Center for Political and Economic Studies was founded to meet this need for policy research and analysis.

The Joint Center's early projects included the collection and dissemination of data on the rapidly growing number of black elected officials (eventually this became its annual *Roster of Black Elected Officials*), the publication of a monthly newsletter, and the provision of technical training, workshops, and publications to black elected officials. The center also from the outset encouraged black elected officials to form caucuses and was instrumental in creating the National Coalition on Black Voter Participation.

In 1972 Eddie Williams became president of the Joint Center. Williams set about to broaden the center's work beyond educational and technical assistance and research support for black elected officials. The result was an announcement that the center would become a "national research organization in the tradition of Brookings and the American Enterprise Institute," rather than simply a "technical and institutional support resource for black elected officials."[b]

Although its budget is modest compared to the budgets of other Washington think tanks, the center has done a remarkable job in facilitating the institutionalization of black politics. Its studies of the growth and development of black elected officials, its work on the implementation of the Voting Rights Act, its work on the development of a consensus black agenda, and its monthly newsletter *Focus* have made the Joint Center the recognized, authoritative source on black politics in the post–civil rights era.[c]

[a]For an analysis of the increasingly important roles played by think tanks in policy making, see James Smith, *Think Tanks and the Rise of the New Policy Elites* (New York: Free Press, 1991).

[b]Joint Center for Political Studies, *Annual Report*, 1991, p. 3.

[c]For a more detailed analysis of the history and development of the Joint Center, see Robert C. Smith, *We Have No Leaders: African Americans in the Post–Civil Rights Era* (Albany: SUNY Press, 1996): 113–20.

Kwesi Mfume, former president of the NAACP, arrested outside Supreme Court while protesting the lack of minority clerks at the Court in 1998.   *Source:* AP Images

lobby for gay and lesbian rights. The black groups, however, have a multiple-issue agenda that focuses on rights- and material-based issues in both domestic and foreign affairs.

The size of an interest group's membership and budget are important resources. A large membership permits grassroots mobilization by letters and phone calls to the media and members of Congress as well as voter mobilization on election day. Money is, as former California House Speaker Jesse Unruh once said, "the mother's milk of politics." It can be employed in a wide range of activities, such as grassroots organizing, voter mobilization, polling, radio and television ads, and litigation. A large financial base is critically important because it permits interest groups to form PACs—political action committees—to raise and give campaign contributions to candidates for office. Since the passage of campaign finance reform laws in the 1970s, PACs have become very important in the lobbying-election process, contributing nearly half the money raised by incumbent congressional candidates. Many nonblack groups (the NRA, the trial lawyers, the AFL-CIO) have large PACs that contribute millions of dollars to congressional candidates. None of the black interest groups have PACs, although several unsuccessful efforts to form one were made in the 1970s by a number of black groups.[3]

Given their multiple rights- and material-issue agendas and their relative lack of resources compared to other interest groups, black groups are at a considerable disadvantage unless they can form coalitions with other groups. On most rights-based issues, civil rights lobbying is done through a broad, multiethnic coalition: the Leadership Conference on Civil Rights. (There are, however, tensions within this group; see Box 8.2.) On welfare

BOX 8.2 THE LEADERSHIP CONFERENCE ON CIVIL RIGHTS

The theory of African American coalitions we have developed in this book suggests that such coalitions, whether rights- or material-based, tend to be unstable and frequently short-lived. While this is generally true, there is one coalition—the Leadership Conference on Civil Rights—that has now lasted almost a half century, although in recent years it too has experienced tensions and conflicts.

The Leadership Conference on Civil Rights (LCCR) is a rights-based coalition. It was founded in 1949 by A. Phillip Randolph, the African American labor leader; Roy Wilkins, assistant director of the NAACP; and Arnold Aronson, a Jewish labor activist. Initially it was a coalition of about 40 black, labor, and Jewish and other religious groups whose principal objective was to secure legislation ensuring the civil rights of African Americans, especially those in the South. This coalition, along with the NAACP, was the principal lobby group for the 1964 Civil Rights Act (at that time, Clarence Mitchell, head of the NAACP's Washington office, also was head of the LCCR).

The African American civil rights movement of the 1960s and its successes served as a model for other groups facing various forms of discrimination. These groups (women, gays, and other minorities) joined the LCCR, expanding its memberships from about 40 groups in 1949 to more than 150 today. In 1949, most of the organizations in the LCCR were black and it was widely viewed as an African American coalition. Today, this is no longer the case, as black organizations constitute little more than a third of the LCCR's membership.[a] The expansion of the coalition has inevitably led to tensions and conflicts along racial, ethnic, and gender lines.

From the beginning there were gender conflicts within the civil rights coalition. African Americans, labor leaders, and spokespersons for working-class women opposed the inclusion of a ban on sex discrimination in employment in the 1964 Civil Rights Act. Labor opposed gender equality in favor of preferential treatment for women: laws limiting working hours and the physical burden of work for women and providing such special benefits as rest and maternity leave. African American leaders (mainly men) opposed the inclusion of gender because they argued that it would take jobs from black men—the putative family breadwinner—and give them to white women. By contrast, support for the inclusion of gender came from conservatives (the amendment on sex was introduced by Howard Smith of Virginia, an opponent of civil rights, who thought the inclusion of sex would kill the entire bill) and white upper-class women's groups such as the National Federation of Business and Professional Women. Although African Americans and labor leaders now support gender equality in employment, sex–race tensions continue over affirmative action, with some African Americans arguing that white women are the principal beneficiaries of a program originally set up for blacks. Affirmative action has also caused conflict with some Jewish groups in the LCCR; these groups tend to object to racial quotas and preferences (especially in higher education) because quotas historically were used to exclude Jews and because some Jewish leaders see them as a violation of merit and the principle of equality for all persons. Jewish–black tensions in the coalition have also been exacerbated in recent years by conflicts over black support for the Palestinians in the Middle East conflict, Israeli support

(continued)

> **BOX 8.2** *continued*
>
> for the apartheid regime in South Africa, and the antisemitic remarks of the Nation of Islam's Louis Farrakhan.
>
> Another source of tension in the LCCR is between African Americans and Mexican Americans. When the 1965 Voting Rights Act was renewed in 1975, the NAACP opposed the inclusion of an amendment to prohibit discrimination against language minorities. Decisions of the LCCR require a unanimous vote of its executive committee, thus the NAACP's opposition effectively killed coalition support, forcing Latino groups in the coalition to act alone in a successful effort to get language groups covered by the Voting Rights Act.[b] Although this issue is now settled, it left a residue of bad feeling between blacks and Latinos. In addition, some African Americans have expressed concerns about the impact of illegal immigration on the employment opportunities of low-income urban blacks, a position that upsets the Asian American and Hispanic American groups in the coalition.
>
> The LCCR is a rights-based coalition that has endured for 50 years, but its successes in the 1960s, the development of new rights groups in the 1970s and 1980s, and the expansion of the coalition have inevitably created some instability. However, as a broad-based coalition that embraces universal rights for all Americans, it is likely to endure, although not without continuing conflicts and tensions.[c]
>
> [a]Dianne Pinderhughes, "Black Interest Groups and the 1982 Extension of the Voting Rights Act," in Huey Perry and Wayne Parent, eds., *Blacks and the American Political System* (Gainesville: University Press of Florida, 1995): 206.
>
> [b]Ibid., p. 211.
>
> [c]Dianne Pinderhughes, "Divisions in the Civil Rights Community," *Political Science and Politics* 25 (1992): 485–87.

and poverty issues, the Center for Budget Priorities (a white group) is an effective lobby and advocacy group, and on national health insurance and full employment, the AFL-CIO and the Conference of Catholic Bishops are, with blacks, part of a broad labor–liberal reform coalition. But as shown by the failure to secure effective full employment legislation in the 1970s and by the defeat of President Clinton's universal health care plan in the 1990s, this reform coalition has not been able to effectively counterbalance the power of those interests opposed to universal health and employment.

African American Women and the Quest for Universal Freedom

Although some black male leaders were ardent feminists—supporters of universal freedom for women—most were not and even those who were always were more concerned with ending racism and white supremacism than sexism and male supremacism. Thus, African American women in politics have tended to embrace a more universal version of freedom than African American men, a version encompassing the elimination of both race and gender barriers to equality. But, feminism—the ideology of gender equality and freedom—has historically been an ambivalent phenomenon in the black community and in African American politics. This is because African American women historically have faced the double burden of oppression on the basis of racism, and discrimination on the basis of sexism. This double burden creates dilemmas—whether elimination of racism or sexism is to be the main focus of the struggles of black women and to what extent black women should identify and form coalitions with white women, who frequently are as racist and white supremacist in their thinking as white men. Also, historically in the United States the struggle for women's rights and the struggle for the rights of blacks have been symbiotic and conflictual. The earliest movement for women's rights originated from the activism of white women in the abolitionist movement. However, these largely middle- to upper-class women tended to view sexism as equal as or more important than racism. The modern feminist movement that originated in the late 1960s and early 1970s also has its roots in black movements for freedom, specifically in the activism of middle-class white women in the protest phase of the civil rights movement during the 1960s.[4] The modern movement for women's liberation also drew on the black power movement for parts of its militancy in rhetoric, strategies, and organizing principles. But, as during the abolitionist movement, tensions emerged as these middle-class white women also tended to see sexism as equal as or more important than racism.

The roots of black feminism go back to the Antebellum Era in the writings and activism of women like Maria B. Stewart and Sojourner Truth, and in the late-nineteenth-century writings of women like Anna Julia Cooper, whose 1892 book *A Voice from the South* is an important early work in the development of a distinctive black feminist thought. Black feminism is also rooted in the activities of the black club movement among women. These activities led to the formation in 1896 of the National Association of Colored Women and later the National Council of Negro Women. The National Association of Colored Women, organized a decade before the NAACP, was the first national black organization to deal with race issues, and the National Council of Negro Women led by Dorothy Height dealt with women's issues as well as broader issues of civil rights during the 1950s and 1960s.

In the 1970s, however, it was clearly the feminist movement among white women that revitalized the ideology among black women, in spite of the skepticism and even hostility of many black women to the middle-class-dominated white feminist movement. The success of the civil rights movement in removing the obvious barriers to racial equality allowed for a renewed focus on gender equality among black women. Shirley Chisholm's election as the first black woman in Congress in 1968 and her 1972 campaign for the presidency were important symbolically in inspiring black female political activism. Finally, the Supreme Court's 1973 decision in *Roe* v. *Wade* to legalize abortion was a catalyst to action, since the decision was opposed by virtually the entire male-dominated black leadership establishment, including the NAACP and the Urban League. The National Black Political Convention in 1972 rejected a resolution supporting legal abortions; leading black nationalists denounced the decision as genocidal and Jesse Jackson equated *Roe* v. *Wade* with the *Dred Scott* decision. (Of major black organizations only the Black Panther Party endorsed *Roe* and a woman's right to choose an abortion.)

In 1973 black women formed the National Black Feminist Organization, which advocated a specifically black agenda of gender equality. In 1974 radical black feminists and lesbians formed the Combahee River Collective (taking its name from a campaign led by Harriet Tubman that freed several hundred slaves), which issued a manifesto defining itself as a group of black women "struggling against racial, sexual, heterosexual and class oppression." (This group is heavily influenced by the writings of Audre Lorde, a young black lesbian feminist and political activist who saw sexuality as an important part of black feminism.)[5] In 1984 politically active black women formed the National Political Caucus of Black Women in order to pursue a distinctive gendered role in African American politics, focusing on issues and the election and appointment of black women to office.

Black Nationalist Movements

Black nationalist organizations are movement rather than interest group organizations. Interest groups accept the legitimacy of the system and seek to have it accept their demands for rights and freedoms; movements challenge system legitimacy and seek fundamental system transformation. Historically, black nationalists have certainly challenged the legitimacy of the American system; in their view, it is incapable of delivering universal freedom and equality. This is shown clearly in the system-challenging rhetoric of nationalist leaders. In 1901 Bishop Henry M. Turner caused a national furor when he said "to the Negro in this country the American flag is a dirty and contemptuous rag. Not a star in it can the colored man claim, for it is no longer a symbol of our manhood rights and freedom."[6] Similar controversial remarks about the flag were made by Louis Farrakhan 95 years later in a speech to his followers in Chicago.

Bishop Henry M. Turner and the First Mass-Based
Black Nationalist Movement

The ideology of black nationalism is as old as the African American experience in the United States; until the Post-Reconstruction Era, however, it was simply the thought of a few intellectuals or the poorly organized efforts of a few remarkable men.[7] The first effort at a nationalist movement on a mass basis was launched by Bishop Henry M. Turner in the 1890s. Faced by the withdrawal of African American freedom, the terrorism of white southern racists, and Booker T. Washington's seeming acceptance of this turn of events, Turner sought to organize blacks for a mass return to Africa. As he frequently said in his speeches and writings, for blacks the choice was simple: "emigrate or perish."[8]

Turner was born a free man of color in 1834. A bishop of the African Methodist Episcopal church, he served as a chaplain in the Union army and as a member of the Reconstruction Georgia constitutional convention. Once Reconstruction ended, Turner attempted to organize a back-to-Africa movement. From 1890 until his death in 1915, Turner organized numerous conferences and filed many petitions with Congress requesting support for his plan. He, for example, was the first African American leader to petition Congress for reparations, calling for a $40 billion payment to blacks for their 200 years of slave labor.

Turner, like most advocates of back-to-Africa schemes, met with little success. Most African Americans—especially the small middle class—opposed Turner's efforts, apparently preferring to go along with the accommodationist approach of Booker Washington than to risk the perils of emigration across the Atlantic. This is an enduring dilemma of nationalist emigrationists; most African Americans do not wish to leave the United States. In addition, absence of support from middle-class blacks makes it difficult to finance emigration schemes. Turner did organize the Colored Emigration League, publish a monthly newsletter, and establish the Afro-American Steamship Company. For a time he was an honorary vice president of the American Colonialization Society, an organization of racists formed in the 1770s shortly after the Revolutionary War. This group favored emigration because, in its view, the United States should be a white man's country. Also, Turner was able to persuade several racist southern congressmen to introduce emigration legislation. This is another dilemma for black nationalist groups: Their potential white coalition partners tend to be racists and white supremacists. Marcus Garvey in the 1920s and more recently Louis Farrakhan have talked to representatives of the KKK and other racist groups about forming coalitions to secure emigration or separation.

Although Turner's movement ended with his death and with little success (it is estimated that perhaps a thousand blacks emigrated to Africa),[9] Turner's rhetoric (he was the first black leader to declare that God was black, a notion later advanced by Marcus Garvey and some sects of the Black Muslims) and strategy of organization was followed by subsequent nationalist leaders and organizations.

Marcus Garvey and the Universal Negro Improvement Association

The second major black nationalist movement was organized in Harlem by Marcus Garvey in 1914. Garvey's organization was called the Universal Negro Improvement Association. At its peak in the 1920s, it claimed a membership of two million in the United States and the West Indies.[10] Like Turner, Garvey declared that God, Jesus, and the angels were black, that whites were an inferior race, and that blacks should return to Africa and restore its past glories. He also founded a steamship company, a newspaper, and a number of small factories and businesses. A charismatic leader and powerful orator, like Louis Farrakhan, today he would draw huge crowds to his rallies. An autocratic leader, in 1921 Garvey declared himself provisional president of Africa although he had never set foot on the continent and never would.

Like Turner's movement, Garvey's was opposed by most blacks, with his strongest base of support coming from among the poor and working classes of the big-city ghettos of the North. Also, like Turner's movement, Garvey's was opposed by the mainstream, middle-class black leadership establishment (an especially bitter critic was W. E. B. Du Bois). Unlike Turner's movement, Garvey's attracted the attention of the federal government, since its mass following and radicalism appeared to be a threat to internal security. In 1925, Garvey and several of his associates were indicted on federal mail fraud charges of using the mail to sell phony stock in his steamship company. His associates were found not guilty, but Garvey was convicted, sentenced to prison for several years, then deported. He died in London in 1940. With his deportation in 1927, his organization and movement split into a number of small sects and factions and lost its effectiveness.

Louis Farrakhan and the Nation of Islam: The Resurgence of Black Nationalism in the Post–Civil Rights Era

The most influential black nationalist leader and organization of the post–civil rights era is Minister Louis Farrakhan and the Nation of Islam. The Nation of Islam—popularly known as the Black Muslims—was founded by W. D. Fard in 1931. After Fard's disappearance it was led by Elijah Muhammad until his death in 1976.[11] Like Garvey's movement, the Nation was based on racial chauvinism, glorifying everything black and condemning whites as devils.

The Nation grew slowly until the charismatic Malcolm X became its national spokesman in the 1960s. Malcolm helped to build a large following for the group among the urban poor and working class.[12] The Nation, like the Garvey movement, established chapters (mosques) throughout the country, operated small businesses and farms, and published a weekly newspaper. Unlike the Garvey and Turner movements, the Nation did not establish a steamship line since it does not favor emigration to Africa. Instead, it desires the creation of a separate black nation within the boundaries of the United States.

When Elijah Muhammad died in 1976, the Nation of Islam split into a series of sects and factions; the main body of the group, led by Wallace Muhammad, Elijah Muhammad's son, was transformed into a mainstream, integrationist (including whites as members), orthodox Islamic group.[13] For a short time in the 1970s, the Nation of Islam disappeared. This was the objective of J. Edgar Hoover and the FBI. Sometime before the death of Elijah Muhammad (the date is not clear), Hoover sent a memorandum to the special agent in charge of the Chicago office, which in part said:

> The NOI (Nation of Islam) appears to be the personal fiefdom of Elijah Muhammad. When he dies a power struggle can be expected and the NOI could change direction. We should be prepared for this eventuality. We should plan now to change the philosophy of the NOI to one of strictly religious and self-improvement orientation, deleting the race hatred and the separate nationhood aspects. In this connection Chicago should consider what counter intelligence action might be needed now or at the time

Malcolm X with Elijah Muhammad, leader of the Nation of Islam.   *Source:* Eve Arnold/Magnum Photos

BOX 8.3 THE AFRICAN AMERICAN REPARATION MOVEMENT

In the Post-Reconstruction Era, Bishop Henry M. Turner was the first African American leader to demand reparation—repayment for the damages of slavery—from the American government. After the Civil War, there was talk of providing a kind of reparation to blacks in the form of "40 acres and a mule." In the 1865 Freedmen's Bureau Act, Congress included a provision granting blacks 40 acres of abandoned land in the southern states. President Andrew Johnson, however, vetoed the bill, arguing that to take land from the former slave owners was "contrary to that provision of the Constitution which declares that no person shall 'be deprived of life, liberty and property without due process of law.' "[a] The closest the U.S. government ever came to paying reparation was General William Sherman's Special Order #15 issued on January 16, 1865.[b] It provided 40 acres to black families living on the Georgia and South Carolina coasts (some of the descendants of these families still live or own property on these lands). Blacks, however, never abandoned their claims for reparation, and the payment by the Congress and several American cities of reparation to Japanese Americans for their World War II incarceration contributed to the rebirth of an African American movement seeking similar remuneration.

The contemporary reparation movement is led by Imari Obadele, a former professor of political science at the historically black Prairie View A & M University and the former provisional president of the Republic of New Africa. The Republic of New Africa is a black nationalist organization founded in 1968 by Obadele (who was then known as Richard Henry). The organization favors the creation of a separate, all-black nation in the southern part of the United States. In 1989 Obadele and others formed the National Coalition of Blacks for Reparations (NCOBRA), a nonprofit coalition of black religious, civic, and fraternal organizations. Since its formation the coalition has engaged in a variety of tactics to advance the cause of reparation, including petitions to Congress and the president, lawsuits, and protest demonstrations at the White House.

African American supporters of reparation cite a number of precedents regarding reparation.[c] But the one cited most frequently and the one that gave impetus to this new movement was the decision by Congress in 1988 to issue an apology and pay $20,000 to each Japanese American (or his or her survivors) incarcerated during World War II.[d] Earlier the cities of Los Angeles and San Francisco had taken similar actions. Using the Japanese case as a precedent, NCOBRA has made a proposal to Congress, called "An Act to Stimulate Economic Growth in the United States and Compensate, in Part, for the Grievous Wrongs of Slavery and the Unjust Enrichment Which Accrued to the United States Therefrom." The proposal indicates no dollar amount for payment (suggesting that the figure be established by an independent commission, as was done in the Japanese American case) but requires that one-third of the payment go to each individual African man, woman, and child; one-third to the Republic of New Africa; and one-third to a national congress of black church, civic, and civil rights organizations.[e]

In the Japanese case, the first step was the appointment by the Congress of a commission to study the issue. Thus, in 1995, Congressman John Conyers, an African American, and Congressman Norman Mineta, a Japanese American, introduced a bill to establish a "Commission to Study Reparations for African Americans."[f] Also, in 1995 several African Americans filed a suit in a federal court in California asking the court to direct the government to pay

(continued)

BOX 8.3 *continued*

reparation. The Court of Appeals of the Ninth Circuit rejected the suit, holding that the United States could not be sued unless it waived its "sovereign immunity" and that the "appropriate forum for policy questions of this sort . . . is Congress rather than the courts."[g]

This new reparation movement is just getting under way, and given the present climate of race relations in the United States, the prospects for its success in the near term do not appear good.[h] However, in part because of the publication in 2000 of *The Debt: What America Owes Blacks* by Randall Robinson, the head of Trans Africa, the issue has at least received increased attention. Articles have appeared in leading newspapers and magazines; local and state legislative bodies have taken up the issue; it has been the topic of lively debate on college campuses, on the Internet, and local and national talk radio programs; and in 2001 the *Philadelphia Inquirer* published two full-page editorials urging the creation of a national commission on reparations. Following the 1992 decision of the state of Florida to pay reparations to the survivors and descendants of Rosewood (a black town that was destroyed by a white mob in 1923), the Oklahoma Commission to Study the Tulsa Race Riots of 1921 recommended that the survivors and descendants be paid reparations for the riots in which white mobs attacked a black neighborhood, destroying homes and businesses and killing hundreds of people.

[a]The text of the Freedmen's Bureau bill and President Johnson's veto message are in *The Forty Acres Documents,* Introduction by Amitcar Shabazz (Baton Rouge, LA: The House of Songhay, 1994): 65, 74, 75–94.

[b]The text of Sherman's Order is also in *The Forty Acres Document,* pp. 51–58.

[c]See Boris Bittker, *The Case for Black Reparations* (New York: Random House, 1973); and Daisy Collins, "Reparations for Black Citizens," *Howard University Law Review* 82 (1979).

[d]Tom Kenworthy, "House Votes Apology, Reparations for Japanese Americans," *Washington Post,* September 18, 1987, p. A1.

[e]Chokwe Lumumba, Imari Obadele, and Nkechi Taifa, *Reparations NOW!* (Baton Rouge, LA: The House of Songhay, 1995): 67.

[f]The text of the Conyers-Mineta bill is in Lumumba, Obadele, and Taifa, *Reparations NOW!* pp. 97–107.

[g]*Cato et al. v. United States of America,* United States Circuit Court of Appeals, Ninth Circuit #94-17102 (1995): 151–62.

[h]An ABC News poll found that overall, 77 percent of Americans were opposed to reparation for blacks. Sixty-five percent of blacks supported the idea, while it was opposed by 88 percent of whites. See ABC News *Nightline,* July 7, 1997.

of Elijah Muhammad's death to bring about such a change in the NOI philosophy. Important considerations should include the identity, strengths and weaknesses of any contender for NOI leader. The alternative to changing the philosophy of the NOI is the destruction of the organization. This might be accomplished through generating factionalism among the contenders for Elijah Muhammad's leadership or through legal action in probate court.[14]

For a while Minister Farrakhan acquiesced in the transformation of the Nation into a strictly religious, integrationist organization. However, after a year or so, he set about to rebuild the Nation on the basis of the original principles of Elijah Muhammad.[15] However, in his clearest break with the traditions of the Nation, Farrakhan in 1993 abandoned the doctrine of nonparticipation in American electoral politics. Under Elijah Muhammad, members of the Nation were strictly forbidden to participate in American politics, which he described as the "devil's" system. Farrakhan abandoned this position first by encouraging his followers to register and vote for Chicago mayoral candidate Harold Washington in 1983. He also supported Jesse Jackson's campaign for president in 1984.

Unlike most African American organizations, the Nation of Islam receives no money from white corporations or businesses. It has approximately 120 mosques in various cities around the country, operates a series of modest small business enterprises, and has a somewhat effective social welfare system for its members. It publishes a weekly newspaper—*The Final Call*—and Farrakhan may be seen and heard on more than 120 radio and television stations around the country. The organization does not reveal the size of its membership, but it is estimated at no more than 20,000. However, the Nation and Farrakhan have millions of followers. A 1994 *Time* magazine poll found that 73 percent of blacks were familiar with Farrakhan, making him, with Jesse Jackson, the best-known African American leader. Most blacks familiar with Farrakhan view him favorably, with 65 percent saying he was an effective leader, 63 percent that he speaks the truth, and 62 percent that he was good for black America.[16] The *Time* poll that produced these figures was taken prior to Farrakhan's success in calling the Million Man March, the largest demonstration in Washington in American history.

FACES AND VOICES IN THE STRUGGLE FOR UNIVERSAL FREEDOM

MARIA W. STEWART (1803–1879)

Maria W. Stewart contributed to universal freedom and equality by becoming the first African American woman to take a leadership role in the abolitionist movement. Born in Boston in 1803, at age five she was orphaned and became a servant to a white clergyman, where she received her education by attending Sunday school and reading books from the church library. A deeply religious woman, she was widowed after three years of marriage, at which time she began her brief career as an antislavery and feminist lecturer.

Historians describe Stewart as the first black woman lecturer and writer and probably the first woman, black or white, to speak before an audience of both men and women. Stewart's career as a writer and lecturer lasted only three years, during which, while living in Boston, she gave three public lectures and published a political treatise and a religious pamphlet. In addition to her antislavery work, Stewart was also an ardent feminist. Not only did she encourage the formation of black women's rights organizations, she urged black women to pursue education and careers outside the home, writing "How long shall the fair daughters of Africa be compelled to bury their minds and talents beneath a load of iron pots and kettles?"

After the Civil War, Stewart became a teacher in Washington, DC. She died in 1879. Shortly before her death she published a collection of her speeches and essays, *Meditations from the Pen of Mrs. Maria W. Stewart.*

*Marilyn Richardson, *Maria Stewart: America's First Black Women Political Writer* (Bloomington: Indiana University Press, 1987).

Summary

Once a group gains entry into the American political system, if it is to be effective it has to form interest groups. Although there is a fairly diverse structure of interest group organizations representing black interests in Washington, these interests are multifaceted, embracing both rights- and material-based interests. In addition, compared to nonblack interest groups, black groups tend to be relatively underfunded. Historically, a number of black leaders and groups have rejected participation in the system, believing it is not effective because of racism and white supremacy and/or because they desire to pursue independent, autonomous political paths. These individuals and groups have embraced black nationalism. In addition, African American women have developed separate organizations in their quest for universal freedom, dealing with both sexism and racism.

Selected Bibliography

Garson, G. David. *Group Theories of Politics.* Beverly Hills: Sage, 1978. A review and critique of the major theories and the research on the interest group basis of American politics.

Giddings, Paula. *When and Where I Enter: The Impact of Black Women on Race and Sex in America.* New York: William Morrow, 1984. One of the earliest and best studies of the subject.

Hamilton, Dana, and Charles Hamilton. *The Dual Agenda: Social Policies of Civil Rights Organizations from the New Deal to the Present.* New York: Columbia University Press, 1996. Although they do not use the terms *rights-based* and *material-based*, this book is an exhaustive study of the dual agenda of black Americans.

Johnson, Ollie, and Karen Stanford, eds. *Black Political Organizations.* New Brunswick, NJ: Rutgers University Press, 2003. A collection of 11 essays examining the activities and impact of contemporary black interest organizations, including the NAACP, Urban League, the Rainbow/PUSH Coalition, Nation of Islam, and the National Council of Negro Women.

Lowi, Theodore. *The End of Liberalism.* New York: Norton, 1979. An influential study of how interest groups manipulate public policy making in pursuit of narrow, parochial interests.

Pinderhughes, Dianne. "Collective Goods and Black Interest." *Review of Black Political Economy* 12 (Winter 1983): 219–36. A largely theoretical analysis of the role of black interest groups in pursuing the multiple policy interests of blacks in an environment of resource constraints.

Pinderhughes, Dianne. "Black Interest Groups and the 1982 Extension of the Voting Rights Act" (pp. 203–24). In Huey Perry and Wayne Parent, eds., *Blacks and the American Political System.* Gainesville: University Press of Florida, 1995. A case study of African American interest group politics in the context of the contemporary civil rights coalition.

Smith, Robert C. *We Have No Leaders: African Americans in the Post–Civil Rights Era.* Albany: SUNY Press, 1996. A detailed study of the transformation of the 1960s African American freedom struggle from movement to interest groups politics, focusing on African American interest groups, the Congressional Black Caucus, black presidential appointees in the executive branch, and Jesse Jackson's Rainbow Coalition.

Stuckey, Sterling. *The Ideological Origins of Black Nationalism.* Boston: Beacon, 1972. A seminal study that includes some of the classic black nationalist writings.

Notes

1. Harold Wolman and Norman Thomas, "Black Interests, Black Groups and Black Influence in the Federal Policy Process: The Cases of Housing and Education," *Journal of Politics* 32 (November 1970): 875–97.

2. Dianne Pinderhughes, "Racial Interest Groups and Incremental Politics" (unpublished paper, University of Illinois, Urbana, 1980): 36.

3. Ibid., p. 122.

4. Michelle Newman, *White Women's Right: The Racial Origins of Feminism in the United States* (New York: Oxford University Press, 1999).

5. See Audre Lorde, *I Am Your Sister: Black Women Organizing Across Sexualities* (Latham, NY: Kitchen Table Women of Color Press, 1985).

6. Edwin Redkey, "The Flowering of Black Nationalism: Henry McNeal Turner and Marcus Garvey," in Nathan Huggins, Martin Kilson and Daniel Fox, eds., *Key Issues in the Afro-American Experience*, vol. 2 (New York: Harcourt Brace Jovanovich, 1971): 115.

7. On the historical origins of black nationalist thought, see Sterling Stuckey, The Ideological Origins of Black Nationalism (Boston: Beacon, 1972), and Sterling Stuckey, *Slave Culture: Foundations of Nationalist Thought* (New York: Oxford, 1967).

8. Stuckey, *The Ideological Origins of Black Nationalism*.

9. Ibid., p. 114.

10. See Edmund Cronon, Black Moses: *The Story of Marcus Garvey and the Universal Negro Improvement Association* (Madison: University of Wisconsin Press, 1955).

11. Claude Andrew Clegg, *An Original Man: The Life and Times of Elijah Muhammad* (New York: St. Martin's Press, 1997).

12. Bruce Perry, Malcolm: *The Life of a Man Who Changed Black America* (Barrytown, NY: Station Hill Press, 1991).

13. Don Terry, "Black Muslims Enter Islamic Mainstream," *New York Times*, May 3, 1993.

14. The Hoover memorandum is quoted in Imam Sidney Sharif, "Hoover Plotted Against Muslims," *Atlanta Voice*, February 22, 1986.

15. On Farrakhan's strategy to revitalize the Nation of Islam, see Robert C. Smith, *We Have No Leaders: African Americans in the Post-Civil Rights Era* (Albany: SUNY Press, 1996, pp. 99–100); Lawrence Mamiya, "From Black Muslim to Bialian: The Evolution of a Movement," *Journal for the Scientific Study of Religion* 21 (1982): 141; and Mattias Gardell, *In the Name of Elijah Muhammad: Louis Farrakhan and the Nation of Islam* (Durham, NC: Duke University Press, 1996). Gardell's work contains a detailed analysis of the theological underpinnings of the Nation of Islam.

16. William Henry, "Pride and Prejudice," *Time*, February 28, 1994, p. 22."

CHAPTER 9

Political Parties

The impossible has happened. In 2008 an African American won the presidential nomination of one of the two major parties. To understand the extraordinary nature of Obama's capture of the Democratic nomination and its significance in the African American quest for universal freedom, one must locate the 2008 election in the historical context of the African American relationship to the two-party system. It is also necessary to analyze what happened in 2008 in relation to the role of blacks in the Democratic Party since the pivotal 1964 election. Finally, to fully understand the Obama phenomenon, it is useful to compare his campaign for the nomination with previous efforts by African Americans to win major party nominations, especially Jesse Jackson's.

African Americans and the American No-Party System

Virtually all political scientists are committed to the idea that a competitive party system is indispensable to the effective operation of any democracy. The essence of this commitment according to Leon Epstein is the theory "that voters should be able to choose between recognizable competing leadership groups" that offer alternative programs and policies addressing citizen needs and interests.[1] The two-party system in the United States has historically worked reasonably well for white Americans, offering alternative candidates, programs, and policies from which they could choose. For African Americans, this has rarely been the case. The American two-party system, Paul Frymer argues, represents a form of institutional racism, in that it was partly designed to marginalize black interests by keeping the issue of slavery off the national political agenda.[2] Thus, for most of American history, blacks have faced a no-party system as from 1787 until the 1860s both major parties ignored the major issue of concern to blacks—freedom.

African Americans—where they were allowed to vote—supported the anti-slavery Free Soil and Liberty parties from the 1840s to the 1860s. However, these parties, because of the structural characteristics of the electoral system that maintain the two-party system, were rarely able to elect their members to office[3] (see Box 9.1). It was not until the Civil War brought about the emergence of the Republican Party and the destruction of slavery that one of the two major parties began to pay some attention to the interests of blacks.

BOX 9.1   BEYOND THE TWO-PARTY SYSTEM?

Recent polls indicate that more than half the public, black as well as white, is dissatisfied with the two-party system and would like to see another party or parties in addition to the Democrats and Republicans. In spite of this discontent, the structure of the electoral system makes the emergence of a viable third party extremely unlikely. The American electoral structure involves two distinct features that discourage the formation of third parties. The first is the *winner-take-all* method of allocating electoral college votes for president, in which the candidate with the most votes gets all of a state's electoral college votes. (Thus, in 1992 Bill Clinton got 43 percent of the popular vote in California but 100 percent of that state's 55 electoral votes.) The second is the *single-member district* system used in electing members of the House, in which voters vote for only one congressperson and the winner needs only a plurality to win. By contrast, virtually every other democratic country uses some form of *proportional representation* that encourages the formation of third or minor parties, since their candidates have a chance to win. A system of proportional representation in the United States would allocate electoral college votes to a candidate according to the proportion of the popular vote that candidate won. Had such a system been in effect in 1992, Ross Perot, who received 20 percent of the vote, would have been awarded 108 electoral votes (20 percent of 538) instead of the zero he got. Similarly, a *multimember district* system for House elections could allow a minor party to win because seats in the House would be determined by each party's percentage of the vote. For example, if in a ten-member district, the Democrats won 40 percent of the vote, they would get four seats; the Republicans, with 40 percent, would get four seats, and Ross Perot's Reform Party, with 20 percent of the vote, would get two seats.

There is some discussion in academic circles about reform of the American electoral system to encourage proportional representation and a multiparty system[a]; former Congressman and 1980 third-party presidential candidate John Anderson is the head of a group—the Center for Voting and Democracy—that is trying to build public support for the idea, and former African American congresswoman Cynthia McKinney (Democrat, Georgia) introduced a bill to provide for proportional representation in House elections. The bill was referred to committee and no further action was taken. Unless a massive grassroots movement develops, these reform ideas will probably not go very far since the Democrats and Republicans will not easily yield their shared monopoly on political power.

[a]See Lani Guinier, *The Tyranny of the Majority: Fundamental Fairness in American Democracy* (New York: Free Press, 1994); Douglas Amy, *Real Choices/New Voices: The Case for Proportional Representation Elections in the United States* (New York: Columbia University Press, 1993); and Kay Lawson, "The Case for a Multiparty System," in Paul Herrnson and John Green, eds., *Multiparty Politics in America: Performance, Promise, Prospects and Possibilities* (Boulder, CO: Rowman, Littlefield, 1999).

African Americans and the American One-Party System: 1868–1936

During the Civil War–Reconstruction era, when African American men first achieved the right to vote, Frederick Douglass is said to have told a group of black voters, "The Republican Party is the deck, all else the sea."[4] What Douglass meant was that only one of the two major parties—the Republican—was willing to address the concerns of blacks. The

Democratic Party, on the other hand, was the party of racism and white supremacy, committed to denying universal freedom to the newly emancipated Africans. Since Douglass' days, except for the brief period of the New Deal, discussed below, hardly anything has changed; one party is the deck, the other the sea—except that today the deck is the Democratic Party.

The Republican Party became the deck because beginning with the Emancipation Proclamation, it adopted policies that addressed the universal freedom concerns of blacks, including three constitutional amendments and three civil rights bills. It also addressed the material-based concerns of blacks with legislation establishing the Freedmen's Bureau, the government's first social welfare agency (see Chapter 2). Although we do not have precise figures, it is probably the case that from the 1868 election (when African Americans in significant numbers were first allowed to vote) until 1936 the Republican Party averaged more than 80 percent of the black vote in presidential elections.

By the late 1870s, however, a white backlash developed, and in the "Compromise of 1877" the Republicans under the leadership of President Rutherford B. Hayes effectively abandoned the interests of blacks in favor of reconciliation with southern white racists (see Chapter 12). The African American leadership and those blacks who could still vote continued to support the Republicans because the Democratic Party was worse. Thus, as Gurin, Hatchett and Jackson conclude, "The history of the black electorate is characterized by blacks' continual commitment to the electoral system and repeated rejection by one party or the other", but, "black leaders have persistently searched for strategies that would make the party system work for the black electorate."[5] Those strategies have included abandoning the Republican Party in favor of Democrats, attempting to use the black vote as the balance of power between the two parties, and running as candidates for the Democratic presidential nomination.

African Americans, Limited Party Competition, and the Balance of Power, 1936–1964

Most blacks remained loyal to the Republican Party in the Depression era 1932 presidential election, in which FDR defeated Herbert Hoover in a landslide. In 1936, however, a majority of blacks voted Democratic in a presidential election for the first time. Blacks did not vote for FDR because he was a Democrat or because he supported their concerns for civil rights and universal freedom. Rather he was able to win black support in 1936 and thereafter because he embraced their material-based interests in jobs, housing, and social security.

By 1945 a majority of blacks were voting Democratic in national elections, but a significant minority remained Republican and even some black Democrats would vote Republican if the candidate and his policies were attractive. Thus, for the first time in history—and for a brief time—African American voters enjoyed the benefit of a two-party system. Thus, they could operate as the balance of power determining the winner in close elections.

On the eve of the 1948 election, Henry Lee Moon, the NAACP's public relations director, wrote *Balance of Power: The Negro Vote*. This slim volume summarized the strategic significance of the black vote: "The Negro's political influence in national elections derives not so much from its numerical strength as from its strategic diffusion in the balance of power and marginal states whose electoral votes are considered vital to the winning candidate."[6]

The black vote (in the swing states of the Northeast and Midwest) did tip the balance to President Truman in 1948 and to President Kennedy in 1960. But it was not a monolithic vote during this period. Truman's Republican opponent in 1948 received about 25 percent of the black vote, as did Republican Richard Nixon in 1960, and Dwight Eisenhower in the 1950s may have received as much as 35 percent. Both parties during this period attempted to appeal to black concerns. In the 1950s Eisenhower's civil rights record was about as good as the Democratic nominee and Nixon's in 1960 was the equal of Kennedy's.

The Collapse of the New Deal Coalition and the Return of the One-Party System

With the entry of blacks into the New Deal coalition, it became inherently unstable and subject to collapse. The coalition FDR patched together included the industrial working class of the Northeast and Midwest, with such ethnic immigrants as Poles, Italians, and the Irish; it also had Jews, liberal intellectuals, white southerners, and blacks. This coalition of opposites—African Americans and southern white racists—was held together by a common interest in universal material benefits. Once the Democratic Party embraced the African American civil rights agenda—first in 1948 under President Truman and then in the 1960s under Presidents Kennedy and Johnson—the New Deal Coalition began to fall apart. In 1948 southern white supremacists and racists left the coalition and formed a third "Dixiecrat" Party. With South Carolina's Strom Thurmond as its presidential candidate, the new party carried four Deep South states. In 1964 southern racists again left the coalition—this time to support the Republican presidential candidate Barry Goldwater, who had opposed the Civil Rights Act of 1964. Goldwater, like Thurmond, carried the Deep South states. In the 1968 presidential election southern whites supported George Wallace, the racist, white supremacist Governor of Alabama, and in 1972 they supported Richard Nixon. By 1972 the New Deal coalition was dead; southern whites had defected along with elements of the northern white industrial working class. By 1980 the Republican Party had consolidated itself as the conservative party of racial reaction. The New Deal coalition collapsed for many reasons, but the major one was racism. Many whites, especially in the South, were unwilling to be a part of a broad material-based coalition if that coalition also embraced the historic quest of African Americans for equality and universal freedom.

The collapse of the New Deal coalition signaled the return of one-party politics. The Democratic Party was now the deck, all else the sea. While only 10 percent of the overall electorate, blacks since the 1970s have constituted 20 percent of the Democratic Party's electorate.[7] The size and geographic distribution (in the South and Midwest) of the vote within the Democratic Party means that the black vote routinely constitutes the balance of power in determining the Party's presidential nominee. This was the case with the nominations of Jimmy Carter in 1976, Bill Clinton in 1992, and Barack Obama in 2008.

However, since the 1970s and especially since the 1980s the Democratic Party has taken the black vote for granted, just as the Republicans did a century ago. Knowing that it can count on nearly 90 percent of the black vote, the Democrats pocket it at the outset of the elections, while offering little in the way of policies to address the main concerns of blacks—joblessness and racialized poverty (see Chapter 15). Indeed, in order to compete for the votes of "Reagan Democrats" since the 1990s, the Party under Clinton has moved steadily to the right on most issues of concern to blacks.[8] Meanwhile, the Republicans ignore the black vote altogether or, as in the case of President George W. Bush, engage in patronage and symbolism.

Nevertheless, at the beginning of the twenty-first century in the American party system, black identification with the Democrats is near universal. This is because black partisanship is based on "their perceptions of each Party's responsiveness to the needs and interests of the black community."[9] That is, individual black voters hold a group-based perception of the parties. In other words, racial identification determines Democratic partisanship.

It is in this context of the historic one-party system in the United States, and the emergence of blacks since the 1960s as the core Democratic voting bloc, that Barack Obama won the Democratic nomination in 2008. Beyond these broad historical considerations, the Obama nomination emerges out of two other circumstances. First, the efforts spearheaded by blacks to democratize the Democratic Party and universalize access to its nominating process. Second, Jesse Jackson's two campaigns for president helped to universalize access to the Party and laid the foundations for the kind of rainbow coalition that Obama built on in his quest for the nomination.

The Democratization of the Democratic Party and the Role of African Americans

Donald Robinson writes, "ever since the founding a determination to democratize the selection of presidents gradually cast aside every impediment."[10] In the latter half of the twentieth century, African Americans played a major role in this democratization process. The African American role in the process began with the challenge by the Mississippi Freedom Democratic Party to the seating of the all-white Mississippi delegation at the 1964 convention (see Box 9.2). The 1964 challenge was "historically important," writes Walters, because "it ultimately set the stage for other challenges and, thus, some changes in the delegate allocation process."[11] At the 1968 Democratic Convention (where anti-war protesters were beaten by police outside the convention hall), Hubert Humphrey won the nomination although he had not competed in any of the primaries and was clearly not the popular choice of most Democrats. To avoid such a situation in the future, a commission was established to reform the nominating process. Headed by Senator George McGovern, among the commission's findings was that although blacks comprised more than 20 percent of Democratic voters, they were only 5.5 percent of delegates at the 1968 convention. To remedy this inequality, the Commission required the states to take "affirmative measures to encourage the representation of minority groups, young people and women in a reasonable relationship to their presence in the population of the state."[12] The Commission also required each state to establish delegate-selection procedures to "assure that voters in each state, regardless of race, color, creed or national origin will have meaningful and timely opportunities to participate fully in the election or selection of such delegates and alternates."[13]

New York Congresswoman Shirley Chisholm, the first African American to seek a major-party presidential nomination, appears on "Meet the Press" in 1972, with the other candidates, George McGovern, Hubert Humphrey, Edmund Muskie, and Henry Jackson. *Source:* Bettmann/Corbis

The results of these reforms were to take the selection of delegates out of the hands of Party leaders and place it in the hands of the people through primaries and caucuses. (In 1968 only 17 states used primaries or caucuses to select delegates.) In 1972 the Party required all states to use some form of proportional allocation of delegates, instead of the winner-take-all approach which was used by many states.

When Jesse Jackson ran for president in 1984, he won 18 percent of the vote but was allocated only 8 percent of the delegates. Jackson argued that this was undemocratic and pressed for changes in the rules.[14] As a result the 1984 Convention appointed a "Fairness Commission," which revised the delegate allocation rules so that they would more closely reflect the wishes of the voters. Without these reforms in the nominating process, Obama could not have won the Democratic nomination.

In reaction to these democratizing reforms, Party leaders attempted to place some limitations on the role of the people in choosing the nominee. This led in 1980 to the creation of "super delegates" (members of Congress, governors, and national and state party leaders)—delegates who could be seated at the convention without having run in the primaries and could vote for any candidate they wished.[15] In general, as Richard Herrera shows, super delegates are more likely to support establishment candidates than outsiders. In 1988, for example, Jackson got 20 percent of the primary vote but only 9.3 percent of the super delegates' votes, but Congressman Dick Gephardt, a congressional leader, received 5 percent of the primary vote but 19 percent of the super delegates' votes.[16]

BOX 9.2 "NO TWO SEATS"

In 1964, a poor sharecropper from Mississippi challenged Lyndon Johnson and the Democratic Party and helped to set in motion a process that fundamentally changed the relationship of the Democratic Party and African American voters.

Fannie Lou Hamer was born in rural Mississippi in 1917, the youngest of 20 children. She spent most of her life working as a sharecropper on a plantation; in 1962 her life was changed forever when she was inspired by a civil rights rally to attempt to register to vote. For this she was fired and ordered off the plantation. From this point until her death at the age of 59 in 1977, she was a major leader of the southern civil rights movement.

In 1964 Fannie Lou Hamer cofounded the Mississippi Freedom Democratic Party, an interracial party that challenged the white supremacist, all-white regular Mississippi Democratic Party. In 1964 the Mississippi Freedom Democratic Party (MFDP) challenged the seating of the all-white Mississippi delegation at the Democratic convention. Mrs. Hamer, the party's cochair, in a dramatic, nationally televised testimony, recounted the atrocities committed against Mississippi blacks who tried to register and vote, including a vivid description of her own brutal beating in a Mississippi jail. Despite the eloquence of her testi-

Fannie Lou Hamer, speaking at the 1968 Democratic National Convention on behalf of the Mississippi Freedom Democratic Party. *Source:* Bettmann/ Corbis

mony, the convention, under instructions from President Johnson, rejected the MFDP challenge, voted to seat the all-white delegation, and as a compromise offered the MFDP two honorary "at large" seats. The MFDP, despite the urgings of Martin Luther King Jr. and white liberal leaders such as Hubert Humphrey, rejected the compromise because, as Mrs. Hamer said, it represented "token rights" and "we didn't come all this way for no two seats." Later, she led a demonstration on the convention floor, protesting the compromise and singing freedom songs.

Although Mrs. Hamer and the MFDP did not succeed in 1964, they were seated at the 1968 convention, and it was their uncompromising position at the 1964 convention that helped to spark the reforms of 1972 that eventually opened the Democratic Party to full or universal participation by all Americans. In 1977 Fannie Lou Hamer died, poor and humble despite her fame and still uncompromising in the struggle for universal freedom.[a]

[a]See Mamie Locke, "Is This America? Fannie Lou Hamer and the Mississippi Freedom Democratic Party," in Vicki Crawford et al., eds., *Women in the Civil Rights Movement: Trailblazers and Torchbearers, 1941–1965* (Brooklyn: Carlson Publishing, 1990): 27–37. See also Kay Mills, *This Little Light of Mine: The Life of Fannie Lou Hamer* (New York: Dutton, 1993).

In 2008 these super delegates accounted for 20 percent of the total. Senator Hillary Clinton, as the establishment candidate, expected these super delegates to be a "reliable firewall against the Obama insurgency."[17] This was one of several strategic miscalculations on her part, since in the end most super delegates ended up supporting Obama.

Jesse Jackson and the Rainbow Coalition: Implications for the Obama Campaign

Not only did Jackson's two campaigns for the presidency bring about changes in the delegate allocation rules that helped Obama's campaign, they also established in their demography the kind of coalition Obama would build on to win the nomination.

Unlike Obama, Jackson did not expect to win the nomination or the presidency. Rather, the strategic purposes of his campaigns were to exercise "leverage" on the party and its nominee.[18] The leverage Jackson wished to exercise was to use the campaigns to halt the conservative drift of the party, to inject progressive perspectives on foreign and domestic issues into the campaign debates and party platform, to mobilize the black vote by increasing registration and turnout, to serve as the balance of power in determining the nominee, and to lay the groundwork for the mobilization of a multiethnic rainbow coalition that might in the future become an electoral majority in presidential politics.[19]

Although Jackson achieved few of these objectives, the coalition he assembled in 1988 in its race–class composition resembles the winning coalition Obama assembled in 2008. First, both candidates relied on the African American vote as their core or base of support, each receiving nearly 90 percent. In 1988, college-educated middle-aged blacks were more likely to support Jackson.[20] Second, their white support was drawn disproportionately from the young, well-educated, and high-income group rather than the elderly, less-educated, poor, or working class.[21] Although there was chatter in the media about Obama's failure to attract white working-class voters, scholars of biracial politics in America have long understood that the "natural ally of the Negro for foreseeable future is the cosmopolitan white bourgeoisie."[22] This is because, as Bostch writes, working-class whites "exhibit enough racial prejudice so that they could be separated from their black working class peers on a number of issues."[23]

Although the age and race–class bases of the Obama and Jackson coalitions are identical, the size of Obama's white "bourgeoisie" support was much larger—large enough, with the support of white young people, to allow him to win the nomination.

Deracialization and the Obama Campaign

The theory of deracialization was developed after the elections of 1989, in which several blacks were elected to office in majority white constituencies, including most prominently Douglass Wilder as governor of Virginia but also the election of David Dinkins as mayor of New York City. McCormick and Jones understand deracialization as "conducting a campaign in a stylistic fashion that defuses the polarizing effects of race by avoiding explicit reference to race specific issues, while emphasizing those issues that are perceived as racially transcendent, thus mobilizing a broad segment of the electorate for the purpose of capturing or maintaining public office."[24] The fundamentals of this theory require black candidates running for high office (senator, governor, president) to avoid references to issue of concern to blacks such as affirmative action or anti-poverty policies. Instead, a deracialized campaign focuses on issues important to the white middle class, such as tax cuts, health care, and education. The theory also requires that the candidate project a "non-threatening" image; for example, she should avoid association with race leaders such as Jesse Jackson and Al Shartpton. In other words, the black candidate should avoid any association with "blackness."

While deracialization may be the only way an African American can successfully compete for high office in the United States, to the extent that it requires downplaying or ignoring altogether issues of concern to blacks, it undermines their quest for universal freedom. This was the critique of the deracialization theory advanced by many black scholars at the time. Professor Robert Starks wrote that the theory cannot be "permitted to divert from the substance of what constitutes African American politics—using electoral politics as a lever to maximize group power in the fight against racism, exclusion, and marginalization while promoting African-American–specific policy preferences within the political system."[25] Professor Ronald Walters wrote, "blacks have a right to demand a useful product from the political system in exchange for their participation and to evaluate the worthiness of politics on that basis. Thus, it is valid for them to ask 'what difference does it make?'—to the satisfaction of their interests that blacks are elected in majority white districts."[26] And one of the authors of this text compared the deracialization of black politics to the deracialization of black music, writing, "Like the transformation of black music, it will be a hollow victory if in order to achieve equitable descriptive-symbolic representation blacks are required to sacrifice their substantive policy agenda. The new black politician would then be a shell of himself, more like a Prince or Michael Jackson than a B.B. King or Bobby Blue Bland."[27]

As we will discuss later in this chapter, during the campaign there was debate about whether Obama, because of his African heritage, was "black enough." However, the real question of his blackness was not his family background but the political imperatives of the deracialization theory.

The Obama Phenomenon

The Obama campaign was a genuine phenomenon, not in the technical sense that scientists use the word but rather as a rare, exceptional, unexpected occurrence. That an African American—any African American—could win a major party nomination for the presidency is phenomenal in itself. However, that an African American of African heritage with a foreign-sounding name and less than four years' experience in national politics could be nominated is even more phenomenal. In winning the nomination, Obama, 46, defeated some of the leading Democratic politicians of the era: Joseph Biden, the 65-year-old 36-year veteran of the Senate and Chair of the Foreign Relations Committee; Christopher Dodd, the 63-year-old 28-year Senate veteran and Chair of the Banking Committee; Bill Richardson, the 60-year-old, Hispanic governor of New Mexico, former Congressman, Energy Secretary, and UN ambassador; John Edwards, the 51-year-old, 2004 vice presidential nominee; and of course Hillary Clinton, the 60-year-old former first lady and two-term U.S. senator.

Obama has always been ambitious. Friends and associates report that he began talking about running for high office while he was in law school,[28] and during the campaign Mrs. Clinton claimed that Obama had mused about running for president when he was in kindergarten. After he graduated from Columbia, Obama moved to Chicago, where he spent time as a community organizer. After a brief visit to his father's ancestral village, Obama entered Harvard. At Harvard, he graduated *magna cum laude* and was the first African American elected president of the law review. After Harvard, rather than accept a position as a law clerk or at a prestigious law firm, he returned to Chicago to start a political career.

Refusing to "wait his turn," three years later he was elected to the Illinois State Senate. Four years later in 2000 he challenged Bobby Rush, the eight-term congressman and former leader of the Black Panther Party. Easily defeated by the popular Rush, Obama was undaunted and in 2004 he ran for the U.S. Senate. After he won the Democratic nomination, Obama was immediately recognized as a "rising star" in the Democratic Party. John Kerry, the 2004 Democratic nominee, invited Obama to deliver the keynote address at the Democratic convention. The speech was a sensation, leading the conservative columnist Michael Barone to write, "Immediately, and not without justification, commentators were hailing this state senator from Hyde Park as a national leader and possible future president."[29]

As the 2008 election approached, Obama was again told to wait his turn—to get some experience in the Senate and national politics before seeking the nation's highest office (see Box 9.3). He refused and in February, 2008, he traveled to Springfield, Illinois, and in front of the old state house where Abraham Lincoln began his career he audaciously announced his candidacy.

Obama's campaign was premised on the idea that after 16 years of Clinton and Bush, the American people wanted change and a new kind of post-partisan coalition politics. But in a fundamental sense, his campaign was based on his biography. In his books (a gifted writer, Obama, unlike most politicians, actually wrote his books) *Dream from My Father: A Story of Race and Inheritance*, a memoir, and *The Audacity of Hope*, a campaign manifesto, Obama presents himself not as a deracialized politician but as a new kind of "post-" or "trans-" racial politician who, because of his background, was uniquely qualified to lead the nation in bridging its racial and partisan divisions. In his March 18, 2008, speech on race, Obama summarized the biographical case for his campaign:

> I chose to run for president at this moment in history because I believe deeply that we cannot solve the challenges of our time unless we solve them together, unless we perfect our union by understanding that we may have different stories, but we hold common hopes; that we may not look the same and may not have come from the same place, but we all want to move in the same direction: toward a better future for our children and our grandchildren.
>
> And this belief comes from my unyielding faith in the decency and generosity of the American people. But it also comes from my own story. I am the son of a black man from Kenya and a white woman from Kansas. I was raised with the help of a white grandfather who survived a Depression to serve in Patton's army during World War II and a white grandmother who worked on a bomber assembly line at Fort Leavenworth while he was overseas.
>
> I've gone to some of the best schools in America and I've lived in one of the world's poorest nations. I am married to a black American who carries within her the blood of slaves and slave owners, an inheritance we pass on to our two precious daughters.
>
> I have brothers, sisters, nieces, nephews, uncles and cousins of every race and every hue scattered across three continents. And for as long as I live, I will never forget that in no other country on earth is my story even possible.[30]

Campaign Organization and Strategy

As the 2008 campaign got underway, it was widely recognized that Hillary Clinton's campaign organization was the most formidable of any Democratic candidate. This was because she was able to draw on the personnel and resources of her husband's previous two successful presidential campaigns. She also could draw on, free of charge, the advice of her husband, who was widely regarded as one of the best political strategists in the country. Nevertheless, in a first test of the strength of the Obama campaign, he was able to put together a sophisticated political organization, headed by David Axelrod, a Chicago-based political consultant (see Chapter 10).

The campaign organization first demonstrated its sophistication in fundraising. The campaign relied on the Internet and small donors (less than $100) and ads on Yahoo, Google, and Microsoft search engines (more than half of the online donations of less than $100 came from 1.5 million donors, the highest in the history of any presidential campaign). The Obama campaign "shattered fundraising records and challenged ideas about the way presidential bids are financed."[31] Table 9.1 compares Clinton and Obama campaign receipts in the critical early months of the campaign. Overall, Obama raised $240 million compared to Clinton's $195 million. By the end of the primary process, Clinton's campaign was in debt of more than $20 million, having to borrow $10 million from herself in order to remain competitive. Meanwhile, Obama finished the primaries with $43 million in cash on hand and a debt of only $300.000.

BOX 9.3   OBAMA'S CONGRESSIONAL RECORD

As a freshman senator in a body with a Republican majority, Obama had little chance in his first two years in the Senate to establish a record of major legislative achievements. As he put it, "contrary to popular perceptions, only about two dozen bills come up for a roll-call vote on the Senate floor every year, and almost none of these are sponsored by a member of the minority party."[a] Thus "most of my major initiatives—the formation of public school innovation districts, a plan to help US automakers pay for their retiree health care cost in exchange for increased fuel standards, an expansion of the Pell Grant program to help low income students meet rising college tuition costs—languished in committee."[b] During his two and a half years in the Senate, Obama introduced 129 bills. Seven passed the Senate and two were enacted into law: a bill to promote democracy and security in the Democratic Republic of Congo and to name a post office in East St. Louis, Illinois, after Katherine Dunham (the famed African American dancer and choreographer, who was born in Chicago).

Obama was appointed to the committees on Foreign Relations, Environment and Public Works, and Veterans' Affairs. On the Foreign Relations Committee, he co-sponsored legislation with the Committee Chairman (Republican Richard Lugar) dealing with weapons proliferation and the black-market trade in arms. He joined with most Democrats to confirm Condoleezza Rice as Secretary of State and to oppose the confirmation of John Roberts as Chief Justice.

[a]Barack Obama, *The Audacity of Hope* (New York: Crown, 2006): 325.

[b]Ibid, p. 326.

Table 9.1 Clinton—Obama Campaign Contributions, January–March, 1968

	CLINTON	OBAMA
January	$20 million	$38 million
February	35	58
March	20	40

Source: Federal Election Commission.

Although Obama relied disproportionately on small donors, like all presidential candidates he received contributions from wealthy, corporate-connected individuals and Hollywood celebrities. However, he received relatively little support from the African American corporate elite. A study by Bloomberg of 191 black members of the boards of the nation's 250 largest corporations found that less than one third contributed to the Obama campaign.[32]

To some extent, the Obama campaign also rewrote the rules for winning the nomination.[33] The Clinton campaign strategy was based on winning the popular vote in the big states on Super Tuesday (March 4), when 24 states voted. Indeed, early in the campaign she predicted she would win the nomination on Super Tuesday. Obama by contrast focused on winning delegates in the small, largely white caucus states, while holding down her margin in the big states so that he would get a reasonable share of their delegates. The strategy worked. On Super Tuesday, Clinton won eight states (including all of the big ones except Illinois), but Obama won in the smaller states, winning 14 states to her 8 and 847 delegates to her 834. Thereafter, he went on to win 11 consecutive states, which gave him an insurmountable delegate lead. Although Clinton went on to win most of the remaining states (including Ohio and Pennsylvania), Obama won enough delegates in those states to win a majority of the delegates.

Obama's delegate triumph was based in part on the overwhelming support to him in African American congressional districts. The Democratic Party awards bonus delegates to districts with a history of strong support for the Party, giving them in some cases twice as many delegates as less loyal Democratic or Republican districts. Since African Americans are the Party's strongest supporters, winning in their districts gave him an advantage over Clinton in the states she won, like Ohio, Texas, California, and New York.

Obama, then, won—paradoxically—the nomination by winning in the blackest and most Democratic places and in the whitest and most Republican places—states like Alaska, Idaho, Utah, Wyoming, and Nebraska.

Once it was clear that Obama had an insurmountable lead in pledged delegates, the unpledged super delegates began to throw their support to him and the race was effectively over by late April although Clinton continued to campaign until the last primaries on June 3.

Ideology and Issues

All of the Democratic candidates in 2008 were liberals, and there was widespread agreement among them on the issues including taxes, health care, education, immigration, the environment, and the Iraq war. Of the major candidates, however, Obama was the only one

Obama Debating Clinton and John Edwards on CNN. *Source:* Landov Media

to oppose the Iraq war from the beginning. During the campaign debates, he used his early opposition to the war to make the case that while he did not have the long Washington experience of his opponents, his opposition to the war showed he had better judgment. (By January 2008 more than 80 percent of Democratic voters were opposed to the war.)

On issues of specific concern to blacks, there were little differences between Clinton and the deracialized Obama. In early 2008, the NAACP submitted 37 questions to Clinton and Obama asking them their position on issues ranging from affirmative action to reparations. The Obama and Clinton positions on all of the issues were almost identical in content, if not style.[34] On welfare, Obama indicated that he supported the legislation signed by President Clinton in 1996, although this legislation was opposed at the time by virtually the entire black leadership (see Chapter 15). On the death penalty, Obama flip-flopped. When he ran for the state senate in 1996, he opposed the death penalty but in his 2004 U.S. Senate campaign he said he accepted it for "the most heinous crimes."[35] On affirmative action, he implied that it should be a class- rather than race-based program, saying he did not think his daughters should be eligible for affirmative action in university admissions.

Since there were no ideological differences between Clinton and Obama, the campaign came down to style or symbolism. Obama emphasized change—"change we can believe in." Clinton emphasized experience—that she would be ready to be president on day one. The media coverage (see below) and the opinions of voters matched these symbolic differences between the candidates.

Table 9.2 displays the opinions of 2008 Democratic primary voters on the most important candidate attributes, the most important issues, and their ideology.

Table 9.2 2008 Democratic Primary Vote for Clinton and Obama by Ideology and Issues

	PERCENT CLINTON	PERCENT OBAMA
Liberal (47)[a]	47	48
Moderate (40)	50	45
Conservative (13)	47	44
MOST IMPORTANT CANDIDATE ATTRIBUTE		
Bring change (50)	29	68
Cares (14)	48	42
Right experience (23)	91	6
Best chance to win (9)	50	47
MOST IMPORTANT ISSUE		
Economy (51)	51	47
Iraq war (27)	42	53
Health care (19)	52	43

[a]Numbers in parenthesis represent proportion of the electorate.

Source: ABC News.

Ideological liberals, moderates, and conservatives did not differ significantly in their candidate preference. On candidate attributes, those who said they believed bringing about change was the most important candidate attribute (50 percent of voters) supported Obama over Clinton by 39 points, 68-29. Those who wanted a candidate with the "right experience" (23 percent) favored Clinton by 85 points, 91-6. Pointing toward one source of Obama's triumph, the change voters were more than twice as large as the experience voters.

On the issues, the voters overwhelmingly viewed the economy as the most important issue and on this issue Clinton had a slight 7-point advantage. Voters who saw the Iraq war as the most important issue (27 percent) gave Obama an 11-point advantage, while Clinton had a similar advantage on health care. Throughout the campaign, Clinton was viewed as having more detailed and comprehensive plans on health care and the economy.

There were some tensions around race in the course of the campaign. Bill Clinton accused the Obama campaign of using "the race card," by attacking him for comparing Obama's victory in South Carolina to Jesse Jackson's and for his dismissal of Obama's opposition to the war as a "fairy tale." Some African Americans did attack Clinton for these remarks, claiming they were intended to diminish or dismiss Obama's campaign. Some African Americans were also disturbed by Mrs. Clinton's remarks suggesting that Martin Luther King Jr.'s "rhetoric" was not enough to pass the civil rights laws of the 1960s. Rather, she said it took the "experience" of President Johnson. But these were minor flaps. In the sense that Tali Mendelberg used the concept in her book *The Race Card*, it was not played in the 2008 primaries. In her work Mendelberg shows that the race card in American elections historically revolves around appeals, whether explicit or implicit, to African American sexuality, criminality, economic dependency, laziness, and their desire to subjugate whites.[36]

Media Coverage

Although President and Mrs. Clinton both complained that media coverage of the campaign was biased in favor of Obama, the most comprehensive study of the campaign (conducted by Harvard's Joan Shorenstein Center on Press & Politics) concludes, "The findings here also belie the idea that Obama enjoyed the most positive coverage, or that the press has somehow gone easier on him than on Clinton during the primaries. In the roughly 10 weeks studied, the former first lady had just as much success in the press as her rival in projecting the narratives she wanted about her personality, history, leadership and character. Fully 67 percent of the assertions about her as a person were positive, versus one third (33 percent) negative—numbers almost identical to Obama."[37]

The study examined coverage in all media—the major newspapers, websites, network and cable television, and talk radio. It found both Clinton and Obama were about equally successful in getting positive coverage, and that the media fairly conveyed each candidate's "master narratives." The most prevalent master narrative about Obama was he represented "hope and change" (28 percent of media coverage projected this idea). The second most prominent narrative about Obama in the media (17 percent) was that he had a "special and rare charisma, someone whose rhetorical skills could move crowds in ways not often seen."[38] The most negative narrative about Obama was that he was too young and inexperienced (12 percent).

Clinton had the "most success projecting the idea of her preparedness to lead the country—to take the 3 AM phone call as her well-known ad proclaimed." A full 38 percent of all character assertions spoke to this trait. This message was much more clearly asserted than any other about Clinton.[39] The most negative narrative about Clinton (13 percent) was that she represented the past or the status quo.

Obama Campaigning with Oprah. *Source:* Getty Images

Overall, coverage of the candidates in the newspapers, on the evening newscasts, and MSNBC were similar; however, CNN was somewhat more favorable to Clinton, while Fox was somewhat more favorable to Obama.[40] Obama received more positive coverage on talk radio—liberal and conservative—than Clinton, while network morning programs were especially favorable to her. (The authors of the study speculate that the morning programs may have been more favorable to Clinton because their audiences are composed disproportionately of women.)

As usual in presidential campaigns, most of the coverage of the 2008 primaries focused on the "horse race" and political tactics and strategy; 78 percent of the stories dealt with these concerns, while a mere 7 percent were public policy stories.[41]

Coverage of Clinton was generally consistently positive, but over time Obama's coverage became consistently more negative even before the firestorm caused by the controversial remarks of his pastor (see Box 9.4).

BOX 9.4 REV. JEREMIAH WRIGHT AND THE AFRO-AMERICAN JEREMIAD

Going back to the Puritans, the jeremiad—an often prophetic, always passionate outcry against injustices—has been a part of the American tradition. And as David Howard-Pitney ably demonstrates in *The Afro-American Jeremiad: Appeals for Justice in America*, African American leaders from Frederick Douglass to Malcolm X have used this tradition to cry out against racial injustices in America.[a] Malcolm X's "Ballot or the Bullet" and Martin Luther King Jr.'s "Why I Am Opposed to the War in Vietnam" are two of the most famous contemporary examples of speeches in this tradition.

Rev. Jeremiah Wright, Barack Obama's former pastor and spiritual advisor, preaches in this tradition. Wright, a theologian named by *Ebony* in 1998 as one of the 15 leading preachers in black America, also preaches in the tradition of black liberation theology. This theology holds that God is committed to the liberation of his most oppressed people—African Americans— and it requires preachers to be unapologetically committed to the liberation of African peoples and to militant protests against racism and white supremacy.

During the course of the 2008 Democratic primary, excerpts from some of Rev. Wright's jeremiads were played over and over again on television, the Internet, and talk radio. In these excerpts, Wright suggested that 9/11 was God's punishment for the injustices of America's foreign policy and that AIDS may have been created by the U.S. government to harm blacks. On 9/11, Wright preached, "We bombed Hiroshima, we bombed Nagasaki, and we nuked far more than the thousands in New York and the Pentagon, and we never batted an eye. . . . America's chickens are coming home to roost." And on America he preached, "The government gives them drugs, builds bigger prisons, passes a three-strike law and then wants us to sing 'God Bless America.' No, no, no, God damn America! That's in the Bible for killing innocent people."[b]

After these excerpts, among others, were broadcast, Obama "condemned" them in "unequivocal terms" but went on to say, "I can no more disown him than I can disown the black community. I can no more disown him [Rev. Wright] than I can disown my white

(continued)

> **BOX 9.4 continued**
>
> grandmother, a woman who helped raise me, a woman who sacrificed again and again for me . . . but a woman . . . who on more than one occasion has uttered racial or ethnic stereotypes that made me cringe."[c]
>
> Later, however, Obama did condemn Wright after the minister repeated his damnations in a histrionic appearance at the National Press Club. Subsequently, he and his wife resigned from Wright's church after a white Catholic priest, in a guest sermon, made racially insensitive remarks mocking Hillary Clinton's campaign.
>
> The excerpts from Wright's jeremiads were widely viewed by commentators in the mainstream media as racist and anti-American, forcing a reluctant Obama for the first time during the campaign to address the issue of race, which he did in a widely praised speech in Philadelphia on March 18. Yet, his association with Rev. Wright remained a cause of concern to many voters throughout the campaign.
>
> [a]David Howard-Pitney, *The Afro-American Jeremiad: Appeals for Justice in America* (Philadelphia: Temple University Press, 1990).
>
> [b]"Preacher with a Penchant for Controversy", *Washington Post*, March 15, 2008.
>
> [c]Transcript ,"Senator Barack Obama's Address on Race", Constitution Center, Philadelphia, *Washington Post*, March 18, 2008.

After Wright's remarks, stories about him and his relationship to Obama received more coverage than any other story that did not deal with the horse race.[42]

In some ways, the biggest media event of the campaign was the endorsement of Obama by talk show host Oprah Winfrey and her campaigning with him in the early primary and caucus states. This was the first time that the immensely popular Winfrey (The *Oprah* program's audience is composed disproportionately of white suburban women.) had ever endorsed a presidential candidate. Although political scientists usually discount the effects of celebrity endorsements on how citizens vote, a study by University of Maryland economists estimated that Winfrey's endorsement gave Obama as much as a million votes in the primaries and caucuses.[43] Her endorsement may have cost her in terms of ratings (her audience fell 7 percent during the year), as she may have alienated some of her white female audience who were Clinton supporters.[44]

The fact that a black and a woman were the leading Democratic candidates led to more diversity among the "talking heads" on cable television. White men dominate the cable and Sunday morning talk shows, but as a result of the Obama–Clinton campaign, media executives were under pressure to bring in more women and minorities. As one observer wrote, "There is suddenly a demand for smart Negroes. You're seeing a lot less of the Jesse Jackson and the Al Sharptons and more academics and thought leaders. This is expressly in response to Barack Obama, less so Hillary. Because of the combination of Hillary and Barack, you're seeing more black women."[45]

Obama's Rainbow

Table 9.3 displays the Democratic primary vote for Obama and Clinton by selected demographic categories. Obama won majority support among two categories: African Americans, where he had a 67-point advantage over Clinton, and young whites

Table 9.3 2008 Democratic Primary Vote for Clinton and Obama, by Selected Demographic Categories

	PERCENT CLINTON	PERCENT OBAMA	DIFFERENCE
Overall[a]	48	46	2
Men (43)[b]	43	50	7
Women (57)	52	43	9
Whites (65)	55	39	16
Blacks (19)	15	82	67
Hispanics (12)	61	35	26
White Men (28)	48	45	3
White Women (37)	60	34	24
Whites, 18–29 (7)	41	53	12
Whites 65+ (13)	63	29	34
Whites—no college (32)	62	31	31
Whites—college grad (32)	48	47	1
Whites <$50k (21)	60	33	27
Whites $50–100k (22)	54	39	15
Whites $100k + (17)	48	47	1
Urban (34)	44	52	8
Suburban (47)	50	44	6
Rural/small town (19)	52	40	12

[a]The overall or total vote includes Florida, which held its primary outside the Democratic Party's schedule. Neither candidate, therefore, campaigned in the state.

[b]Numbers in parenthesis represent proportion of the electorate.

Source: ABC News.

(18–29), where he had a 9-point advantage. Clinton won among white women with a 24-point advantage, white men (3 points), Latinos (26 points), whites without a college education (31), whites over 65 (34), and low income whites (less than $50,000 in annual income) with a 27-point advantage. Clinton and Obama received roughly the same proportion of the white college-educated and upper income vote. Obama won the urban vote by 8 points, Clinton the rural vote by 12 and the suburban vote by 4. Overall, including Florida, Clinton won 48 percent of the vote, to Obama's 46 percent.[46]

Table 9.4 displays the regional distribution of the Obama vote among whites. He had his best showing in the selected western states and his worst showing in the southern states. The pattern of his supporters, however, was consistent: the young, the well-educated, and the upper income group. But in the southern states his support among young whites resembles more his support among elderly whites in other parts of the country, as does his support among the college-educated and upper income groups. For example, nationally Obama received 53 percent of the white youth vote, but in Kentucky, Alabama, and Louisiana he received about a third, which is roughly the same as the 29 percent of the elderly white vote he received nationally.

Table 9.4 2008 White Primary Vote for Obama, by Selected States and Demographic Categories[a]

NORTHEAST

	PA	VT	CT	NJ	NH
Overall vote	37%	59%	51%	43%	37%
Male	43	64	57	39	38
Female	32	56	42	27	33
18–29	48	NA	58	51	50
65+	30	58	47	26	32
No college	29	56	38	14	35
College graduate	45	62	55	38	37
<$50k	33	61	41	25	31
$50–100k	37	57	49	32	38
$100k+	44	66	53	36	39

MIDWEST

	OH	WI	MO	IA[b]	IN
Overall vote	44%	57%	49%	34%	49%
Male	39	63	41	33	41
Female	31	47	38	32	39
18–29	48	66	57	56	54
65+	23	41	26	18	47
No college	27	52	33	NA	34
College graduate	45	59	61	NA	49
<$50K	28	50	35	31	38
$50–100k	36	57	43	32	41
$100K+	44	61	63	40	41

SOUTH

	Ky	AL	MD	VA	LA	SC
Overall vote	30	56	58	64	57	54
Male	26	27	48	58	31	27
Female	21	23	38	47	29	22
18–29	30	33	53	72	36	50
65+	16	13	34	40	24	11
No college	25	19	32	42	27	16
College graduate	40	38	47	58	39	52
<$50k	20	23	40	35	27	19
$50–100k	28	23	45	48	34	25
$100k+	26	NA	41	63	36	32

(continued)

Table 9.4   (continued)

WEST

	OR	NM	CA	UT	MT
Overall	58	49	42	56	58
Male	66	59	55	64	65
Female	51	51	36	49	48
18–29	72	65	63	70	74
65+	45	57	35	40	40
No College	49	41	37	47	49
College graduate	66	60	51	62	62
<$50k	52	47	39	49	53
$50–100k	62	55	42	54	61
$100k+	65	55	55	64	59

[a]In Illinois Obama won every demographic category except whites 65 and older (41 percent) and whites with no college (46 percent). In New York, Clinton had her best showing among blacks of any state (37 percent).

[b]The Iowa caucuses involved all the major candidates. Most of the other contests involved only Clinton and Obama.

Source: ABC News.

With African Americans as his base and with strong support among young and well-educated whites, Obama's 2008 rainbow coalition resembles Jackson's in 1988. The difference is that the magnitude of his support among whites was much greater. In Table 9.5 data are displayed comparing the 1988 Jackson vote among whites with Obama's in selected

Table 9.5 A Comparison of the Jesse Jackson and Obama White Vote in Selected States, 1988 and 2008

	JACKSON	**OBAMA**	**DIFFERENCE**
Alabama	6%	25%	19
Arkansas	6	16	10
Georgia	6	43	37
Kentucky	7	23	16
Louisiana	6	30	24
Maryland	11	42	31
Massachusetts	16	40	24
Mississippi	6	26	20
Missouri	12	39	27
North Carolina	7	37	30
Oklahoma	8	29	21
Rhode Island	16	37	21
Tennessee	5	26	21
Texas	14	44	30
Virginia	14	52	38

Source: ABC News.

states. In all except Arkansas, Obama's vote was at least three times greater than Jackson's and in most states it was four times as great.

Although Obama lost the Latino vote decisively, he did much better than Jackson. While Jackson received an estimated 15 percent of the Latino vote in 1988, Obama won 35 percent. Many media commentators attributed the relatively low level of support for Obama among Latinos to the negative stereotypes about blacks held by some Latinos (see Chapter 7).[47] It is more likely, however, that the Latino vote for Clinton is more a result of loyalties to the Clintons than hostility to blacks or to Obama as a black candidate. That is, it is likely that if Bill Richardson, a Latino, had remained in the race, most Latinos would nevertheless have supported Clinton. Similarly, if Obama had not become a viable candidate, most blacks in 2008 would probably have voted for Clinton because of similar loyalties.

After blacks, Jews are the most liberal voting bloc in the United States. Jews have also been more willing to vote for black candidates than other white ethnic groups. In 1988 Jackson received very little Jewish support, an estimated 7 percent. This was partly because of Jackson's close identification with the Palestinian cause and his making of alleged anti-Semitic comments during the 1984 campaign (he referred to Jews as "Hymie" and New York City as "Hymietown"). Some Jewish leaders and Israeli commentators raised questions about Obama's commitment to Israel, and rumors and lies about his being Muslim were circulated to Jewish voters. In response, the leaders of nine major Jewish organizations issued a joint letter stating, "Attempts of this sort to mislead and inflame voters should not be a part of our political discourse and should be rebuffed by all who believe in our democracy. Jewish voters, like all voters, should support whichever candidate they believe would make the best president."[48]

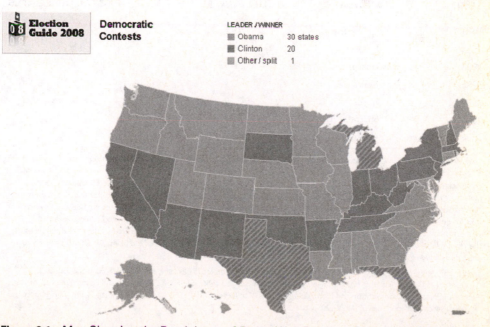

Election Guide 2008

Democratic Contests

LEADER / WINNER
- Obama   30 states
- Clinton   20
- Other / split   1

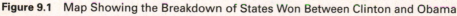

Figure 9.1   Map Showing the Breakdown of States Won Between Clinton and Obama

Jews constituted an important but small part of Obama's coalition. He narrowly won the Jewish vote in California and Massachusetts, with an overall average of 42 percent in the five states (in addition to Massachusetts, California, New York, Pennsylvania, and New Jersey) where there was a significant Jewish vote (excluding Florida).

Finally, data from California indicate that Clinton defeated Obama by a margin of two to one among Asian Americans and she won the gay and lesbian vote 60 to 25 percent.

The Obama Campaign Compared to All Major Party African American Candidates

Tables 9.5 and 9.6 compare the Obama campaign with all previous African American candidates for major party presidential nominations, going back to Shirley Chisholm's pioneering 1972 campaign. The tables show that comparatively Jackson's 1988 campaign is the closest parallel to Obama's in terms of percentage of votes by states and number and percentages of delegates.

Race and Gender

As we indicate in Chapter 7, the African American and women's freedom movements existed in a tentative, tenuous, unstable coalition for universal freedom. Although the two movements have shared ideas and objectives—the right to vote, equality under the law, and an end to racism and sexism generally—going back to the abolitionist movement

Table 9.6 The Number and Percentage of Delegates Received by African American Presidential Candidates at Major-Party Conventions, 1972–2008[a]

YEAR	CANDIDATE	DELEGATES	% OF TOTAL DELEGATES
1972	Chisholm	152	5
1984	Jackson	466	12
1988	Jackson	1,219	29
1996	Keyes	1	0
2000	Keyes	0	0
2004	Sharpton	27	0
2008	Obama	2,158.5	50.5

[a]The data are for African Americans who have run for president in major-party primaries. However, blacks also have received delegates for president while not running in the primaries. In 1888 Frederick Douglass received one delegate at the Republican convention. In 1968 Channing Phillips as the District of Columbia's "Favorite Son" candidate received 68 delegates, Ronald Dellums three in 1980, and Barbara Jordan one in 1976. Blacks have also received symbolic delegates for the vice presidential nomination. Blanche Bruce, the Reconstruction Era senator, received eight vice presidential delegates in 1888 and Edward Brooke one in 1968. During the 1960s, 1970s, and 1980s, Chisholm, Julian Bond, Barbara Jordan, and Dellums received vice presidential delegates, ranging from 20 for Dellums in 1976 to 49 for Bonds in 1968. The Obama delegate count is as of the close of the primaries. Of his total delegates, 394.5 are super delegates. At the end of the primaries Clinton had 1,920 delegates including 280 super delegates.

Source: The delegate numbers are from Congressional Quarterly, *Guide to US Elections,* 4th ed. vol. 1 (Washington, DC: Congressional Quarterly Press, 1994): 615–40, as reported in revised Table 4 in Hanes Walton, Jr. and Lester Spence, "African American Presidential Convention and Nominating Politics: Alan Keyes in the 1996 Republican Primaries and Convention," *National Political Science Review* 7 (1999): 205.

there have been, seemingly inevitable, conflicts and tensions. African American women have sometimes been conflicted, trying to balance their racial and gender interests. So, it was perhaps inevitable that such tensions would emerge when the first woman with a realistic chance of winning a major party nomination would compete with the first African American, a man, with a chance to win.

As Table 9.3 shows, the Democratic electorate was divided, with a huge race–gender chasm in voting. African American women, as we discussed in Chapter 5, tend to prioritize race over gender because race is a more salient basis for identification than gender and they consider racism a greater barrier to universal freedom than sexism. Thus, from the earliest voting in the Iowa caucuses, there was no gender gap in black voting behavior. Black women were as likely to vote for Obama as black men.

There were, however, significant gender gaps in the white electorate. Among white men there was only a modest 3-point gap in voting: Clinton 48, Obama 45. But among white women, the gap was 24; 60 to 34 in favor of Clinton. This gap was especially pronounced among older white women, who overwhelmingly supported Clinton. Clinton's core constituency was white women, who constituted 37 percent of the primary electorate and comprised nearly half of her total vote. Obama's core constituency of African Americans constituted 19 percent of the electorate and provided him more than a third of his vote. Put another way, Clinton won the votes of almost three million more white women than Obama but he won more than four million more black votes than she.

Obama was supported by several white female governors and senators, and Clinton was supported by a large number of black members of Congress, including some of its best known female members. As discussed below, there was debate in the black community about whether Obama was black enough. Similarly, in the feminist community, there were divisions over Clinton's feminist credentials, partly because she had achieved her prominence in politics through marriage rather than on her own (as was not the case, for example, with House Speaker Nancy Pelosi, the first woman Speaker of the House). Finally, Clinton's support among white women was divided by class as well as age; she was less likely to be supported by young and college-educated women.

Nevertheless, some white feminist leaders suggested that Obama was clearly less qualified than Clinton and that he won because he was a man, a "dashing dreamer" and "arrogant interloper" who was able to thwart the dream of the first woman president because of sexism.[49] Gloria Steinem, the feminist icon, wrote, "Be honest: Do you think [Obama's background] is the biography of someone who could be elected to the United States Senate? After less than one term there, do you believe he could be a viable candidate to head the most powerful nation on earth?"[50] And Geraldine Ferraro, the first female major party vice presidential nominee, implied that Obama was an affirmative action candidate who was winning only because he was black.[51] After Obama won the nomination, she said that she might not vote for him because "I think Obama was terribly sexist."[52]

As discussed above, the most comprehensive study on media coverage of the campaign shows the coverage of Clinton and Obama was roughly balanced with, if anything, a slight tilt toward Clinton. But at the end of the campaign, her supporters charged the media with sexism. Citing such things as a fixation on her clothes, her laugh, and even her cleavage, these supporters suggest that sexism denied her the presidency.[53] The available evidence does not support these allegations. But at the end of the primaries, polls indicated that as much as 20–30 percent of Clinton's white female supporters indicated they would vote for McCain. Thus, at the start of the general election, one newspaper headlined "Now Obama Must Mend Broken Hearts."[54]

Racial Identities and Loyalties

Initially, the Obama campaign divided the African American community. For reasons discussed in Chapter 12, African Americans were extraordinarily supportive of Bill Clinton, although many of his policies were conservative and his record on race was ambivalent. In the earliest stages of the 2008 election, support for President Clinton translated into support for his wife. A late November 2007 poll found that Clinton's favorability rating among blacks (83 percent) was higher than Obama's (75 percent).[55] Early preference polls showed her leading Obama among blacks by as much as 30 points. However, by the time of the South Carolina primary—the first where black voters were a significant part of the electorate—Obama won nearly 90 percent of the black vote, and ultimately it was black voters who propelled him to victory.

Not only were black voters initially divided between Clinton and Obama, but the leadership as well. Just as several prominent white female political leaders supported Obama, Clinton was supported by prominent African American leaders. Her supporters included Congressman John Lewis, the civil rights icon; Ervin "Magic" Johnson, the former basketball player; poet Maya Angelou; Robert Johnson, the founder of BET; the black mayors of Oakland and Philadelphia; and more than half of the Congressional Black Caucus. This leadership support was all based on loyalty to the Clintons, as well as lack of knowledge of Obama and the belief that he was too young and inexperienced to be elected.

But some blacks also expressed sentiment that he was not "black" or, at least, not black enough. Indeed, shortly before Obama was to address the group, the National Association of Black Journalists held a panel discussion on Obama's blackness. Debra Dickerson, an African American writer, expressed these sentiments about Obama's "unblackness":

> "Black", in our political and social reality, means those descended from West African slaves. Voluntary immigrants of African descent (even those descended from West Indian slaves) are just that, voluntary immigrants of African descent with markedly different outlooks on the role of race in their lives and politics. At a minimum, it can't be assumed that a Nigerian cabdriver and a third-generation Harlemnite have more in common than the fact a cop won't bother to make the distinction. They're both "black" as matter of skin color and DNA, but only the Harlemnite, for better or worse, is politically and culturally black . . . .[56]

Dickerson went on to aver, "and more subtly, when the handsome Obama doesn't look eastern (versus western) African, he looks like his white mother; not so subliminally, that's partially why whites can embrace him but blacks fear that one day he'll go Tiger Wood on us and get all race transcendent (he might well not be in the running without a traditionally black spouse and kids)."[57]

Other blacks questioned Obama's blackness because of his mixed race heritage and the fact he was raised mainly by his white grandparents. Although there was a lot of chatter in the media about Obama's blackness, there is no evidence this was ever a concern of the black mass public. And the election data indicate it was not, because as soon as Obama demonstrated that he was a credible candidate (by winning the virtually all-white Iowa caucuses),

African Americans gave him overwhelming support in every subsequent primary or caucus except in Clinton's home state of New York, where he won only two-thirds of the vote.

As the black community began to rally around Obama—to become "increasingly protective"—as the *Washington Post* put it,[58] questions were raised about the blackness of those blacks supporting Clinton. Members of the Congressional Black Caucus came under increasing pressure, leading Congressman John Lewis to switch his support to Obama. Newark, New Jersey, Congressman Donald Payne also switched his support, telling his hometown paper he had only supported Clinton because he thought Obama's campaign was "just a trial balloon."[59] Several members of the Congressional Black Caucus who supported Clinton were challenged in the Democratic primaries, with their challengers asserting that their opposition to Obama proved they were "out of touch with the black community."[60] In Brooklyn, one black voter went even further, telling the *New York Times* it was "Racial self-hatred. It was as if they [black leaders who supported Clinton] were saying: we're people of color are not ready yet, we're not ready to be in the White House. Self-hatred does that to you."[61]

Ultimately, the idea of Obama—a talented, handsome, charismatic young black man—becoming president captivated the entire black community and support for him became a marker of one's blackness and loyalty to the black community. After hundreds of years of slavery, lynching, and Jim Crow segregation, Obama's candidacy came to embody Dr. King's dream. As Valerie Grim, Chair of Indiana University's African American Studies Department, put it:

> I have parents who are still living who are very enthusiastic about Obama. They live in Mississippi. For a time my parents couldn't vote, and when they could, their only choice was a white person. This means more than just seeing a black person on the ticket. It represents things they had been denied. It's being able to see the unbelievable, that the impossible might be possible. It represents for them a new day.[62]

In this historic atmosphere, even black conservatives and Republicans were captivated. Rev. Kirby John Caldwell, President Bush's long-time spiritual advisor, announced he was supporting Obama. And Armstrong Williams, the ardent black conservative talk show host, who said he had never before voted for a Democrat, declared, "I don't necessarily share his policies; I don't like much that he advocates, but for the first time in my life, history thrusts me to seriously think about it. I can honestly say I have no idea who I am going to pull that lever for in November. And to me, that's incredible."[63]

Not all African Americans, however, were captivated. From the right, Stanford University's Thomas Sowell dismissed Obama as an "upscale demagogue" who "for decades [has] been promoting the far left vision of victimization and grievances. . . . Later, when the ultimate political prize—the White House—loomed on the horizon, Obama did a complete makeover, now portraying himself as a healer of divisions."[64]

From the left, the University of Pennsylvania's Adolph Reed Jr. wrote, "He's a vacuous opportunist. I've never been an Obama supporter. I've known him since the very beginning of his political career, which was a campaign for the seat in my state senate district in Chicago. He struck me then as a vacuous opportunist, a good performer with an ear for how to make white liberals like him. I argued at the time that his fundamental political center of gravity, beneath empty rhetoric of hope and change and new directions, is neoliberal."[65]

While the Reed and Sowell views are distinctively minority ones, they are indicative that Obama and his history-making campaign did not transcend all division in the black community.

Summary

For most of their history, African Americans have had to deal with a no-party system or a one-party system. Until the Civil War Reconstruction Era, blacks confronted a no-party system since they were excluded from both major parties. Since Reconstruction, except for the brief period from 1936 to 1968, blacks have confronted a one-party system, with one party ignoring the black vote and the other taking it for granted. Since the 1960s blacks have been the most loyal and reliable voters in the Democratic Party coalition, but since the 1970s the Democrats have been reluctant to embrace black concerns, especially their material-based interests. In order to leverage their influence in the Democratic Party, blacks have sought the party's presidential nomination. None, however, came close until Barack Obama in 2008. What impact the nomination of the deracialized Obama will have on the party system and the capabilities of African Americans to use it in their continuing struggle for universal freedom cannot now be known. One thing is clear, however: It is likely for the foreseeable future that blacks will reinforce their attachment to the Democratic Party, thus reinforcing the one-party system.

Selected Bibliography

Baer, Kenneth. *Reinventing the Democrats: The Politics of Liberalism from Reagan to Clinton*. Lawrence: University of Kansas Press, 2000. A Study of how and why the Democratic Party moved in a more conservative direction.

Chisholm, Shirley. *The Good Fight*. New York: Harper & Row, 1973. A memoir of her run for the presidency in 1972.

Eldersveld, Samuel, and Hanes Walton, Jr. *Political Parties in American Society*. Boston: Bedford/St. Martin's Press, 2000. A comprehensive assessment of the status of the American party system.

Frady, Marshall. *Jesse: The Life and Pilgrimage of Jesse Jackson*. New York: Random House, 1996. A comprehensive, full-length biography of the civil rights leader and presidential candidate.

Frymer, Paul. *Uneasy Alliances: Race and Party Competition in America*. Princeton: Princeton University Press, 1999. A study of the two party system and how it operates to create a one party system for blacks.

Henry, Charles. *Jesse Jackson: The Search for Common Ground*. Oakland, CA: Black Scholar Press, 1991. A brief, readable account of the Jackson campaigns.

Ladd, Everett C., and Charles Hadley. *Transformation of the American Party System: Political Coalitions from the New Deal to the 1970s*. New York: Norton, 1975. An analysis of the decline of the New Deal coalition.

Lawson, Kay, ed. *Political Parties and Linkage*. New Haven, CT: Yale University Press, 1980. A collection of papers examining the decline of political parties as the linkage between citizens and government.

Mills, Kay. *This Little Light of Mine: The Life of Fannie Lou Hamer*. New York: Dutton, 1993. A biography of the famous Mississippi freedom fighter.

Morris, Lorenzo. "Race and the Rise and Fall of the Two Party Systems." In Lorenzo Morris, ed., *The Social and Political Implications of the 1984 Jesse Jackson Campaign*. New York: Praeger, 1990. An important article analyzing the functional limitations of the two-party system in terms of black voter choice.

Obama, Barack. *Dreams from My Father.* New York: Crown, 1995. A memoir of his journey to adulthood and his search for community.

———. *The Audacity of Hope.* New York: Crown, 2006. A campaign manifesto.

Walters, Ronald. *Black Presidential Politics: A Strategic Approach.* Albany: SUNY Press, 1988. An influential study of the strategic use of the black vote in presidential elections.

Walter, John C. *The Harlem Fox: J. Raymond Jones and Tammany Hall.* Albany: SUNY Press, 1989. A memoir of the first African American head of Tammany Hall, the New York City Democratic party organization.

Walton, Hanes, Jr. *Black Political Parties: A Historical and Political Analysis.* New York: Free Press, 1972. A comprehensive analysis of African American political parties.

———. "Democrats and African Americans: The American Idea." In Peter Kover, ed., *Democrats and the American Idea.* Washington, DC: Center for National Policy Press, 1992. A brief history of African Americans in the Democratic Party.

Weiss, Nancy. *Farewell to the Party of Lincoln: Black Politics in the Age of FDR.* Princeton, NJ: Princeton University Press, 1983. A historical account of the shift of blacks from the Republican to the Democratic Party.

Wilson, John. *Barack Obama: This Improbable Quest.* New York: Paradigm, 2008. An examination of Obama's candidacy from liberal and conservative perspectives.

Notes

1. Leon Epstein, "The Scholarly Commitment to Parties," in Ada Finifter, ed., *The State of the Discipline* (Washington, DC: American Political Science Association, 1983): 129.

2. Paul Frymer, *Uneasy Alliances: Race and Party Competition in America* (Princeton: Princeton University Press, 1999).

3. Hanes Walton, Jr., *The Negro in Third Party Politics* (Philadelphia: Dorrance, 1969).

4. This section draws on Robert C. Smith and Richard Seltzer, "The Deck and the Sea: The African American Vote in the Presidential Elections of 2000 and 2004," *National Political Science Review* 22 (2008): 263–70.

5. Patricia Gurin, Shirley Hatchett, and James Jackson, *Hope and Independence: Black Response to Electoral and Party Politics* (New York: Russell Sage, 1991): 64.

6. Henry Lee Moon, *Balance of Power: The Negro Vote* (Garden City, NY: Doubleday, 1948): 198.

7. Robert Axelrod, "Where the Votes Come From: An Analysis of Electoral Coalitions," *American Political Science Review* 66 (1972): 11–20 and his "Communications," *American Political Science Review* 76 (1982): 393–96.

8. Kenneth Baer, *Reinventing the Democrats: The Politics of Liberalism from Reagan to Clinton* (Lawrence: University Press of Kansas, 2000).

9. Michael Dawson, *Behind the Mule: Race, Class and African American Politics* (Princeton: Princeton University Press, 1994): 112. See also Katherine Tate, *From Protest to Politics: The New Black Vote in American Elections* (Cambridge: Harvard University Press, 1994).

10. Donald Robinson, *To The Best of My Ability: The Presidency and the Constitution* (New York: Norton, 1987): 173.

11. Ronald Walters, *Black Presidential Politics: A Strategic Approach* (Albany: SUNY Press, 1988): 53.

12. Quoted in Ibid., p. 55.

13. Ibid.

14. E. J. Dionne, "Jackson Says Delegate Rules Have Been Unfair," *New York Times*, May 5, 1988.

15. Samuel Eldersveld and Hanes Walton, *Political Parties in American Society*, 2nd ed. (New York: Bedford/St. Martin's Press, 2000): 215, 216.

16. Richard Herrera, "Are Super Delegates Super," *Political Behavior* 16 (1994): 79–92.

17. Katherine Seelye, "For Clinton, a Key Group Didn't Hold," *New York Times*, June 5, 2008.

18. Walters, *Black Presidential Politics.*
19. Robert C. Smith, "From Insurgency Toward Inclusion: The Jackson Campaigns of 1984 and 1988," in Lorenzo Morris, ed., *The Social and Political Implications of the 1984 Jesse Jackson Presidential Campaign* (Westport, CT: Praeger, 1990). See also Charles Henry, *Jesse Jackson: The Search for Common Ground* (Oakland, CA: Black Scholar Press, 1991).
20. Katherine Tate, *From Protest to Politics: The New Black Voters in American Elections Enlarged Edition* (Cambridge: Harvard University Press, 1994): 144–45.
21. Michael Preston, "The 1984 Presidential Primary Campaign: Who Voted for Jesse Jackson and Why," in Lucius Barker and Ronald Walters, eds., *Jesse Jackson's 1984 Presidential Campaign: Challenge and Change in American Politics* (Urbana: University of Illinois Press, 1989). See also Smith, "From Insurgency Toward Inclusion," pp. 225–28.
22. James Q. Wilson, "The Negro in Politics," in Talcott Parsons and Kenneth Clark, eds., The Negro in Politics," *The Negro American* (Boston: Houghton Mifflin, 1966): 427.
23. Robert Bostch, *We Shall Not Overcome* (Chapel Hill: University of North Carolina Press): 196.
24. Joseph McCormick and Charles Jones, "The Conceptualization of Deracialization," in Georgia Persons, ed., *Dilemmas of Black Politics* (New York: HarperCollins, 1993): 76.
25. Robert Starks, "Commentary and Response to Exploring the Meaning and Implications of Deracialization in African American Urban Politics," *Urban Affairs Quarterly* 27 (1990): 216.
26. Ronald Walters, "Two Political Traditions: Black Politics in the 1990s," *National Political Science Review* 3 (1992): 207.
27. Robert C. Smith, "Recent Elections and Black Politics: The Maturation or Death of Black Politics," *PS: Political Science & Politics* 28 (1990): 161.
28. Lize Mundy, "A Series of Fortunate Events," *Washington Post Magazine*, August 12, 2007.
29. Michael Barone, *The Almanac of American Politics, 2006* (Washington: National Journal, 2005): 560.
30. Transcript, "Senator Barack Obama's Address on Race," Constitution Center, Philadelphia, *Washington Post*, March 18, 2008.
31. Matthew Mosk, "Obama Rewriting Rules for Raising Campaign Money Online," *Washington Post*, March 28, 2008.
32. Jonathan Salant, "Obama's Bid Doesn't Have Support of Most Black Corporate Elite," *Bloomberg News.com*, http://www.blomberg.com/apps/news?pid=20670001.refer=politics, March 18, 2008.
33. Jonathan Weisman, Shailagh Murray, and Peter Slavin, "Strategy Was Based on Winning Delegates, Not Battlegrounds," *Washington Post*, June 4, 2008.
34. "The NAACP 2008 Presidential Candidate Civil rights Questionnaire," http://www.naacp.org/news/press/2008-12-01, Responses.
35. Bob Egelko, "Where Candidates Stand on Crime, Death Penalty," *San Francisco Chronicle*, February 10, 2008.
36. Tali Mendelberg, *The Race Card: Campaign Strategy, Implicit Messages and the Norm of Equality* (Princeton: Princeton University Press, 2001): 95.
37. Project for Excellence in Journalism "Character and the Primaries of 2008: What Were the Media Master Narratives About the Candidates During the Primary Season?" Joan Shorenstein Center for Press & Politics, Harvard University, 2008, pp. 6–7.
38. Ibid., p. 5.
39. Ibid., p. 7.
40. Ibid., p. 30.
41. Ibid., p. 35.
42. Ibid., p. 37.
43. Brian Stetler, "Endorsement From Oprah Winfrey Quantified: A Million Votes," *New York Times*, August 11, 2008.

44. Edward Wyatt, "A Few Tremors in Oprahland," *New York Times*, May 26, 2008.
45. Felicia Lee, "Like the Candidates, TV's Pundits Show Signs of Diversity," *New York Times*, April 2, 2008.
46. Since neither candidate actively campaigned in Florida the results there may not be a fair reflection of the candidates' support. Clinton and Obama declined to campaign in Florida because it moved its primary date ahead of schedule in violation of Party rules.
47. James Traub, "The Emerging Minority," *New York Times*, March 2, 2008.
48. James Barron, "9 Jewish Leaders Say E-mail Spread Lies About Obama," *New York Times*, January 16, 2008.
49. Jonathan Tilove, "Now Obama Must Mend Broken Hearts," *Real Clear Politics*, http://www.realclearpolitics.com, May 23, 2008.
50. Gloria Steinem, "Women Are Never Front-Runners," *New York Times*, January 8, 2008.
51. Geraldine Ferraro, "Healing the Wounds of Democrats Sexism," *Boston Globe*, May 30, 2008.
52. Jodi Kantor, "Gender Issues Lives on as Clinton's Hopes Dim," *New York Times*, May 19, 2008.
53. Katherine Seelye and Julie Bosman, "Media Charged with Sexism in Clinton Coverage," *New York Times*, June 13, 2008.
54. Tilove, "Now Obama Must Mend Broken Hearts."
55. "Senators Clinton, Obama Well Ahead of the Pack in the Minds of Likely African American Primary Voters," Joint Center for Political and Economic Studies, press release, November 27, 2007.
56. Debra Dickerson, "Colorblind," *Salon.Com*, http://www.salon.com/opinion/feature/2007/01/22obama/print.html.
57. Ibid.
58. Darryl Fears, "Black Community Is Increasingly Protective of Obama," *Washington Post*, May 10, 2008.
59. Quoted in Robin Abcarian and Bob Drogin, "Obama Picks up Nine Super delegates," *Los Angeles Times*, May 10, 2008.
60. Raymond Hernandez, "A New Campaign Charge: You Supported Clinton," *New York Times*, July 1, 2008.
61. Ibid.
62. Fears, "Black Community Increasingly Protective of Obama."
63. Frederic Frommer, "Black Conservatives Conflicted on Obama Campaign," *San Francisco Chronicle*, June 14, 2008.
64. Thomas Sowell, "Don't Need to Go Backward," *Contra Costa Times*, May 9, 2008.
65. Adolph Reed, Jr., "Obama No," *The Progressive*, http://www.progressive.org/mag-reedo508, May 2008.

CHAPTER 10

Voting Behavior and Elections

In 1984, during his campaign for the presidency, Jesse Jackson would frequently tell black audiences, "Hands that picked cotton can now pick presidents." The African American vote was critical in picking the president in 2008. To understand the significance of the black vote in American politics, we must place the phenomenon in its historical and systemic contexts.

The Historical and Systemic Dimensions of African American Voting Behavior

The first presidential election in American history in which virtually all African Americans could vote was 1968, three years after passage of the Voting Rights Act in 1965.

Between the Constitutional Convention of 1787 and the end of the Civil War in 1865, only six states permitted the "Free" Negroes to vote; enslaved persons, of course, could not vote in any state. The Revolutionary War, with all its discussion of freedom, did not change the nonvoting status of African Americans. In fact, between the Revolutionary and Civil Wars, Tennessee in 1834, North Carolina in 1835, and Pennsylvania in 1838, all withdrew the right to vote from "Free Negroes."

New York, on the other hand, did not deny the right; rather, it restricted voting by requiring that "Free Negroes" show ownership of property valued at $200. When this rule went into effect, the number of voters dropped. New York subsequently held three statewide suffrage referenda in which the state's white voters were asked to decide whether to give "Free Negroes" full, universal voting rights. The first referendum was held in 1846, the second in 1860, and the third in 1869. All three were voted down by the state electorate.[1]

However, if the northern and Midwestern states opposed a simple aspect of universal freedom such as voting rights prior to the Civil War and thereafter, the South would become the central opponent after the Civil War until the present day. Beginning with the Compromise of 1877, which the South brought about through the fraud, corruption, and violence of the 1876 election, African Americans' newly won voting rights were once again restricted and curtailed, the Fifteenth Amendment notwithstanding. The South's drive to eliminate African Americans from the ballot box culminated in the "era of disenfranchisement" (1890–1901), when all 11 of the states of the Old Confederacy adopted new state constitutions that prevented, prohibited, or manipulated African Americans out of their voting rights. Because of a series of inventive, innovative, and amazingly effective devices like the Grandfather Clause, white primaries, preprimaries, poll taxes, reading and interpretation tests, multiple ballot boxes, single-month registration periods, party- instead of state-administered primaries, single-state party systems, evasion, economic reprisals, terror, fraud, corruption, violence, mayhem, and murder, African Americans found it exceedingly difficult to register, much less to vote.[2] In Louisiana, one of the southern states where voter registration data were kept by race, it is possible to see in empirical terms just how effective these tactics were in crippling African American voters. Figure 10.1 shows percentages for an entire century comparing the eligible African American voting age population with those who overcame the obstacles and became registered voters. African American registered voters plummeted from a high of 130,444 in 1897 to a low of 5,320 in 1910. The new state constitution in Louisiana disenfranchised, in a very short span of time, more than 95 percent of the entire African American electorate. Nearly the same reality prevailed in the other states of the Old Confederacy.

But as had happened in the antebellum period, African Americans once again organized and lobbied to regain their suffrage rights, doing so from 1895 to 1965. With the NAACP taking the lead nationally and numerous courageous individuals and groups spearheading efforts at the local and state levels, the drive to regain the ballot met with some success.[3] Although the success was uneven, painfully slow, and in numerous places quite deadly, some partial success was achieved.

Initially, victories came from Supreme Court cases, like *Guinn and Beal* v. *U.S.* (1914), which declared the Grandfather Clause unconstitutional; *Lane* v. *Wilson* (1939),

Figure 10.1   The Percentage of African American Registered Voters in Louisiana, 1867–1964

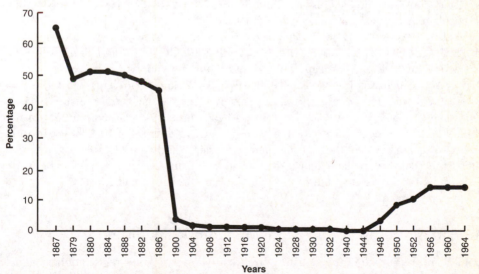

Sources: Adapted from *Annual Cyclopaedia and Register of Important Events of the Year 1867*, vol. VII (New York: D. Appleton and Company, 1869): 461 for the year 1867; Perry H. Howard, *Political Tendencies in Louisiana*, revised and expanded (Baton Rouge: Louisiana State University Press, 1971): 421–22 for the years 1879–1964. Calculations prepared by the authors.

Table 10.1 Percentage of African Americans of Voting Age in the Southern States: 1900–2000

SOUTHERN STATES	1900	1910	1920	1930	1940	1950	1960	1970	1980	1990	2000
Alabama	43.9	41.7	37.7	35.6	33.4	29.5	26.2	21.1	22.5	23.2	20.0
Arkansas	27.8	28.2	27.4	26.6	24.6	20.5	18.5	14.8	13.9	13.6	14.3
Florida	44.2	42.0	34.0	29.0	26.0	20.1	15.2	11.9	11.6	11.9	13.6
Georgia	44.6	43.0	39.8	36.6	32.8	28.6	24.5	22.7	23.9	24.5	26.8
Louisiana	45.4	42.2	38.2	36.6	34.4	30.3	28.5	26.0	27.3	28.0	29.4
Mississippi	56.9	54.9	51.3	49.4	47.1	41.3	36.1	30.3	31.2	31.7	33.0
North Carolina	30.7	29.4	28.1	27.2	25.6	23.8	21.6	18.7	19.6	20.2	20.2
South Carolina	54.0	50.5	47.2	42.0	38.7	33.9	29.2	25.4	27.7	27.5	27.4
Tennessee	23.1	21.6	19.9	19.2	18.1	16.1	15.0	13.4	14.0	14.7	15.0
Texas	18.7	16.7	15.4	14.6	14.0	12.3	11.7	11.0	11.7	11.4	12.1
Virginia	32.7	30.5	28.8	25.3	23.1	21.1	18.9	16.2	17.4	17.8	19.1

Source: Adapted from U.S. Bureau of the Census, *Statistical Abstract of the United States: 1910–2000* (Washington, DC: Government Printing Office, 1911–2000). Calculations prepared by the authors.

which voided the single-month registration scheme; *Smith* v. *Allwright* (1949), which outlawed white primaries; *Terry* v. *Adams* (1953), which eliminated privately administered elections; and a federal district court decision in 1949 that declared "understanding and explaining clauses" to be unconstitutional.[4]

Later, congressional legislation assisted the court decisions. The Civil Rights Acts of 1957 and 1960 and Title I of the 1964 Civil Rights Act added limited federal protection for African American voting rights. Then in 1965, Congress passed Voting Rights Act, which was renewed in 1970, 1975, 1982, and 2006. This law permitted federal registrar, to go into the states covered by the law and register African Americans to vote. However, by the 1960s, the African American community in the South had lost considerable political power. For example, as Table 10.1 shows, in 1900 blacks were a majority of the population in Mississippi and South Carolina, but by the 1960s they constituted less than a third. Similar declines in voting power between 1900 and 1970 are observed in Louisiana, Georgia, Alabama, and Florida.

African American Voting Behavior: Empirical Renderings

Data from the Bureau of the Census permit us to compare voter registration to actual voting in Table 10.2. From the mid-1960s until the present, nearly two-thirds of the African American community have registered to vote. With the exception of the 1976 presidential election, more than half of all African American registered voters voted in presidential elections. There is, however, an almost 10 percent gap between African American registered voters and those who actually vote.

Table 10.2 Percentage of African Americans Registered and Voting, 1964–2006

YEAR	PERCENTAGE REGISTERED	PERCENTAGE VOTING
1964	60[a]	59
1966	60	42
1968	66	58
1970	61	44
1972	66	52
1974	55	34
1976	59	49
1978	57	37
1980	60	51
1982	59	43
1984	66	56
1986	64	43
1988	65	52
1990	39	39
1992	64	54
1994	59	37
1996	64	51
1998	60.2	39.6
2000	68	57
2002	62.4	67.5
2004	68.7	60.0
2006	60.9	41.0

[a]*Estimated Data*

Sources: For the presidential election data, see Jerry T. Jennings, "Voting and Registration in the Election of November 1992," *Current Population Reports, Population Characteristics, Series P20-422* (Washington, DC: Government Printing Office, 1993); for congressional election data, Jerry T. Jennings, "Voting and Registration in the Election of November 1990," *Current Population Reports, Population Characteristics, Series P10-453* (Washington, DC: Government Printing Office, 1991); U.S. Bureau of the Census, "Voting and Registration in the Election of November 1998," *Current Population Survey P20-523RV* (Washington, DC: Census Bureau, 2000); U.S. Bureau of the Census, "Voting and Registration in the Election of November 2000," *Current Population Reports, Population Characteristics, Series P20-542* (Washington, DC: Census Bureau, 2000): 5; U.S. Bureau of the Census, "Voting and Registration in Election of November 2002," *Current Population Reports, Population Characteristics, Series P20-552* (Washington, DC: Census Bureau, 2004): 5; U.S. Bureau of the Census, "Voting and Registration in Election of November 2004," *Current Population Reports, Population Characteristics, Series P20556* (Washington, DC: Census Bureau, 2006): 4; and U.S. Bureau of the Census, "Voting and Registration in Election of November 2006," *Current Population Reports, Population Characteristics, Series P20557* (Washington, DC: Census Bureau, 2008): 4.

Table 10.3 reveals the demographic correlates of the 2000 and 2004 black vote. African American voters tend to be female and over 45 years of age. The majority live in the South, four-fifths have a high school education or better, two-thirds earn more than $25,000 per year, and almost half own their own homes.

Table 10.3 Demographic Correlates of African American Voters in the 2000 and 2004 Presidential Elections

DEMOGRAPHIC VARIABLES	PERCENTAGE OF 2000 VOTERS	PERCENTAGE OF 2004 VOTERS
Sex		
Male	46.0	46.5
Female	54.0	53.5
AGE		
Under 45	61.0	52.4
Over 45	39.0	47.6
REGION		
Northeast	17.6	16.0
Midwest	18.8	20.5
South	54.8	53.9
West	8.9	9.6
EDUCATION		
Grade school	7.1	8.1*
High school	49.7	28.6
Some college	26.8	31.0
College	16.5	21.1
LABOR		
Employed	60.8	62.7
Unemployed	5.0	6.7
Not in labor force	34.2	30.6
FAMILY INCOME		
Under 25,000	39.7	32.6*
25,000–49,999	29.7	20.1
50,000 and above	23.7	35.2
TENURE		
Owner occupied	47.1	62.3
Renter occupied	52.9	36.7

Sources: Adapted from U.S. Bureau of the Census, "Voting and Registration in the Election of November 2000," *Current Population Reports, Population Characteristics, Series P20-542* (Washington, DC: Census Bureau, 2002); and from the Bureau of the Census, "Detailed Tables for Voting and Registration in the Election of November, 2004," *Current Population Reports, Population Characteristics, Series P20556 Series* (Washington, DC: Census Bureau, 2006). Calculations prepared by the authors.

Beyond the Boundaries of Race: Blacks Running for Governor and U.S. Senate, 2006

To understand the extraordinary significance of the Obama campaign, one must know that most of the more than 8,000 black elected officials in the United States are elected from majority black places or majority–minority (blacks and Latinos) local, state, or federal legislative districts. This means that very few blacks have been elected to the Senate or as governors of states, since there are no majority black states in the United States. Since the people began to directly elect U.S. senators in 1914, only three African Americans have been elected, and in the history of the nation, only one black—Douglas Wilder of Virginia in 1979—has been elected governor. (In 2008, Basil Patterson, New York's Lt. Governor, succeeded to the governorship of the state after the incumbent resigned as a result of a sex scandal.) This is because, in general, enough whites have been unwilling to vote for a black candidate—whatever his ideology or qualifications—to make such candidacies politically realistic. Racism is part of the explanation for this unwillingness, as is the perception among some whites that blacks are too liberal for their conservative ideological inclinations.

In the face of these perceived political realities, only two black members of the congress have left the House to seek statewide office, which is frequently the career path of White House members. Alan Gerber summarizes the situation as follows:

> African American members of Congress rarely seek higher office. Prospects for winning statewide are discouraging. No African American has moved from the House to the Senate or to the governor's mansion. The liberal voting record that African American representatives typically compile does not provide a strong foundation for winning statewide elections and there remains some resistance to voting for African Americans for higher office.[5]

And even when blacks run, they tend to lose. Since the 1960s there have been 21 major-party nominees for the Senate (11 Democrats, 10 Republicans) and 10 for governor (9 Democrats, 1 Republican).[6] Table 10.4 lists these candidates by year, state, name, party, and percent of

Table 10.4 Major-Party African American Nominees for Governor and U.S. Senate, 1966–2004, and Percent of Vote

SENATE

1966	Massachusetts	Edward Brooke	R	60.7
1972	Massachusetts	Edward Brooke	R	63.5
1974	Connecticut	James Brannen	R	34.3
1978	Massachusetts	Edward Brooke	R	44.8
1988	Maryland	Alan Keyes	R	38.2
	Virginia	Maurice Dawkins	R	28.7
1990	North Carolina	Harvey Gantt	D	47.4
1992	Illinois	Carol Moseley Braun	D	53.0
	Maryland	Alan Keys	R	29.0
1994	Missouri	Alan Wheat	D	35.7
	Washington	Ron Sims	D	45.1
1996	North Carolina	Harvey Gantt	D	45.8
1998	Illinois	Carol Moseley Braun	D	47.0
	Connecticut	Gary Franks	R	32.0

(continued)

Table 10.4   (continued)

2000	Massachusetts	Jack E. Robinson	R	13.0
	Mississippi	Troy D. Brown	D	31.0
2002	Texas	Ron Kirk	D	43.0
2004	Georgia	Denise Majette	D	39.0
	Illinois	Barack Obama	D	70
	Indiana	Marvin Scott	R	37.0
GOVERNOR				
1982	California	Tom Bradley	D	48.1
1986	California	Tom Bradley	D	37.4
	Michigan	William Lucas	R	31.4
1989	Virginia	Douglas Wilder	D	50.1
1990	South Carolina	Theo Mitchell	D	27.9
1995	Louisiana	Cleo Fields	D	37.0
1999	Louisiana	William Jefferson	D	30.0
2002	Nevada	Joe Neal	D	22.0
	New York	H. Carl McCall	D	33.0

Source: Adapted from the Joint Center for Political and Economic Studies, "Political Report," *Focus* (May/June 2006), p. 6.

the vote received. It shows that only four of the Senate nominees were successful. (Edward Brooke twice in Massachusetts and Carol Mosley Braun and Barack Obama once each in Illinois.) Of the ten nominees for governor, only Wilder was successful. Los Angeles Mayor Tom Bradley ran a very competitive race for governor in California in 1982 and Harvey Gantt for Senate from North Carolina in 1990. Otherwise, the African American nominees listed in Table 10.4 ran largely symbolic campaigns with little realistic chance of winning.

Despite these seemingly daunting odds, in 2006 a bumper crop of blacks ran for either the Democratic or Republican nominations for governor or Senate. In Maryland Lt. Governor Michael Steele was the Republican Senate nominee (Kwesi Mfume, the former congressman and head of the NAACP, ran unsuccessfully for the Democratic nomination in Maryland). In Tennessee, Harold Ford left the House to become the Democratic Senate nominee and Keith Bulter, a former Detroit city councilman and pastor of one of the city's largest churches ran unsuccessfully for the Republican Senate nomination. In Mississippi, Erik Flemming, a state representative, won the Democratic nomination for the Senate. Meanwhile, two African American Republicans won their party's nomination for governor; Lynn Swann, the former Pittsburgh Steelers star football player, in Pennsylvania and Ken Blackwell, Ohio's controversial (controversial because many African Americans alleged that he played a key role in suppressing the Ohio black vote in 2004 and thereby facilitated Bush's victory) Secretary of State. Finally, in Massachusetts, Deval Patrick, the former assistant attorney general for civil rights in the Clinton administration, won the Democratic gubernatorial nomination.

In these six states the black population is relatively small, ranging from a high of 36 percent in Mississippi to 5 percent in Massachusetts (for an average of 16 percent). The most extensive study of blacks running for higher office in the United States finds that the presence of a black Democrat on the ballot increases black turnout by 2.3 percent (the presence of a black Republican has no effect on black turnout), while the presence of a black of either party increases white turnout by 2.2 percent.[7] Although the percentage increases are about the same for both races, the actual increase is much greater for whites given the larger size of the white population. And both white Democrats and Republicans are less likely to vote for their party's nominee when she or he is black.[8] Thus, the barriers were considerable for these 2006 African American candidates seeking to cross the boundaries of race to become governors or senators. These barriers are especially high for the black Republicans since they can expect little or no increased turnout among blacks and less support from their fellow white partisans.

Table 10.5 displays outcomes in 2006 for the six major party candidates running for governor and senate.[9] In Massachusetts Deval Patrick made history by becoming only the second African American elected governor in the United States. Patrick won 56 percent of the vote, including 89 percent of the black vote and 51 percent of the white vote. All of the other candidates lost. The three Republican candidates—Swann, Steele, and Blackwell—received relatively little black support and only Steele received more than half of the white vote. In Tennessee Harold Ford received 95 percent of the African American vote but only 40 percent of the votes of whites. The results in Mississippi suggest an almost completely racially polarized electorate, with Flemming receiving 35 percent of the vote, which matches almost exactly the black proportion of the state's population. The experience of African Americans running beyond the boundaries of race in 2006 suggests that a new structure of ambition was emerging in black politics, where a new generation of politicians perceive that the white electorate in the twenty-first century is willing to vote for an ideologically and culturally mainstream black candidate for any office.[10]

Table 10.5 African American Major Party Nominees for Governor and U.S. Senate 2006, by Percent of Total Vote and Percent of White and Black Vote

CANDIDATE VOTE	PERCENTAGE OF TOTAL VOTE	PERCENTAGE OF BLACK VOTE	PERCENTAGE OF WHITE VOTE
Lynn Swann	40	13	43
Kenneth Blackwell	37	20	40
Deval Patrick	56	89	51
SENATE			
Harold Ford	48	95	40
Michael Steele	44	27	52
Erick Flemming	35	NA	NA[a]

[a]No exit polls were conducted in Mississippi because the race was considered noncompetitive. Flemming, for example, raised only $13,959 compared to the nearly $3 million raised by his Republican opponent, incumbent Senator Trent Lott.
Source: CNN

The 2008 General Election: Presidential and Congressional

The Conventions and Vice Presidential Nominees

At the Democratic convention in Denver, African Americans constituted 24 percent of the 4,440 delegates, up from 20 percent in 2004. In 1988, when Jesse Jackson ran a second time for the nomination, blacks constituted 23 percent of the delegates.

Obama selected Senator Joseph Biden as his vice presidential running mate. A majority of Democrats supported Hillary Clinton for the vice presidential nomination, including 78 percent of those who voted for her in the primaries.[11] Since the nomination contest between Obama and Clinton was almost a tie, many Clinton supporters thought she had earned second place on the ticket. This was especially the case among some of her female supporters, as almost certainly would have been the case among blacks if the situation had been reversed and Obama had come in a close second to Clinton.

However, only 37 percent of Obama's primary voters supported the selection of Clinton (60 percent of Clinton delegates at the Convention favored her selection but only 3 percent of Obama's).[12] Although Clinton had favorable ratings among Democrats (especially white women), there was "intense dislike" for her among Republicans (67 percent had a "very unfavorable" view of her) and among independents, where 37 percent had a very unfavorable view.[13] Looking at these numbers, Obama strategists likely calculated that the experienced and less controversial Biden was a safer choice than Clinton. Nevertheless, Biden's selection likely alienated some of Clinton's supporters (especially white women) and reinforced the race–gender tensions that emerged during the Democratic primaries.

Partly in response to Obama's choice, John McCain, the Republican nominee, selected Sarah Palin, the 21-month first-term governor of Alaska. McCain, the 72-year-old, 22-year Senate veteran and Vietnam prisoner of war with a reputation as a maverick, won the nomination by default. That is, he was more acceptable to the conservative base and evangelical Christians than his principal opponents, former New York City Mayor Rudy Guliani and former Massachusetts governor Mitt Romney (Guliani is a supporter of abortion and gay rights, as was Romney while he was governor of Massachusetts). However, McCain was not viewed as a reliable conservative. Thus, Governor Palin, an ideological conservative and opponent of abortion and gay rights, could shore up McCain's support among the Republican base, as well among women disaffected by Obama's choice of Biden rather than Clinton.

Although Palin probably did help McCain among Republican base voters, her lack of experience and poor performance in a series of television interviews led even conservative commentators to question McCain's judgment in selecting a person with such minimal qualifications for the vice-presidency. (By early October, only 43 percent of voters thought Palin was qualified to be president, compared to 79 percent for Biden.)[14] And there is little evidence that she was able to appeal to Clinton's disaffected female supporters.

African American delegate representation at the 2008 Republican Convention was the lowest in 40 years. Of the 2380 delegates at the convention, only 36 were black. A mere 1.5 percent compared to 7 percent in 2004 and 1 percent in 1968.

Campaign Finance and Media Coverage

Although Obama had promised to participate in the public finance system established in 1976 to fund presidential campaigns, shortly after he won the nomination, he changed his mind, becoming the first major party nominee not to participate since the system was established. In his statement explaining his decision, Obama charged that Republicans had become "masters at gaming the system" by using unaffiliated groups that could raise unlimited funds (so-called 527s) to launch "smear attacks" on Democratic nominees. While there is an element of truth to Obama's allegations (the so-called swift boat ads against John Kerry in 2004 are an often-cited example), Obama's unparalleled fundraising capabilities were probably the decisive factor in his decision to forego public financing. Under the public financing system, each candidate in 2008 was limited to $84 million. Meanwhile, Obama raised more than $225 million by the end of September. In September, McCain and the Republicans spent $108 million compared to the Democrats and Obama's $134 million. (The two parties are allowed to raise and spend separately from the candidates.)

This financial advantage allowed Obama to outspend McCain in television and radio ads by an estimated 4.1 margin (in some battleground states, the margin was as much as 7.1), including advertising in traditional Republican states and purchasing a half-hour "informercial" on seven networks (including BET and Univision, the Spanish language network) at a cost of $4 million.[15] Broadcast a week before the election, the infomercial reached an estimated audience of 35 million. These funds also allowed Obama to fund an extensive, nationwide grassroots voter registration, mobilization, and get-out-the-vote campaign. As Table 10.6 shows, this allowed the Obama campaign to directly contact (in person or by phone, e-mail, or text message) a much larger percentage of likely voters: 21 to 14 percent. The Obama campaign was especially more likely to contact the campaign's core constituencies of blacks (56 to 16 percent) and young people (29 to 11 percent). The McCain campaign was more likely to have contacted white evangelical Christians (26 to 15 percent) but Obama

Table 10.6 Percentage of Likely Voters Contacted by Obama and McCain Campaigns, by Selected Demographic Categories

	OBAMA	McCAIN
All Voters	21%	14%
Democrats	44	—
Republicans	—	25
Conservatives	22	23
White Evangelical Christians	15	26
Independents	26	20
Youth (−35)	29	11
Seniors (55+)	32	25
Blacks	56	16

Source: "Behind the Numbers," *Washington Post*, October 24, 2008, based on ABC News/*Washington Post* poll conducted October 19–22, 2008.

had greater contact with senior citizens and independents and almost the same level of contact with conservatives.

As in the primaries, most of the press coverage of the general election focused on the "house race" (campaign tactics, strategies, and polls) rather than policy. According to a study by the Pew Center, more than twice as many stories focused on this topic as compared to the issues.[16] Coverage of the candidates in general was fairly balanced until the near collapse of the economy in mid-September. Thereafter stories about McCain became much more negative; 57 percent negative compared to 29 percent negative stories about Obama. The authors of the Pew Center report suggest that this shift came about because Obama was perceived as responding to the economic crisis more effectively than McCain and as a result his approval rating in the polls increased. As his approval ratings increased, press coverage became more positive; and as coverage became more positive, his approval ratings increased. In other words, both the press and the public like winners. The authors of the report conclude, "The financial crisis and particularly Obama's steadier reaction to it in relation to McCain's were clearly a turning point in the media coverage. The more positive coverage was then reflected in the polls, which in turn were reinforced in the horse race coverage that played off the polls. In that sense, the data show Obama was the beneficiary of the tactical, strategic bias of the press."[17]

Issues

The 2008 election was a "retrospective" election.[18] That is, it was a referendum on the last eight years of the Bush administration. This made for an ideal situation for Obama or any Democrat to compete. (Throughout 2008, the Democrats maintained a double-digit lead on the "generic" ballot, which asks voters which party they would like to see win the presidency.) As the general election approached, 90 percent of the population thought the country was headed in the wrong direction; the nation faced rising gas prices, a collapse in the housing market, a massive budget deficit, rising unemployment, an unpopular war, and an incumbent president whose popularity was in the low 20s. Finally, a month before the election the stock market dramatically declined and the credit markets collapsed, requiring a $700 billion bailout from the federal treasury. Newspaper headlines and television newscasts raised the spectra of another Great Depression. *Time*, for example, in its cover story of October 13, under the caption "The New Hard Times," showed men in long, Depression-era soup lines.

The 2008 election was therefore a classic bread and butter election. Theodore White, who chronicled presidential elections from 1960 to 1972 in his *The Making of the President* series of books, quipped there are only three issues in American politics: bread and butter, war and peace, and black and white. After 1972, a fourth issue complex emerged—"right and wrong"—revolving around social-moral issues such as prayer in school, abortion, and gay rights. In 2008 the right and wrong issues were ignored; the war and peace issue faded as bread and butter overshadowed all else. (In mid-October, 70 percent of voters said the economy was the number-one issue, followed by the Iraq war at 9 percent.)

In this dismal strategic situation, the McCain campaign attempted to make black and white the issue by focusing on Obama's "character." In the three televised debates

Obama and McCain in the third debate. *Source:* Landov Media

between McCain and Obama, polls indicate that voters thought Obama won each of them. For example, a CNN poll found that 51 percent of voters declared Obama the winner of the first debate, 24 percent thought McCain won, with the remainder calling it a tie.[19] Shortly thereafter, polls indicated Obama had a 6–10 percent lead nationally, with a similar or larger margin in the so-called battleground states. At this point, McCain strategists announced that the campaign was conceding Michigan and would in the future focus on Obama's character and "associations" rather than the issues. As one said, "We're going to get a little tougher. We've got to question this guy's associations, very soon. There's no question that we have to change the subject here."[20] Change the subject from bread and butter to black and white.

Governor Palin began the attacks by accusing Obama of "palling around with terrorists," referring to his relationship with William Ayres, a University of Illinois education professor and one of the founders of the 1960s Weather Underground. The Weather Underground was responsible for bombing the Capitol and the Pentagon during the Vietnam War.[21] News reports pointed out that Obama was eight years old when the bombings occurred and that he and Ayres were not friends, although they lived in the same Chicago neighborhood, served on charitable boards together (in 1997 the City of Chicago named Ayres its citizen of the year), and Ayres hosted a coffee for Obama when he first ran for office.[22]

In its analysis, the Associated Press wrote that Palin's comments were "tinged with racism," concluding, "Palin's incendiary charge draws media attention away from the worsening economy . . . [But] whether intended or not by the McCain campaign, portraying Obama as 'not like us' is another potential appeal to racism . . . . Palin's words avoid repulsing voters with overt racism. But there is another subtext for creating the false image of a black presidential nominee 'palling around' with terrorists while assuring a predominantly white audience that he doesn't see their America."[23]

In the last weeks of the campaign, McCain and Pallin said that Obama was a socialist because of his plan to raise taxes on the wealthy in order to, in Obama's words, "spread the wealth around." The charge of socialism was part of the campaign's continuing effort to portray Obama as a liberal or radical whose policies and past associations put him "out of the mainstream."[24] Meanwhile, Obama and Biden continued to emphasize the economy and McCain's association with the "failed policies" of the Bush administration.

Forecasting the Election

Political scientists have developed sophisticated mathematical models to forecast the outcome of presidential elections. Using the state of the economy as the main variable, these models typically also include the strength of the two parties, the popularity of the incumbent president, and the appeal of the candidates.[25] Michael Lewis-Beck of the University of Iowa, perhaps the leading presidential election forecaster, employed this model to forecast the 2008 election (variations of the model have correctly forecast virtually every presidential election since 1948). Although Lewis-Beck predicted an Obama victory, his initial model forecasted a 56.58 margin of victory, but after including variables taking account of Obama's race, the margin dropped to a razor-thin 50.07.[26] Other forecasters found similar results, suggesting that race played some role in determining the outcome of the election. How much of a role can only be known when detailed post-election studies are available.

The Mobilization of the Black Vote and Obama's Minority–Majority Coalition

The Obama campaign mobilized the black community in an unprecedented way. More so than even the Jackson campaigns, blacks participated in the process to a greater extent than whites. Forty-six percent of blacks compared to 48 percent of whites reported following the election "closely," 31 percent reported making a campaign contribution (compared to 21 percent of whites), and twice as many blacks (14 percent) reported working in a campaign. Again, this is extraordinary since whites generally participate in presidential campaigns more than blacks.[27]

This heightened participation, however, was not universal. In late September, the *Washington Post* conducted a series of interviews with blacks in the poor Mississippi Delta town of Canton (population 13,000; 80 percent black). Only one person (the Chair of the County Democratic Party) had put up an Obama campaign sign and the *Post* reporter concluded:

> . . . there remains pockets of Americans who are deeply skeptically of the candidates and uninterested in participating. Their detachment is bred of years of disappointment and the pervasive feeling that no matter who wins, little in their lives will

change . . . . There's a hardened sense among many in this town . . . that Obama does not know about and could not understand their problems. Others know a black man is running but can't quite remember his name. Some are excited by Obama' candidacy but have never voted, cannot recall the last time they went to the polls, or have no idea how or where to register.[28]

Nevertheless, Obama received a larger proportion of the black vote than any previous Democratic nominee; 95 percent compared to Lyndon Johnson's 94 percent in 1964 and John Kerry's 88 percent in 2004 (since 1964 Democratic nominees have received an average 88 percent of the black vote). The African American proportion of the electorate also increased, from 11 percent in 2004 to 13 percent in 2008.

Obama's minority–majority coalition resembles the typical Democratic presidential coalition since the late 1960s, winning 86 percent of the Jewish vote, 67 percent of Latinos', 66 percent of Asian Americans', and 70 percent of the gay and lesbian vote. As Table 10.7 indicates, this is comparable to the coalition of minorities assembled by Kerry in 2004.

Although Obama lost the white vote to McCain 43 to 55 percent, this margin is slightly better than the 41 percent of the white vote won by Kerry in 2004. And as in the Democratic primaries, Obama also won the vote of young whites by a margin of 10, 54 to 44 percent (data not displayed in table).

Overall, preliminary data indicate Obama won approximately 65 million votes to McCain's 57 million, giving him a winning margin of 53 percent to McCain's 46 percent (the remainder was won by minor party candidates). Obama won 28 states and the District of Columbia with 364 electoral college votes, to McCain's 163 electoral votes. Early estimates of turnout indicate it was 62.5 percent, the highest since 1964. The total estimated vote was 133 million, compared to 122 million in 2004.

Obama, unlike Gore and Kerry in 2000 and 2004, ran virtually a 50-state campaign, not wanting to depend on victory in only a few states in order to win. He was able to do this because during the long primary contest, he had established campaign organizations in every state. These organizations and his financial advantage enabled him to attain a broad national victory, winning nine of the ten so-called battleground states (all except Missouri).

One area of the country where Obama did not make significant inroads was the South. Although he carried the three states of the "suburban south" (Virginia, North Carolina, and Florida), he lost by substantial margins in the eight other states of the region. In many of these states, McCain won the white vote by margins of 9 to 1, with neither age nor education altering support for Obama. Clearly, traditional southern racism played a role in these outcomes. In interviews by the *New York Times*, many white southerners made it clear they were apprehensive about an Obama presidency. One respondent said she was bothered by the idea of a black man "over me," while another said Obama's election would make blacks "more aggressive."[29] The fact, however, that Obama won without significant southern support suggests that the region's influence in presidential elections is declining.[30] Obama was not the only African American running for president in 2008. Cynthia McKinney, the former Georgia Congresswoman, was the Green Party candidate, perennial candidate Alan Keyes ran on the America's Independent Party ticket and James Harris was the Socialist Workers Party nominee. All of the minor party candidates (including independent Ralph Nader and Libertarian Bob Barr) got less than 2 percent of the vote.

Table 10.7 A Comparison of the 2000, 2004 and 2008 Vote in the Presidential Elections, by Selected Demographic Categories

	2000			2004			2008		
	PERCENTAGE OF ELECTORATE	PERCENTAGE OF GORE	PERCENTAGE OF BUSH	PERCENTAGE OF ELECTORATE	PERCENTAGE OF BUSH	PERCENTAGE OF KERRY	PERCENTAGE OF ELECTORATE	PERCENTAGE OF OBAMA	PERCENTAGE OF McCAIN
Gender									
Women	52	54	43	54	48	51	53	56	43
Men	48	42	53	46	55	44	47	49	48
Race/Ethnicity									
Whites	81	42	54	77	58	41	74	43	55
Blacks	10	90	9	11	11	88	13	95	4
Latinos	7	62	35	8	44	53	9	67	31
Asian Americans	2	55	41		44	56	3	66	31
Religion (whites only)									
Protestant	56	34	63	54	59	40	42	34	65
Evangelicals	14	18	80	23	78	21	26	24	74
Catholic	25	45	52	27	52	47	19	47	52
Jewish	4	80	17	3	25	74	2	86	16
Other	5	53	35	7	74	23	NA	NA	NA
None	9	57	63	10	31	67	NA	NA	NA
Region									
Northeast	23	56	39	22	43	56	21	59	40
Midwest	26	48	49	26	51	48	24	54	44
South	31	43	55	32	58	42	32	45	54
West	21	48	46	20	49	50	23	57	40

(*continued*)

Table 10.7 *(continued)*

	2000			2004			2008		
	PERCENTAGE OF ELECTORATE	PERCENTAGE OF GORE	PERCENTAGE OF BUSH	PERCENTAGE OF ELECTORATE	PERCENTAGE OF BUSH	PERCENTAGE OF KERRY	PERCENTAGE OF ELECTORATE	PERCENTAGE OF OBAMA	PERCENTAGE OF McCAIN
Education									
Some high school	15	59	38	4	49	50	4	63	35
High school graduate	21	48	49	22	52	47	20	52	46
Some college	32	45	51	32	54	46	31	51	47
College graduate	24	45	51	26	52	46	28	50	48
Postgraduate	18	52	44	16	44	55	17	58	40
Sexual Orientation									
Gay/lesbian	4	70	25	4	23	77	4	70	27
Heterosexual	96	47	50	96	53	46	96	53	45

Note: NA—Data not available

Sources: The 2004 data are from the Edison Media Research and Milofsky Exit Poll as reported on CNN.Com/ELECTION/2004/pages/results/states/US/p/oo/epolls.o.html. The 2008 data are from "President: National Exit Poll," http://www.cnn.comELECTION/2008/results/polls/#USPOp1.

BOX 10.1 DAVID AXELROD: THE STRATEGIST

Obama's success in winning the Democratic nomination is widely attributed to his success in putting together a formidable campaign organization. At the head of this organization as chief strategist and media consultant was David Axelrod, the 51-year-old former *Chicago Tribune* political writer and a columnist. In 1984 Axelrod left journalism to work in the U.S. Senate campaign of Paul Simon. His success in helping to elect Simon led to the establishment of Axelrod & Associates, a political consultant firm. Axelrod's firm did strategic and media work for some of the leading Democratic politicians, including Christopher Dodd, Hillary Clinton, and John Edwards. However, Axelrod has also worked in the political campaigns of some of the nation's leading African Americans, including black mayoral candidates in Chicago, Detroit, Washington, Houston, and Cleveland, as well as Deval Patrick's successful run for Massachusetts governor in 2006.

Source: Landov Media

Obama met Axelrod shortly after he returned to Chicago and they became friends and political allies. A consultant in Obama's 2004 U.S. Senate campaign, Axelrod is credited with helping to develop the Obama delegate and caucus strategy and his campaign narratives of hope and change in the 2008 presidential campaign. He also supervised the creating and marketing of many of the television ads and Internet videos.

Although some African Americans (including Obama's pastor Rev. Jeremiah Wright) criticized Obama for relying too heavily on Axelrod and other white advisors, over the years Axelrod has demonstrated his capabilities in selling deracialized black candidates to majority white constituencies.

The Democrats increased their margins in both houses of Congress, partly due to Obama's coattails. In the House, they won 20 additional seats, giving the Party 260 of the 435. Democrats won six additional Senate seats, bringing their majority to 57 (including two independents). Although this is less than the 60 votes needed to break a Senate filibuster, it provides the new president with working majorities in both houses. The size of the black congressional delegation will decline from 43 to 42. The Illinois governor appointed an African American, Roland Burris, to succeed Obama but New Orleans Congressman William Jefferson was defeated.

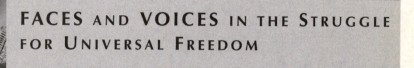

FACES AND VOICES IN THE STRUGGLE FOR UNIVERSAL FREEDOM

JOHN MERCER LANGSTON (1829–1897)

John Mercer Langston was the first African American elected to office in the United States. Born free in Virginia, he was the son of a wealthy white slaveholder and a mother of mixed African and Indian ancestry. When his father died he left Langston an inheritance, which he used to get a good education and accumulate a substantial fortune. After graduating from Oberlin College in Ohio in 1850, he aspired to become a lawyer. Ohio law prohibited African Americans from practicing law, but because of his light skin color it was decided that Langston was entitled to the privileges of a white man. A successful practice led to his election to the Oberlin town council, making him not only the first black elected to office but also the first from a majority white constituency (ironically, blacks were not allowed to vote in Ohio, so a special exception had to be made in order that Langston could vote for himself). In many ways Langston resembles Barack Obama; born to mixed-race parents, highly educated and charismatic, he was able to appeal across racial boundaries to establish a minority–majority coalition. Langston was also mentioned as a possible Republican vice presidential candidate.

After the Civil War Langston returned to Virginia where he was elected to Congress, where he fought for free and fair elections as the indispensable foundation for universal freedom. (Because of a long dispute about irregularities in the election, Langston was able to serve only three months of his two-year term.) In addition to holding elective office, Langston organized the National Equal Rights League (a forerunner to the NAACP) and was the founding dean of Howard University law school. He was appointed by President Rutherford B. Hayes as minister to Haiti and the Dominican Republic. In 1894, three years before his death, he wrote his autobiography, *From the Virginia Plantation to the National Capital.**

---

*William and Aimee Lee Cheek, *John Mercer Langston and the Fight for Black Freedom* (Urbana: University of Illinois Press, 1989)

Summary

Until the adoption of the Fifteenth Amendment in 1870, African Americans were denied the right to vote even in northern states such as New York. Even after the adoption of the amendment, it would take passage of the Voting Rights Act of 1965 before African Americans gained the universal right to vote throughout the United States. Today, blacks vote at about the same rate as whites when social class is taken into account. From time to time the black vote has been the balance of power in presidential elections, determining the outcome when the white vote is closely divided. This process is episodic, however, because generally the black vote is a "captive vote" in national elections, ignored by the Republicans and taken for granted by the Democrats. In 2008, however, the black vote was in a sense "liberated," playing a crucial role in the election of the first African American president.

Selected Bibliography

Guinier, Lani. *The Tyranny of the Majority*. New York: Free Press, 1994. President Clinton's failed nominee for assistant attorney general for civil rights explains the limitations of the Voting Rights Act and blacks' use of the ballot to achieve race reform.

Jarvis, Sonia. "Historical Overview: African Americans and the Evolution of Voting Rights." In R. Gomes and L. Williams, eds., *From Exclusion to Inclusion: The Long Struggle for African American Political Power*. Westport, CT: Greenwood Press, 1992. A concise overview of the long struggle of blacks to obtain the ballot.

Pinderhughes, Dianne. "The Role of African American Political Organizations in the Mobilization of Voters." In R. Gomes and L. Williams., eds., *From Exclusion to Inclusion: The Long Struggle for African American Political Power*. Westport, CT: Greenwood Press, 1992. A study of the role that black political organizations play in registering and turning out the black vote.

Reid, John. "The Voting Behavior of Blacks." *Intercom* 9 (1981): 8–11. A brief but very useful analysis of the factors shaping the black vote.

Tate, Katherine. *From Protest to Politics: The New Black Voter*. Cambridge, MA: Harvard University Press, 1994. A sophisticated study of the black vote intention and the vote itself, focusing on their determinants.

Walton, Hanes, Jr., ed. "Black Voting Behavior in the Segregationist Era." In *Black Politics and Black Political Behavior: A Linkage Analysis*. Westport, CT: Praeger, 1994. An examination of how blacks registered and voted in Georgia during the era of disenfranchisement.

Notes

1. Phyllis Field, *The Politics of Race in New York: The Struggle for Black Suffrage in the Civil War Era* (Ithaca, NY: Cornell University Press, 1982): 59, 124–26, 198.
2. On these various schemes used in the South to deprive blacks of the vote, see Hanes Walton, Jr., *Black Politics* (Philadelphia: J. B. Lippincott, 1992): 33–54.
3. For an engaging memoir of one of these courageous individuals, see John H. Scott (with Cleo Scott) *Witness to the Truth: My Struggle for Human Rights in Louisiana* (Columbia: University of South Carolina Press, 2003).

4. For citations to and discussions of these cases, see Walton, *Black Politics*, pp. 33–40.
5. Alan Gerber, "African Americans' Congressional Careers and the Democratic House Delegation," *Journal of Politics* 58 (1996): 831–45.
6. Although few blacks have been elected senator or governor, a number in various parts of the country have been elected to lower-level statewide offices such as Lt. governor, secretary of state, and superintendent of education. Also, in addition to the major party nominees, uncounted numbers of blacks have ran for governor or senator as minor-party and independent candidates.
7. Ebonya Washington, "How Black Candidates Affect Turnout," Cambridge, MA: National Bureau of Economic Research, Working Paper #11915, 2006.
8. Ibid.
9. For case studies of five of six of these elections (all except Pennsylvania), see the symposium "Beyond the Boundaires: A New Structure of Ambition in American Politics," *National Political Science Review* 12 (2009, forthcoming).
10. Andrea Gillespie "The Third Wave: A Theoretical Introduction to the Post Civil Rights Era Cohort of Black Elected Leadership." Paper presented at the annual meeting of the National Conference of Black Political Scientists, San Francisco, March 22–24, 2007.
11. Ken Garber, "New Poll Finds More Than Half Democrats Want Clinton as Obama's Vice President," *U.S. News*, July 10, 2008.
12. Ibid.
13. "Polls: Mixed Feelings on Clinton as VEEP," http://cbss.com/campaign08/clinton.vice. president.2.744025.html. On the polarized attitudes toward Clinton see Gil Troy, *Hillary Rodham Clinton: Polarizing First Lady* (Lawrence: University Press of Kansas, 2008).
14. James Rainey, "Conservative Intellectuals Slam McCain," *Los Angeles Times,* September 28, 2008 and Kathleen Parker "The Palin Problem," *Washington Post*, September 28, 2008.
15. Jim Rutenberg, "Nearing Record, Obama's Ad Efforts Swamps McCain," *New York Times*, October 17, 2008.
16. See "Winning The Media Campaign, Pew Research Center, Project for Excellence in Journalism," http://www.journalism.org/nide/13309.
17. Ibid.
18. Morris Fiorina, *Retrospective Voting in American National Elections* (New Haven: Yale, 1981).
19. Associated Press, "Two Polls Give Obama the Edge," *West County Times*, September 28, 2008.
20. Michael Shear, "McCain Vows to Go On Offensive Against Obama," *West County Times*, October 5, 2008.
21. Jim Kuhenhenn, "Palin Says Obama 'Palling Around' with Terrorists," *West County Times*, October 5, 2008.
22. Scott Shane, "Obama and 60s Bomber: A Look into Crossed Paths," *New York Times*, October 3, 2008.
23. Douglass Daniel, "Analysis: Palin's Words Carry Racial Tinge," *West County Times,* October 5, 2008.
24. David Lightman and William Douglas, "Analyst: Obama's Tax Plan Doesn't Qualify as Socialism," *West County Times,* October 23, 2008.
25. Michael Lewis-Beck, *Forecasting Elections* (Washington: CQ Press, 1992). See also the symposium edited by James Campbell, "Forecasting the 2008 National Election," *PS: Political Science and Politics* 41 (2008).

26. "Baraka Obama Will Win the Presidency, Political Scientists Forecast," http://www.britannica.com/blogs/2008/08/barack_obama_will_win-t.

27. Gary Langer, "Blacks Political Engagement Spikes: Though Racial Division Remain," http://abcnews.go.com/print?id=3143.

28. Krissah Williams Thompson, "In Mississippi, Deep-Rooted Doubt," *Washington Post*, September 28, 2008.

29. Adam Nossiter, "For South, A Waning Hold on National Politics," *New York Times*, November 10, 2008.

30. Thomas Schaller, *Whistling Past Dixie: How Democrats Can Win Without the South* (New York: Simon & Shuster, 2006).

CHAPTER 11

The Congress and the African American Quest for Universal Freedom

The framers of the Constitution intended for Congress to be the dominant branch of the government. Of the legislative power, John Locke had written, it "is not only the supreme power of the commonwealth, but sacred and unalterable in the hands where the community have once placed it."[1] Following Locke's logic the framers made the Congress the first branch of government (Article I), preceding the presidency (Article II) and the judiciary (Article III). Article I is also by far the longest of the three articles, specifying in detail the broad powers of the U.S. government.

Legislation is understood as a general rule of broad application *enacted by a broadly representative body*.[2] We emphasize the words to make the point that in democratic societies, legislation and representation are closely connected, such that a defining property of a legislative institution is the extent to which it fairly represents the people. The English philosopher John Stuart Mill stated the case for the necessary relationship between legislation, representation, and democracy in his 1869 book *Considerations on Representative Government*.

> In a really equal democracy, every or any section would be represented, not disproportionately, but proportionately. A majority of electors would always have a majority of the representatives but a minority of electors would always have a minority of representatives, man for man, they would be as fully represented as the majority; unless they are, there is not equal government, but government of inequality and privilege: one part of the people rule over the rest: There is a part whose fair and equal share and influence in representation is withheld from them contrary to the principle of democracy, which professes equality as its very root and foundation.[3]

The Representation of African Americans in Congress

Given that in a democracy the legislature should represent the people equally, a first question becomes, How representative of African Americans is the Congress? Political scientists usually measure the representativeness of a legislative institution on the basis of three criteria: descriptive, symbolic, and substantive.[4] *Descriptive representation* is the

181

extent to which the legislature looks like the people in a demographic sense. *Symbolic representation* concerns the extent to which people have confidence or trust in the legislature, and *substantive representation* asks whether the laws passed by the legislature correspond to the policy interests or preferences of the people. We discuss the extent to which Congress represents the substantive interests of African Americans later in this chapter. With respect to symbolic representation, African Americans, like white Americans, have relatively low levels of confidence or trust in Congress (see Chapter 3).[5]

Historically, the Congress has not been descriptively representative of African Americans. Of more than 11,000 persons who have served in the Congress, only 112 have been black (107 in the House, 5 in the Senate).[6] From 1787, the year of the first Congress, until 1870, no African American served in Congress. In 1870–1871 six blacks were seated in the House of Representatives. From the 1870s to 1891, blacks averaged two representatives in the House, and in the next decade there was only one black congressman to represent the nation's population of more than 8 million blacks. In 1901 George White of South Carolina became the last Reconstruction Era African American to serve in Congress. In his farewell speech, White told his white colleagues, "This, Mr. Chairman, is perhaps the Negroes' temporary farewell to the American Congress; but let me say like the Phoenix he will rise again. These parting words are in behalf of an outraged, heart broken, bruised and bleeding but God fearing people, faithful, industrious loyal, rising people—full of potential force."[7]

From 1901 to 1929 no blacks served in the Congress. In 1928 Oscar DePriest was elected from Chicago, and in 1944 Adam Clayton Powell was elected from Harlem. Until the post–civil rights era, only five blacks served in the House. Then in 1969 and again in 1992 there was a fairly rapid rise in black representation in the House, reaching an all-time high of 43 in 2006. The growth in black representation is a function of several factors: the concentration of blacks in highly segregated urban neighborhoods, the Supreme Court's "one person, one vote" decisions in *Baker* v. *Carr* and *Wesberry* v. *Sanders*, and the implementation of the 1965 Voting Rights Act.[8]

In the Senate's more than 200 years, only five blacks have served in it: Hiram Revels and Blanche K. Bruce from Mississippi during Reconstruction; Edward Brooke from Massachusetts, who served from 1966 to 1978; Carol Mosley Braun, elected in 1992 from Illinois but defeated for reelection in 1998; and Barack Obama, elected from Illinois in 2004. Senators are elected on a statewide basis, and since no state has a black majority, it has been very difficult for blacks to win Senate seats. Because of racist and white supremacist thinking, whites have been reluctant to vote for black candidates. Although blacks have made substantial progress in achieving fair and equitable representation in the House, the Congress, as Table 11.1 shows, is still best described as a body of middle-age, middle-class, white men. In the House and Senate, Asian Americans are reasonably represented, in part because they are a voting plurality in Hawaii. However, blacks and Latinos are not equitably represented; African Americans, for example, are 12 percent of the population but 1 percent of the Senate and 9 percent of the House. Women, who constitute more than half the population, are only 16 percent of the House and 13 percent of the Senate. These numbers for women are small, but they are much better than the numbers of a decade ago when there were only one or two female senators and women constituted only 5 percent of the House. The nation's major religious groups— Protestants, Catholics, and Jews—are equitably represented in both the House and the

Table 11.1 Selected Demographic Characteristics of Members of the 109th Congress, 2004–2006

PERCENTAGE POPULATION	DEMOGRAPHIC CHARACTERISTICS	HOUSE	SENATE[a]
	Race/ethnicity		
69.1	White	86%	95%
12.5	Black	9	1
12.5	Latino	4	2
3.6	Asian American	1	2
0.7	Native American[b]	0	0
	Religion		
62	Protestant	57	53
27	Catholic	29	24
2.5	Jewish	6	13
	Other[c]	8	12
	Education		
23	College	96	97
77	Noncollege	4	3
	Average Age		
32.8		55	60

[a]Senator Ben Nighthorse Campbell of Colorado, the Native American member, retired at the end of the 108th Congress.

[b]There is one Native American in the House: Congressman Tom Cole from Oaklahoma.

[c]The other religious faiths are mainly Mormon and Greek Orthodox.

Source: The Associated Press, "New Congress More Diverse," November 6, 2004.

Senate. (Jews to some extent are "overrepresented," constituting less than 3 percent of the population but about 6 percent of the House and 13 percent of the Senate.) In sum, the Congress is not a representative body insofar as its African American, Latino, and female citizens are concerned.

Congressional Elections and African Americans

Reapportionment and Redistricting

The Constitution requires that every ten years the government conduct a census, an "enumeration" of the population. The primary constitutional purpose of the census is to provide a basis for reapportioning seats in the House. The size of the House is fixed by law at 435. *Reapportionment* involves the allocation of these 435 seats among the 50 states on the basis of changes in population—for example, the movement of the population in the last four decades from the "snowbelt" states of the Midwest and Northeast to the "sunbelt" states of the South and West. After reapportionment, the states then engage in the process of *redistricting,* the allocation of seats within a state on the basis of populations within each congressional district, with each district containing roughly

700,000 persons. The census is therefore important as a basis of allocating political power among and within the states. This has particular implications for America's racial minorities since it is well known that the census regularly undercounts blacks and Latinos, thereby depriving them of a fair share of political power as well as other social and economic benefits that are allocated on the basis of population. In the 1990 census, an estimated 4.8 percent of the black population and 5.2 percent of the Latino population were not counted.[9] Although it is possible for the Census Bureau to "statistically adjust" the census count to include those left out, the Supreme Court has held that such an adjustment is not required by the Constitution.[10] However, for the 2000 census, the Census Bureau agreed to employ statistical sampling as a means to count those persons most often missed by traditional methods of counting. The Republican leadership in the House pledged to block this change, saying the plan violated the Constitution's requirement that there be an actual "enumeration" of the population; also, it would likely help Democrats by increasing the number of minorities and urban dwellers.

However, in January 1999 the Supreme Court ruled that federal law bars the use of statistical sampling for apportioning seats in the House. Instead, the Court, in a 5-4 decision upholding the ruling of a special three-judge federal district court in Richmond, Virginia, said that while sampling could be used for other purposes (such as redistricting state legislatures and allocating federal money to the states), Congress had mandated that an actual enumeration or "head count" be used in congressional reapportionment. The decision split the Court on ideological lines, with the four more liberal justices dissenting, holding that while sampling could not be a substitute for an enumeration it was a permissible "supplement" to "achieve the very accuracy that the census seeks and the Census Act itself demands."[11]

The 2000 census did include both the actual enumeration and a statistically adjusted figure based on sampling. Although statistical experts declared that the 2000 census was probably the most accurate ever, there was nevertheless an estimated undercount of 1.2 percent (about 3.3 million persons) of the overall population compared to 1.6 percent in 1990. It is estimated that 2.1 percent of blacks and 2.9 percent of Latinos were missed in the 2000 count.

Black Congressional Districts, Campaigns, and Elections

Of the 42 congressional districts represented by blacks in the House, four are majority white and the rest are either majority black or majority–minority (blacks and Latinos).[12] Each of these districts is represented by Democrats. Until 1992, virtually all the black majority districts were urban, northern, and disproportionately poor.[13] As a result of the 1992 redistricting, the large southern (52 percent of the total) and rural (25 percent) black population is now represented in the House (all the southern states except Arkansas send at least one black to the House).[14]

The black districts are overwhelmingly Democratic in party registration and invariably elect Democrats. Like most members of the House, once elected, blacks are routinely reelected. The *advantages of incumbency* make it virtually impossible to defeat an incumbent congressperson; more than 90 percent who seek reelection are reelected.

Finally, except for their race and the greater representation of women, blacks in Congress are quite similar to whites: well-educated, middle-class men. Women, however,

Members of the Congressional Black Caucus meeting with President Bush.   *Source:* Pablo Martinez Monsivais/AP Images

are better represented, constituting 31 percent of the black congressional delegation compared to about 10 percent among whites.[15]

The Color of Representation: Does Race Matter?

In 1993 Carol Swain in a controversial book *Black Faces, Black Interests: The Representation of African Americans in Congress* argued that white members of Congress could represent the interests of blacks as well as and in some cases, perhaps, better than blacks.[16] That is, she argued that taking into account a representative's party and region, whites in the House represented the black community as well as blacks. Swain's study, however, was limited, based on the roll-call votes of a limited number of congress people (nine blacks and four whites) during a two-year time frame. More comprehensive and detailed studies have disproven Swain's argument. Kenny Whitby in *The Color of Representation: Congressional Behavior and Black Interests* found that racial differences in congressional voting are more likely to show up when bills are amended than on the final roll-call votes studied by Swain. Studying congressional voting behavior from 1973 to 1992, Whitby found that race matters even after controlling for party and region.[17] In general, he found that the policy payoffs in the form of more effective antidiscrimination policies in education, employment, and housing are more likely to come from black than white representatives. David Canon in *Race, Redistricting and Representation: The Unintended Consequences of*

Black Majority Districts found that race matters in Congress, not just in terms of substantive voting but also in various forms of symbolic representation. For example, black members of the House are more likely than whites to make speeches concerning race (50.8 percent of the speeches by blacks compared to 12.8 percent of whites); more likely to sponsor and introduce bills dealing with race (42 percent for blacks, 5 percent whites); more likely to hire blacks for top staff positions (72.3 percent, 6.7 percent); and more likely to raise race issues in their press releases and newsletters (24.6 percent compared to 12.6 percent).[18] Finally, Katherine Tate in *Black Faces in the Mirror: African Americans in the U.S. Congress* substantiates the work of Whitby and Canon, finding that black members are the most reliable and consistent supporters of substantive black interests in Congress. She also found an important symbolic dimension to this representation in that in general black constituents feel they are better represented in Congress when their representatives are black.[19]

African American Power in the House

Power or influence in the House of Representatives is best gauged by committee and subcommittee assignments, seniority, and party leadership positions.[20] In addition, in the last two decades House members have increasingly attempted to exercise power outside the formal committee and party leadership positions by forming caucuses of like-minded members.

The Congressional Black Caucus: Increasing Size, Declining Solidarity

There are now more than 100 legislative caucuses in the House. These groups are organized by members with a common interest or policy agenda so that they can exchange research and information, develop legislative strategies, and act as a unified voting bloc to bargain in support of or against particular bills and amendments.[21]

The Congressional Black Caucus (CBC) is one of the oldest House caucuses, formed in 1969 as an outgrowth of the black power movement's call for racial solidarity and independent black organization. In addition to its role as an internal House legislative caucus, the CBC also plays an external role by forming coalitions with interest groups outside the Congress and operating as one of the two or three major African American interest organizations in Washington.[22] The work of the caucus includes such activities as lobbying the president, presenting various black legislative agendas and alternative budgets in floor debates, and holding its annual legislative weekends. The legislative weekends, held in the fall of each year, usually bring several thousand African American scholars, elected officials, and civil rights leaders to Washington to participate in panels and workshops on issues affecting African Americans.

Power in the House is allocated first on the basis of party. The majority party (the party with one more seat than the other) leads the House and its committees and establishes its agenda, deciding which bills and which, if any, amendments will be allowed to come to a vote. Thus, between 1995 and 2007 blacks exercised relatively little power in the House because the Republicans were the majority party. With the Democrats winning a majority in the 2006 elections African Americans are poised to exercise some leverage in fashioning the Party's legislative agenda. In addition with Democrats in the majority African Americans will chair five full committees and seventeen subcommittees.

However, even with the Democratic majority in the House the power of the Caucus will depend on its being a *unified* minority. Although the Caucus is still a relatively cohesive, liberal voting bloc, its unity or solidarity has declined as it has grown in size. When it was first organized in 1969 it had 13 members, all of whom represented urban areas generally in the North or West. It operated during its early history as a small, highly unified group that was a reliable source of voting cues for its members.[23] Today the Caucus has 42 members (including Senator Burris) and they represent diverse districts, with many in the rural South and others with substantial Latino populations.

Inevitably, this growth in size results in declining solidarity. Five members of the Caucus (Ford of Tennessee, Davis of Alabama, Scott and Bishop of Georgia, and Wynn of Maryland) were also members of the conservative Democratic Leadership Council, or the so-called House "Blue Dogs," the coalition of moderate–conservative southern Democrats. On several issues including the Iraq War, the bankruptcy bill (the credit card industry supported legislation that makes it virtually impossible for persons to completely liquidate their debts), and legislation lowering the estate tax, several Caucus members voted with the conservative, Republican majority.

The decline in Caucus solidarity is not surprising since it is axiomatic in politics that the larger a group the greater the likelihood of internal conflicts and divisions. For a minority group like the Caucus, however, any decline in solidarity represents a potential loss of power.

In the 2007 Democratic congressional primaries, one of the longest serving of these black "blue dogs"—Albert Wynn of Maryland—was defeated for renomination. Wynn, who had served in the House for 15 years, was defeated by Donna Edwards, an African American attorney. National liberal and labor organizations targeted Wynn and supported Edwards in an effort to send a message that moderate–conservative Democrats would be held accountable by their liberal constituents. Also, in 2007 the second Muslim was elected to the Congress. Andre Carson, an African American, was elected from Indianapolis to complete the unexpired term of his grandmother, Representative Julia Carson. The Carsons' district is 63 percent white, 29 percent black.

African Americans in the Congressional Power Structure

Party Leadership

The principal members of the Democratic Party power structure in the House are the speaker, majority leader, the majority whip, the deputy whips, the members of the Steering and Policy Committee (which makes committee assignments and establishes broad party policy), and the officers of the Democratic Caucus. From 1989 to 1991 when he resigned to become president of the United Negro College Fund, Pennsylvania Congressman Bill Gray served as majority whip, the number three leadership position behind the speaker and the majority leader. In 2004, Congressman James Clyburn was elected majority whip.

In 1999, third-term Congressman J. C. Watts of Oklahoma was elected chairman of the Republican Party Conference, the fourth-ranking position in the Republican leadership structure in the House. This was widely interpreted as a move by the party to reach out to black and other minority voters. Watts's selection marked the first time an African American had held a leadership position in the House Republican Party.

In 2002, however, Congressman Watts decided to retire from the Congress, leaving the Republican Party in Congress once again all white or, put another way, leaving the black congressional delegation entirely Democratic. Watts cited personal reasons for retirement (wanting to spend more time with family and to pursue business interests), but reportedly he privately complained that he was not adequately respected by some of his colleagues in the Republican leadership.[24]

Committees and Committee Leadership

In the 109th Congress, blacks served on every standing committee of the House except one (Natural Resources). In Table 11.2, data are displayed on black membership and seniority on the major or "power" committees of Congress and on those committees that are especially important to black interests. The major or power committees are the ones dealing with money: the Budget Committee; the Committees on Ways and Means (taxes) and Appropriations (spending); the Rules Committee; the Energy and Commerce Committee (because of its broad jurisdiction under the commerce clause); and the Armed Services Committee (because of the importance of military policy

Table 11.2 African American Members of the House, Assignments on Major/Power Committees and Committees of Special Interest to Blacks, 109th Congress, 2002–2006

MAJOR/POWER COMMITTEES	DEMOCRATIC MEMBERS	BLACK MEMBERS AND RANKS
Appropriations	29	Clyburn (19)[a]
		Jackson (23)
		Kilpatrick (24)
		Fattah (26)
		Bishop (28)
Armed Services	28	Meek (25)
Budget[b]	19	Ford (11)
		Scott (10)
		Majette (18)
Energy and Commerce	26	Towns (6)
		Rush (11)
		Wynn (15)
Rules	4	Hastings (4)
Ways and Means[c]	17	Rangel (1)
		Lewis (8)
		Tubbs-Jones (17)

(continued)

Table 11.2 *(continued)*

*COMMITTEES OF SPECIAL
INTEREST TO BLACKS*

Financial Services	32	Waters (3)
		Watt (8)
		Carson (10)
		Meek, G. (12)
		Lee (13)
		Ford (18)
		Clay (22)
		Scott, GA (31)
Education and Workforce	22	Owens (3)
		Payne (4)
		Davis (16)
Judiciary	16	Conyers (1)
		Waters (9)
		Watt (6)
		Jackson-Lee (8)
		Scott (VA) (5)
		Watt (7)
		Waters (10)

[a]The number in parentheses represents the member's rank or seniority among Democratic members of the committee.

[b]The Budget Committee prepares the annual congressional budget, setting targets for taxation, spending, and borrowing.

[c]In addition to its power to impose taxes on personal, corporate, and other income, the Ways and Means Committee also has responsibility for Social Security, Medicare, Medicaid, welfare, and international trade. Congressman William Jefferson of Louisiana was a member of the Ways and Means Committee, but was removed in 2006 by the Party Caucus after it was reported he was under investigation by the FBI for bribery.

and the size of the military budget). The Judiciary Committee is important to black interests because of its jurisdiction over civil rights legislation; the Financial Services Committee because of its jurisdiction over urban and housing policy; and the Education and Workforce Committee because of its jurisdiction over education, labor, and parts of welfare policy.

Table 11.2 shows that African Americans are represented on each of the major or power committees, and they are heavily represented on those committees of special relevance to black interests—Judiciary, Financial Services, and Education and Workforce. Blacks also chair one of the power committees, Ways and Means (arguably the most powerful committee in the Congress), and one of the interest committees, Judiciary. In addition, African Americans chair three other committees (Standards of Official Conduct, Homeland Security, and Administration) and 17 subcommittees. (The chair of Administration and Standards of Official Conduct died during the last Congress).

Because of the operation of the seniority system and the ability of African Americans to be routinely reelected to the Congress, black members have gained considerable power in the House (see Box 11.1).

Congressional Responsiveness to the African American Quest for Universal Rights and Freedom

Rights-Based Issues: From Arguing About Slavery to the Civil Rights Act of 1991

Like each of the major institutions of the American government, the Congress's response to the black demand for universal freedom and equality has been hesitant, tentative, and unstable. Interestingly, the first congressional response to the African American demand for universal freedom was a debate over whether the Congress should listen—simply hear—let alone respond to the demand for African freedom. From 1835 to 1844, Congress debated whether it should even receive African American petitions for freedom. Until 1836, black petitions to end slavery were received, printed in the record, and referred to committee. But in 1836 Congressman James Hammond of South Carolina demanded that these petitions not even be received by Congress because to do so was an unconstitutional infringement on slavery. For nine years the House debated this "gag rule," with the opponents (led by former president John Quincy Adams, by then a House member) arguing that to ban slave petitions was a violation of the First Amendment right of petition, which, they claimed, should be accorded even to slaves. In 1844, the House finally defeated the gag rule on slave petitions.[25]

Before Congress enacted the first wave of civil rights legislation during Reconstruction, it took three other actions dealing with the issue of slavery. First, in 1787 in the Northwest Ordinance Act, Congress banned slavery in the new territories of the upper Midwest, which prevented the spread of slavery into places like Illinois and Indiana.[26] Second, in 1808 Congress abolished the slave trade. Although this was an important law, the illegal importation of additional slaves actually continued until the Civil War.[27] Finally, in 1862 in the middle of the Civil War, Congress abolished slavery in the District of Columbia.

Congressional responsiveness to the African American agenda of universal rights and freedom occurred in two periods: the 1860s during Reconstruction and the 1960s during the civil rights movement. As Table 11.3 shows, from 1866 to 1875 Congress passed six civil rights bills including three civil rights enforcement acts. Between 1957 and 1968 the Congress passed five civil rights bills, including the crucially important Civil Rights Act of 1964, the Voting Rights Act of 1965, and the Fair Housing Act of 1968.

In many ways the civil rights laws of the 1960s simply duplicate those passed in the 1860s. The Supreme Court invalidated the 1860s laws as unconstitutional or declined to require their enforcement; thus, the Congress in the 1960s had to repass them, which again shows the tenuousness and instability of rights-based coalitions. Similarly, the Civil Rights Restoration Act of 1985 and the Civil Rights Act of 1991 were passed to overturn Supreme Court decisions that made parts of the 1964 act difficult to enforce (see Chapter 13). In addition to these major civil rights laws, Congress in the 1970s passed a series of amendments to the 1964 act allowing the government to engage in affirmative action to achieve equality in employment for African Americans, other minorities, and women.[28] (See Box 11.2.)

BOX 11.1   TERM LIMITS, SENIORITY, AND AFRICAN AMERICAN POWER IN THE HOUSE

For decades, more than 90 percent of the members of the House who have sought reelection have won. The advantages of incumbency—name recognition, access to the media, staff support, and campaign contributions—make it virtually impossible to defeat an incumbent congressperson. Even with the massive turnover in Congress after the Republican victory in 1994, 93 percent of the incumbents running for reelection won. As a result, in recent years a movement developed that would limit the terms of members of Congress by law (usually the proposal is that members of the House be limited to six 2-year terms and members of the Senate to two 6-year terms). The Supreme Court, in the 1995 case *U.S. Term Limits, Inc. v. Thornton,* held that the terms of members of Congress could be limited only by an amendment to the Constitution, not by actions of the states or the Congress. In 1995 the House voted on a term-limits amendment to the Constitution, but it failed to get the necessary two-thirds majority (227–204).

Proponents of term limits argue that members who serve long periods of time lose touch with their constituents back home, becoming "professional" rather than "citizen" legislators and eventually becoming the captives of the Washington interest group establishment. Opponents of term limits argue that it would result in an inexperienced Congress that could easily be dominated by special interest groups, the media, and the bureaucracy. Often overlooked in the debate on term limits is the effect on African American political power in the House. Black members of the House are more likely to be reelected than whites; as a result, they have greater seniority, and seniority translates into power in terms of committee leadership. Thus, blacks in the House hold major leadership positions on some of that body's most important committees and are the most senior Democrats on 17 House subcommittees. Not everyone in Washington is pleased with this development. After the Republican victory in 1994, two prominent Washington columnists, Cokie and Steven Roberts, wrote that blacks have too much power in the House and "accordingly, the Democratic leadership in the House will become increasingly weighted toward minorities and thus toward liberal ideas and principles. And to party moderates, this is exactly the wrong direction."[a]

It is the wrong direction, the Roberts argue, because the presence of so many blacks in powerful positions sends the wrong signal to suburban white voters. All African American Democratic members of the House voted against the term-limit amendment in 1995, perhaps because they saw it as a means to deprive them of power. The political scientist Bruce Oppenheimer wrote, "Although I would be among the first to resist conspiratorial explanations for the recent popularity of congressional term limits, it is ironic that one clear effect of its adoption would be to deprive nonwhites of the only power base advantage they currently have in American government."[b]

[a]Cokie and Steven Roberts, "Democrats Must Face Race Issue," *West County Times,* December 16, 1994, p. A11. On this point see also Andrew Taylor, "Liberal Wing Poised to Seize Control of Committees," *West County Times,* May 7, 2006; and Alan Gerber, "African American Congressional Careers and the Democratic House Delegation," *Journal of Politics* 58 (1996): 831–45.

[b]Bruce Oppenheimer, "House Term Limits: A Distorted Picture," *Social Science Quarterly* 76 (December 1995): 728.

Table 11.3 List of Civil Rights Laws Enacted by Congress: Reconstruction Era, Civil Rights Era, and Post–Civil Rights Era

RECONSTRUCTION ERA

Civil Rights Act, 1866

Civil Rights Act, 1870

Civil Rights Act, 1875

Enforcement Act, 1870

Enforcement Act, 1871

Enforcement Act, 1875

CIVIL RIGHTS ERA

Civil Rights Act, 1957

Civil Rights Act, 1960

Civil Rights Act, 1964

Voting Rights Act, 1965

Fair Housing Act, 1968

POST–CIVIL RIGHTS ERA

Equal Employment Opportunity Act of 1972

Civil Rights Restoration Act, 1988

Civil Rights Act of 1991

Civil Rights in the Republican Congress

When the Republicans took control of the Congress in 1995, black leaders expressed alarm that they might roll back civil rights gains, especially affirmative action. However, in 1998 both the House and Senate rejected amendments to the transportation bill that would have prohibited the use of a 10 percent "goal" in the allocation of contracts to minority- and female-owned businesses. The amendment was rejected in the Senate by a vote of 58 to 37, with all Democratic senators voting no except one (Senator Ernest Hollings of South Carolina), and with 15 of the 55 Republican Senators also opposing the amendment. In the House, the amendment was defeated by a vote of 225 to 194. All except three House Democrats opposed the amendment and it was also opposed by 29 Republicans. Note that this amendment was supported by Republican congressional leaders, including House Speaker Gingrich, who made a passionate floor speech calling on his colleagues to end this form of affirmative action.

Several weeks later the House also defeated by an even larger margin an amendment prohibiting colleges and universities from using affirmative action in their admission policies if they receive federal funds. The vote was 249 to 171. Although Republican leaders supported the amendment, 55 Republicans joined with 193 Democrats to defeat the legislation.[29]

The Renewal of the 1965 Voting Rights Act

The Voting Rights Act of 1965 and the Civil Rights Act of 1964 are the major legislative achievements of the 1960s civil rights movement. Unlike the 1964 act, several

BOX 11.2   TWO MASSACHUSETTS SENATORS[a] AND THE AFRICAN AMERICAN QUEST FOR UNIVERSAL FREEDOM

Massachusetts is often referred to as "freedom's birthplace" and as the "citadel of American liberalism." Whether this reputation is deserved or not, in Senator Charles Sumner and in Senator Edward "Ted" Kennedy,[a] Massachusetts has sent to the Senate two men who have distinguished themselves in the African American quest for universal freedom.

Frederick Douglass described Senator Sumner as the greatest friend the Negro people ever had in public life. Born in 1811, Sumner served in the Senate from 1852 until his death in 1874. During his career in the Senate he was that body's most outspoken champion of the freedom of the enslaved African. In an 1856 Senate speech he bitterly attacked two of his colleagues for their support of slavery. Two days later Congressman Preston Brooks entered the Senate chamber and nearly beat Sumner to death, arguing that his remarks were a libel on the South. After a three-year recovery period, Sumner returned to the Senate to continue his struggle for black freedom, both rights- and material-based.

Sumner made his greatest contribution to the African American freedom struggle after the Civil War. With Congressman Thaddeus Stevens, he led the fight in Congress for civil rights legislation and passage of the Fourteenth and Fifteenth Amendments. Stevens and Sumner were also responsible for the idea of "40 acres and a mule," introducing legislation to confiscate the slaveholders' plantations, divide them up, and give them to the slaves as compensation or reparation and as a means to punish the slaveholders for treason.

At the time of his death, Sumner was fighting for a civil rights bill that would have banned discrimination and segregation in every public place in the United States—from schools to churches, from cemeteries to hospitals. On his deathbed, surrounded by Frederick Douglass and other African American leaders, Sumner's last words were said to have been, "Take care of my civil rights bill—take care of it—you must do it."

One hundred years later another senator from Massachusetts took up Sumner's cause. Senator Edward Kennedy, elected to the Senate in 1962 to take the seat vacated by his brother when he became president, is the second most senior Democrat in the Senate. Throughout his more than four decades in the Senate, Kennedy has been a leader in the passage of every civil rights bill, from the Civil Rights Act of 1964 to the Civil Rights Act of 1991. Especially after the murder of his brother Robert in 1968, Kennedy made the cause of the poor and racially oppressed his cause. As the senior Democrat on both the Labor and Public Welfare Committee and the Judiciary Committee, he has led the fight for minimum wage legislation, national health insurance, immigration reform, and education and employment legislation. In 1993, his Labor and Public Welfare Committee was the only committee to report and send to the floor national health insurance legislation, largely due to his leadership as chair. In 1996 he was the floor leader of the fight to increase the minimum wage, to provide health coverage for laid-off workers, and to ban discrimination against homosexuals in employment.

Perhaps the Senate's most famous member, Kennedy is regarded as one of the body's most passionate and skilled legislators on issues of civil rights and social justice. In 1980

(continued)

BOX 11.2 continued

he challenged President Jimmy Carter for renomination, charging that the president had abandoned the liberal cause. After his loss to Carter, Kennedy returned to the Senate, where he became a leading opponent of the Reagan administration's civil rights and social welfare policies. Although his goal of succeeding his brother as president was not to be, he has left his mark, as there is no major piece of civil rights or liberal reform legislation of the last four decades that was not influenced by the senator from Massachusetts.

[a]On Sumner, see Frederick Blue, *Charles Sumner and the Conscience of the North* (New York: Norton, 1976); and on Kennedy, see Adam Clymer, *Edward M. Kennedy: A Biography* (New York: Morrow, 1999).

provisions of the Voting Rights Act are temporary, requiring periodic renewals by the Congress. These provisions were last renewed for 25 years in 1982 and were set to expire in 2007. Of the provisions requiring renewal or "reauthorization," two are controversial. The first is Section 5, which requires states with a history of racial discrimination to apply to the U.S. Justice Department or the U.S. District Court in Washington before making any change in their election laws or procedures. The second controversial provision is Section 203 (added when the act was renewed in 1975) requiring jurisdictions with large numbers of foreign-language-speaking persons to provide multilingual ballots. The so-called "preclearance" requirements of Section 5 cover several southern states and parts of several northern states, including California and New York.

President Bush and the leaders of both parties in the House and Senate enthusiastically endorsed renewal of the act for 25 more years. (The House bill to renew the act was "HR9," indicating it was among the Republican leaders' top ten priorities). However, some southern conservative Republicans in the House and Senate objected to renewal of Section 5, claiming preclearance is unnecessary because their states no longer engage in racial discrimination. They also allege that Section 5 is unconstitutional because it results in the creation of legislative districts based on race, and is discriminatory against the South. Conservative Republicans also objected to Section 203, arguing, in the words of Iowa Congressman Steven King, that use of multilingual ballots "encourages the linguistic division of the nation."[30] African American and Latino leaders strongly supported renewal of the act, contending that there is still evidence of racial discrimination at the polls, and that the act is responsible for the steady increase in the number of black and Latino elected officials.

In the summer of 2006 the House approved renewal of the act by 309 to 33 (all negative votes cast by Republicans). An amendment to delete Section 5 was defeated 302 to 18 and an amendment to drop Section 203 was defeated 238 to185. Two weeks after the House approved the bill, the Senate passed it 98 to 0.

Restoring Civil Rights

Twice before (in 1988 and 1991), Congress passed civil rights laws designed to overturn unfavorable Supreme Court decisions: decisions that made it difficult to enforce the Civil

Rights Act of 1964. In 2008, two similar bills were proposed. Both were introduced by Senator Edward Kennedy.

The first was the Fair Pay Restoration Act. In 2007, in *Ledbetter* v. *Goodyear Tire* the Court in a 5-4 decision ruled that employees complaining of pay discrimination had to file the charges within 180 days of the initial act of discrimination. But as Justice Ruth Bader Ginsberg noted in her dissent, often an employee would not know it when the initial act of discrimination takes place, because salaries and raises of employees are often confidential. (Lilly Ledbetter, the plaintiff in the case, did not learn that she was given smaller raises than her male counterparts until years later.) The Fair Pay Restoration Act would over-turn the Court's decision by establishing that the 180-day deadline starts when the employee receives the unequal pay, not when the employer made the decision to discriminate. The Act also requires that the 180 days begin anew with each discriminatory paycheck. President Bush threatened to veto the bill and Republicans in the Senate used a filibuster to keep it from coming to a vote.

The second bill, the Civil Rights Act of 2008, was introduced in the House by Congressman John Lewis. It would reverse the Court's decision in *Alexander* v. *Sandoval* (see Chapter 13, p. 242) and restore to individuals the right to sue in cases of institutional racism as well as individual discrimination, whether it involves race, age, gender, ethnicity, or disability. The House easily passed the bill but, like the fair pay bill, it was blocked in the Senate.

Material-Based Rights: From 40 Acres and a Mule to the Humphrey-Hawkins Full Employment Act

If Congress has been reluctant and tentative in terms of responsiveness to the rights-based black agenda, it has been even less responsive to the material-based agenda. The Constitution, after adoption of the Fourteenth Amendment, may be interpreted to guarantee universal civil and political freedoms; however, many, perhaps most, Americans tend to think that access to material benefits (land, health care, jobs) should not be universal but rather individual. That is, in a free enterprise, capitalist system, it is up to each individual to get his own land, health care, and employment. This view was expressed very clearly by President Andrew Johnson when he vetoed the Freedmen's Bureau Act, which, in addition to granting blacks land, also provided other welfare and educational benefits to the former slaves. In his veto message the president wrote, "The idea on which the slaves were assisted to freedom was that on becoming free they would be a self-sustaining population. Any legislation that shall imply they are not expected to attain a self-sustaining condition must have a tendency injurious alike to their character and their prospects."[31] The ideas of President Andrew Johnson were echoed by Newt Gingrich and Bill Clinton, who argued that welfare is injurious to the character, individual responsibility, and sense of self-reliance of the African American community.

The Humphrey-Hawkins Act

The 1963 March on Washington during which Dr. King gave his famous "I Have a Dream" speech was a march for "jobs and freedom." However, as we pointed out in

Chapter 7, rights-based demands usually take precedence over material-based ones. Thus, the demand for jobs had to wait for the gaining of freedom in the form of the 1960s civil rights laws. But the problem of joblessness was clearly a major problem in the African American community, especially in the cities of the North where blacks already had basic civil and political rights. Since the end of the Depression, African Americans have never experienced full employment (see Chapter 15). In general, in the post–World War II era, black unemployment has been twice that of whites, generally at about 10 percent of the adult labor force.[32] Thus, at the end of the civil rights era, the material-based demand for jobs—full employment guaranteed by the federal government—became the principal African American demand, the priority item on the black agenda.

At the time of his death in 1968, Dr. King was planning to lead a multiracial coalition of poor people to march on Washington, the principal demand of which was a guaranteed job or income. After Dr. King's death this demand for jobs became the principal priority of African American interest groups.[33] In the late 1960s the Congressional Black Caucus, under the leadership of California Congressman Augustus Hawkins, developed a broad coalition of blacks, liberal, labor, and religious groups to try to persuade Congress to pass legislation "guaranteeing a job to all willing and able to work." Once before, in 1946, a broad liberal–labor coalition had sought similar legislation. By the time the bill was passed as the Employment Act of 1946, however, the job guarantee provision had been deleted and the act was little more than a policy-planning mechanism, creating the President's Council of Economic Advisors and a Joint Economic Committee in the Congress.[34]

Critics of the Employment Act of 1946, including business leaders, academic economists, the mainstream media, and conservative politicians, argued that the idea of full employment guaranteed by the federal government was "socialistic," "anti-free enterprise," "utopian," "un-American," and would result in "runaway inflation." Similar criticisms were made of the 1978 legislation introduced by Congressman Hawkins and former vice president Senator Hubert Humphrey. The bill, "The Full Employment and Balanced Growth Act," as originally introduced provided each American citizen with a legal right or entitlement to a job and required the Congress, if necessary, to create public-sector jobs if an individual could not find a job in the private economy. By the time the bill was passed and signed by President Carter, these provisions, as was the case in 1946, had been deleted, making the bill little more than a symbolic statement of principles.[35]

In the Clinton administration, the black unemployment rate fell below 10 percent for the first time since the Vietnam War (the comparable white unemployment rate was below 4 percent). Generally, economists have considered 5–5.5 percent unemployment to be "full employment"—the rate reached during the Clinton administration. But this leaves large numbers of adult blacks unemployed. Thus, even in relatively good economic times the African American community remains in a recession. The fate of the Humphrey-Hawkins Act suggests that there is little that can be done about it. We discuss this problem in Chapter 15, which deals with domestic public policy.

FACES AND VOICES IN THE STRUGGLE FOR UNIVERSAL FREEDOM

JOHN LEWIS (1940–)

John Lewis's contribution to universal freedom and equality derives from his leadership of the SNCC (the Student Nonviolent Coordinating Committee) during the civil rights movement and his work in Congress. Born in Troy, Alabama, Lewis was inspired to join the civil rights movement in 1958 after meeting Dr. Martin Luther King Jr. In 1961 Lewis was among the founding members of the SNCC, a minority–majority coalition of black and white college students. In 1963 he was elected chairman of the SNCC. The SNCC was the most radical of the civil rights organizations, and the young women and men in the group displayed extraordinary courage in confronting vicious racists throughout the South. But of all the brave people in the SNCC, perhaps none was more courageous than Lewis. In 1961 he was beaten unconscious in Montgomery, Alabama, on one of the first freedom rides. In 1965 he suffered a similar fate as he led a march from Selma to Montgomery. Arrested more than 40 times, Lewis always responded nonviolently and with expressions of Christian love. Decades later, reflecting on Lewis's work in the civil rights movement, *Time* magazine referred to him as a "living saint."

Source: Ric Feld/AP Images

In 1986 Lewis was elected to Congress from Atlanta, forging a minority–majority coalition composed of 90 percent of the white vote and 40 percent of the black vote. In the House he continued to emphasize coalition building. His status as a genuine American hero facilitated his capacity to build multiracial coalitions. A member of the powerful Ways and Means Committee, Lewis has devoted much of his time to persuading the Congress to recognize the contributions of African Americans and the civil rights movement to American history. Among his achievements are the establishment of a Washington memorial to Dr. King and a national museum of African American history. In 1999 he wrote a memoir, *Walking with the Wind: A Memoir of the Movement.*

Summary

Congress as a legislative body in theory should represent all the people of the United States. Historically, the American Congress has not represented its black citizens in a fair and equitable way. Although some progress has been made in enhancing the representation of blacks in Congress in the last two decades, they are still not equitably represented, especially in the Senate, where only one black serves and only five have served in the more than 200-year history of that body. Although African Americans are not equitably represented in Congress, because they are routinely reelected through the operation of the seniority system, blacks in the House have accumulated considerable power in terms of positions of committee leadership. In two periods—the 1860s and 1960s—Congress has responded to the black quest for universal freedom by passing several major civil rights bills. However, Congress has been less responsive to the African American quest for material rights and benefits such as land in the 1860s and jobs in the 1970s.

Selected Bibliography

Baker, Ross. *House and Senate,* 2nd ed. New York: Norton, 1995. A comparative analysis of the two houses focusing on how the differences in their sizes affect their operations.

Barone, Michael, and Grant Ujifusa. *The Almanac of American Politics 2004.* Washington, DC: National Journal, 2005. The biannual compilation of data on the districts and members of the House and Senate.

Berg, John. *Unequal Struggle: Class, Gender and Race in the U.S. Congress.* Boulder, CO: Westview Press, 1994. A perceptive analysis of how the structure of the capitalist economy constrains progressive action that would benefit minorities, workers, and women.

Canon, David. *Race, Redistricting and Representation.* Chicago: University of Chicago Press, 1999. A comprehensive analysis of how blacks in Congress more effectively represent black interests than whites.

Champagne, Richard, and Leroy Rieselbach. "The Evolving Congressional Black Caucus: The Reagan–Bush Years." In Huey Perry and Wayne Parant, eds., *Blacks and the American Political System.* Gainesville: University Press of Florida, 1995. A historical survey of the Caucus from its founding in 1969 to the last years of the Bush administration.

Congressional Quarterly. *Origins and Development of Congress.* Washington, DC: Congressional Quarterly, 1976. A concise account of the history of Congress.

Congressional Quarterly. *Powers of Congress.* Washington, DC: Congressional Quarterly, 1976. A concise overview of the powers of Congress.

Graham, Hugh Davis. *The Civil Rights Era: Origins and Development of National Policy.* New York: Oxford University Press, 1990. A comprehensive study of the passage and implementation of the 1960s civil rights laws.

Jones, Charles E. "An Overview of the Congressional Black Caucus, 1970–85." In F. Jones et al., eds., *Readings in American Political Issues.* Dubuque, IA: Kendall/Hunt, 1987. An overview of the Caucus's operations from its founding through the middle Reagan years.

Loevy, Robert, ed. *The Civil Rights Act of 1964: The Passage of the Law That Ended Racial Segregation.* New York: SUNY Press, 1996. Firsthand, behind-the-scenes accounts of how the Civil Rights Act was passed.

Singh, Robert. *The Congressional Black Caucus: Racial Politics in the U.S. Congress.* Thousand Oaks, CA: Sage, 1998. An analysis of the limited effectiveness of the Caucus as a lobby for black interests in Congress.

Smith, Robert C. "Financing Black Politics: A Study of Congressional Elections." *Review of Black Political Economy* 17 (1988): 5–30. A study of the role of money in the election of blacks to Congress.

Swain, Carol. *Black Faces, Black Interests: The Representation of African American Interests in Congress.* Cambridge, MA: Harvard University Press, 1993. A controversial analysis suggesting that whites in Congress represent the interests of blacks as well as blacks do.

Tate, Katherine. *Black Faces in the Mirror: African Americans and Their Representatives in Congress.* Princeton: Princeton University Press, 2003. A study of black House members and the symbolic and substantive impact of their representation.

Wilson, Woodrow. *Congressional Government: A Study in American Politics.* Gloucester, MA: Peter Smith, 1956. The 28th president's still-insightful study of how the organization and procedures of Congress make it an inefficient, irresponsible, and ineffective legislative institution.

Notes

1. John Locke, *The Second Treatise of Government,* edited by Thomas Peardon (Indianapolis: Bobbs-Merrill, 1952): 75.
2. Benjamin Akzin, "Legislation: Nature and Function," *International Encyclopedia of the Social Sciences* (New York: Free Press, 1972): 223.
3. John Stuart Mill, *Considerations on Representative Government* (Indianapolis: Bobbs-Merrill, 1869, 1952): 146.
4. Hanna Pitkin, *The Concept of Representation* (Berkeley: University of California Press, 1972): 5.
5. In a 1995 survey, only 14 percent of Americans said they have a "great deal" or "quite a lot" of confidence in Congress. See *Why Don't Americans Trust the Government?* (Cambridge, MA: *The Washington Post*/Kaiser Family Foundation/Harvard University Survey Project, 1996): 3. For detailed data on African American attitudes toward Congress, refer to chap. 3, Table 3.3.
6. For a list and biographical and related information on each person who has served in the Congress, see *Biographical Directory of the American Congress, 1774–1996* (Washington, DC: Congressional Quarterly, 1998).
7. Quoted in Rayford Logan, *The Betrayal of the Negro* (New York: Collier Books, 1965): 98.
8. In *Baker* v. *Carr* (369 U.S. 186, 1962), the Supreme Court held that the Fourteenth Amendment's equal protection clause required that state legislative districts be equal in population, and that each legislator represent roughly the same number of people. In *Wesberry* v. *Sanders* (376 U.S. 1, 1964), the Court applied this equality in representation principle to congressional districts.

9. Linda Greenhouse, "Supreme Court Agrees to Hear Case on Government's Refusal to Adjust Census," *New York Times,* September 28, 1995, p. A14.

10. *Wisconsin* v. *City of New York* #94-1614, 1996 (slip opinion).

11. Linda Greenhouse, "In Blow to Democrats, Court Says Census Must Be by Actual Count," *New York Times on the Web* (January 26, 1999).

12. Congresswoman Eleanor Holmes Norton, who is black, represents the District of Columbia. Each of the U.S. territories—Puerto Rico, Guam, the Virgin Islands, and American Samoa—are allowed to send delegates to the House. These delegates are allowed to vote in committees and participate in floor debates but they are not allowed to vote on the floor. The delegate from the Virgin Islands is also black.

13. Robert C. Smith, "The Black Congressional Delegation," *Western Political Quarterly* 34 (June 1981): 204–5.

14. David Bositis, *The Congressional Black Caucus in the 103rd Congress* (Washington, DC: Joint Center for Political and Economic Studies, 1994): 10–12.

15. Ibid.

16. Carol Swain, *Black Faces, Black Interests: The Representation of African Americans in Congress* (Cambridge: Harvard University Press, 1993).

17. Kenny Whitby, *The Color of Representation: Congressional Behavior and Black Interests* (Ann Arbor: University of Michigan Press, 1998): 110–111.

18. David Canon, *Race, Redistricting and Representation: The Unintended Consequences of Black Majority Districts* (Chicago: University of Chicago Press, 1999): 189, 191, 209, and 219.

19. Katherine Tate, *Black Faces in the Mirror: African Americans and Their Representatives in the US Congress* (Princeton: Princeton University Press, 2003). Recent research also shows that black voters attach less significance to descriptive representation but are more likely than whites to contact black members of Congress. See Claudine Gay, "Spirals of Trust: The Effect of Descriptive Representation on Relationships Between Citizens and Their Government," *American Journal of Political Science* 46 (2000): 714–32.

20. Richard Fenno, "The Internal Distribution of Influence: The House," in David Truman, ed., *The Congress and America's Future* (Englewood Cliffs, NJ: Prentice Hall, 1965): 52.

21. Susan Webb Hammond, Daniel Mulhollan, and Arthur Stevens, "Informal Congressional Caucuses and Agenda Setting," *Western Political Quarterly* 38 (1985): 583–605; and Burdett Loomis, "Congressional Caucuses and the Politics of Representation," in Lawrence Dodd and Bruce Oppenheimer, eds., *Congress Reconsidered* (Washington, DC: Congressional Quarterly, 1981): 204–20.

22. On the Congressional Black Caucus's origins and evolution, see Charles Jones, "An Overview of the Congressional Black Caucus," in Franklin Jones et al., eds., *American Political Issues* (Dubuque, IA: Kendall/Hunt 1987): 219–40; Richard Champagne and Leroy Rieselbach, "The Evolving Congressional Black Caucus," in Huey Perry and Wayne Parant, eds., *Blacks and the American Political System* (Gainesville: University Press of Florida, 1995): 130–61; and Robert Singh, *The Congressional Black Caucus: Racial Politics in the U.S. Congress* (Thousand Oaks, CA: Sage, 1998).

23. Arthur B. Levy and Susan Stoudinger, "Sources of Voting Cues for the Congressional Black Caucus," *Journal of Black Studies* 7 (1976): 29–46.

24. Juliet Eilperin, "GOP's J. C. Watts Will Leave Congress," *West County Times,* July 2, 2002.

25. The story of the battle to lift the gag rule on slave petitions is told in William Lee Miller, *Arguing About Slavery: The Great Battle in the United States Congress* (New York: Knopf, 1995).

26. William Freehling, "The Founding Fathers and Slavery," *American Historical Review* 77 (1972): 87. To get around the law, Illinois and Indiana passed black indentured servant laws; these, although not law, in effect legalized African slavery.

27. Ibid.

28. Robert C. Smith, *We Have No Leaders: African Americans in the Post–Civil Rights Era* (Albany: SUNY Press, 1996): chap. 6. The Senate during the 1970s also killed in close votes or blocked through filibusters House-passed bills that would have banned school busing for purposes of school desegregation.

29. A "dear colleague" letter from J. C. Watts, then the only House black Republican, was said to have been influential in persuading some Republican members to oppose the amendment. See Juliet Eilperin, "House Defeats Bill Targeting College Affirmative Action," *Washington Post,* May 7, 1997, p. A4.

30. Charles Babington, "GOP Rebellion Stops Voting Rights Act," *Washington Post,* June 22, 2007.

31. Veto message of President Andrew Johnson, The Freedmen Bureau's Act, February 19, 1966, as reprinted in Amilcar Shabazz, ed., *The Forty Acres Documents* (Baton Rouge: House of Songhay, 1994): 84.

32. On black joblessness and its effects on the origins of the so-called black underclass, see William Wilson, *The Truly Disadvantaged* (Chicago: University of Chicago Press, 1987).

33. C. Hunter-Gault, "Black Leaders Agree Full Employment Is Overriding Issue of the 1970s," *New York Times,* August 31, 1977, p. A1.

34. Stephen K. Bailey, *Congress Makes a Law: The Story Behind the Employment Act of 1946* (New York: Vintage Books, 1964).

35. For a detailed case study of the Humphrey-Hawkins Act, see Smith, *We Have No Leaders,* chap. 7.

CHAPTER 12

The Presidency and the African American Quest for Universal Freedom

My paramount object in this struggle is to save the union, and is not either to save or destroy slavery—If I could save the union without freeing any slave I would do it, and if I could save it by freeing all the slaves I would do it; and if I could save it by freeing some and leaving others alone I would also do that—what I do about slavery and the colored race, I do because I believe it helps to save the union—I shall do less whenever I shall believe what I am doing hurts the cause, and I shall do more whenever I shall believe doing more will help the cause—I shall try to correct errors when shown to be errors; and I shall adopt new views so fast as they shall appear to be true views—I have here stated my purpose according to my view of official duty; and I intend no modification of my oft-expressed personal wish that all men everywhere could be free.[1]

—Abraham Lincoln (1862)

We begin this chapter with the famous quotation from Abraham Lincoln's letter to newspaper editor Horace Greeley. We do so first because Lincoln was the first American president to deal in a positive, antiracist way with the African American quest for universal freedom. Second, in his timid, cautious, moderate approach to dealing with the freedom of African Americans, Abraham Lincoln is the paradigmatic president, setting an example—a pattern or model—for the handful of other American presidents who have dealt in a positive way with the African American freedom quest.[2]

Abraham Lincoln: The Paradigmatic President

Horace Greeley, a former congressman and liberal reform leader (best known for his famous saying, "Go West, young man"), urged President Lincoln to turn the Civil War into a moral crusade against slavery. Lincoln refused. Writing to Greeley that while he personally opposed slavery and supported universal freedom for all men everywhere, his principal objective in the war, according to his view of "official duty" as president, was to save the Union, and that what he did about slavery was secondary to this "paramount objective." What President Lincoln was saying and what all other American presidents from George

Washington to George W. Bush have said is that the problem of African American freedom must take second place to what is good for the nation—the Union—as a whole.

Lincoln, as a recent biographer shows in detail, was a skilled politician, despite his reputation as a back-country lawyer from Illinois.[3] Thus, he might also have said that what he did about slavery was also secondary to what was good for him as a politician in terms of public opinion (white public opinion) and his chances for reelection. While American presidents perhaps should attempt to lead public opinion on issues important to the nation's well-being—and occasionally some have done so—most have not, choosing instead to follow rather than lead. This may be an enduring dilemma of the American democracy on all kinds of issues but especially on issues of race and racism, where Bryce's description of presidential leadership is apt: "timid in advocacy . . . infertile in sugges-tion . . . always listening for the popular voice, always afraid to commit himself to a point of view which may turn out unpopular."[4] Alexis de Tocqueville's *Democracy in America*, published in 1835, is generally considered the most perceptive and prophetic book ever written on the subject of America's democracy. In it he argued that universal freedom and equality for blacks and whites were unlikely to occur in any country, but it was especially unlikely in the United States precisely because of its democracy. Tocqueville wrote:

> I do not imagine that the white and black races will ever live in any country upon an equal footing. But I believe the difficulty to be still greater in the United States than elsewhere. . . . A despot who should subject the Americans and their former slaves to the same yoke, might perhaps succeed in commingling the races, but as long as the American democracy remains at the head of affairs, no one will undertake so difficult a task; and it may be foreseen that the freer the white population of the United States becomes, the more isolated it will remain.[5]

One hundred fifty years after Tocqueville's pessimistic assessment, political scientist Richard Riley writes of the history of the presidency and the African American struggle for freedom:

> These incentive structures made it extremely unlikely that someone fervently commit-ted to racial equality would rise through the popularly based electoral process to the presidency in the first place, or that, once there he or she would feel free (or compelled) to invest presidential power in the controversial enterprise. . . . At bottom, on the ques-tion of African American rights, the presidency became an agency of change only when movements for equality had successfully reoriented the incumbent's perception of those role requirements, by preparing public opinion and illuminating the risks of inequality in periods of heightened danger to the nation's peace and security.[6] (See Box 12.1.)

Lincoln, Emancipation, and Colonialization

Historian George Fredrickson describes President Lincoln as a "pragmatic white supremacist."[7] Throughout his public career, Lincoln opposed slavery—because he thought it was morally wrong but also because he thought it was economically unwise, favoring instead "free labor on free soil."[8] But Lincoln also was a white supremacist, holding that the African people were "inferior in color and perhaps moral and intel-lectual endowment."[9] While Lincoln was antiracist in his attitudes toward slavery, he was racist in the sense that he, like the overwhelming majority of northern whites, opposed social and political equality for blacks. Whether Lincoln's views on racial

BOX 12.1 EXECUTIVE POWER, EXECUTIVE ORDERS, AND CIVIL RIGHTS[a]

Executive orders have been frequently employed by American presidents in the development of civil rights policy. Although the legislative power is vested exclusively in the Congress, presidents since Lincoln have claimed the right to issue directives of broad and general application that have the same legal effect as a law passed by Congress. Presidents trace their authority to engage in this kind of quasi-legislative activity to the general grant of the "executive power" to the president and to the command of Article II: "He shall take care that the laws be faithfully executed." The Supreme Court has upheld this broad interpretation of presidential power by holding that executive orders have the full force of law unless they conflict with a specific provision of the Constitution or of the law. Presidents use executive orders to establish policies when Congress refuses to do so. For example, when Congress refused to pass legislation prohibiting businesses from firing workers who go on strike, President Clinton issued an executive order prohibiting businesses with government contracts from doing so (most large corporations and many small companies have contracts with the federal government to deliver products or services).[b]

Until the 1960s, Congress refused to legislate in the area of civil rights; thus, presidents, beginning with Franklin Roosevelt, began to use executive orders as a way to get around congressional inaction on civil rights policy. Here are the most important executive orders (E.O.s) dealing with civil rights:

E.O. 8802 (1941): Establishes policy of nondiscrimination in employment by companies with defense contracts and creates the Committee on Fair Employment Practices—Franklin Roosevelt

E.O. 9980 (1948): Establishes policy of nondiscrimination in government employment and creates a Fair Employment Board within the Civil Service Commission—Harry Truman

E.O. 9981 (1948): Establishes policy of nondiscrimination in the armed forces and creates the President's Committee on Equality of Treatment and Opportunity in Armed Services—Harry Truman[c]

E.O. 10479 (1953): Establishes Government Contract Committee to ensure that government contractors and subcontractors comply with nondiscrimination provisions in employment—Dwight Eisenhower

E.O. 10925 (1961): Establishes President's Committee on Equal Employment Opportunity and requires government contractors to take "affirmative action to ensure that applicants are treated equally during employment, without regard to their race, creed, color or national origin"—John Kennedy

E.O. 11063 (1962): Prohibits discrimination in federally assisted housing and creates President's Committee on Equal Housing—John Kennedy

(continued)

BOX 12.1 *continued*

E.O. 11246 (1965): Requires government contractors to take affirmative action as a prerequisite to the award of a contract and requires the Labor Department to enforce the order—Lyndon Johnson

E.O. 11245 Revised (1971): Requires government contractors to develop affirmative action plans with goals and timetables for hiring, training, and promoting African Americans and other minorities—Richard Nixon[d]

Executive orders are an easy way for a president to establish public policy; however, Congress, if it wishes, may vote to overturn such orders. Since they are the policy decisions of a single individual, what one president gives, another may take away by a simple "stroke of his pen."

[a]On the use of executive orders to make civil rights policy from the Roosevelt to the Johnson administration, see Ruth Morgan, *The President and Civil Rights: Policy Making by Executive Order* (New York: St. Martin's Press, 1970).

[b]A three-judge federal appeals court in Washington ruled that President Clinton's striker replacement order was illegal because it conflicted with federal labor law. The administration declined to appeal this ruling to the Supreme Court, fearing the conservative court might issue a sweeping ruling undermining the president's power to issue executive orders. See "Clinton Accepts Defeat on Strikers' Protection," *San Francisco Chronicle,* September 10, 1996, p. A9.

[c]President Truman based this order on his authority as commander-in-chief as well as the executive power and the "take care" clause.

[d]This order is the basis and model for the affirmative action programs and policies discussed in Box 12.3.

equality were sincere or simply politically expedient is not known. However, as Frederick Douglass said, "Clearly, if opposition to black equality constituted a strong and general conviction of the white community, Lincoln would be prepared to accept it as a fact of life, not readily altered even if morally wrong."[10] (See Box 12.2.)

As Lincoln told Greeley in his letter, if he could save the Union without freeing any slave he would do it; if he could do it by freeing some he would do it; and if he could do it by freeing some and leaving others alone he would do that. As the war progressed, Lincoln eventually concluded that to save the Union, he must *promise* freedom to *some* of the slaves. Thus, on January 1, 1863, the president, using his authority as commander in chief of the army and navy, issued the Emancipation Proclamation. The Proclamation was issued as a war measure, a measure necessary to win the war. Lincoln called it a "fit and necessary war measure for suppressing said rebellion."[11] The Emancipation Proclamation applied only to those parts of the country under Confederate control—"the states and parts of states . . . wherein the people are this day in rebellion."[12] It specifically exempted Union border slave states such as Maryland and those parts of the South controlled by the Union army (New Orleans, for example). Thus, at the time the Emancipation Proclamation was issued, it freed very few slaves.[13] Rather, it was important as a war measure to encourage blacks in the South to rise and join the struggle because once the war was won, the Proclamation promised that they "henceforward shall be free." In addition to being a war measure, the Proclamation had a diplomatic purpose, which was to encourage European support for the Union cause by transforming the war into a moral crusade against slavery.

Lincoln's use of the commander-in-chief clause to promise freedom to the slaves was unprecedented and of questionable constitutionality since it may have violated the Fifth

BOX 12.2   THE FIRST THIRTEENTH AMENDMENT[a]

As the prospects of secession and civil war increased, the House and Senate appointed special committees to investigate the situation and make recommendations that might avoid war. Among the recommendations proposed by the House committee was an amendment to the Constitution that would have prohibited any amendment to the Constitution granting the Congress the power to interfere in any way with slavery in any state. The text of the amendment read:

> No amendment shall be made to the Constitution which will authorize or give to Congress the Power to abolish or interfere, within any state, with the domestic institutions thereof, including that of persons held to labor or service by the laws of said state.

This extraordinary amendment, intended to freeze slavery into the Constitution forever, was adopted on March 2, 1861, by a Congress that was overwhelmingly northern, since by that time the senators and representatives from seven southern states that had already seceded were not present. President Lincoln took the extraordinary and completely unnecessary step of personally signing the amendment, the first time a president has signed a constitutional amendment. Three states—Ohio, Illinois, and Maryland—quickly ratified the amendment. However, the attack one month later on Fort Sumter that brought on the Civil War ended any prospect of preserving the Union by preserving slavery, and no other state ratified this first Thirteenth Amendment. Ironically, the second Thirteenth Amendment, adopted four years later, abolished slavery throughout the United States. (Lincoln also signed this amendment.)

[a]For a history of the first Thirteenth Amendment and an analysis of whether it would have been constitutional if it had been ratified, see Mark Brandon, "The 'Original' Thirteenth Amendment and the Limits to Formal Constitutional Change," in Sanford Levinson, ed., *Responding to Imperfection: The Theory and Practice of Constitutional Amendment* (Princeton, NJ: Princeton University Press, 1995).

Amendment provision against the "taking of private property without just compensation."[14] The Thirteenth Amendment, however, settled the question of the constitutionality of the Proclamation. What should be done with the African Americans, once they were free, became the central question before the president and the country.

Lincoln's position was similar to that of Thomas Jefferson and it was clear and long-standing: colonialization. Once freed, the Africans should be deported out of the country. In his first message to Congress, Lincoln urged recognition of Liberia and Haiti and colonialization of blacks there or in some other places where the climate is "congenial to them."[15] Why colonialization? Why not instead integration and universal freedom? Lincoln's response was public opinion, telling a delegation of black leaders at the White House that "insurmountable white prejudice made racial equality impossible in the United States."[16] And "on this broad continent, not a single man of your race is made the equal of a single man of ours. Go where you are treated the best and the ban is still on you."[17] Colonialization was an impractical scheme, costly and complex. Thus, nothing ever came of it although Lincoln supported it until the day of his death.

Lincoln was the first president to act decisively in favor of African American freedom, but his actions were partial (promising limited rather than universal freedom), limited by his own prejudices, by public opinion, and by the exigencies of winning the war. Lincoln

President Lincoln reading the draft of the Emancipation Proclamation to his cabinet on July 22, 1862.   *Source:* Missouri Historical Society, Photographs and prints Collection

is near universally considered the nation's greatest president. Yet, in his approach to the problem of race, he was timid and cautious, "always listening for the popular voice, always afraid to commit himself to a point of view that may turn out unpopular." This is how it has always been with American presidents and race—and perhaps, as Tocqueville said, must be. Frederick Douglass summed up the paradigmatic Lincoln in a speech unveiling a monument to the president on April 14, 1876. He told the whites in the audience, "You are the children of Lincoln, we are at best his step-children," but Douglass said:

> Viewed from the genuine abolition ground, Mr. Lincoln seemed tardy, cold, dull and indifferent, but measuring him by the sentiment of his country, a sentiment he was bound as a statesman to consult, he was swift, zealous, radical and determined.[18]

Lincoln himself could not have summed it up better.

The Racial Attitudes and Policies of American Presidents from George Washington to George W. Bush

The American presidency is an office of great power and majesty, and therefore the racial attitudes and policies of American presidents have been a crucial factor in the African American quest for universal freedom.

Of the 43 men who have served as president, very few have been allies in the African American freedom struggle. On the contrary, most have been hostile or at best neutral or ambivalent. Table 12.1 lists the American presidents in terms of their racial attitudes and policies. Twenty-three (more than half) were white supremacists, including, as we have said,

Table 12.1 A Typology of the Racial Attitudes and Policy Perspectives of American Presidents, from George Washington to George W. Bush[a]

WHITE SUPREMACIST[b]	RACIST	RACIALLY NEUTRAL	RACIALLY AMBIVALENT	ANTIRACIST
George Washington (1789–1797)	George Washington[c]			
	JOHN ADAMS (1798–1801)			
Thomas Jefferson (1801–1809)	Thomas Jefferson[c]			
James Madison (1809–1817)	James Madison[c]			
James Monroe (1817–1825)	James Monroe[c]			
	John Q. Adams (1825–1829)			
Andrew Jackson (1829–1837)	Andrew Jackson[c]			
Martin Van Buren (1837–1841)	Martin Van Buren			
William H. Harrison (1841)	William H. Harrison			
John Tyler (1841–1845)	John Tyler			
James Polk (1845–1849)	James Polk[c]			
Zachary Taylor (1849–1850)	Zachary Taylor[c]			
Millard Fillmore (1850–1853)	Millard Fillmore			
Franklin Pierce (1853–1857)	Franklin Pierce			
James Buchanan (1857–1861)	James Buchanan			
Abraham Lincoln (1861–1865)				Abraham Lincoln
Andrew Johnson (1865–1869)	Andrew Johnson[c]			Ulysses S. Grant (1869–1877)
			Rutherford B. Hayes (1877–1881)	
		CHESTER ARTHUR (1881–1885)	JAMES GARFIELD (1881)	
Grover Cleveland (1885–1889, 1893–1897)		Grover Cleveland		
				BENJAMIN (1889–1893)

(continued)

Table 12.1 (continued)

WHITE SUPREMACIST[b]	RACIST	RACIALLY NEUTRAL	RACIALLY AMBIVALENT	ANTIRACIST
HARRISON				
William Mckinley (1897–1901)	William Mckinley	William Mckinley		
Theodore Roosevelt (1901–1909)	Theodore Roosevelt			
		WILLIAM H. TAFT (1909–1913)		
Woodrow Wilson (1913–1921)	Woodrow Wilson			
Warren G. Harding (1921–1923)		Warren G. Harding		
		CALVIN COOLIDGE (1923–1929)		
		HERBERT HOOVER (1929–1933)		
		FRANKLIN D. ROOSEVELT (1933–1945)		
Harry S. Truman (1945–1953)				Harry S. Truman
Dwight Eisenhower (1953–1961)			Dwight Eisenhower	
				John F. Kennedy (1961–1963)
				Lyndon B. Johnson (1963–1969)
Richard Nixon (1969–1974)				Richard Nixon (1969–1974)
			Gerald Ford (1974–1977)	
				Jimmy Carter (1977–1981)
			Ronald Reagan (1981–1989)	
			George Bush (1989–1993)	
			William Clinton (1993–2000)	
			George Bush (2001)	

(continued)

Table 12.1 (continued)

[a]We classify a president as a white supremacist if the historical record indicates that he held a belief in the inferiority of the African people. A racist is one who supported the institutions of slavery and segregation. A racial neutral is a president whose record shows no positions on racial issues, while a racial ambivalent is a president whose actions on race issues vary from antiracist to racial neutral. An antiracist president is one whose record is characterized by actions to dismantle at least parts of the system of racial subordination. All presidents until Lincoln were racist since they defended the institution of slavery, as sanctioned by the Constitution. After Lincoln, we do not classify presidents as racists or white supremacists unless there is evidence in the historical record that they believed blacks were an inferior people or they supported racial segregation and inequality. There is unavoidably some ambiguity in these classifications. For example, as president, John Q. Adams took no antiracist or antislavery actions, but he was not personally racist; after leaving the presidency, Adams, as a congressman, was a vigorous opponent of slavery and the slave trade. And Jefferson—clearly a white supremacist and a racist—acted as soon as the Constitution permitted to abolish the slave trade.

[b]Information on the attitudes and racial policies of the presidents were obtained from various biographical sources including the entire University Press of Kansas American Presidency series and the summary works of George Sinkler, *Racial Attitudes of American Presidents: From Abraham Lincoln to Theodore Roosevelt* (Garden City, NY: Doubleday, 1971); Kenneth O'Reilly, *Nixon's Piano: Presidents and Racial Politics from Washington to Clinton* (New York: Free Press, 1995); and Richard Riley, *The Presidency and the Politics of Racial Inequality: Nation-Keeping from 1831 to 1965* (New York: Columbia University Press, 1999). Years in parentheses indicate tenure in office.

[c]Indicates slaveowners.

Abraham Lincoln. Eighteen have also been racists, supporting either slavery (including eight slaveowners) or segregation and racial inequality. Thirteen have been neutral or ambivalent in their attitudes toward African American freedom. Eight—Lincoln, Grant, Benjamin Harrison, Truman, Kennedy, Johnson, Nixon, and Carter—have pursued antiracist policies in terms of emancipation of the slaves and their freedom and equality in the United States. Although we classify Lincoln as an antiracist president on the basis of the Emancipation Proclamation, as we indicated, he was ambivalent, favoring freedom for the slaves but not racial equality and universal rights. Table 12.1 also shows that with the exception of Lincoln, Grant, and Harrison, all the antiracist presidents have served in the mid-twentieth century, most since the 1960s.[19] Of the 10 greatest American presidents, according to the most recent poll of American historians—Lincoln, Washington, Franklin Roosevelt, Jefferson, Jackson, Theodore Roosevelt, Wilson, Truman, Polk, and Eisenhower—eight were white suprema- cists, six were racists, and only two—Lincoln and Truman—were antiracists.[20]

The Presidency and the African American Quest for Universal Freedom: From the Revolutionary Era to the Post–Civil Rights Era

This part of the book is necessarily brief since, as we indicated in the previous section, most American presidents have been unresponsive to the African American quest for universal freedom.

The Revolutionary Era

Perhaps all the early American presidents supported the institution of slavery because they thought it was economically necessary or because doing so was politically expedient. O'Reilly in his book on the racial attitudes of American presidents indicates that several Revolutionary era presidents (Washington, Jefferson, Madison, and John Q. Adams) saw slavery as morally wrong and hoped that it would wither away.[21] Yet, none of these early presidents favored universal freedom for blacks; rather, they, like Lincoln, tended to favor colonialization.[22] The only action against slavery by an American president during this period was Jefferson's decision to stop the slave trade as soon as the Constitution permitted. In fact, he proposed to end slavery in 1807, one year before the constitutionally permissible year of 1808. In his annual message to Congress on December 2, 1806, Jefferson wrote,

> I congratulate you fellow citizens on the approach of the period when you may inter- pose your authority constitutionally [to stop Americans] from further participation in those violations of natural rights which have been so long continued on the unoffending inhabitants of Africa, and which the morality, reputation and best interests of our coun- try have long been eager to proscribe.[23]

The Antebellum Era

None of the nine presidents who served during the Antebellum Era (1830–1860) took any action in response to the African American quest for universal freedom, ignoring or attempting to repress the increasingly militant demands for freedom coming from the abolitionist movement.

The Reconstruction Era

Andrew Johnson, who succeeded Lincoln after his murder, was one of the more racist of American presidents in his attitudes and policies. A white supremacist and racist slave-owner from Tennessee, Johnson vetoed civil rights legislation and the Freedmen's Bureau Act. When Congress overrode his vetoes, he refused to faithfully carry out the law as required by the Constitution—one of the factors that led to his impeachment by the House (he came within one vote of being convicted in the Senate and removed from office). By contrast, Ulysses S. Grant, Johnson's successor, was one of the most antiracist presidents in American history. Although he owned one slave, Grant freed him early, and once Grant became president he attempted to enforce the civil rights laws vigorously, urging his white countrymen to grant African Americans universal suffrage and equality under the law. Grant also appointed blacks to federal office for the first time. Frederick Douglass said of Grant that he never exhibited "vulgar prejudices of any color."[24] Even so, when Grant left office, most of the southern states were under the control of white racists and the tide of public opinion in the North was shifting against his policies.

Grant was followed in office by Rutherford B. Hayes. While antiracist in his personal convictions, Hayes, to win the presidency, agreed in the famous "Compromise of 1877" to withdraw federal troops from the South, effectively bringing the brief era of Recon-struction to an end.[25]

The Post-Reconstruction Era

Most presidents after Hayes ignored the problems of race and racism. White public opinion was indifferent or hostile to the African American quest for freedom, and American presidents, whatever their personal attitudes, followed rather than led during this period: 1880s–1930s. Presidents Grover Cleveland and Theodore Roosevelt were attacked because they had eaten dinner with blacks. Cleveland denied it and Roosevelt, who invited Booker T. Washington to the White House for dinner, promised never to do it again. Woodrow Wilson, the first Democratic candidate for president to receive significant black support, nevertheless once in office immediately sought to impose racial segregation throughout the federal workplace in Washington (see Chapter 14).

Benjamin Harrison was the first antiracist president since Grant and the last before Truman. Among his antiracist policies was a proposed constitutional amendment to over-turn the Supreme Court decision invalidating the Civil Rights Act of 1875, legislation to allow the federal government to enforce African American voting rights in the South, and antilynching legislation.[26] Harrison also responded to the material-based interests of blacks by supporting legislation—the Blair Act—that would have provided large sums of federal money to improve southern schools.

From Benjamin Harrison to Franklin Roosevelt, American presidents were largely silent on the issues of race and racism. Roosevelt, the first Democratic president to receive a majority of the black vote, is typical of the political expediency of American presidents on issues of race and racism. In more than 13 years in office, Roosevelt never took any stand on issues of racial discrimination, refusing, despite the urging of his wife Eleanor, even to speak out against lynchings. Like President Kennedy a generation later, Roosevelt's response was always, "I can't take the risk."[27] That is, the president argued that he could not risk losing the support of the powerful white supremacist southern Democrats for his New Deal economic program. Thus, he was willing to sacrifice or trade off the civil rights of blacks to obtain material benefits for all Americans. Blacks benefited from Roosevelt's material-based reforms—public works, housing, and agricultural programs—although the programs were administered on a racially discriminatory basis.

Roosevelt was also concerned that support for civil rights would jeopardize his renomination and reelection, since southern whites controlled an important bloc of votes at the Democratic convention and in the electoral college.

Roosevelt did respond to one black demand during his term in office. This was the material-based demand for jobs in the war industries, but he did so only after the threat of a massive march on Washington by African American workers. Charging that there was widespread discrimination in the growing war industries, A. Phillip Randolph threatened to bring hundreds of thousands of blacks to Washington in a massive protest demonstration. To convince Randolph to call off the march, Roosevelt in June 1941 issued Executive Order 8802, prohibiting discrimination in employment of workers in industries with government contracts. The order also created a committee on Fair Employment Practices; however, it was poorly funded and staffed and was not very effective in ending employment discrimination.[28]

The Civil Rights Era

Although President Truman shared the same white supremacist views of his native Missouri, as president he took a strong antiracist position. He did so for two reasons. First, faced with a third-party challenge from the liberal, progressive Henry Wallace, Truman judged that a strong civil rights program would help him rally the black vote in the big cities of the electoral-vote-rich northeastern and midwestern states. Second, Truman judged that support for civil rights was a cold war imperative. That is, as the leader of the "free world," the United States would be embarrassed and ridiculed by the Soviet Union if it continued to adhere to racism as a national policy.[29]

Thus, President Truman became the first president in history to propose a civil rights reform agenda to the Congress, including a ban on employment discrimination, anti-lynching legislation, and a proposal to end the poll tax. President Truman also issued Executive Order 9981 banning discrimination in the armed services, ordered an end to discrimination in federal employment, was the first president to address an NAACP convention, and directed the Justice Department to file a brief in support of school desegregation cases then pending before the Supreme Court. Although the Congress did not pass Truman's civil rights proposals, his administration was the first in 50 years to place the issue of civil rights on the national agenda.[30]

Two minor civil rights bills were passed during the administration of President Eisenhower (the first since Reconstruction); however, his support for them was reluctant. Eisenhower was a white supremacist and a race ambivalent, preferring to avoid taking any action on civil rights or race-related issues if at all possible. He did issue executive orders prohibiting discrimination in government employment and by companies with government contracts, and he appointed a few blacks to minor positions in his administration. The major civil rights issue during the Eisenhower administration was the Supreme Court's *Brown* desegregation decision. Eisenhower opposed the Court's decision and was reluctant to enforce it. However, when Arkansas Governor Orval Faubus used the state's national guard to block the admission of nine black schoolchildren to

Little Rock's Central High School, Eisenhower felt he had no choice as president but to "take care that the laws be faithfully executed." Thus, he reluctantly dispatched the U.S. Army to enforce the Court's order that the black children be admitted.

John F. Kennedy would not have won the closest election in American history without the support of black voters. But like Franklin Roosevelt, he was reluctant to risk losing the support of white southerners by introducing civil rights legislation. Only after the civil rights demonstrations led by Dr. King created a national crisis did Kennedy finally propose civil rights legislation. In his 1963 speech proposing what was to become the Civil Rights Act of 1964, Kennedy became the first American president to declare that racism was morally wrong.

President Kennedy also appointed a number of blacks to high-level posts in his administration and was the first president to openly entertain blacks at the White House. He also reluctantly issued Executive Order 11063 banning discrimination in federally assisted housing. During the 1960 campaign, Kennedy had promised with a "stroke of the pen" to end discrimination in the sale and rental of housing. Yet, he delayed, and blacks sent hundreds of pens to the president in case he had misplaced his. Finally, in late 1962, he signed the order, but it was limited, excluding all existing housing and covering only housing owned or directly financed by the federal government. Also, President Kennedy, like President Eisenhower, reluctantly sent the army into Mississippi to enforce a court order desegregating the state's university.

President Johnson signing the Civil Rights Act of 1964.   *Source:* Cecil Stoughton/LBJ Library Collection

Unlike Presidents Kennedy and Roosevelt, President Johnson was willing "to take the risk" of losing the support of white southern Democrats by enthusiastically and unequivocally supporting civil rights legislation (when he signed the 1964 Act he told his aides, "We have just lost the South for a generation"). In addition to signing three major civil rights bills, Johnson also initiated the Great Society and the "war on poverty" designed to deal with the material-based needs of urban and rural poor people, many of whom were African Americans. Johnson also made a number of historic appointments, placing the first black in the cabinet and the first black on the Supreme Court.

The Post–Civil Rights Era

Although Richard Nixon was a white supremacist and his 1968 campaign was based on a strategy of attracting the white racist vote in the South,[31] as the first post–civil rights era president he presided over the successful desegregation of southern schools, the renewal of the Voting Rights Act in 1970, implementation of Executive Order 11246 establishing affirmative action, and the appointment of scores of blacks to high-level positions in the government. In addition Nixon proposed a far-reaching material-based reform—the Family Assistance Plan—that would have guaranteed an income to all families with children. Although this reform was defeated by an odd coalition of blacks and liberals (who thought the income guarantee was too low) and conservatives (who wanted no guarantee at all), if it had passed it would have substantially raised the income of poor families, many of whom were black.[32] Historians are unclear as to why Nixon took such a strong civil rights policy stance (especially on affirmative action),[33] but the political climate in the late 1960s probably made such positions seem politically expedient.

In his 18 months in office, President Gerald Ford distinguished himself on race by appointing the second black to the cabinet and by waging a year-long campaign to get the courts and the Congress to end busing for purposes of school desegregation.

Jimmy Carter appointed a number of blacks to high-level positions in his administration and to the federal courts,[34] supported affirmative action in the form of the *Bakke* case (see Box 12.3), and reorganized the civil rights enforcement bureaucracy.[35] However, he rejected an ambitious proposal by his African American Housing Secretary Patricia Roberts Harris for a new urban antipoverty program,[36] and supported only a watered-down version of the Humphrey-Hawkins full employment bill.

Ronald Reagan's two terms in office were characterized by ambivalence on race. He came into office determined to dismantle the Great Society and affirmative action programs. Several Great Society programs were eliminated and the budgets for others were substantially cut. But Reagan also signed a 25-year extension of the Voting Rights Act, strengthened the Fair Housing Act, and (reluctantly) signed the Martin Luther King Jr. holiday bill. He also refused to issue an executive order eliminating affirmative action, as he had implied he would during the 1980 campaign (see Box 12.3).

George Bush's administration was also characterized by ambivalence on civil rights. In 1990 he vetoed the Civil Rights Act (designed to overturn several Supreme Court decisions that made it difficult to enforce employment discrimination laws), calling it a "quota bill," but in 1991 he signed essentially the same bill he had vetoed a year earlier.[37] Bush also appointed the second black to the Supreme Court, but the appointee was a man described by most black leaders as an "Uncle Tom" and a "traitor to the race."[38]

Justice Thomas was also accused by Anita Hill, a former black female employee, of sexual harassment. Additionally, Bush rejected proposals by his aides for new antipoverty programs, arguing that they were too expensive and too liberal.[39]

The Clinton Administration

Bill Clinton was arguably the first authentically nonracist, non–white supremacist president in American history. American presidents are a product of the culture and socialization process of their time, and Bill Clinton was the first president to come of age in the nominally nonracist, non–white supremacist post–civil rights era. By all accounts, Clinton was as free of racist and white supremacist thinking as any white person can be.[40] Yet, to win the presidency, Clinton ran on a strategy of deliberately distancing himself from black voters in order to win over the so-called Reagan Democrats who had voted Republican because of the Democrats' close identification with African Americans.[41]

In his first term in office, Clinton appointed a large number of blacks to high-level positions in the administration (one-fourth of the cabinet) and to the courts. He also refused to support proposals to eliminate affirmative action (see Box 12.3) and was responsive to black concerns to use military force to restore the democratically elected president to office in Haiti (see Chapter 16), and became the first U.S. president to make state visits to several African countries. On material-based issues, Clinton proposed a complicated yet comprehensive plan to guarantee health care to all Americans. Although Clinton's plan was not enacted, if Congress had passed it, it would have universalized access to health care and been of enormous benefit to African Americans (see Chapter 15). Clinton's major initiative on race during his second term was to propose a dialogue on race.[42]

BOX 12.3   AFRICAN AMERICANS AND PRESIDENTIAL POLICY MAKING: THE CASE OF AFFIRMATIVE ACTION

Affirmative action—a variety of programs and policies designed to enhance the access of racial minorities and women to education, employment, and government contracts—is one of the most controversial civil rights policies of the day, as it has been since it was created by African American policy makers in the Johnson and Nixon administrations. Although affirmative action as national policy was developed by African Americans and is widely supported by African Americans and their leaders, in the Carter administration African American policy makers sought to abolish such programs.

Late in the Johnson administration, Edward Sylvester, an African American who headed the Labor Department's office of Federal Contract Compliance, developed the "Cleveland Plan" designed to assure equal employment opportunity for blacks in the Cleveland, Ohio, construction industry. The Cleveland Plan required that construction companies with government contracts develop detailed plans specifying the precise number of blacks they planned to hire in all phases of their work. This plan brought protests from labor unions, business groups, conservatives, and liberals who argued that it established racial hiring quotas. Eventually, the comptroller general (head of the General Accounting Office, the congressional

(continued)

BOX 12.3 continued

watchdog agency) ruled that the plan was illegal, not because it required quotas but because it violated standard contract bidding procedures. Sylvester's plan was dropped. To the surprise of most observers, Sylvester's plan was resurrected in the conservative, business-oriented Nixon administration, again under the policy leadership of African Americans. President Nixon appointed Arthur Fletcher as an assistant secretary of labor and John Wilks as director of the Office of Federal Contract Compliance. Immediately these two African Americans set about to revive Sylvester's plan. Using Philadelphia as the model city, the "Philadelphia Plan" required government contractors to set specific numerical goals for the employment of minority workers. Unlike Sylvester's Cleveland Plan, the Philadelphia Plan complied with standard contracting procedures but the comptroller general again ruled it was illegal, this time because it used race as a factor in determining employment. President Nixon, however, rejected the comptroller general's ruling, arguing that as president he had the inherent "executive power" to implement the Philadelphia Plan by executive order (E.O. 11246). The Senate later passed an amendment upholding the comptroller general's decision, but after intense lobbying by President Nixon and his secretary of labor, George Shultz, the House by a vote of 208 to 156 rejected the Senate's amendment and affirmative action effectively became the law of the land. Ironically, given Democratic support for affirmative action and Republican opposition to it today, in 1971 a majority of Democrats in Congress voted against affirmative action while it was supported by a majority of Republicans.

The Philadelphia Plan became the model for affirmative action throughout American society, including admission to colleges and universities. In the late 1970s the University of California at Davis established an affirmative action program at its medical school in order to increase the number of minority students enrolled there. Under its plan, 16 of its 100 openings were set aside for minorities only. Allan Bakke, a white applicant who was rejected for admission, sued the university, arguing that for a university to consider race in making its admission decisions was a violation of the Civil Rights Act of 1964 and the Fourteenth Amendment's equal protection clause. The California Supreme Court in the case of *Regents of the University of California* v. *Bakke* (1978) declared the Davis plan unconstitutional. The university appealed this decision to the U.S. Supreme Court.

A sharply divided Supreme Court upheld the university's right to use race in making admission decisions but agreed that setting a quota of 16 slots for minorities only was unconstitutional. We discuss the details of the Court's opinion in *Bakke* and other affirmative action cases in Chapter 15; here we focus on the role of African American policy makers. In important cases, the Supreme Court will "invite" the administration to submit an *amicus curiae* ("friend of the court") brief explaining how it thinks the case should be decided. In the Carter administration, the two policy makers responsible for preparing the administration brief were Wade McCree, who was solicitor general, and Drew Days, III, assistant attorney general for civil rights (and later solicitor general in the Clinton administration). In the first draft of the brief prepared by the solicitor general, the very principle of affirmative action—that race could be considered in admissions or employment decisions—was rejected as a violation of the equal protection clause. It read, "we doubt that it is *ever* proper to use race to close any portion of the class for competition by members of all races" and that "racial classifications favorable to minority groups

(continued)

BOX 12.3 continued

are presumptively unconstitutional."[a] If this position had been adopted by the Court, affirmative action would have been eliminated, not just in university admissions but in employment and government contracting. McCree's brief, however, was leaked to the press and after intense lobbying by the NAACP, the Congressional Black Caucus, and others, President Carter instructed the attorney general to request the solicitor general to rewrite the brief. Although McCree was reportedly outraged by what he considered unseemly political pressure, the brief was rewritten to uphold the right of the university to use race in its admissions decisions. Again, the irony here is that affirmative action created by black men serving in a conservative Republican administration was almost eliminated by black men serving in a liberal Democratic administration.

Three decades after the Philadelphia Plan and two decades after *Bakke,* affirmative action is still under attack. President Reagan implied during the 1980 campaign that he would abolish affirmative action in the federal government by revoking Nixon's 1971 order. But he backed off at the urging of former Nixon administration labor secretary George Shultz (then Reagan's secretary of state) and Samuel Pierce, the secretary of housing and urban development and the only African American in his cabinet. In his review of affirmative action policy—a review led by Christopher Edley, an African American White House staff assistant—President Clinton concluded that while some reforms might be appropriate, affirmative action programs were still necessary to assure equal opportunities for minorities and women. Thus, his formulation: "mend it, don't end it."[b]

However, Republican congressional leaders are opposed to affirmative action; the 1996 Republican presidential nominee Bob Dole also opposed affirmative action; the Supreme Court in a series of cases has been edging away from the principle of affirmative action (led by African American Justice Clarence Thomas); and in 1996, the trend-setting voters of California—by 56 to 44 percent—approved Proposition 209, the ballot initiative ending affirmative action in that state's education, employment, and contracting.[c] A leader of the California antiaffirmative action initiative was Ward Connerly, an African American.

In the George W. Bush administration the Supreme Court took up the issue of affirmative action in university admissions for the first time since the *Bakke* case, involving two cases from the University of Michigan. Black appointees in the administration were divided on what position the administration brief to the Supreme Court should take. Three administration blacks— Ralph Boyd, the assistant attorney general for civil rights; Gerald Reynolds, the assistant secretary of education for civil rights; and Brian Jones, the general counsel in the Department of Education—all argued that *Bakke* should be reversed and any consideration of race in university admission should be unconstitutional.[d] African American Secretary of Education Rodney Paige, African American Deputy Attorney General Larry Thompson, and National Security Advisor Condoleezza Rice supported the position eventually adopted by Bush, which sidestepped the constitutional question but argued that the Michigan programs in question were racial quotas and therefore prohibited by *Bakke*. Rice, a former professor and Provost at Stanford, reportedly helped Bush to make the decision and write his speech on the cases.[e] Finally, Secretary of State Powell firmly and publicly opposed the president's position, saying he fully supported affirmative action in principle as well as the specific Michigan programs.[f]

(continued)

BOX 12.3 continued

[a]Quoted in Robert C. Smith, *We Have No Leaders: African Americans in the Post–Civil Rights Era* (Albany: SUNY Press, 1996): 149–50. For a detailed analysis of the evolution of affirmative action from the Kennedy to the Nixon administration, see Hugh Davis Graham, *The Civil Rights Era: Origins and Development of National Policy* (New York: Oxford, 1990): chaps. 10–13; on policy developments from the Nixon to the Bush administration, see Smith, *We Have No Leaders,* chap. 5.

[b]See "Remarks by the President on Affirmative Action," The White House, Office of the Press Secretary, July 19, 1995. The Clinton administration's detailed review of affirmative action is *Affirmative Action Review: Report to President Clinton* (Washington, DC: Bureau of National Affairs, 1995). This report was prepared by White House advisors George Stephanopoulos and Christopher Edley, Jr.

[c]Several days after Proposition 209 was approved, Federal District Court Judge Thelton Henderson suspended its implementation because he said it probably violated the Fourteenth Amendment's equal protection clause. Judge Henderson's order was later reversed by the Ninth Circuit Court of Appeals and the proposition took effect in the late summer of 1997. See John Bourdeau, "Appeals Court Upholds Support for Prop. 209," *West County Times,* August 22, 1997, p. A1.

[d]"Black Lawyer Behind Bush's Affirmative Action Stance," *The Crisis* (March/April 2003), p. 9.

[e]Mike Allen and Charles Lane, "Rice Helped Shape Bush Decision on Admissions," *Washington Post,* January 17, 2003.

[f]Scott Lindlow, "Powell Backs Affirmative Action," *West County Times,* January 20, 2003.

However, if Clinton sought to universalize health care and establish it as a right for all citizens, he did the exact opposite with respect to welfare. During the 1992 election, Clinton campaigned on the pledge, "End Welfare as We Know It," by imposing a two-year time limit on eligibility for Aid to Families with Dependent Children. The Congress did not act on Clinton's welfare bill in his first two years in office. But once the Republicans took control of Congress, they enacted a much more radical proposal: one that abolished the 60-year-old New Deal guarantee of welfare as a universal, federally guaranteed right. Clinton vetoed two versions of this bill, but as the 1996 election approached, he was persuaded (against the advice of his policy advisors on welfare) by his political advisors that the politically expedient and popular thing to do was sign the bill. So, in July of 1996 he signed this radical reform bill (we discuss the welfare reform bill in Chapter 15).

In addition, in spite of the opposition of the Black Caucus and most civil rights and civil liberties groups, Clinton signed a harshly punitive anticrime bill that included mandatory sentencing for a variety of crimes including first-time drug offenses, the punishment of juveniles as adults, life in prison for persons convicted of three felonies (the so-called "three strikes and you're out"), and expansion of the death penalty to cover more than 50 federal crimes. (The three-strikes law is widely viewed as responsible in part for the growing incarceration of young black men, discussed in Chapter 15.)

On the Clinton administration and race, Steven Shull concludes, "Bill Clinton was the most rhetorical but also most symbolic and least supportive Democrat in his public statements. . . . Even such long-accepted remedies as affirmative action based on race alone were challenged, with Clinton suggesting that women and even economically disadvantaged white men should be eligible for government remedies."[43]

In spite of these policy differences between blacks and Clinton when he left office and in his postpresidency, he remains extraordinarily popular among African American leaders and ordinary people. (Clinton located his postpresidential office in Harlem.) In a series of interviews with prominent blacks after Clinton left office, journalist Dewayne Wickham found that Clinton was viewed as among the best, if not the best, president in terms of African American interests.[44] Black public opinion was also highly favorable toward Clinton throughout his tenure, and especially during the investigations leading up to his impeachment, trial, and acquittal. By contrast, when Jimmy Carter, the last Democratic president, left office, his performance was approved of by only 30 percent of blacks compared to 70 percent approval of Clinton during his last year.[45]

Since many of Clinton's policies were conservative, how can one account for his popularity among blacks? How did he capture the imagination of blacks, such that Nobel laureate Toni Morrison could call him the first black president and the Arkansas Black Hall of Fame could make him its first white member? Although scholars disagree on the sources of Clinton's popularity, many attribute it to the prosperous economy (which led to a substantial reduction in black unemployment), his appointments (see Chapter 14), various symbolic gestures, his obvious familiarity with and comfort among blacks, and to the fact that he became president after 12 years of Reagan and Bush, who were viewed as overtly hostile to black interests.[46]

The George W. Bush Administration

President Bush entered the presidency with less support from African Americans than any president of the post–civil rights era, with black leaders and voters questioning the very legitimacy of his election. Partly as a result, Bush attempted to reach out to the black community with appointments, symbolic gestures, and substantive policies. Appointments are discussed in Chapter 14; among the symbolic gestures was a visit to several African countries. On Goree Island in Ghana (where enslaved Africans began their sojourn to America) while he did not formally apologize for slavery (as Clinton also refused to do on his visit), he described it as "one of the greatest crimes of history." Bush also hosted half of Africa's leaders at a Washington summit and held one of his rare state dinners for the president of Uganda. Among other symbolic gestures, Bush hung a portrait of Martin Luther King Jr. in the White House, laid a wreath at King's tomb, hosted Thomas Jefferson's black relatives at the White House, and signed legislation creating a National Museum of African American History and Culture.

In terms of policy, the Bush record, like Clinton's, is mixed. He issued broad guidelines prohibiting racial profiling by federal law enforcement agencies (except for cases involving terrorism and national security), proposed to Congress a program to increase low-income and minority home ownership, pushed through the No Child Left Behind Act designed to raise the performance of low-income and minority students, and proposed the "Faith Based Initiative" to allow churches to provide social services to the poor. In foreign policy he dispatched a special envoy to mediate the Sudanese civil war, sent a small U.S. peacekeeping force to Liberia, and proposed substantial increases in funds to combat AIDS in Africa. However, over the vigorous objections of the Congressional Black Caucus and other African American leaders, Bush brought about the removal of Jean Claude Aristride, the democratically elected president of Haiti. During the Clinton administration U.S. forces were used to restore Aristride to office after he had been overthrown in a military coup. But the Bush administration, charging that Aristride was corrupt and engaged in drug trafficking, cut off all U.S. aid to Haiti and encouraged the World Bank and the International Monetary Fund to do the same. And then as insurgents threatened to take over the country, the United States told Aristride that if he did not leave the country it could not guarantee his safety. African American leaders had urged the United States to intervene to preserve Aristride's presidency (charging the insurgents were "thugs" and "terrorists"). Instead, Bush blamed Aristride for the crisis and forced him into exile in Africa. Later, Secretary of State Powell threatened to prosecute Aristride on corruption charges in U.S. courts.[47]

African American leaders also objected to the centerpiece of Bush's domestic policy agenda—his tax cuts—and of his foreign policy, the war on Iraq. The Iraq War is discussed in Chapter 16. African American leaders objected to Bush's tax cuts because they claimed they went mainly for the rich and disproportionately benefited whites. For example, it is estimated that blacks and Latinos received tax cuts 35–40 percent smaller than whites.[48] Black leaders also opposed a series of Bush proposals to cut funding for housing, Head Start, and Medicaid, and to increase the hours parents on welfare had to work and shift control over health and welfare programs to the states.[49]

However, the most controversial race issue of the Bush administration was its decision on what kind of brief to file in the cases challenging the University of Michigan affirmative action programs. These two cases were the most important on the issue since the Supreme Court's landmark 1978 ruling in *Regents of University of California* v. *Bakke,* in which it banned quotas but held that race could be taken into consideration as a "plus factor" in university admissions in order to achieve diversity.

The Bush administration was divided on what position it should argue before the Court (we discuss the Supreme Court's decision in the case in Chapter 13, and the role of black administration officials in the decision is discussed in Box 12.3). Conservatives in the administration led by the attorney general and the solicitor general argued that the administration should ask the Court to overrule *Bakke* and declare that the Fourteenth Amendment prohibited any consideration of race in university admissions. The solicitor general, Theodore Olson, the official responsible for writing the brief, was adamant, since in 1996 he persuaded the Fifth Circuit Court of Appeals in *Hopwood* v. *Texas* to overrule *Bakke.* Moderates in the administration including Alberto Gonzalez, the president's Hispanic general counsel, urged President Bush to avoid the constitutional question of whether race could ever be used in admission decisions. Instead, they said the administration should simply ask the Court to declare the Michigan programs unconstitutional because they constituted racial quotas. Olson was reportedly furious and threatened to go public with his opposition until he received a call from the vice president telling him in effect to "shut up."[50]

In a seven-minute, late-afternoon speech Bush adopted the position of Gonzalez and the other moderates, saying that while he supported "diversity of all kinds" the Michigan programs were "fundamentally flawed" because they constituted "racial quotas," which are "divisive, unfair, and impossible to square with the Constitution."[51]

Summary

Most American presidents have been white supremacists and many have been racists. And of those who have been neither, they have generally been reluctant to act decisively against racism and in favor of universal freedom unless forced to do so during times of crisis. Abraham Lincoln established the pattern, the paradigm for how American presidents would deal with the African American freedom quest, when he said he would only grant blacks freedom if it would help save the union. Otherwise, he said he would do nothing despite his personal antislavery convictions.

The American presidency is an office of great power and majesty, but the 43 men who have held the office have been reluctant (with the exception of Lyndon Johnson) to use that power and majesty to further African American freedom, preferring "not to take the risk" of alienating white public opinion, jeopardizing other policy priorities, or damaging their chances for election and reelection.

Selected Bibliography

Bennett, Lerone. *Forced into Glory: Abraham Lincoln's White Dream.* Chicago: Johnson Publishing, 2000. A highly critical assessment of Lincoln, by one of the nation's leading African American historians.

Donald, David. *Lincoln.* New York: Simon & Schuster, 1995. One of the best and most recent biographies of the sixteenth president.

Fehrenbacher, Don. "Only His Stepchildren: Lincoln and the Negro." *Civil War History* 12 (1974): 293–309. A generally favorable analysis of the president's posture toward African Americans.

Fredrickson, George. "A Man Not a Brother: Abraham Lincoln and the Negro." *Journal of Southern History* 41 (1975): 39–58. A balanced assessment of the subject.

Hine, Darlene Clark, and Pero Dagbovie, eds. *African Americans and the Clinton Presidency: The Need for a Third Reconstruction* (Unpublished Manuscript 2005). A collection of papers critically assessing the Clinton administration's relationship to blacks.

Holden, Matthew, Jr. "Race and Constitutional Change in the Twentieth Century: The Role of the Executive." In John Hope Franklin and Genna Rae MacNeil, eds., *African Americans and the Living Constitution.* Washington, DC: Smithsonian Institution Press, 1995. An analysis of the policy initiatives on race of American presidents, focusing on the context of presidential decision making.

Morgan, Ruth. *The President and Civil Rights: Policy Making by Executive Order.* New York: St. Martin's Press, 1970. A study of presidential use of executive orders to advance civil rights.

O'Reilly, Kenneth. *Nixon's Piano: Presidents and Racial Politics from Washington to Clinton.* New York: Free Press, 1995. A useful study of the subject.

Quarles, Benjamin. *Lincoln and the Negro.* New York: Oxford University Press, 1962. The definitive study of the subject.

Riley, Richard. *The Presidency and the Politics of Racial Inequality: Nation-Keeping from 1831 to 1965.* New York: Columbia University Press, 1999. The most recent book-length study of the subject.

Rossiter, Clinton. *The American Presidency,* rev. ed. New York: Harcourt Brace Jovanovich, 1960. The standard study of the role of the president and the presidency's central role in American politics.

Shull, Steven. *American Civil Rights Policy from Truman to Clinton.* Armonk, NY: M. E. Sharpe, 1999. A detailed empirical study, focusing mainly on the Reagan, George H. W. Bush, and Clinton administrations.

Sinkler, George. *The Racial Attitudes of American Presidents: From Abraham Lincoln to Theodore Roosevelt.* Garden City, NY: Doubleday, 1971. A comprehensive analysis of the subject.

Walton, Hanes, Jr. *African American Power and Politics: The Political Context Variable.* New York: Columbia University Press, 1996. A detailed study of how the Reagan and Bush presidencies changed the political context of discussions on race.

Notes

1. Letter to Horace Greeley, *Abraham Lincoln: Collected Works,* vol. V, pp. 388–89.
2. Richard Riley explains the role of the president on issues of race in terms of "nation-maintaining." He writes, "The central finding of this study is that the presidency has routinely

served as a nation-maintaining institution on the issue of racial inequality. Indeed, the evidence arrayed here strongly suggests that one of the enduring roles each president is required to execute is that of nation-keeper, a protector of the inherited political and social order and a preserver of domestic tranquility." See *The Presidency and the Politics of Racial Inequality: Nation-Keeping from 1831 to 1965* (New York: Columbia University Press, 1999): 10.

3. David Donald, *Lincoln* (New York: Simon & Schuster, 1995).
4. As quoted in George Sinkler, *The Racial Attitudes of American Presidents: From Abraham Lincoln to Theodore Roosevelt* (Garden City, NY: Doubleday, 1971): 11.
5. Alexis de Tocqueville, *Democracy in America,* edited by Phillips Bradley (Garden City, NY: Doubleday, 1848, 1969): 356.
6. Riley, *The Presidency and the Politics of Racial Inequality,* pp. 18–19.
7. On Lincoln's racial attitudes, see Benjamin Quarles, *Lincoln and the Negro* (New York: Oxford University Press, 1962); George Fredrickson, "A Man Not a Brother: Lincoln and the Negro," *Journal of Southern History* 41 (1975): 39–58; and Don Fehrenbacher, "Only His Stepchildren: Lincoln and the Negro," *Civil War History* 12 (1974): 293–309.
8. Lincoln did not favor the abolition of slavery (frequently calling abolitionism "dangerous radical utopianism") but rather opposed its extension beyond the South to the Midwest and the West because he wanted these lands preserved for free (white) labor on free land. See Eric Foner, *Free Soil, Free Labor: The Ideology of the Republican Party Before the Civil War* (New York: Oxford University Press, 1970).
9. Fredrickson, "A Man Not a Brother," p. 46.
10. Quoted in Ibid., p. 45.
11. Abraham Lincoln, "The Emancipation Proclamation," in Kermit Hall, William Wiecek, and Paul Finkelman, eds., *American Legal History: Cases and Materials* (New York: Oxford University Press, 1991): 224.
12. Ibid.
13. A standard study of the Emancipation Proclamation is John Hope Franklin, *The Emancipation Proclamation* (Garden City, NY: Doubleday, 1963).
14. The commander-in-chief clause was used by Franklin Roosevelt to incarcerate Japanese Americans as a World War II measure, which at the time was held to be constitutional by the Supreme Court although it was a clear violation of the Fifth Amendment prohibition on the deprivation of liberty without a trial.
15. Fredrickson, "A Man Not a Brother," p. 45.
16. Ibid., p. 48.
17. Fehrenbacher, "Only His Stepchildren," p. 307.
18. *The Life and Times of Frederick Douglass Written by Himself,* introduction by Rayford Logan (London: Collier Books, 1892, 1962): 485, 489.
19. Matthew Holden, Jr., "Race and Constitutional Change in the Twentieth Century: The Role of the Executive," in John Hope Franklin and Genna Rae MacNeil, eds., *African Americans and the Living Constitution* (Washington, DC: Smithsonian Institution Press, 1995): 117–43.
20. Arthur Schlesinger, Jr., "Rating the Presidents: From Washington to Clinton," *Political Science Quarterly* 112 (1997): 179–90.
21. Kenneth O'Reilly, *Nixon's Piano: Presidents and Racial Politics from Washington to Clinton* (New York: Free Press, 1995). O'Reilly argues that Andrew Jackson was the "first (and arguably the only) chief executive in American history not to consider slavery a moral evil," p. 31.
22. Ibid., chap. 1.
23. Quoted in William Freehling, "The Founding Fathers and Slavery," *American Historical Review* 77 (1972): 396.

24. O'Reilly, *Nixon's Piano,* p. 135.

25. Samuel Tilden, governor of New York, apparently won a majority of the vote for president but the Republicans controlled enough southern electoral votes to give the presidency to Hayes in exchange for his promise to withdraw federal troops and leave the South alone with respect to the treatment of blacks. See C. Vann Woodward, *Reunion and Reaction: The Compromise of 1877 and the End of Reconstruction* (Garden City, NY: Doubleday, 1956).

26. Harrison's support for antilynching legislation came about not as a result of the lynching of blacks, but rather after 11 Italian citizens were lynched in New Orleans. The Italian government filed a strong protest and Harrison responded with his proposed legislation. See O'Reilly's *Nixon's Piano,* p. 59.

27. Ibid., p. 111. Roosevelt was even reluctant to send a written message to the annual NAACP convention.

28. Louis Ruchames, *Race, Jobs and Politics: The Story of FEPC* (New York: Columbia University Press, 1953).

29. See Mary Dudziak, "Desegregation as a Cold War Imperative," *Stanford Law Review* 41 (1988): 1147–75.

30. As Franklin Roosevelt had feared, Truman's support did cost him the support of white southern Democrats, who walked out of the 1948 convention, formed a third party, and ran Strom Thurmond for president. Thurmond carried four southern states.

31. See John Ehrlichman, *Witness to Power* (New York: Auburn House, 1982): 222–23; and O'Reilly, *Nixon's Piano,* chap. 7.

32. Daniel P. Moynihan, *The Politics of a Guaranteed Income: The Nixon Administration and the Family Assistance Plan* (New York: Vintage Books, 1973).

33. O'Reilly, Nixon's Piano, chap. 7; and Hugh Davis Graham, *The Civil Rights Era: Origin and Development of National Policy* (New York: Oxford University Press, 1990): chaps. 12–14.

34. Robert C. Smith, "Black Appointed Officials: A Neglected Category of Political Participation Research," *Journal of Black Studies* 14 (March 1984): 369–88.

35. Eleanor Holmes Norton, "The Role of Black Presidential Appointees," *Urban League Review* 9 (Summer 1985): 108–9.

36. Harold Wolman and Astrid A. E. Merget, "The President and Policy Formulation: President Carter and Urban Policy," *Presidential Studies Quarterly* 10 (1980): 402–15; and Robert C. Smith, *We Have No Leaders: African Americans in the Post–Civil Rights Era* (Albany: SUNY Press, 1996): 149–51.

37. On Bush's flip-flop on the 1990 and 1991 civil rights bills, see Smith's *We Have No Leaders,* pp. 170–82.

38. Arch Parsons, "Thomas Nomination Divides the Black Community," *West County Times,* July 28, 1991.

39. Robert Pear, "Administration Rejects Proposals for New Anti-Poverty Programs," *New York Times,* July 6, 1990.

40. O'Reilly, *Nixon's Piano,* chap. 9.

41. See O'Reilly, *Nixon's Piano*; and Smith, *We Have No Leaders,* chap. 9, for discussion of Clinton's electoral strategy.

42. Adolph Reed, Jr., "America Becoming—What Exactly?: Social Policy Research as the Fruit of Bill Clinton's Race Initiative," in Darlene Clark Hine and Pero Dagbovie, eds., *African Americans and the Clinton Presidency Reconsidered* (Unpublished Manuscript, 2006); See also "President Clinton Journeys to Africa," *Jet,* April 20, 1998.

43. Steven Shull, *American Civil Rights Policy from Truman to Clinton* (Armonk, NY: M.E. Sharpe, 1999): 80, 93.

44. Dewayne Wickham, *Bill Clinton and Black America* (New York: Ballantine Books, 2002).

45. Robert C. Smith, "Presidential Leadership and the Quest for Racial Equality: The Clinton Administration," in Hine and Dagbovie, eds., *African Americans and the Clinton Presidency: The Need for a Third Reconstruction.*

46. See Smith, "Presidential Leadership and the Quest for Racial Equality"; Joe Trotter, "Reflections on Bill Clinton, Black America and the Politics of Race"; and Pero Dagbovie, "Reassessing Bill Clinton's Intriguing Relationship with Black America," in Hine and Dagbovie, eds., *African Americans and the Clinton Presidency Reconsidered.*

47. Christopher Marcus, "U.S. Considers Charging Aristide with Corruption," *New York Times,* April 6, 2004.

48. Gene Sperling, "Budget Problems: Bush Economics Leaves Most African Americans Behind," *The Crisis* (March/April 2004), p. 18.

49. Amy Goldstein and Johnath Weisman, "Bush Seeks to Recast Ties to the Poor," *Washington Post,* February 9, 2001.

50. Howard Fine, "The Color of Racial Politics," *Newsweek,* January 27, 2003.

51. Amy Goldstein and Dana Milibank, "Bush Joins Admission Case Fight," *Washington Post,* January 16, 2003. See also Dana Milibank, "Bush Aides Split on Bias Case at U. Mich.," *Washington Post,* December 18, 2002.

CHAPTER 13

The Supreme Court and the African American Quest for Universal Freedom

The question is simply this: can a Negro, whose ancestors were imported into this country, and sold as slaves, become a member of the political community formed and brought into existence by the Constitution of the United States, and as such become entitled to all the rights, and privileges, and immunities, granted by that instrument to the citizens. . . . We think they are not, and they are not included, were not intended to be included, under the word "citizen" in the Constitution, and can therefore claim none of the rights and privileges which that instrument provides for and secures to citizens of the United States. On the contrary, they were at that time [1787] considered as a subordinate and inferior class of beings, who had been subjugated by the dominant race, and, whether emancipated or not, yet remained subject to their authority, and had no rights or privileges but such as those who held the power and the government might choose to grant them.

Chief Justice Roger B. Taney[1]

We begin this chapter with an excerpt from Chief Justice Taney's remarkable opinion in *Dred Scott* v. *Sanford*. The *Dred Scott* decision is historically important because the case marks the first time in the then 70-year history of the Court that it squarely addressed the rights of the African people in the United States, holding that they had no rights—none whatsoever—except those that white people might choose to give them.[2] For the next 70 years of its history, the Court ignored the rights and freedoms of Africans, in spite of the adoption of the Civil War amendments to the Constitution, which granted citizenship to blacks and guaranteed universal rights and freedoms.[3] Then, beginning in the 1940s and lasting until the 1980s, the Supreme Court in a series of cases began slowly to enforce the Constitution's guarantees of universal rights and freedoms. Except for this remarkable 40-year period—1940s to 1980s—the Supreme Court historically has been a racist institution, refusing to support universal freedom for African Americans. On the contrary, as in the *Dred Scott* case, for much of its more than 200 years the Court has taken the position that the rights of African Americans were not universal but rather existed only as whites might "choose to grant them." It now appears, as the Court approaches its third century, that it may once again be reverting to its racist past.[4]

The Supreme Court of the United States is a political institution. That is, unlike the courts in most nations, the courts in the United States are not simply legal institutions deciding questions of innocence or guilt in criminal cases or liability in civil cases. Rather, as Professor Robert Dahl writes, "To consider the Supreme Court of the United States strictly as a legal institution is to underestimate its significance in the American political system. For it is also a political institution, an institution, that is to say, for arriving at decisions on controversial questions of national policy."[5] In its decisions on controversial issues of national policy, the Court responds slowly but surely to public opinion and the fundamental currents of national election majorities. Thus, if the Supreme Court is reverting to racism, it may reflect its understanding of public opinion and the outcome of recent presidential elections, which were often won by candidates perceived by blacks as hostile to their quest for universal freedom. Or in the famous words of humorist Finley Peter Dunne's "Mr. Dooley," "The Supreme Court follows the election returns."

Judicial Appointments and African Americans

One hundred and ten persons have served as Supreme Court justices. Two have been African Americans. The first was Thurgood Marshall, the legendary chief lawyer for the NAACP and one of the greatest African American leaders of all time.[6] Appointed by President Johnson in 1967, Marshall's confirmation was held up for several months by racists and white supremacists but he was eventually approved and went on to serve on the Court for more than two decades until he retired in 1991. When Marshall retired, President George H. W. Bush nominated Clarence Thomas, then a judge on the District of Columbia Court of Appeals, to replace him. Thomas was bitterly opposed by African American leaders because of his opposition to affirmative action and his conservative ideology generally. This opposition was reinforced by the last-minute allegations of sexual harassment by Anita Hill, an African American lawyer and former assistant to Thomas. Although black leaders opposed Thomas's nomination, he was supported by black public opinion and this support continued after the Hill allegation.[7] However, in several southern states this support was diminished to some extent, especially among black women.[8] And in an interesting example of how events can shape the socialization process, African Americans were more informed about the issue (particularly their senator's vote) than whites, closing the traditional gap in political information between the races.[9]

Justice Marshall in his years on the Court became one of the most liberal justices in the Court's history, forging a jurisprudence of activism in which the Court would seek to resolve racial and other social problems.[10] Thomas in his years on the Court has been its most conservative member, forging a jurisprudence of "strict constructionism," which rejects the idea that the Court should attempt to resolve societal problems.[11]

President Franklin Roosevelt was the first president to appoint a black person to the federal courts, naming William Hastie as a judge in the Virgin Islands. President Kennedy appointed three black judges to the federal courts; President Johnson named seven; and President Nixon, three. Generally, appointments to the courts are based on party and ideology. That is, American presidents and senators tend to select judges from their party, who share their ideology, whether liberal or conservative. For example, African Americans who tend to be liberal Democrats are more likely to receive judicial

Table 13.1 Percentage of African American Appointees to the Federal Courts, from the Carter to the George W. Bush Administrations

Carter	13.9%	(28)[a]
Reagan	2.1	(6)
Bush	6.8	(10)
Clinton	19.5	(33)
Bush, George W.	0.7	(18)

[a]The numbers in parentheses represent the number of appointments of black judges in each administration.

Sources: Sheldon Goldman and E. Slotnick, "Clinton's First Term Judiciary: Many Bridges to Cross," *Judicature* 80 (1997): 254–73. Data on George W. Bush appointees from the National Bar Association, January 2007.

appointments from Democratic presidents. This trend is shown in Table 13.1. In the Carter administration, 13.9 percent of all judicial appointments were black, and in the Clinton administration the figure was 19.5 percent. In the Reagan administration, however, 2.1 percent of the appointees were black, and in the Bush administration the figure was 6.8 percent. President George W. Bush nominated 18 blacks to the federal courts, only 0.7 percent of his nominees as of January 2007. These include six circuit court judges, including two (including the first woman) to the previously all-white Fourth Circuit (actually Bush renominated Judge Roger Gregory to the Fourth Circuit—Gregory had been given a temporary, recess appointment by President Clinton). President Bush also nominated California Supreme Court Justice Janice Brown, an African American, to the District of Columbia Circuit, generally considered the second most powerful Court in the nation. Although Senate Democrats, with the support of African American leaders, filibustered her nomination for two years, in 2005 she was confirmed by the Senate.

How Should the Constitution Be Interpreted?: Judicial Restraint Versus Judicial Activism and the Implications for Universal Freedom

Throughout the Court's history, but especially in the twentieth century, there has been a debate among scholars, politicians, and judges over how the Constitution should be interpreted. Conservative scholars and jurists tend to favor *judicial self-restraint,* or "strict constructionism." That is, they argue that justices and judges should look to the intent of the framers of the Constitution and precedents in interpreting the Constitution rather than applying their own political values or changing the Constitution to fit the needs of a changing society. By contrast, liberal scholars and jurists tend to favor *judicial activism,* or "loose constructionism." That is, they argue that the intent of the framers on many issues is vague and unclear, and that the framers designed the Constitution as a "living" document to be interpreted broadly to fit the needs of a changing society.[12]

Although an important legal and political debate, it is in some ways misleading since at times liberals have favored judicial restraint and conservatives have favored activism. For example, an important principle of conservative jurisprudence is that the courts should adhere to precedent (*stare decisis*) and not overturn the decisions of democratically elected legislative bodies unless they clearly violate the Constitution. Yet, the current conservative majority on the Supreme Court has in recent years been active in overturning precedents and congressional and state legislative acts in the areas of commerce, affirmative action, and voting rights. The liberal bloc led by Justice John Paul Stevens, on the other hand, in its dissents has called for restraint, adherence to precedents, and deference to legislative majorities. Thus, whether one is for "strict" or "loose" interpretation depends, as the saying goes, "on whose ox is gored."

Table 13.2 lists the number of federal and state laws declared unconstitutional from 1800 to 2000. The data in the table show that there have been two periods of sustained judicial activism: from 1910 to 1940, and from 1950 to 2000. In the first period, a conservative Supreme Court declared unconstitutional 26 federal laws and 350 state laws. This represents 26 percent of all the federal laws and 30 percent of all the state laws declared unconstitutional in the entire history of the Court. This spate of judicial activism involved a conservative Court overturning a series of progressive reforms regulating private property and the industrial economy. The second period of judicial activism involved a liberal Supreme Court overturning state and federal laws that

Table 13.2 Number of Federal, State, and Local Laws Declared Unconstitutional by the Supreme Court, 1800–2000

YEARS	FEDERAL LAWS	STATE AND LOCAL LAWS
1800–1809	1	1
1810–1819	0	7
1820–1829	0	8
1830–1839	0	3
1840–1849	0	9
1850–1859	1	7
1860–1869	4	23
1870–1879	7	36
1880–1889	4	46
1890–1899	5	36
1900–1909	9	40
1910–1919[a]	6	118
1920–1929	15	139
1930–1939	13	93
1940–1949	2	58
1950–1959[a]	5	60
1960–1969	16	149
1970–1979	20	193
1980–1990	18	125
1990–2000[a]	29	63
TOTAL	153	1,251

[a]Periods of judicial activism.

Sources: Lawrence Baum, *The Supreme Court,* 7th ed. (Washington, DC: Congressional Quarterly Press, 2001). Data from 1990 to 1999 drawn from Baum. Data for 2000 provided to the authors by Professor J. Clay Smith of the Howard University Law School.

restricted civil rights, liberties, and freedoms. In this period, 41 federal laws and 402 state laws were declared unconstitutional, representing more than 32 and 35 percent, respectively, of all federal and state laws declared unconstitutional by the Court.

For African Americans and their quest for universal freedom, the debate on how the Constitution should be interpreted depends on the context and the times. In the Post–Reconstruction Era, when the Court ignored the intent of the framers of the Fourteenth and Fifteenth Amendments and declared unconstitutional several civil rights laws, black interests would have been served by judicial self-restraint. But in the 1960s and 1970s, black interests were served when the Court for the first time began to enforce the Fourteenth and Fifteenth Amendments by declaring state laws unconstitutional and upholding federal civil rights laws. In the current period of judicial activism (1990–2000) African American interests are adversely affected by the Rehnquist Court's state-centered federalism, which limits the authority of the federal government to expand and extend universal rights and freedom (see Chapter 2).

As a result of the activism of the Court under Chief Justice Earl Warren's leadership, liberals and progressives came to view the Court as a defender of minority rights. Historically, however, the Warren Court is an anomaly since for much of the Court's history it has been a racist, antifreedom institution. Legal scholar Girardeau Spann argues that this racist, antiminority stance of the Court is "structurally" inevitable. He writes:

> My argument is that, for structural reasons, the institutional role that the Court is destined to play within our constitutional scheme of government is the role of assuring the continued subordination of racial minority interests. I believe that this subordination function is inevitable; that it will be served irrespective of the Court's composition at any particular point in time; and that it will persist irrespective of the conscious motives of the individual justices.[13]

The Supreme Court and African Americans: Rights- and Material-Based Cases

The Supreme Court was transformed into a liberal institution beginning with the New Deal. President Roosevelt appointed nine justices to the Court and his successor, President Truman, appointed four. Most of the Roosevelt and Truman appointees were more or less liberal, as were the four appointees made by President Eisenhower, including Chief Justice Warren. This liberal tendency of the Court was consolidated by the four appointments made by Presidents Kennedy and Johnson. Among the leading liberal jurists appointed to the Court from the 1930s to the 1960s were Hugo Black, William O. Douglas, William Brennan, Arthur Goldberg, Thurgood Marshall, and Abe Fortas. As a result, by the late 1940s the Court was in the process of shifting its jurisprudence from a focus on protecting property rights and business interests toward a concern with individual civil liberties and the civil rights of minorities.[14]

Simultaneous with this transformation of the Court, the NAACP transformed its approach to civil rights from lobbying to litigation. In 1939 the NAACP Legal Defense Fund was created, and under the leadership of Thurgood Marshall it developed a systematic strategy of using the courts to achieve social change and racial justice, a strategy later employed by many other American groups (see Box 13.1). This strategy was

BOX 13.1   LITIGATION AND SOCIAL CHANGE: THE LEGACY OF *BROWN*

In Chapter 7 we discussed how the African American civil rights and black power movements of the 1960s and 1970s sparked and served as a model for social movements among women, gays, and other minorities. The success of the NAACP Legal Defense Fund's litigation strategy in the *Brown* v. *Board of Education* case also led other groups in the United States to create organizations and develop strategies using litigation to bring about social change.[a]

Following the NAACP model, in the late 1960s scores of groups organized legal defense funds—women, Mexican Americans, Puerto Ricans, Asian Americans, gays and lesbians, and evangelical Christians. Once organized, these groups followed the strategy pioneered by Thurgood Marshall of bringing a series of

Thurgood Marshall, George Hayes, and James Nabrit outside the Supreme Court after it announced its landmark decision in *Brown* v. *Board of Education*. Source: Bettmann/Corbis

well-researched, strategically selected "test cases" before the Court to force it to establish new rights and expand the idea of freedom.

Supreme Court Justice Ruth Bader Ginsberg is sometimes referred to as the "Thurgood Marshall of the women's movement" for her work as an attorney on women's legal projects in the 1960s and 1970s; these were projects that led to an expansion of women's rights and freedoms, including the critical right of a woman to choose an abortion. As a result of the litigation, new rights have been established for the elderly, the poor, language minorities, immigrants, environmentalists, and the handicapped.

The NAACP turned to the Courts in the 1930s to pursue its civil rights agenda because its leaders felt relatively powerless in the ordinary politics of lobbying Congress and the president. Other groups, also feeling powerless and seeing the success of the NAACP in *Brown,* also turned to the Courts, and the process significantly expanded the idea of universal freedom.[b]

[a]See Clement Vose, "Litigation as a Form of Pressure Group Activity," *The Annals of the American Academy of Social and Political Science* 319 (September 1958): 20–31; and Karen O'Connor, *Women's Organizations' Use of the Courts* (Lexington, MA: Lexington Books, 1980).

[b]In recent years, right-wing conservative and religious groups have also adopted the NAACP approach to litigation, filing strategic test cases, for example, on voting rights and affirmative action.

enormously successful, as during the 1960s and early 1970s the Court issued a number of landmark rulings expanding the rights of blacks, other ethnic minorities, women, atheists, communists, and persons accused of crimes.

These successes, however, brought reactions from conservative and racist forces (during the 1950s and 1960s there were billboards throughout the South reading "Impeach Earl Warren"), and conservative Republican presidents began to campaign against the Court's "liberal activism" and promise to appoint "strict constructionists" as justices. Between 1969 and 1991, Presidents Nixon, Ford, Reagan, and Bush appointed 11 justices to the Court. By the late 1980s, as a result of these appointments, the Supreme Court had a narrow five-person conservative majority (see Table 13.3). Immediately, this majority, led by Chief Justice William Rehnquist, began to retreat from the civil rights reforms of the 1960s and 1970s. We examine this retreat on rights- and material-based cases in an analysis of the last three decades of Supreme Court decision making on school desegregation, voting rights, and affirmative action (for the Court's own record on affirmative action see Box 13.2). But first we examine President George W. Bush's first two appointments to the Court.

As a candidate, President Bush promised to appoint Supreme Court justices in the mold of Antonin Scalia and Clarence Thomas, the Court's two most conservative justices and the justices most consistently hostile to civil liberties and civil rights. In 2004 Justice Sandra Day O'Connor retired and Chief Justice Rehnquist died. To replace them President Bush nominated John G. Roberts for chief justice and Samuel Alito to replace O'Connor. The NAACP, the Leadership Conference on Civil Rights, the Congressional Black Caucus, and other national civil rights organizations opposed both nominees, fearing Bush was keeping his promise. Black leaders expressed special

Table 13.3 Justices of the Supreme Court by Ideological Inclination, 1986–2007

JUSTICE	NOMINATED BY
STRICT CONSERVATIVE[a]	
Samuel Alito	George W. Bush (2005)
John Roberts	George W. Bush (2005)
Antonin Scalia	Ronald Reagan (1986)
Clarence Thomas	George Bush (1991)
MODERATE CONSERVATIVE	
Anthony Kennedy	Ronald Reagan (1988)
MODERATE LIBERAL	
John Paul Stevens	Gerald Ford (1975)
David Souter	George Bush (1990)
Ruth Bader Ginsberg	Bill Clinton (1993)
Stephen Breyer	Bill Clinton (1994)

[a]The classifications of Chief Justice Roberts and Justice Alito are tentative, based on their less than one year on the court. However, a study by Georgetown University Law Center found that in their brief tenures, in nonunanimous decisions Roberts sided with Justice Stevens—the Court's most liberal member—only 35 percent of the time and Alito only 23 percent. See Linda Greenhouse "With Robert at Helm, a Supreme Court in Flux," *New York Times*, July 2, 2006.

BOX 13.2   TO BE YOUNG, WHITE, AND MALE: THE SUPREME COURT RECORD ON EQUAL EMPLOYMENT OPPORTUNITY, 1972–1998

A principal responsibility of the Supreme Court in the post–civil rights era is to decide cases involving implementation of the 1964 Civil Rights Act's prohibition on employment discrimination. In its affirmative action jurisprudence, the Court has to deal with issues of "diversity"—the extent to which universities and employers may take race and gender into account in creating a workplace and university class that reflects the diverse ethnic and racial makeup of the nation.

Although the Supreme Court is the ultimate judge of equal employment and affirmative action for the nation, its own record on these matters is itself suspect. Indeed, under ordinary circumstances, the Court's record might lead to its being sued for violations of the Civil Rights Act and for failure to achieve a diverse workplace (the Court is, of course, exempt from such suits).

Each year, each of the nine justices is allowed to select up to four clerks to serve for a one-year term. These young persons—usually selected from among the best students at the nation's elite law schools—play an influential role in screening cases the Court will hear, in doing research, and in writing draft opinions for the justices. Thus, these clerks play powerful behind-the-scenes roles in shaping the kinds of cases the Court will hear and the legal rationales and scope of its opinions.[a]

In 1998, *USA Today* conducted the first ever demographic study of Supreme Court law clerks.[b] The study found that this elite of the Court's workforce was largely composed of young white males. Specifically, the study found that of the 394 clerks hired during the tenure of the

Percentage of Whites Hired as Clerks by Justices of the Supreme Court[*]		
Justice	**Number of Clerks**	**Percentage White**
Rehnquist	79	99%
Stevens	58	86
O'Connor	68	91
Scalia	48	100
Kennedy	45	91
Souter	31	94
Thomas	29	86
Ginsberg	20	90
Breyer	16	80

(continued)

BOX 13.1 continued

justices from 1972 to 1998, 1.8 percent were black, 1 percent were Latino, and 4.5 percent were Asian Americans.[c] Four of the nine justices (including the chief justice, who had served on the Court for more than a quarter of a century) had never hired a black clerk. The following table shows the percentage of white clerks appointed by the justices.

*The justices are listed by length of service on the Court. These data are reported in Tony Mauro, "Schools Urged to Press for Diversity in Court Clerkships," *USA Today*, May 8–10, 1998, p. 4A.

[a]The screening of cases is an especially important role. For example, typically more than 5,000 cases are appealed to the Court annually but it usually hears fewer than a hundred.

[b]In 1996, as part of the research for this book, we tried unsuccessfully to obtain data on the racial composition of the Court's clerks. We were told by the Office of the Clerk of the Court that such information was not available either from the Clerk's office or the chambers of the individual justices. The results of the *USA Today* study are reported in Tony Mauro, "Court Faulted on Diversity," *USA Today*, May 8–10, 1998, p. A1.

[c]Seventy-five percent of the clerks during this period were men. On the role of the clerks, see Artemus Ward and David Weiden, *Sorcerers Apprentices: 100 Years of Law Clerks at the United States Supreme Court* (New York: New York University Press, 2006).

---

concerns about their views on affirmative action, since both men as young lawyers in the Reagan administration wrote memos opposing affirmative action. Alito, for example, in a 1985 memo wrote that he was "particularly proud" of the administration's efforts to convince the Supreme Court that "racial and ethnic quotas" should not be allowed.[15] At their confirmation hearings neither nominee was required or willing to state their current views on affirmative action. Roberts was confirmed 78-22 and Alito 58-42. In their first year on the Court it did not consider any affirmative action cases, but it agreed to hear two cases involving race and school assignments in its next term (see page 240).

Rights-Based Cases

School Desegregation

In 1954 the Supreme Court, in a unanimous decision written by Chief Justice Warren, in effect overruled its decision in the 1896 *Plessy* v. *Ferguson* case by declaring that, at least in the area of public education, the principle of "separate but equal" violated the equal protection clause of the Fourteenth Amendment.[16] "Separate educational facilities," Chief Justice Warren wrote, are *"inherently unequal"* (emphasis added). The *Plessy* decision dealt with segregation on railroad cars but thereafter it was applied to all areas of southern life, including public schools.

Although, according to the Court, separate was constitutionally permissible only if facilities for blacks and whites were equal, the equality part of the principle was never enforced. Three years after *Plessy* in *Cummings* v. *Richmond County Board of Education*, the Court held that it was permissible to provide a high school for whites but not for blacks.[17] Thus, the doctrine of equality in *Plessy* was a lie. *African Americans in violation of the Court's own decision were relegated to separate and unequal schools and other facilities.* The initial strategy of the NAACP, therefore, was to attack not the practice of segregation itself but rather the absence of equality in the education of blacks.

This attack on unequal educational opportunities began at the graduate and professional levels. In 1938 in *Missouri ex rel. Gaines* v. *Canada,* the Court invalidated Missouri's policy of excluding blacks from its law school and instead offering to pay for their attendance at out-of-state law schools.[18] In *Sweatt* v. *Painter* (1939) the Court found that Texas's all-black law school was "inherently inferior" to its school for whites and ordered the admission of blacks to the white school.[19] In *McLaurin* v. *Oklahoma State Regents,* the Court ruled that Oklahoma State University's practice of segregating black students in its graduate school was unconstitutional.[20] After these victories at the graduate level, the NAACP, after extensive research and debate, changed its strategy and decided to launch a direct attack on the doctrine of separate but equal.[21] The result was the Court's 1954 *Brown* decision.

When the Court declared that segregated schools were unconstitutional it did not order the schools to be integrated. Rather, a year later, in what is called "*Brown II,*" the Court ordered the states practicing segregation in public education to "desegregate" with "all deliberate speed."[22] In other words, the states were told to take their time—to desegregate the schools, but slowly. It was not until 1969 in *Alexander* v. *Holmes County Board of Education* that the Court ordered the states to desegregate the schools "at once."[23] Only after this decision—some 15 years after *Brown*—did most southern states begin to desegregate their separate and unequal schools.[24]

In 1971, in *Swann* v. *Charlotte Mecklenburg,* the Court ordered school districts to use busing to achieve racial balance or quotas so that "pupils of all grades are assigned in such a way that as nearly as practicable the various schools at various grade levels have about the same proportion of black and white students."[25] The principles of the *Swann* case were soon applied nationwide, leading to an enormous political controversy and eventually a decision by the Court to reverse its position and put an end to school busing.[26]

Busing for purposes of school desegregation was overwhelmingly opposed by white Americans (in the range of 75–80 percent); African American opinion was about equally divided, with polls showing about half supporting busing. In many cities, court-ordered busing led to mass protests by whites, boycotts, violence, and "white flight" to private or suburban schools.

In *Milliken* v. *Bradley,* the Supreme Court began the process of dismantling busing for purposes of desegregation. Specifically, the Court overturned a lower court order that required busing between largely black Detroit and the largely white surrounding suburbs. The Court majority agreed that Detroit's schools were unconstitutionally segregated but held that cross-district busing between city and suburbs was not required to comply with *Brown.*[27] In an angry dissenting opinion, Justice Thurgood Marshall accused his colleagues of bowing to political pressure and of being unwilling to enforce school busing because it was unpopular with the white majority. Since *Milliken,* the court has continued to retreat from busing as a device to desegregate the schools.

Because of white flight to the suburbs, America's urban school systems cannot be desegregated unless there is cross-district busing between city and suburbs. The Supreme Court, however, will not permit this. Thus, 50 years after *Brown,* most African American schoolchildren remain in schools that are separate and unequal—inequalities that are so great that one observer describes them as "savage."[28]

In 2004 there were numerous conferences, special classes, and seminars at colleges and universities, several books, and scores of newspaper articles and television stories commemorating the 50th anniversary of the May 17, 1954, *Brown* decision. Virtually all commentators celebrated the courage and skill of the individuals who brought the cases and the wisdom of the justices in their decision. *Brown* was also celebrated as the most important Court decision of the twentieth century, and one of the two or three most important in the history of the Court. The historical significance of the case, however, was not in terms of school integration but rather in terms of its symbolism—its symbolism in striking down the constitutional foundations and legitimacy of racism and white supremacy. In terms of school integration, most commentators agreed that *Brown* had been a failure. That is, 50 years after *Brown* most black (and Latino) children in the North and South attend schools that are separate and unequal.[29] The separateness is a function of the segregated housing patterns that characterize most urban areas of the United States, where blacks live mostly in central city ghettos and whites mainly in affluent urban enclaves or suburbia. Thus, in 2000, 40 percent of all public schools were almost all black or minority. The inequality flows from the fact that states generally rely on the local property tax to finance schools. This means that affluent, high-property-value school districts are able to provide much more in per pupil spending than poor districts. And since whites live disproportionately in affluent districts and blacks disproportionately in poor districts, the effect is to create school systems throughout the nation that in some ways are as separate and unequal as they were prior to *Brown*.

Voting Rights and Racial Representation

Prior to the passage of the Voting Rights Act in 1965, very few African Americans were elected to office in the United States. In that year, approximately 280 blacks held elected offices in this country, including six members of Congress. Today there are more than 8,000 black elected officeholders, including 42 members of Congress.[30] Thus, blacks in the last 25 years have made considerable progress in their quest for public office; however, 8,000 offices constitute a minuscule 1.5 percent of the more than 500,000 elective offices in the United States. Even this tiny number of blacks holding elected office may be in jeopardy as a result of recent Supreme Court interpretations of the Voting Rights Act.

When the Voting Rights Act was passed, it was initially used to guarantee southern blacks the simple right to cast a vote. However, in the late 1960s, the Supreme Court issued a series of decisions interpreting various provisions of the act as guaranteeing not just the simple right to vote but also the right to cast an effective vote—a vote that would allow African Americans to choose candidates of their choice, presumably one of their own race.[31] The key case in this regard is *United Jewish Organizations* v. *Carey*.[32]

In 1972, the New York State Legislature redrew Brooklyn's state senate and assembly districts so that several would have black and Puerto Rican majorities ranging from 65 to 90 percent. In doing this, the Legislature divided a cohesive community of Hasidic Jews between separate assembly and senate districts in the Williamsburg section of Brooklyn, where previously they had been located within single districts. The Hasidic Jews alleged that the creation of the majority–minority districts was "reverse discrimination" against whites, and the United Jewish Organizations of Williamsburg filed suit, claiming that the New York Legislature's actions violated the Fourteenth Amendment's equal protection clause.

In a 7-to-1 decision the Supreme Court rejected the claims of the Hasidic Jews, holding that deliberate creation of majority–minority legislative districts was not reverse discrimination and therefore did not violate the equal rights of Brooklyn's white voters. Writing for the majority, Justice White noted that whites made up 65 percent of Brooklyn's population and were majorities in 70 percent of its senate and assembly districts. Therefore, "as long as whites, as a group, were provided with fair representation, we cannot conclude that there was a cognizable discrimination against whites or an abridgment of their right to vote."[33] In 1993 in *Shaw* v. *Reno,* the Supreme Court in effect reversed its holding in *Carey,* deciding that the deliberate creation of majority black districts might indeed violate the equal protection rights of white voters.[34]

After the 1990 census, most of the southern states, following the precedent established in *Carey,* created new majority black congressional districts. These districts in turn elected 12 new black congresspersons. In several states (North Carolina, South Carolina, Florida, Alabama, and Virginia) this was the first time a black had been elected to Congress since Reconstruction. In North Carolina, several white voters sued, alleging, as did the Hasidic Jews in Brooklyn two decades earlier, that the creation of the black districts was "reverse discrimination" and a violation of the Fourteenth Amendment's equal protection clause.

In *Shaw,* a narrow 5-to-4 majority of the Court agreed with North Carolina's white voters. Writing for the majority, Justice O'Connor held that the North Carolina districts were unconstitutional because they were irregularly shaped. (The 12th district in North Carolina stretched approximately 160 miles along Interstate 85 and for much of its length is no wider than the I-85 corridor.) Justice O'Connor said the districts were "so extremely irregular on [their] face . . . that they rationally can be viewed as an effort to segregate the races for purposes of voting." Such segregation, Justice O'Connor wrote, "reinforces the perception that members of the same racial group—regardless of their age, education, economic status or the community in which they live—think alike, share the same political interests and will prefer the same candidate. We have rejected such perceptions elsewhere as impermissible racial stereotyping."[35]

In his dissent, Justice Stevens pointed out the irony and perversity of the situation in which the Fourteenth Amendment, which was enacted to protect the rights of African Americans, was being used in this case to deny them rights and representation. He wrote:

> If it is permissible to draw boundaries to provide adequate representation for rural voters, for union members, for Hasidic Jews, for Polish Americans or for Republicans, it necessarily follows that it is permissible to do the same thing for members of the very minority group whose history in the United States gave birth to the Equal Protection Clause. A contrary conclusion could only be described as perverse.[36]

After eight years of litigation and more than a dozen cases in several states, the Supreme Court in 2001 in *Easley* v. *Cromartie* to some extent clarified the principles of *Shaw* in a way that permits some use of race as a factor in legislative redistricting.[37] This case once again involved the drawing of the lines in North Carolina's

12th congressional district, which was the district in dispute in the original case. After the Court declared the majority black 12th district unconstitutional, the North Carolina legislature redrew the lines of the district to create a 41 percent majority black district. The three-judge federal district court in North Carolina ruled this new district unconstitutional because it had used race as the "predominant factor" in redrawing the lines. In *Easley* a 5-to-4 majority reversed the district court, holding that district court's conclusion that race was the predominant factor in drawing the lines was "clearly erroneous." Rather, Justice Stephen Breyer, writing for the majority (which included Justice O'Connor), concluded that the district lines were based on party affiliation rather than race, and since there is a high correlation between race and party (95 percent of black voters in North Carolina typically vote for Democratic candidates) it was appropriate for the legislature to take race into account as a surrogate for party. Thus, Breyer concluded that race was not an illegitimate consideration in redistricting as long as it was not the "dominant and controlling" one. Justice Clarence Thomas, writing for himself and the other dissenting justices, argued that the majority should not have second-guessed the conclusions of the district court but that even if the majority was correct that party rather than race was the predominant factor, the lines were still unconstitutional because "it is not a defense that the Legislature merely may have drawn the district based on the stereotype that blacks are reliable Democratic voters." While the Court's narrow decision suggested to state legislatures that race could be used in the redistricting process, it still left the situation muddled in terms of the factual determination of when the use of race was "predominant," "dominant," or "controlling."

Material-Based Cases: Affirmative Action

Affirmative action encompasses a variety of policies and programs designed to assure African Americans (and other minorities and women) access to material benefits or rights in the areas of education, employment, and government contracts. These programs and policies were put into place in the late 1960s and early 1970s by the courts, Congress, the president, and many of the states, for one or more of the following reasons: (1) to remedy or compensate African Americans for past discrimination, (2) to enforce or implement provisions of the 1964 Civil Rights Act, and (3) to create diversity in education, employment, and government contracting. These programs are now under attack by the conservative Republicans in Congress and at the state and local levels. Leading this attack is the Supreme Court's five-person conservative majority. Next we review the history of Supreme Court decision making on affirmative action in cases dealing with education, employment, and government contracting.

Education

In 1978 in *Regents of the University of California* v. *Bakke*, the Supreme Court in a split decision upheld the constitutionality of affirmative action.[38] The case involved two issues: first, whether it was constitutionally permissible for a state to take race into account in allocating material benefits—in this specific case, access to medical school;

second, if the use of race was deemed permissible, whether the state could use a numerical racial quota to allocate these benefits (in *Bakke* this involved setting aside 16 of 100 slots for minority students only). In deciding the case, the Court was deeply divided, issuing six separate opinions. Four conservative justices led by Justice Rehnquist argued that the University of California program violated Title VII of the 1964 Civil Rights Act (which prohibits discrimination by institutions receiving federal funds) as well as the equal protection clause of the Fourteenth Amendment. In the view of these four justices, taking race into consideration in allocating material benefits was never permissible. Four liberal justices led by Justices Brennan and Marshall held that a state, in order to remedy past discrimination or create ethnic diversity, could take race into consideration in allocating benefits and could, if it wished, use a fixed quota. Justice Lewis Powell, the Court's only Southerner, split the difference between his liberal and conservative colleagues by holding that a state could use race for purposes of diversity but that a fixed quota was illegal and unconstitutional.

In the 25 years since *Bakke* the country and the courts became increasingly divided about affirmative action in higher education. Of the Thirteenth Circuit courts of appeal four had issued different opinions on the issue. The Fifth and Eleventh Circuits (covering six southern states) overruled *Bakke* and banned affirmative action, and the Sixth and Ninth Circuits (covering several midwestern and nine western states) upheld *Bakke*. Because of these conflicts between the circuits (which meant the Constitution and the law had different meanings depending on what part of the country one lived in), the Supreme Court in 2003 decided to revisit *Bakke*.

The Court considered two cases from the University of Michigan. The first involved the University's undergraduate admissions program in which black, Hispanic, and Native American applicants were automatically awarded 20 points of the 100 needed to guarantee admission. The second dealt with the University's law school admission program, which was designed to achieve a "critical mass" of minority students by requiring admission officials to consider all aspects of an applicant's record (including his or her ethnicity) in an "individualized assessment" of the extent to which the applicant contributed to the University's goal of a well-qualified and diverse law school class. Both programs were challenged by white applicants who had been denied admission. They alleged that the University's use of race as a factor in its admissions decisions violated the Civil Rights Act of 1964 and the equal protection clause of the Fourteenth Amendment. The Sixth Circuit rejected the challenge to the law school's program, and its decision on the undergraduate program was pending when the Supreme Court decided to take both cases. These two cases, *Gratz et al.* v. *Bollinger et al.* and *Grutter* v. *Bollinger et al.* were argued before the Court on April 1 and decided on June 29, 2003.

In its decision the Court upheld the law school program but declared the undergraduate program unconstitutional. Writing for a 5-4 majority in *Grutter,* Justice O'Connor reaffirmed *Bakke*, writing, "Today we endorse Justice Powell's view that student body diversity is a compelling state interest that can justify the use of race in university admissions."[39] The chief justice and Justices Kennedy, Thomas, and Scalia dissented, concluding that the law school admission program operated as a racial quota system. As Justice Scalia wrote, the program was little more than "a sham to cover a scheme of racially proportionate admissions."[40]

In *Gratz,* however, Justice O'Connor joined the other side, voting to strike down the undergraduate program with its automatic 20 points for minorities as a quota system. In his opinion for the majority, the chief justice held that the 20 points awarded to "every single 'underrepresented minority' applicant because of race was not narrowly tailored to achieve educational diversity."[41] In his concurring opinion, Justice Thomas went beyond the chief justice to declare that even if the program was narrowly tailored it would still be unconstitutional because the use of race in admissions decisions is "categorically prohibited by the Fourteenth Amendment."[42]

In her dissent Justice Ginsberg suggested that affirmative action was not only a compelling interest of states to achieve diversity in their universities but also to remedy past and ongoing racism. She wrote, "The racial and ethnic groups to which the College accords special consideration (African Americans, Hispanics and Native Americans) historically have been relegated to inferior status by law and social practice; their members continue to face class based discrimination to this day."[43] She also suggested that Justice O'Connor was somewhat disingenuous in approving the law school program that indirectly took race into consideration, while disapproving the undergraduate program because it did so openly. She wrote, "If honesty is the best policy, surely Michigan's accurately described, fully disclosed college affirmative action program is preferable to achieving similar numbers through winks, nods and disguises."[44]

While the Court in *Grutter* narrowly upheld the use of race to achieve diversity in higher education, in 2008 in two related cases it held that race could not be used to achieve diversity in elementary and secondary education. The two cases, *Parents Involved in Community Schools* v. *Seattle School District* and *Meredith* v. *Jefferson County Board of Education,* involved the use of race as one factor in assigning students to schools in order to maintain diversity or racial integration. White parents sued claiming that the assignment of pupils by race violated the Fourteenth Amendment's equal protection clause. A bitterly divided Court, in a 5-4 decision, agreed. Writing for the majority, the chief justice invoked the famous *Brown* decision, declaring that the Constitution forbids the classification of students on the basis of race, whether for purposes of integration or segregation. In his dissent, Justice Breyer wrote that use of *Brown* in these cases was a "cruel distortion of history" because the "lesson of history is not that efforts to continue racial segregation is constitutionally indistinguishable from efforts to achieve racial integration." Although Justice Kennedy joined the majority, he was unwilling to conclude that the Constitution prevented any consideration of race in order to achieve racial integration. Describing the chief justice's opinion as "all-too unyielding" in its insistence that race can never be a factor in pupil assignments, Kennedy wrote that in some instances race might be used to reach *Brown*'s objective of ending "de facto re-segregation in schooling."

Meanwhile, in Michigan in 2006 the voters approved Proposition 2, prohibiting the use of racial preferences by any state agency including colleges and universities. The Proposition was approved by a margin of 58 to 42 percent. While only 14 percent of blacks voted yes, the Proposition was approved by 62 percent of whites including 68 percent of white men and 57 percent of white women. In 2008 a similar proposition was defeated in Colorado and approved in Nebraska.

Employment

The equivalent to the *Bakke* case in the area of employment is *Griggs et al.* v. *Duke Power Company*, decided in 1971.[45] In this case, a unanimous Supreme Court struck down educational and test requirements that had a discriminatory impact on blacks seeking employment, unless such requirements could be shown to be necessary to the performance of the job. In *Wards Cove* v. *Atonio*, decided in 1989, the Supreme Court by a 5-to-4 vote in effect overruled *Griggs*, holding that a business could engage in racially discriminatory hiring practices if they served "legitimate employment goals."[46] Unlike the Court's decisions in the areas of affirmative action involving education and government contracts, which involved interpreting the Constitution, the employment cases involve interpreting a statute or law (specifically Title VII of the 1964 Civil Rights Act). Thus, the Congress could change the Court's decision by simply passing a new law. This it did in the 1991 Civil Right Act. Specifically, with respect to *Wards Cove*, the Congress reinstated the principles of *Griggs* by requiring that employee qualifications be nondiscriminatory and "job related for the position in question and consistent with business necessity."[47] However, the language of the 1991 act is, according to lawyers specializing in employment discrimination, so riddled with confusing, contradictory, and ambiguous provisions that sorting it out will take years.[48] Since the Supreme Court's misinterpretation of the existing law is what made the 1991 act necessary in the first place, the Court may read the ambiguous new law in a way adverse to the interests of African Americans. Indeed, in 1993 the Court in *St. Mary's Honor Center* v. *Hicks* once again overturned two 20-year-old precedents involving employment discrimination, leading Justice Souter in a dissenting opinion to warn his colleagues that they were ignoring the intent of Congress as expressed in the 1991 Civil Rights Act.[49]

Government Contracts

In 1977, to increase minority access to government contracts, Congress added a provision to the Public Works Act requiring that at least 10 percent of federal funds granted for local projects be awarded to minority-owned businesses. White businessmen challenged this 10 percent set-aside as an unconstitutional racial quota, but the Court in *Fullilove* v. *Klutznik* rejected their claims.[50] In *Fullilove* the Court held that Congress, to remedy past discrimination, had the authority to establish the 10 percent set-aside as a reasonable method to assure minority access to contracts. In 1989 in *Metro Broadcasting* v. *Federal Communications Commission*, the Court upheld similar minority set-aside programs in the allocation of broadcast licenses.[51] Both these decisions were overruled by the conservative Court majority.

In 1983, Richmond, Virginia, established a minority set-aside program for its contracts modeled on the plan passed by Congress and approved by the Supreme Court in *Fullilove*. In *J. A. Croson* v. *City of Richmond*, the Court in a 5-to-4 decision declared the Richmond plan unconstitutional.[52] Writing for the majority, Justice O'Connor declared that Congress as a coequal branch of government had the authority to establish such set-asides, but the states and localities were prohibited by the Fourteenth Amendment's equal protection clause from doing so unless the plans were "narrowly tailored" to meet identified discriminatory practices. In one of his many angry dissents during his last years on the Court, Justice Marshall described his colleagues' overturning of Richmond's set-aside program as a "deliberate and giant step backward in this Court's affirmative action jurisprudence" that assumes "racial discrimination is largely a phenomenon of the past, and that governmental bodies need no longer preoccupy themselves with rectifying racial injustice."[53]

In *Croson,* Justice O'Connor implied that Congress had the authority to do what the city of Richmond could not do in remedying racial discrimination. Six years later, in *Adarand Constructors* v. *Pena,* she rejected this view and ruled that Congress had to follow the same strict standards as the states.[54] In *Adarand,* the Court, again by 5 to 4, overturned the *Fullilove* and *Metro Broadcasting* precedents. As a result of the *Croson* decision there was a dramatic decline in minority access to contracts in Richmond and other states and localities.[55] A similar result may follow in the wake of *Adarand.* For example, after *Adarand,* President Clinton suspended most federal affirmative action programs that reserved contracts exclusively for minorities and women.[56]

Institutional Racism: Rights Without Remedies

In its 2000–2001 term the court went out of its way to take a case in civil rights law that dealt a death blow to the right of individuals to challenge practices of institutional racism by the states. In doing so it overruled the decisions of 9 of the 12 circuit courts that had ruled on the issue in more than two decades of litigation.

Institutional racism (which the Court refers to as "disparate impact") deals with policies or programs that have a racially discriminatory impact or effect. By contrast, individual racism (which the Court refers to as "disparate treatment") deals with intentional acts of discrimination. Since the adoption of the Civil Rights Act of 1964 individuals have had the right to sue states for both types of discrimination. But in a 5-to-4 decision the Court's conservatives in *Alexander* v. *Sandoval* (#99-1908, 2000) took away the individual right to sue states practicing institutional racism. The case involved a challenge to an Alabama law requiring all applicants to take the state's written driver's license examination in English. The suit alleged that in its impact or effect the requirement discriminated on the basis of language or ethnic origin. The district court and the Eleventh Circuit agreed. But in *Sandoval* the Court, without reaching the merits of the case as to whether the requirement was discriminatory, held that the Civil Rights Act of 1964 allowed individuals to sue only in disparate treatment cases. In another one of his unusually harsh dissents (parts of which he read; a step a justice takes to signal the importance or significance of a decision), Justice Stevens condemned his colleagues for reaching out to take the case when there was no conflict between the circuits and for overturning two decades of precedent, and concluded that "it makes no sense" to distinguish between types of discrimination in terms of an individual's right to sue. *Sandoval* is a potentially far-reaching decision since disparate treatment cases are difficult to prove (it is not likely, for example, that the authorities in Alabama openly discussed their intent to use the English requirement as a means to discriminate on the basis of ethnic origins), which is why individuals in the post–civil rights era resorted to disparate impact suits in the first place.

FACES AND VOICES IN THE STRUGGLE FOR UNIVERSAL FREEDOM

EARL WARREN (1891–1974)

As the 14th chief justice of the United States, Earl Warren did more to address the cause of equality and universal freedom than all of his predecessors combined. Indeed, Chief Justice Warren is one of the best friends of freedom ever to hold a high position in the U.S. government.

Warren was appointed to the Court by President Eisenhower in 1953 as a political favor because as governor of California he had helped Eisenhower win the Republican nomination (Eisenhower later said Warren's appointment was one of the worst mistakes he made as president). Although a popular and progressive governor, Warren had no experience as a judge and his record had not

Source: Collection of the Supreme Court of the United States

shown any particular concern for civil rights or civil liberties. (For example, he had strongly supported the incarceration of Japanese Americans during World War II.) Once on the Court, however, he showed remarkable skills in leading the most pro–universal freedom court in the history of the United States.

Warren is most famous for the *Brown* v. *Board of Education* school desegregation decision. Although his opinion in *Brown* was narrowly focused on education, Warren used it as a precedent to end segregation in all government-operated institutions. In 1967 in *Loving* v. *Virginia,* in the name of freedom and equality the Court declared state bans on interracial marriage unconstitutional.

Although best known for *Brown* and related civil rights cases, the Warren Court extended universal freedom and equality to many other oppressed and stigmatized minorities, including persons accused of crimes, atheists, religious minorities, communists, and women. Warren said he was most proud of the Court's decision in *Baker* v. *Carr,* which established the principle of "one man, one vote." This decision was important, he said, because it helped to make democracy a reality for all Americans.*

---

*Bernard Schwarz, *Super Chief: Earl Warren and His Supreme Court* (New York: New York University Press, 1983).

Summary

For much of its history the Supreme Court has been a racist institution. From its 1857 decision in *Dred Scott* declaring that African Americans had no rights whatsoever, until the remarkable period of the Warren Court in the 1960s, the Court generally ruled against the freedom interests of blacks. In its decisions on race, as with most other cases, the Court tends to reflect the opinions of the white majority and to follow the ideological directions established by the electorate.

In his last year on the Court, Justice Thurgood Marshall in a speech characterized the Court's 1988–1989 term as a deliberate retrenching of the civil rights agenda. Marshall then suggested that in order to protect their rights and freedoms blacks should look to Congress not the courts. Blacks did turn to the Congress after the 1988–1989 term and the result was the Civil Rights Act of 1991. Such legislation, however, has to be reviewed by the Court. Therefore, ultimately, the African American quest for freedom will be profoundly shaped by five people.

Selected Bibliography

Abraham, Henry. *The Judicial Process,* 4th ed. New York: Oxford University Press, 1980. A general overview of the judicial process in the United States, including local, state, and federal courts.

Dahl, Robert. "Decision Making in a Democracy: The Supreme Court as a National Policy Maker." *Journal of Public Law* 6 (Fall 1957): 257–88. A classic analysis of the Court's role in the political process.

Hall, Kermit, William Wiecek, and Paul Finkelman. *American Legal History: Cases and Materials.* New York: Oxford University Press, 1991. A nearly comprehensive collection of cases and commentary on the development of law in the United States, focusing on all areas of law including race and civil rights.

Howard, John R. *The Shifting Wind: The Supreme Court and Civil Rights from Reconstruction to Brown.* Albany: SUNY Press, 1999. A sprightly and often moving analysis of the Court's role in pushing and subverting the African American quest for freedom. Especially valuable for its insights into the internal dynamics of Supreme Court decision making.

Leuctenburg, William. *The Supreme Court Reborn: The Constitutional Revolution in the Age of Roosevelt.* New York: Oxford University Press, 1995. A lucid account of the transformation of the Supreme Court into a liberal reform institution beginning with the New Deal and ending with the Warren Court.

Rosenberg, Gerald. *The Hollow Hope: Can Courts Bring About Social Change?* Chicago: University of Chicago Press, 1996. An analysis of the limited capacity of the courts to foster social change, including detailed study of school desegregation.

Spann, Girardeau. *Race Against the Court: The Supreme Court and Minorities in America.* New York: New York University Press, 1993. An argument that the Supreme Court will enforce minority rights only to the extent that whites are not disadvantaged.

Vose, Clement. "Litigation as a Form of Pressure Group Activity." *The Annals of the American Academy of Political and Social Science* 319 (September, 1958): 20–31. The classic analysis of the use of litigation as a means of influencing the making of public policy.

Walton, Eugene. "Will the Supreme Court Revert to Racism?" *Black World* 21 (1972): 46–48. A cogent analysis of the racist history of the Court.

Notes

1. *Dred Scott* v. *Sanford,* 19 Howard, 60 U.S. 393 (1857), as cited in Kermit Hall, William Wiecek, and Paul Finkelman, eds., *American Legal History: Cases and Materials* (New York: Oxford University Press, 1991): 208.
2. Dred Scott was a slave residing in Illinois, a free state. When his owner returned to Missouri, a slave state, Scott argued that as a result of living in Illinois he had become free and remained

free even in Missouri. The Supreme Court of Missouri rejected Scott's claims and he appealed to the Supreme Court of the United States, which upheld the decision of the Missouri court. Historians contend that this decision (described by Horace Greeley at the time as "wicked," "atrocious," "abominable," and "detestable hypocrisy") was one of the factors that helped to cause the Civil War. Greeley is quoted in Hall, Wiecek, and Finkelman, *American Legal History,* p. 213.

3. J. Morgan Kouser, *Dead End: The Development of Nineteenth Century Litigation on Racial Discrimination* (New York: Oxford University Press, 1986).

4. Eugene Walton, "Will the Supreme Court Revert to Racism?" *Black World* 21 (1972): 46–48.

5. Robert Dahl, "Decision Making in a Democracy: The Supreme Court as a National Policy-Maker," *Journal of Public Law* 6 (Fall 1957): 281. In his analysis of the Court, Dahl concluded that its main function is to confer legitimacy on decisions taken by the political branches.

6. Robert C. Smith, "Rating Black Leaders," *National Political Science Review* 8 (2001): 124–38.

7. See Robert C. Smith and Richard Seltzer, *Contemporary Controversies and the American Racial Divide* (Lanham, MD: Rowman & Littlefield, 2000): 68–72.

8. Vincent Hutchings, "Political Context, Issue Salience and Selective Attentiveness: Constituent Knowledge of the Clarence Thomas Confirmation Vote," *Journal of Politics* 63 (2002): 846–68.

9. Ibid.

10. See J. Clay Smith, Jr., *Supreme Justice: the Speeches and Writings of Thurgood Marshall* (Philadelphia: University of Pennsylvania Press, 2003).

11. Scott Gerber, *First Principles: The Jurisprudence of Clarence Thomas* (New York: New York University Press, 1999).

12. On this debate, see Edwin Meese (Reagan's attorney general, for the judicial self-restraint view), *The Great Debate: Interpreting Our Written Constitution* (Washington, DC: Federalist Society, 1986); and William Brennan (the former justice, for the activism view), *The Great Debate: Interpreting Our Written Constitution* (Washington, DC: Federalist Society, 1986).

13. Girardeau Spann, *Race Against the Court: The Supreme Court and Minorities in Contemporary America* (New York: New York University Press, 1993).

14. William Leuchtenburg, *The Supreme Court Reborn: The Constitutional Revolution in the Age of Roosevelt* (New York: Oxford University Press, 1995).

15. David Savage, "Court to Hear Cases on Race in Schools," *Los Angeles Times,* June 6, 2006.

16. *Brown* v. *Board of Education,* 347 U.S. 483 (1954).

17. 175 U.S. 528 (1899).

18. 305 U.S. 337 (1938).

19. 339 U.S. 629 (1950).

20. 339 U.S. 737 (1950).

21. For detailed analysis of this strategy shift, see Richard Kluger, *Simple Justice: The History of* Brown v. Board of Education (New York: Vintage Books, 1977).

22. *Brown* v. *Board of Education,* 349 U.S. 294 (1955).

23. 392 U.S. 430 (1969).

24. In addition to the impact of the Court's unequivocal order in *Alexander* v. *Holmes,* southern school districts began to rapidly desegregate because the 1964 Civil Rights Act provided that schools practicing racial segregation could not receive federal financial assistance. In 1969 the Nixon administration began to enforce this provision vigorously.

25. 402 U.S. 1 (1971).

26. See Nicholas Mills, ed., *The Great School Bus Controversy* (New York: Teachers' College Press, 1973).

27. *Milliken* v. *Bradley,* 418 U.S. 717 (1974).

28. Jonathan Kozol, *Savage Inequalities: Children in America's Schools* (New York: Crown, 1991).

29. See Charles Ogletree, *All Deliberate Speed: Reflections on the First Half Century of* Brown v. Board of Education (New York: W.W. Norton, 2004); and Sheryl Cashin,

The Failure of Integration: How Race and Class Are Undermining the American Dream (New York: Public Affairs Press, 2004).

30. On the growth of black elected officials since the Voting Rights Act, see Theresa Chambliss, "The Growth and Significance of African American Elected Officials," in R. Gomes and L. Williams, eds., *From Exclusion to Inclusion* (Westport, CT: Praeger, 1992): 53–70.

31. For a review of these cases, see Robert C. Smith, "Liberal Jurisprudence and the Quest for Racial Representation," *Southern University Law Review* 15 (Spring 1988): 1–51.

32. 430 U.S. 144 (1977).

33. Ibid.

34. *Shaw* v. *Reno,* 509 U.S. 690 (1993).

35. Ibid.

36. Ibid.

37. *Easley* v. *Cromartie* (#99-1864, 2001). The case was originally *Hunt* v. *Cromartie* (after James Hunt, the governor of the state at the time of the appeal); however, the Court renamed the case to reflect the name of the new governor, Michael Easley.

38. 438 U.S. 265 (1978).

39. *Grutter* v. *Bollinger et al.* (slip opinion) #0-241 (2003).

40. Ibid.

41. *Gratz et al.* v. *Bollinger et al.* (slip opinion) #02-516 (2003).

42. Ibid.

43. Ibid.

44. Ibid.

45. 401 U.S. 424 (1971).

46. Another important affirmative action case in the area of employment is *Steelworkers* v. *Weber* (99 S.Ct. 2721, 1979). In this case, the Court approved a plan by the steelworkers' union and Kaiser Aluminum that set aside half the slots in a training program for skilled and craft workers for African Americans. This decision too is jeopardized by the Supreme Court's recent line of decisions.

47. "The Compromise on Civil Rights," *New York Times,* December 12, 1991.

48. Steven Holmes, "Lawyers Expect Ambiguities in New Rights Law to Bring Years of Lawsuits," *New York Times,* December 12, 1991.

49. (slip opinion) 90-602 (1993).

50. 448 U.S. 448 (1980).

51. 110 S.Ct. 2997 (1990).

52. 488 U.S. 469 (1989).

53. Ibid.

54. (slip opinion) 903-1841 (1995). This case involved a suit by white contractors challenging a minority set-aside in federal highway construction.

55. Augustus Jones and Clyde Brown, "State Responses to *Richmond* v. *Croson:* A Survey of Equal Employment Opportunity Officers," *National Political Science Review* 3 (1992): 40–61. See also W. Avon Drake and Robert Holsworth, *Affirmative Action and the Stalled Quest for Racial Progress* (Urbana: University of Illinois Press, 1996): chap. 7.

56. Steven Holmes, "White House to Suspend a Program for Minorities," *New York Times,* March 8, 1996, p. A1; and Steven Holmes, "Administration Cuts Affirmative Action While Defending It," *New York Times,* March 16, 1998, p. A17.

CHAPTER 14

The Bureaucracy and the African American Quest for Universal Freedom

The Nature of the Federal Bureaucracy

In his classic studies, Max Weber defined *bureaucracy* as a form of power based on knowledge—rationally and hierarchically organized. In other words, a bureaucracy is a system of bureaus and agencies that carry out laws and policies on a routine, day-to-day basis, using a hierarchy, standardized procedures, knowledge, and a specialization of duties.[1]

What are the functions of the bureaucracy? Essentially, the bureaucracy serves three major functions. First, it must execute the law. Second, it must write the rules so as to execute the law. Finally, it must adjudicate between claimants and resolve disputes when disagreements arise about proper procedures, regulations, guidelines, and federal practices. Collectively, these three major functions are subsumed under the rubric of *implementation*. Hence, the purpose of the federal bureaucracy is to implement the laws.

Table 14.1 shows the structure, organization, and types of federal agencies and bureaucracies. Basically, the bureaucracy can be grouped into five major categories. First are the agencies within the *Executive Office of the President,* such as the Office of Management and Budget and the National Security Council. Second are the 15 *cabinet departments.* There are also numerous *independent agencies* such as the Environmental Protection Agency, the National Aeronautics and Space Administration, and the Social Security Administration.

In addition to these administrative units, there are the *government corporations,* which can function like private corporations. Examples are the United States Postal Service and Amtrak.

Finally, there are the *independent regulatory commissions,* which are supposed to be beyond direct presidential and congressional influence. Members of these commissions serve for fixed terms and therefore may not be fired by the president, so these commissions may in theory act in the public interest without political pressure. Table 14.1 shows that only 2 of the 61 independent commissions and government corporations deal explicitly with issues of race or civil rights: the Civil Rights Commission and the Equal Employment Opportunity Commission. They represent 3.3 percent of the total commissions and corporations.

Table 14.1 Structure of the Federal Bureaucracy

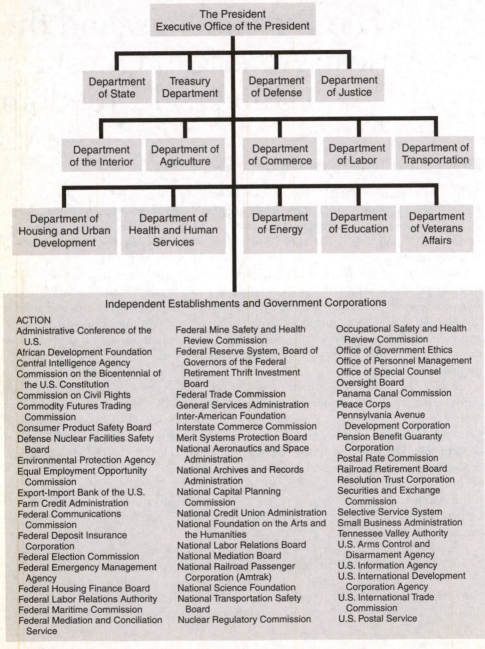

Source: *United States Government Manual, 2000–2001* (Washington, DC: Government Printing Office).

Bureaucracies with Race Missions

In 1865 the Bureau of Refugees, Freedmen and Abandoned Lands, better known as the Freedmen's Bureau, was established. The Bureau was the first federal agency with a race mission. Its purposes were to address problems of the refugees displaced by the Civil War; to provide social, educational, and medical benefits to the newly freed slaves; to provide for the cultivation of abandoned lands; and to make sure the freed slaves received fair wages for their labor. However, because of the opposition of conservative Republicans and white supremacist and racist Democrats, Congress dissolved the Bureau in 1872.

In 1939 Attorney General Frank Murphy issued an order establishing a civil liberties unit within the Justice Department. The purpose of this unit was to put the federal government on the side of those fighting for civil liberties and civil rights, especially African Americans.

Then, in the 1957 Civil Rights Act, Congress created the Commission on Civil Rights—a fact-finding agency that makes recommendations to the president and Congress. In addition, this new law upgraded the civil rights unit in the Justice Department to a full-fledged Civil Rights Division (CRD).

Congress followed up with the 1960 Civil Rights Act which expanded the power of the CRD of the Justice Department. The Civil Rights Act of 1964 created three new race-oriented federal bureaucratic units, although with different structural arrangements. Title VI created inside all federal agencies, departments, and commissions an Office of Civil Rights Compliance (OCRC), which monitored state and local governments to ensure that they did not spend federal funds in a racially discriminatory fashion. The Office of Federal Contract Compliance (OFCC) was also created in the Department of Labor to assure nondiscrimination and affirmative action by employers with government contracts.

Title VII created the Equal Employment Opportunity Commission (EEOC) to ensure nondiscrimination in federal employment, in private employment, and in employment by state and local governments. In 1972, legislation sponsored by African American Congressman Augustus Hawkins made the EEOC a completely independent commission.

Title X of the 1964 act created the Community Relations Agency, a federal bureaucracy designed to improve race relations in communities having racial conflicts. The agency was empowered to use the carrot-and-stick approach: Provide money and assistance, and also use legal recourse to minimize racial conflict. Eventually this agency was reduced in size and shifted to unit status within the Justice Department.

The 1965 Voting Rights Act created a unit inside the Justice Department's CRD to handle matters of racial discrimination in voter registration and voting, particularly in the southern states where efforts had been persistent in denying African Americans their voting rights.

Last, in 1984 Congress created the Martin Luther King, Jr., Federal Holiday Commission and eventually provided some small funding, empowering it to help in the celebration and promotion of the national holiday.

Thus, necessity forced the government to create two types of federal agencies with a racial mission: (1) relief agencies (material-based) and (2) protection agencies (rights-based).

Both types have faced strong public criticism, driven in part by southern racial hostilities. By the time of the Reagan administration, the president himself attacked these agencies.[2] First, President Reagan appointed members to the Commission on Civil Rights who were hostile to civil rights, including its African American chairman Clarence Pendelton. Second, Attorney General Edwin Meese and the Assistant Attorney General for Civil Rights William Bradford Reynolds attempted to undermine civil rights enforcement. Clarence Thomas at the EEOC did the same thing. Thus, Reagan's ideological appointees diminished the enforcement role of the bureaucracy. President George Bush followed Reagan's approach, and Clinton moved away from appointing anyone who had an activist orientation toward promoting stronger and better civil rights enforcement efforts.[3]

Overall, there are four federal bureaus devoted to an explicitly racial mission: (1) the Commission on Civil Rights, (2) the Equal Employment Opportunity Commission, (3) the Martin Luther King, Jr., Federal Holiday Commission, and (4) the Civil Rights and Voting Rights units in the Justice Department. Each of these bodies, as President Reagan showed, is subject to political influences and pressures (as well as budgeting ones) that can reduce their enforcement effectiveness. Thus, the federal bureaucracy has not been a consistently useful tool in the African American quest for universal freedom, and occasionally it has been hostile to that quest (see Box 14.1).

Running the Bureaucracy: African American Political Appointees

When one analyzes and evaluates the federal bureaucracy, however, the entire story is not captured by focusing on federal agencies designed to deal with race and race relations. An important part was played by African Americans who obtained leadership roles in the federal bureaucracy in general.

During the New Deal, Mary McLeod Bethune announced, "My people will not be satisfied until they see some black faces in high places."[4] When she uttered these words, no African American had ever headed a federal agency or bureau.

More than three decades after her comment, there had still been no African American in such a capacity (although Roosevelt did appoint Mrs. Bethune director of the Division of Negro Affairs of the National Youth Administration). Although President Eisenhower made a couple of token appointments, this situation would not change in a major way until the administration of President Kennedy in 1961. Thus, for the greater part of America's history, African Americans, though subject to the federal bureaucracy, were outside it. Therefore, the first quest of African Americans in terms of the bureaucracy was to make it representative of all the people.

President Grant began the initial process of appointing African American Republican leaders to minor federal posts in Washington, DC, and in the southern states, and to diplomatic posts in African and Caribbean nations. Posts such as custom collector and minister to foreign countries became the manner in which the Republican party enhanced and enlarged its alliance with the African American electorate.

The first Democratic president to deal with black appointments was Grover Cleveland, elected in 1884, who appointed blacks as ministers to Haiti and Liberia and a Recorder of Deeds in Washington, DC.[5]

BOX 14.1   THE BUREAUCACY AT WORK: DR. MARTIN LUTHER KING JR. AND THE FBI

The Federal Bureau of Investigation (FBI), a part of the Justice Department, is the nation's principal law enforcement and investigative agency, made famous in scores of television programs and movies. This agency, charged with enforcing the civil and constitutional rights of citizens, consistently failed to provide protection to civil rights workers in the South during the 1960s, claiming, in the words of its director, J. Edgar Hoover, that it was not a police force and therefore could not protect the civil rights of southern blacks. Yet the FBI and Hoover set about to systematically harass, discredit, and destroy America's preeminent civil rights leader.

From 1963 until Martin Luther King Jr.'s death in 1968, the FBI systematically attempted to destroy his effectiveness as the leader of the civil rights movement. According to the FBI agent in charge, "No holds were barred. We have used [similar] techniques against Soviet agents. [The same methods were] brought home against any organization which we targeted. We did not differentiate. This is a rough, tough business."[a] Among the many "rough, tough" tactics used against Dr. King were efforts to prove that he was a communist or that he was being manipulated by communists: wiretaps and microphone surveillance of his home, office, and hotel rooms; attempts to prove he had secret foreign bank accounts; attempts to prove that he had numerous affairs with women; and attempts to prevent him from publishing his books and from receiving the Nobel Peace Prize. Derogatory information about Dr. King's private life was given to members of Congress, the press, university and church leaders (including the Pope), and other leaders of the civil rights movement. Finally, in an act of desperation, the FBI sent a letter to Dr. King urging him to commit suicide or face exposure as a "liar" and "pervert," leading Dr. King to exclaim that the FBI, the nation's chief law enforcement bureaucracy, was "out to break me."

To his eternal credit, Dr. King did not yield to the efforts of the FBI. However, for a time the Bureau's dirty tricks caused deep distress for Dr. King, his family, and his associates. The FBI's attempt to destroy Dr. King is thoroughly documented in the Senate's investigation and in David Garrow's *The FBI and Martin Luther King, Jr.*[b] Many critics of the FBI's campaign against Dr. King contend that it was a product of J. Edgar Hoover's paranoia and a bureaucracy gone amok; however, Garrow, a political scientist, argues that this view is not correct. Granted, the FBI under Hoover had unprecedented power and autonomy; even so, the presidents and members of Congress in Hoover's time were mostly white men of narrow conservative views,[c] and Garrow contends that the FBI faithfully represented these same American values and was not an out-of-control bureaucracy. Garrow concludes, "The Bureau was not a renegade institution secretly operating outside the parameters of American values, but a virtually representative bureaucracy that loyally served to protect the established order against adversary challenges."[d]

[a]*Supplementary Detailed Staff Reports on Intelligence Activities and the Rights of Americans, Book III.* Final Report of the Select Committee to Study Government Operations with Respect to Intelligence Activities, United States Senate, 94th Congress, April 1976, p. 81.

[b]David Garrow, *The FBI and Martin Luther King, Jr.* (New York: Penguin Books, 1983).

[c]Ibid., pp. 224–25.

[d]Ibid., p. 213.

Mary MacLeod Bethune, the informal leader
of Franklin D. Roosevelt's black cabinet.
Source: Gordon Parks/Getty Images.

But no matter whether the appointments were by the Democratic or the Republican Parties, they were based on a single reality: "The . . . strategy was to identify and then latch onto a black leader who could coalesce a potentially powerful black vote."[6] Hence, "the motives of the Republicans (or Democrats) who aligned themselves with blacks were utilitarian and shortsighted."[7] Listen as one white politician writes President Grant urging the appointment of an African American state leader to an ambassadorial post. In a letter dated January 28, 1871, Carmen A. Newcombe, a party faithful and personal friend of the president, wrote:

> If [James Milton Turner] can go to Liberia for two years he will gain a national reputation which will make him the universally trusted leader of the colored men in the campaign of [18]72. . . . He can come back in '72 and take his place as the chosen leader of his race and whose [sic] claims to leadership will not be disputed.[8]

Simply put, African American political appointees in the bureaucracy had the exposure to make them potential leaders in their own communities.

However, in the midst of such political appointments, white supremacists took over the southern governments and displaced most African American state and local appointive officials by violence, fraud, and corruption. These displaced officials then turned to Presidents Grant, Arthur, and Harrison as a source of federal appointments and patronage positions.[9] Thus, what started out as a trickle of federal jobs emerged into a full-fledged effort to find employment for black party loyalists.

In sum, the Republican Party's need for the black vote launched African Americans into the federal bureaucracy. Eventually this trend, coupled with the need for political jobs for the African American community, made federal patronage appointments all the more important and useful for the African American community. Thus, political patronage became a way in which blacks could gain access to the federal bureaucracy. Necessity again proved vital in forging a connection between the African American community and the federal bureaucracy. These two links—the party's need for votes and the community's need for employment—continued and expanded. The period of greatest expansion came in the New Deal Era, 1932–1945, as President Roosevelt appointed a significant number of African American advisors who became known informally as "the black cabinet."

The New Deal formalized the role of African American advisors to presidents, which had started with Frederick Douglass, who advised Presidents Lincoln and Grant, and continued with Booker T. Washington, who advised Cleveland, Harrison, Theodore Roosevelt, and Taft. These individuals, however, had served in informal, nebulous, and unofficial positions. Roosevelt was the first to give his political appointees and advisors institutional positions in the bureaucracy.

Following the New Deal, the next great step came with Presidents Kennedy and Johnson, who appointed a number of blacks to high-level positions. In 1966, President Johnson became the first president to appoint an African American to cabinet rank, as Robert Weaver became secretary of the Housing and Urban Development (HUD) Department. President Gerald Ford appointed William Coleman secretary of Transportation. President Carter placed Patricia Harris first at HUD then at HEW and appointed Andrew Young and later Donald McHenry as UN ambassadors; Reagan named Samuel Pierce secretary of HUD.

In 1992, President Clinton broke new ground. Usually African Americans were given one cabinet position, frequently at HUD or HEW (now HHS). Clinton placed four blacks in his cabinet—at Energy, Agriculture, Veterans Affairs, and Commerce—and named numerous others to subcabinet positions. Between 1966, when one black was appointed, and 1992, when four were appointed, Democratic presidents made the largest number of political appointments. Toward the end of his first term, Clinton named an African American—Franklin Raines—to head (with cabinet rank) the powerful Office of Management and Budget. Clinton also appointed blacks to head two important regulatory commissions: the National Labor Relations Board and the Federal Communications Commission. Table 14.2 shows the appointment patterns of recent American presidents.

President George W. Bush's record on the appointment of blacks and other minorities to high-level positions in the bureaucracy resembles more the record of his Democratic predecessors than it does his father's or Ronald Reagan's. As the data in Table 14.2 show, about 10 percent of his appointments were black compared to 5 and 6 percent, respectively, for the Reagan and Bush administration. In the Clinton administration 13 percent of the appointments were black. Not only did Bush appoint a relatively large number of blacks compared to prior Republican presidents, his overall appointments were the most ethnically diverse in history, including 6 percent Latino and 3 percent Asian American (compared to Clinton's 4 percent Latino and 1 percent Asian American). Like Clinton, Bush appointed blacks to many high visibility and powerful positions throughout the government, including three cabinet positions: secretary of state (the senior cabinet post), secretary of Education, and secretary of Housing and Urban Development. Condoleezza Rice, an African American political scientist, became the first woman and the second black

Table 14.2 Percentage of African American Political Appointees, from the Kennedy–Johnson Administrations to the George W. Bush Administration[a]

ADMINISTRATION	PERCENTAGE[b]
Kennedy–Johnson	2
Nixon–Ford	4
Carter	12
Reagan	5
Bush	6
Clinton	13
George W. Bush	10

[a]The Kennedy–Johnson administrations were treated as one for purposes of data collection, as were the Nixon–Ford administrations.

[b]Percentages are based on all presidential appointments, excluding judges and military officers.

Sources: The data on appointees from Kennedy–Johnson to Bush are from Robert C. Smith, *We Have No Leaders: African Americans in the Post–Civil Rights Era* (Albany: SUNY Press, 1996): 131. The data on the George W. Bush administration was collected by the authors.

(after Colin Powell in the Reagan administration) to serve as national security advisor. (The vice president, the secretaries of State and Defense, the heads of the CIA, the Joint Chiefs of Staff, and the national security advisor constitute the principal national security decision makers in government. Thus, under Bush blacks held one-third of these positions.) Bush also appointed blacks to the number-two positions in the departments of Health and Human Services, Justice, and HUD, as head of the Civil Rights Division in the Justice Department, as vice chair of the Federal Reserve Board, as chair of the Federal Communications Commission (Michael Powell, the son of the secretary of state), and as assistant secretary of commerce in charge of postwar Iraqi reconstruction. In his second administration, Bush promoted Rice from national security advisor to secretary of State.

Staffing the Bureaucracy: African American Civil Servants

African American political appointees cannot, in and of themselves, do the job alone.[10] All political appointees are transients. The average length of service is 22 months out of a four-year cycle. Thus, to influence and impact bureaucratic rule making and policy, any group needs a continuing presence and permanency inside the bureaucracy, a day-to-day involvement. This means African Americans had to become permanent bureaucrats through the civil service process. After a brief probationary period, individuals hired through this process—*civil servants*—may not be fired. They become part of the *permanent government*.

When political scientists treat the federal bureaucracy and the question of race, their focus is usually on African American employment in this permanent bureaucracy. Although black employees were appointed after the Civil War, by the time of the passage of the Pendleton Act (which created the civil service), there were only 620 black civil servants in the federal government. By 1893, the report of the Civil Service Commission indicated that the number had risen to 2,393, but this 74 percent increase was to run headlong into southern opposition and the ideology of white supremacy and its emerging social and political context of segregation.[11]

Segregation occurred in federal government departments before 1913, but it was limited, received little White House consideration, depended largely on individual administrations, and did not prevent some black Americans from gaining promotions.[12] However, this rising federal acceptance of the southern system of segregation started slowly and gradually to have an impact in the federal bureaucracy despite the civil service merit system. For instance, the percentage of black employees fell from 6 percent in 1910 to 4.9 percent in 1918.[13] But the influence of the gradual and evolving southern forces of white supremacy and segregation coalesced into a tidal wave with the election of a Democratic Congress and a southern Democratic president, Woodrow Wilson, in 1912.[14]

Southern forces started to work on President Wilson from the first day of his administration. Thomas Dixon was the southern novelist who wrote the racist *Clansman,* which became D. W. Griffith's racist film *The Birth of a Nation.* (President Woodrow Wilson saw this film at the White House and endorsed it, saying it was "history written with lighting.")[15] Dixon wrote President Wilson on his nomination of a black American to a post in the Treasury: "I am heartsick over the announcement that you have appointed a Negro to boss white girls as Register of the Treasury."[16] With these types of pleas pouring in, President Wilson permitted most federal bureaucracies in 1913 to segregate African Americans from whites; even the toilets and restrooms were segregated.

In May 1914, the U.S. Civil Service Commission, finding itself in a changed political context and environment, "made photographs mandatory on all application forms. . . . [This practice became] an obvious instrument of discrimination in the appointment of applicants, since it abrogated the principle of merit."[17] With the president and the Commission supporting the segregation of the federal bureaucracy, in 1913 and 1914 Congress joined the process. First, southern congressmen in 1913 formed the Democratic Fair Play Association (DFPA), made President Wilson an honorary member, and held numerous public meetings to discuss their central principle of "the segregation of the races in government employment" and "the reorganization of the civil service" in light of these principles.[18] Chief among the leaders of the DFPA were southern white supremacists: Hoke Smith of Georgia, Benjamin Tillman of South Carolina, and James Vardaman of Mississippi. There was a similar group in the House of Representatives.[19]

Overall, the federal government's embrace of segregation outlasted the Wilson administration, since the succeeding Republican presidencies continued Wilson's policies.[20] Thus, the federal government's acceptance of the policies of white supremacy and segregation "determined the relationship between Black Americans and the federal government for the ensuing fifty years."[21] Hence, the legacy the Wilson presidency left African Americans in the bureaucracy was devastating. Desmond King concludes, "After 1913 Black American employees in Federal Agencies were disproportionately concentrated in custodial, menial and junior clerical positions and were frequently passed over for appointment at all."[22] The federal bureaucracy became a pillar of segregated race relations.

African Americans, through the NAACP and other African American groups, fought this trend; and while some of the worst features, such as photographs on applications, were removed in 1940, the final dismantling did not occur until the 1964 Civil Rights Act. Figure 14.1 displays the rise, fall, and gradual evolution of federal employment of African Americans. The graph shows that African Americans have slowly risen in the staffing of

Figure 14.1 Percentage of African Americans in the Federal Bureaucracy: 1881–1990

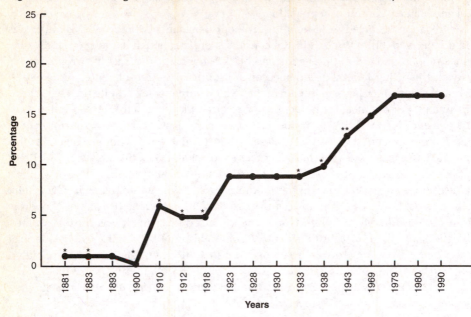

*These percentages were taken from the King book cited below.

**These percentages are based on a partial survey covering only 44 federal agencies.

Sources: Adapted from L. J. Hayes, *The Negro Federal Government Worker* (Washington, DC: The Graduate School, Howard University, 1941): 1, 153; and Desmond King, *Separate and Unequal: Black-Americans and the U.S. Federal Government* (London: Oxford University Press, 1995): 81, 221–37.

the federal bureaucracy, but their presence has not yet made the federal bureaucracy representative of the nation's population.[23]

Shaping Bureaucratic Policy: Antidiscrimination Rule Making

Another characteristic of African Americans and the federal bureaucracy is their role in rule making, especially in antidiscrimination policy. The federal bureaucracy cannot protect and promote African American civil and voting rights unless it has the rules and regulations in place to implement the laws. The federal bureaucracy is severely restricted in its role and function when these rules and regulations do not exist.

When the 1960s civil rights laws were passed, the federal bureaucracy could begin writing antidiscrimination rules and regulations. Given the racial history of the federal bureaucracy, most departments did not move swiftly to develop and promulgate rules designed to achieve antidiscrimination in America. Rather, most of the federal bureaucracy was very slow to develop antidiscrimination rules and regulations. Even so, by the late 1970s, antidiscrimination rules and regulations were well established.

In the first week of his second term, President Reagan signed Executive Order #12498, requiring all units of the federal bureaucracy to submit to the Office of Management and Budget (OMB) any rule or regulation that was being contemplated for approval.[24] With the OMB in the Executive Office of the President, all antidiscrimination policies could be stopped even before they were drafted. And they were.[25]

When President Bush entered the White House in 1988, he not only permitted the Reagan executive order to stand (presidential executive orders can be repealed or revoked by the next president),[26] but he also shifted federal regulations away from race to discrimination against the aged and handicapped. Few antidiscrimination civil rights rules and regulations were promulgated during the Bush presidency.

The Clinton administration took over in 1992 with four African American cabinet secretaries, whereas Bush and Reagan had only one. Did the presence of a Democratic president and four African American top political appointees change the civil rights regulatory policies of the Clinton administration? The answer is no. First, President Clinton, like Bush, permitted Reagan's executive order to continue in force. Second, the large number of African American cabinet secretaries had little impact or influence on antidiscrimination rule making. They simply did not advance such rules or regulations. Neither the Democratic president nor his African American appointees took any major initiatives to shift the rule-making process toward protection of the civil rights of African Americans.

The George W. Bush administration continued the practices of past administrations by ignoring race-related antidiscrimination rules and regulations. However, it added a new wrinkle. Beginning in 2003, the OMB, which has the responsibility for coordination and oversight of federal regulatory policies, started to issue what are called "prompt letters" to all federal agencies. These letters highlight the regulations the administration believes should be revised, rescinded, pursued, or further investigated.[27] In effect, these letters allow the president on an informal basis to establish the regulatory priorities of all federal agencies. In the past, agencies determined their own priorities.

What were the priorities of the administration with respect to civil rights regulations and rules? In a word, none. Analysis of the 2001–2004 regulatory agenda of all federal agencies at the various stages of rule making shows that the current Bush administration, like the previous one, has ignored race-related antidiscrimination rules in favor of rules dealing with discrimination against the disabled and the aged.[28] Occasionally, one finds an agency like the Institute of Museum and Library Services in the National Foundation of the Arts and Humanities just getting around to completing rules for the implementation of Title VI of the 1964 Civil Rights Act, but race-related antidiscrimination rule making generally has disappeared from the federal government.[29]

BOX 14.2   THE BUREAUCRACY AND YOUR RACE

In the United States—*and only in the United States*—a person of *any* known African ancestry is defined as black or African American. This peculiar definition of one's race was established early by the U.S. Bureau of the Census, which declared:

> A person of mixed white and Negro blood should be returned as a Negro, no matter how small the percentage of Negro blood. Both black and mulatto persons are to be returned as Negroes, without distinction. A person of mixed Indian and Negro blood should be returned as a Negro. . . . Mixtures of non-white races should be reported according to the race of the father, except that Negro Indian should be reported as Negro.[a]

(continued)

BOX 14.2 *continued*

At the founding of the Republic, the Census Bureau recognized three races: black, white, and red. However, as the nation became more ethnically diverse or multicultural, this definition became inadequate. Thus, in 1977 the bureaucracy changed the definition or meaning of race. The bureaucracy responsible for defining race is not the Census Bureau (an agency within the cabinet-level Department of Commerce) but the Office of Management and Budget (OMB), an agency within the Executive Office of the President, whose principal responsibility is to prepare the annual budget the president submits to Congress. In addition to its budget responsibilities, the OMB also has overall management or oversight responsibility for the federal bureaucracy. In this latter role, in 1977 it issued Statistical Policy Directive #15 defining the meaning of race for purposes of federal policy. According to this definition, there are four "races" in the United States: black, white, American Indian or Alaskan native, and Asian or Pacific Islander. To determine ethnic identification, black and white respondents are asked to check "Hispanic origin" or "not of Hispanic origin," in effect creating a fifth "race." The five categories are used by the Census Bureau and all other government agencies that collect statistical data. Such data are used to determine the racial composition, of the country; to reapportion the House and state and local legislative bodies, to monitor enforcement of civil rights and affirmative action laws, and for other purposes.

In recent years, however, this bureaucratic definition of race has been challenged by many Americans, especially the growing number of biracial or mixed-race couples. In 1967 the Supreme Court declared in *Loving* v. *Virginia* that a state was in violation of the Fourteenth Amendment's equal protection clause if it prohibited interracial or mixed marriages.[b] Since that time the number of mixed black–white marriages has increased dramatically—from 149,000 to 964,000 (a 547 percent increase).[c] Increasingly, some of these mixed couples, their offspring, and others are demanding that the OMB change its 1977 directive to include the category "mixed race" or "multiracial."[d] According to a 1995 *Newsweek* poll, 49 percent of blacks but only 36 percent of whites support adding this new category.[e] However, most African American leaders and civil rights organizations have opposed the change, arguing that the new category will result in a loss of black political power, undermine affirmative action, and lead to increased discrimination and stigmatization of African Americans.[f]

In 1993 the OMB agreed to consider adding the multiracial category in time for use in the 2000 census. However, a task force appointed to study the issue recommended that instead of a new multiracial category, people be allowed to check more than one race on the census questionnaire. The task force contended that a new multiracial category would "add to racial tensions and further fragmentation of our population."[g]

The 2000 census allowed individuals for the first time to check more than one race on the census questionnaire. Therefore, it included the traditional definition of who is black, as well as those persons who elected to select any other racial categories. Ninety-eight percent of Americans selected a single race and 2 percent—6.8 million persons—selected a second race, including 1.7 million blacks (about half the blacks who selected a second race reported they were white). This 1.7 million (25 percent of those who selected multiple categories) represents 4 percent of the "all-inclusive" black population or the population combining single- and mixed-race blacks. The all-inclusive figure is about 5 percent higher than the black

(continued)

BOX 9.4 *continued*

figure, and adding the two together increases the black population percentage from 12.3 to 13.9 percent of the nation's population (from 34,658,190 to 36,419,434). The OMB decided that those blacks (and other minorities) who selected white would be assigned—following the practice of the first census—to the black category. However, it left ambiguous how those blacks who selected another minority group would be categorized. Thus, the compromise on meaning of race for the 2000 census likely creates as many problems as it resolves and is likely to be revisited before the next census, especially as the number of mixed-race marriages or relationships increases and as the nation becomes more ethnically diverse. (According to the 2000 census 3.1 percent of whites indicated they had a spouse of a different race, 5.7 percent of blacks, 16.3 percent of Asian Americans, and 16.3 percent of Latinos.) But one thing is clear—the meaning of race in America will continue to be determined more by politics than by biology.

[a]This definition from the first census is quoted in Langston Hughes and Milton Meltzer, *A Pictorial History of the Negro in America* (New York: Crown, 1964): 2. On the historical origins of America's definition of race, see F. James Davis, *Who Is Black: One Nation's Definition* (University Park: Pennsylvania State University Press, 1991). See also Melissa Nobles, *Shades of Citizenship: Race and the Census in Modern Politics* (Palo Alto: Stanford University Press, 2000).

[b]380 U.S. 1 (1967).

[c]See Michael Frisby, "Black, White or Other," *Emerge* (December/January 1996): 49.

[d]Jon Michael Spencer, *The New Colored People: The Mixed Race Movement in America* (New York: New York University Press, 1997).

[e]Tom Morganthau, "What Color Is Black?" *Newsweek*, February 13, 1995, p. 65.

[f]Frisby, "Black, White or Other," p. 51.

[g]Steven Holmes, "Panel Balks at a Multiracial Census Category," *New York Times*, July 9, 1997, p. A8.

Bureaucratic Implementation: Federalism and States' Rights

Ultimately, the bureaucracy must act as an implementor and manager of public policy. And to lower its effectiveness and efficiency in these rules, critics, particularly southern critics, have turned to federalism to support, undergird, and structure their attack. Hence, every attempt of the federal government in general and of the federal bureaucracy in particular to regulate these social systems has been met with protests about the intrusion on states' rights and the violation of the constitutional principle of federalism. When federal departments have been created with a racial mission, they have been denounced as a federal grab for power and the usurpation of states' rights. Hence, such agencies have tended to pursue only voluntary, cautious, temporary, and persuasive enforcement efforts. Political appointees cannot have or take aggressive stances toward protecting civil rights. This situation leads to the diminution of antidiscriminatory rules and regulations.

Federalism therefore has been used as a device to limit the influence and impact of the federal bureaucracy in advancing the quest for universal freedom of African Americans.

Civil Rights Enforcement in the Bush Administration

Generally, the bureaucracies under Republican presidents are less aggressive in enforcing the nation's civil rights laws, and there are frequently tensions and conflicts between the permanent civil service professionals in the civil rights bureaucracies and the political appointees of the president who supervise their work. Studies of George W. Bush's administration find evidence of both these phenomena. A study by a Syracuse University research institute found that "federal enforcement of civil rights laws has sharply dropped since 1999."[30] Specifically, the study found that while the level of complaints had remained relatively constant (about 12,000 annually), the number of criminal charges brought by the Justice Department had declined. Also, the number of recommendations for prosecutions by the FBI or other federal agencies declined by more than one-third between 1990 and 2004, from 3,000 to 1,900 in 2004.[31] The study found that only civil rights and environmental enforcement was down during this period, while enforcement of illegal immigration, weapons violations, and drug laws remained constant or increased. Overall, between 1999 and 2004, Justice Department statistics indicate that prosecution of racial and gender discrimination cases declined by 40 percent.[32]

The Justice Department's Civil Rights Division (CRD) is the bureaucracy responsible for enforcing civil rights laws. As a result of its slowdown in enforcement and conflicts with the Bush appointees who ran the CRD, more than 20 percent of its staff lawyers left in 2005. They complained that political appointees were ignoring their professional recommendations and making decisions on the basis of ideology.[33] As a result of these complaints, the Justice Department prohibited staff attorneys from making recommendations in major voting rights cases, a significant change in bureaucratic procedures that were designed to insulate professional decisions from politics.[34] The Justice Department also changed the procedures for hiring staff lawyers. Instead of a hiring committee of career civil servants, the responsibility for such decisions was turned over to political appointees. These appointees then filled these positions with persons with conservative ideological credentials, but little experience in civil rights (except defending employers against discrimination lawsuits or fighting affirmative action). After studying the resumes of successful applicants from 2001 to 2006, the *Boston Globe* concluded that the Bush administration had "effectively turn[ed] hundreds of career jobs into politically appointed positions."[35]

As we pointed out, this is not a new development. Since the Nixon administration there have been "clashing beliefs in the executive branch" between liberal-leaning civil servants in the civil rights bureaucracies and conservative appointees of Republican presidents.[36]

On one issue in which the recommendations of the career lawyers were overturned the courts subsequently overruled the decision of the political appointees. The issue involved a program established by the state of Georgia requiring voters to present government-issued identification cards in order to vote. The staff lawyers recommended rejection of the program as a violation of the Voting Rights Act. The Fifth Circuit Court of Appeals agreed, suggesting that the identification card requirement resembled the "Jim Crow era poll tax."[37]

In 2008, however, the Supreme Court upheld a similar voter identification system in Indiana. In a 6-3 opinion written by the Court's leading liberal, Justice Stevens wrote that photo identification was "amply justified by the valid interest in protecting the integrity and reliability of the electoral process." In dissent, Justice Souter wrote, "Indiana's voter ID law threatens to impose . . . burdens on the voting rights of tens of thousands of the state's citizens and a significant percentage of those individuals are likely to be deterred from voting." The case was *Crawford* v. *Marion County Election Board*.

FACES AND VOICES IN THE STRUGGLE FOR UNIVERSAL FREEDOM

ARTHUR FLETCHER (1924–2005)

Arthur Fletcher's contribution to universal freedom and equality is controversial. In 1969 as an assistant secretary of labor in the Nixon administration, Fletcher was principally responsible for the design and implementation of affirmative action as the policy of the U.S. government. (Refer to Box 12.3.) As he told one of the authors of this text in a 1971 interview, "affirmative action was my baby." In fathering affirmative action, Fletcher used his position to advance the cause of racial equality more effectively than any other African American who has served in the bureaucracy. As one of the highest-ranking blacks in the bureaucracy during the Nixon administration, he was a leader in organizing other blacks in the administration to advocate for the interests of African Americans.

Born in Phoenix, Arizona, the son of a career military man, Fletcher was raised in Kansas. A star football player at Washburn University in Topeka, in 1954 he became the first African American player for the Baltimore Colts. After graduation he became active in Kansas Republican politics, and

Source: Michael Bryant/MCT/Newscom

was one of the individuals who helped to finance the *Brown vs. Board of Education* lawsuit. In the 1960s he moved to the West Coast, eventually settling in the state of Washington, where he ran successfully for lieutenant governor. Fletcher's Republican Party activism lead to his appointment by Nixon and subsequently, as one of the most visible black Republicans in the nation, he served as an advisor to Presidents Ford and Reagan and under the first President Bush he was named chairman of the U.S. Commission on Civil Rights. Although Fletcher considered himself a loyal Republican, he did not hesitate to criticize Republican presidents and policies, describing President Reagan, for example, as "the worst president for civil rights in the twentieth century."

As affirmative action became increasingly controversial in the 1980s and 1990s and the Republican Party dropped its support for it, Fletcher briefly considered running for the party's presidential nomination in 1996 in order to defend "his baby." However, he ultimately declined to run, recognizing that as a liberal in a party that now stood strongly for conservatism, he would get little support in terms of money or votes.

Summary

The bureaucracy—the hundreds of departments, agencies, bureaus, and commissions that enforce the law and implement public policies—is integral to the black quest for universal freedom and equality. That is, a law enacted by Congress or a decision by the Supreme Court are mere words on paper unless the bureaucracy acts to enforce or implement them. Although black inclusion in the bureaucracy started after the Civil War, effective representation did not begin to occur until the 1960s. Bureaucratic rules and regulations to enforce and implement civil rights laws since the 1960s have depended on the priorities of the president. Federalism has also sometimes been a barrier to the universal application of these laws.

Selected Bibliography

Altshuler, Alan, and Norman C. Thomas, eds. *The Politics of the Federal Bureaucracy.* New York: Harper & Row, 1977. A good collection of papers examining the structure and operation of the federal bureaucracy and its place in the political system.

Hayes, L. J. *The Negro Federal Government Worker.* Washington, DC: Howard University Press, 1941. A pioneering work on the subject.

King, Desmond. *Separate and Unequal: Black Americans and the U.S. Federal Government.* London: Oxford University Press, 1995. A historical account of African Americans in the federal bureaucracy.

Krislov, Samuel. *The Negro in Federal Employment: The Quest for Equal Opportunity.* Minneapolis: University of Minnesota Press, 1967. Generally considered the standard work on the subject.

Naff, Katherine. *To Look Like America: Dismantling Barriers for Women and Minorities in Government.* Boulder, CO: Westview Press, 2001. An examination of the barriers to full inclusion of minorities and women in the bureaucracy.

Smith, Robert C. "Black Appointed Officials: A Neglected Category of Political Participation Research." *Journal of Black Studies* 14 (March 1984): 369–88. A study of African American presidential appointees from the Kennedy to the Carter administrations.

Smith, Robert C. "Blacks and Presidential Policy Making: Neglect, Policy Symbols and Cooptation." In Robert C. Smith, *We Have No Leaders: African Americans in the Post–Civil Rights Era* (chap. 5). Albany: SUNY Press, 1996. A study of the policy-making roles of black presidential appointees from the Nixon to the first Bush administration.

Walton, Hanes, Jr. *When the Marching Stopped: The Politics of Civil Rights Regulatory Agencies.* Albany: SUNY Press, 1988. A comprehensive study of the ups and downs of the implementation of the 1964 Civil Rights Act, from the Johnson to the Reagan administrations.

Notes

1. See Max Weber, "Bureaucracy," in H. H. Gerth and C. Wright Mills, eds., *From Max Weber: Essays in Sociology* (New York: Oxford University Press, 1969).

2. Hanes Walton, Jr., *When the Marching Stopped: The Politics of Civil Rights Regulatory Agencies* (Albany: SUNY Press, 1988): p. 6.

3. See Steven Shull, *American Civil Rights Policy from Truman to Clinton: The Role of Presidential Leadership* (Armonk, NY: M. E. Sharpe, 1999): chap. 5.

4. Quoted in Hanes Walton, Jr., *Invisible Politics* (Albany: SUNY Press, 1985): 262. See also Mary McLeod Bethune, "Certain Unalienable Rights," in Rayford Logan, ed., *What the Negro Wants* (Chapel Hill: University of North Carolina Press, 1944): 248–58.

5. Lawrence Grossman, "Democrats and Blacks in the Gilded Age," in P. Kolver, ed., *Democrats and the American Idea* (Washington, DC: Center for National Policy Press, 1992): 149–61.

6. Gary Kremer, *James Milton Turner and the Promise of America: The Public Life of a Post–Civil War Black Leader* (Columbia: University of Missouri Press, 1991): 40.

7. Ibid.

8. Ibid., p. 53.

9. Ibid., p. 50.

10. For analysis of policy roles of black presidential appointees from the Nixon to the Bush administrations, see Robert C. Smith, *We Have No Leaders: African Americans in the Post–Civil Rights Era* (Albany: SUNY Press, 1996): chap. 5.

11. John Hope Franklin and Alfred Moss, *From Slavery to Freedom: A History of Africans* (New York: Knopf, 2000): 336.

12. Ibid., p. 9.

13. Ibid., p. 49.

14. Ibid., p. 9.

15. Thomas Cripps, "The Reaction of the Negro to the Motion Picture, *The Birth of a Nation*," *Historian* 25 (May 1963): 224–62.

16. Desmond King, *Separate and Unequal: Black Americans and the U.S. Federal Government* (London: Oxford University Press, 1995): 5.

17. Ibid., p. 48.

18. Ibid., p. 22.

19. Ibid., p. 25.

20. Ibid., pp. 20, 49.

21. Ibid., p. 20.

22. Ibid., p. 4.

23. See Katherine Naff, *To Look Like America: Dismantling Barriers for Women and Minorities in Government* (Boulder, CO: Westview Press, 2001).

24. Walton, *When the Marching Stopped*, p. 134.

25. Ibid., pp. 135–36.

26. Ibid., pp. 137–57.

27. "Introduction to the Fall 2003 Regulatory Plan," *Federal Register,* vol. 68 (December 22, 2003): 72409; and "Introduction to the Fall 2002 Regulatory Plan," *Federal Register,* vol. 67 (December 9, 2002): 74057–62.

28. Hanes Walton, Jr., et al., "The Civil Rights Regulatory Agenda of the Bush Administration," *Urban League Review* 14 (1990): 17–28.

29. "Institute of Museum and Library Services—Completed Action," *Federal Register*, vol. 68 (December 22, 2003): 73738.

30. Associated Press, "Enforcement of Civil Rights Law Declined Since 1999, Study Finds," *New York Times*, November 11, 2004.

31. Ibid.

32. Ibid.

33. Dan Eggen, "Civil Rights Focus Shift Roils Staff," *Washington Post,* November 13, 2005.

34. Dan Eggen, "Staff Opinions Banned in Voting Rights Cases," *Washington Post,* December 10, 2005.

35. Charlie Savage, "Civil Rights Hiring Shifted in Bush Era," *Boston Globe,* July 23, 2006.

36. Joel Aberbach and Bert Rockman, "Clashing Beliefs in the Executive Branch: The Nixon Administration Bureaucracy," *American Political Science Review* 70 (1976): 456–68. On the Reagan administration, see Donald Robinson, *To the Best of my Ability: The Presidency and the Constitution* (New York: Norton, 1987): 191–99.

37. Eggen, "Staff Opinions Banned in Voting Rights Cases."

CHAPTER 15

Domestic Policy and the African American Quest for Social and Economic Justice

In this chapter we examine the efforts by African Americans to secure universal freedom with respect to access to material benefits, focusing mainly on the interrelated domestic policies of full employment and welfare reform. We focus primarily on these two issues because along with national health insurance they have consistently been priority items on the post–civil rights era black agenda for social and economic justice. We also discuss other policy issues of importance to blacks, including the criminal justice system, health, and the HIV/AIDS epidemic.

The Federal Government, the Economy, and the Welfare State

Until the Great Depression, the federal government took little responsibility for managing the economy or seeing to the social security of its citizens. Rather, the generally accepted belief was that in a free enterprise, capitalist economy the government should follow Adam Smith's principle of "laissez-faire" (leave it alone). This meant that the economy should be self-regulating, without interference from the government, and that each individual should be responsible for his and his family's welfare. Thus, at the height of the Depression, with 13 million people—25 percent of the labor force—unemployed, President Hoover declined to propose any major plan or program to get the economy back on its feet or to help those in misery, arguing that the federal government lacked the constitutional authority to act and that, in any event, anything the government did would simply make things worse.

This view changed with the coming of the New Deal. Under Franklin Roosevelt's leadership, the federal government for the first time assumed responsibility for managing the economy, seeking full employment, and assisting in providing for the social security and welfare of the American people.[1] In the Employment Act of 1946, the law explicitly spells out the responsibility of the government to manage the economy in order "to promote maximum employment, production and purchasing power."[2] To achieve these objectives of the 1946 act, the Congress created within the Executive Office of the President a three-person Council of Economic Advisers (staffed by academic economists) and directed the president to submit an annual economic report on his plans to achieve the act's objectives of economic growth, maximum employment, and price stability (low inflation). To oversee the president's economic report and plan, the Congress also created the Joint Economic Committee, which has members from both the House and the Senate.[3]

The Failure of "Universal" Employment

Can full or universal employment be achieved in the American economy? Some scholars suggest that through a combination of sound fiscal and monetary policies and targeted job creation, public works, and service programs, the American economy can be made to operate at full employment without unacceptably high levels of inflation.[4] Yet these scholars are a minority: Most economists and political leaders argue that full employment cannot be achieved in the United States without unacceptably high levels of inflation or some permanent system of government wage and price controls.

For example, during congressional hearings on the Humphrey-Hawkins Act, two leading liberal economists said flatly that full employment (defined as 4 percent unemployment) was not possible. Charles Shultz, later to become chair of President Carter's Council of Economic Advisers, told the Senate Labor Committee that "the chief obstacle is inflation. I believe S. 50 [the Full Employment and the Balanced Growth Act] does not sufficiently recognize that fact, and hence needs to be changed in a number of important respects. Moreover, the combination of 'employer of last resort' provisions in this bill and the wage standards that go with it threaten to make the inflation problem worse."[5] Also, John Kenneth Galbraith, long-time liberal Democratic economist, presidential advisor, and Harvard professor, told the Senate Banking Committee:

> At a four percent unemployment rate, there is no question the American economy can be dangerously inflationary. . . . I must specifically and deliberately warn my liberal friends not to engage in the wishful economics that causes them to hope that there is still some undiscovered fiscal or monetary magic which will combine low unemployment and low inflation.[6]

In the 24 years since passage of the Humphrey-Hawkins Act, neither the president, nor the Congress, nor the Federal Reserve has sought to use the planning process established by the act to move toward a 4 percent unemployment rate. As Congressman Hawkins woefully wrote in a 1986 article, "Since the passage of the Act, we have yet to see an economic report from the President, a Federal Reserve report or a Joint Economic Committee report that constructs the actual programmatic means for achieving full employment."[7] To the contrary, economic policy makers today generally consider 5–5.5 percent unemployment as the so-called natural rate of unemployment. This natural rate of unemployment, which translates into 10–12 percent for blacks, is accepted by Democrats and Republicans and liberals and conservatives—what one writer calls "a bipartisan fear of full employment."[8]

In 1999 the overall unemployment rate fell to 4.3 percent, the lowest rate in 24 years, which led immediately to fears that the Federal Reserve would raise interest rates to slow the growth of the economy and prevent a rise in inflation. Yet, as the numbers in Table 15.1 show, this "dangerously low" level of unemployment still left the black community in a recession, with an adult unemployment rate of 7.7 percent; the black male teenage unemployment rate was 23.5 percent, compared to 11.6 percent for white teenagers. Meanwhile,

Table 15.1 Rate of Unemployment in the United States by Race, Gender, and Age, April 1999

OVERALL RATE	4.3%
Adult Whites	3.8
Adult White Men	3.0
Adult White Women	3.6
White Teenagers	11.6
Adult Blacks	7.7
Adult Black Men	6.1
Adult Black Women	6.8
Black Teenagers	23.5

Source: United States Department of Labor, Bureau of Labor Statistics, May 1999 press release. These data are seasonally adjusted. Adult is 20 years and older; teenager is 16–19.

whites were experiencing full employment at 3.8 percent as defined by the Humphrey-Hawkins Act. Since it is not likely that the Federal Reserve will permit the unemployment rate to fall much below 4 percent, blacks in this country will *never* experience full employment (on the role of race and racism on black unemployment, see Box 15.1).

BOX 15.1   RACE, RACISM, AND AFRICAN AMERICAN UNEMPLOYMENT

Until the passage of the Civil Rights Act of 1964, it was perfectly legal for white employers to post signs or simply say to black job seekers, "We don't hire coloreds." Since the passage and implementation of the 1964 act and the development of affirmative action policies, racism has declined in the employment of blacks. However, studies still show continuing discrimination as African Americans seek work.

In 1991, the Urban Institute conducted a "hiring audit" to determine the degree of racial discrimination in entry-level employment in Washington, D.C., and Chicago. The research used selected black and white "job testers" carefully matched in age, physical size, education (all were college educated), and experience, as well as such intangible factors as poise, openness, and articulateness. They were then sent to apply for entry-level jobs advertised in Washington and Chicago area newspapers. The study found what the authors call "entrenched and widespread" discrimination at every step in the hiring process, with whites three times as likely to advance to the point of being offered a job.[a]

Similarly, a study by Kirschenman and Neckerman, titled "We'd Love to Hire Them But, . . ." found that Chicago area white employers were extremely reluctant to hire blacks, especially black men. Speaking of potential black workers, these employers told the researchers, "They are lazy; they steal; they lack motivation; they don't have a work ethic." Or, "I need someone who will fit in"; "my customers are 95 percent white . . . I wouldn't last very long if I had a black"; and "my guys don't want to work with blacks."[b]

(continued)

BOX 15.1 *continued*

In an experimental study of racism in employment between 2001 and 2002, researchers sent 5,000 applications to prospective employers in Boston and Chicago. The applications were identical except one group had names identified with African Americans, the other whites. The names were randomly assigned so that applicants with black and white identified names applied for the same set of jobs with the same resumes. Applicants with white-sounding names were 50 percent more likely to be called for interviews than those with black-sounding names.[c] In a similar experiment, Dorvah Pager, a graduate student at the University of Wisconsin, found that a white man with a criminal record had a better chance to get a job than an identically qualified black man without a record. For her dissertation research, Pager sent teams of black and white young men—well groomed, well spoken, college educated, and with identical resumes—to seek entry-level jobs. The only difference was that some indicated they had an 18-month prison sentence for cocaine possession. She found that the employer call-back rate for a black with this criminal record was 5 percent, and 14 percent without a record. But for whites the rate was 17 percent with the record and 34 percent without the record.[d]

[a]Margery Turner, M. Fix, and R. Struyk, *Opportunities Denied, Opportunities Diminished: Discrimination in Hiring* (Washington, DC: Urban Institute, 1991).

[b]Joleen Kirschenman and Kathryn Neckerman, "We'd Love to Hire Them But . . . The Meaning of Race for Employers," in C. Jencks and P. Peterson, eds., *The Urban Underclass* (Washington, DC: Urban Institute, 1991).

[c]M. Bertrand and S. Mullainathan, "Are Emily and Brendan More Employable Than Lakisha and Jamal?: A Field Experiment on Labor Market Discrimination," http://gsb.uchicago.edu/pdf/bertrand.pdf (November 8, 2002).

[d]Brooke Koreger, "When a Dissertation Makes a Difference," *New York Times*, April 20, 2004.

One reason that blacks have more difficulty finding employment than whites do is that employers increasingly locate businesses away from the central cities. For example, in testimony to Congress in 1998, HUD Secretary Andrew Cuomo reported that in the most recent growth cycle in the economy (1992–1998), more than 15 million new jobs were created, but only 13 percent were located in central cities.[9]

Consequences of the Failure of Full Employment on the African American Community

What are the consequences of this long-term recession on the well-being of the African American community? First and most obviously, a job is a material benefit, providing the money necessary to support self and family. Less obvious but also important, a job is a psychic benefit, providing individuals with a sense of self-esteem, self-worth, and dignity. Thus, for many people, unemployment means not just a lack of money but lack of a sense of self-worth. We discuss the lack of money—enough money—in a moment, but first, what can be said about the impact of unemployment on things other than a person's pocketbook?

In 1984 Harvey Brenner, a sociologist, prepared a report for the Joint Economic Committee of Congress. In it, he showed that for every 1 percent increase in the rate of

Since the end of slavery, blacks have always faced a disproportionately high rate of unemployment. Indeed, blacks frequently say, "The only time we had full employment was during slavery."   *Source:* Stephen Ferry/Getty Images

unemployment, there is an associated increase of 5.7 percent in murders, 4.1 percent in suicides, 1.9 percent in mortality, 3.3 percent in mental institutionalization, and a 4.7 percent increase in divorce and separation.[10] Other studies have found correlations between increases in unemployment and increases in child abuse, alcoholism, wife battering, and other individual and community pathologies.[11] Multiply Brenner's 1 percent increase by a factor of 10 over several generations to get a feel for the damaging consequences of long-term unemployment on the African American community.

African Americans and the Criminal Justice System

The United States imprisons more people than any other country in the world—about 3 million people or about 3 percent of the population are incarcerated.[12] Nearly 40 percent of these people are African Americans, although blacks constitute little more than 12 percent of the population. Further, in 1995, more than 32 percent of young black men (20–29) were in jail or prison compared to only 7 percent of young white men. Astonishingly, the percentage of young black women in jail (5 percent) is almost as large as the percentage of jailed white men (only 1.5 percent of white women are jailed).[13] A partial explanation of this disproportionately high rate of black incarceration is that young black men who are poor commit more crimes than whites, but also important is the racial discrimination in the criminal justice system and unfairness in the punishment for use of illegal drugs. In 1995 the *Nashville Tennessean* analyzed all 1992–1993 convictions in all federal district courts in the United States. The study found that the sentences of black criminals were up to 40 percent longer than those of white criminals in some courts, and that blacks are less likely than whites to get a break on their sentences. This racial disparity existed in all parts of the country, but it was highest in the West (California) and lowest in the South. And the disparity was only a black–white one, as Hispanics received the same sentences for the same crime as whites (there were too few Asians to make a comparison).[14]

Adding to this disparity in crime and punishment is the war on drugs. Under federal law, a person convicted of selling 5 grams of crack cocaine receives a mandatory five years in prison; a person would have to sell 250 grams of powdered cocaine to get a five-year sentence (a 100-to-1 ratio). Ninety percent of the persons convicted of selling crack cocaine are black; 90 percent of those convicted of selling powdered cocaine are white. Thus, blacks are given sentences five times as great as those of whites because their illegal drug of choice is crack rather than powdered cocaine. These racial sentencing disparities have been challenged and upheld in the federal courts, and shortly after the Million Man March, the House of Representatives voted down a Congressional Black Caucus bill that would have equalized sentences for powdered and crack cocaine.

In the aftermath of the Rodney King beating by the Los Angeles police in 1991, the NAACP in collaboration with Harvard and the University of Massachusetts conducted a study of police–community relations in black America. The study concluded "The beating of Rodney King is part of a long and shameful history of racially motivated brutality and degradation that continues to find expression in powerful places."[15] Ronald Walters, using figures from the Police Foundation, found that during the 1980s, 78 percent of those killed and 80 percent of those nonfatally shot were minorities, and a 1993 study of reports of police brutality in 15 major newspapers between January 1990 and May 1992 found that the majority of the victims were black. Of 131 such victims reported during this period, 87 percent were black, 10 percent Latino, and 3 percent white.[16] By contrast, 93 percent of the officers were white.

In recent years African American leaders have held protest demonstrations and lobbied Congress, the president, and state and local governments to put and end to "racial profiling" (the practice by police of stopping drivers of certain racial groups because they believe these groups are more likely to commit certain types of crimes).[17] Congressman John Conyers, the senior African American member of Congress and the chairman of the House Judiciary Committee, estimates that 72 percent of car drivers stopped by the police are black. Their offense, Conyers says, is "DWB"—driving while black—an offense he says from which no black is immune. In a speech on the House floor Conyers remarked, "There are virtually no African American males—including congressmen, athletes, actors and office workers—who have not been stopped at one time or another for an alleged traffic violation, namely driving while black."[18] According to a 1999 Gallup poll, 56 percent of whites and 77 percent of blacks believe racial profiling is widespread. Also, 57 percent of blacks indicated they believed they had been stopped by the police "just because of their race," a figure that rises to 72 percent among blacks 18–34 years of age.[19]

Unemployment, Poverty, and the African American Family

Using the government's official definition of poverty—about $21,000 for a family of four—roughly a quarter of the African American community is poor. Only about 11 percent of the white population fits this definition. While there are more poor whites than blacks (about 20 million whites compared to 9 million blacks), poverty has a more devastating impact on the black *community* than on the white. For example, the impact of unemployment on the African American family has been nearly disastrous.

In 1965, Senator Daniel Patrick Moynihan, then an assistant secretary of labor, wrote a report on the "Negro" family in which he argued that high unemployment was leading to a breakup of the traditional two-parent family. Moynihan wrote that the "fundamental overwhelming fact" in the decline of the traditional African American family is that "Negro unemployment with the exception of a few years during the Korean War, has continued *at disastrous levels for 35 years*" (emphasis in original).[20] When Moynihan wrote his report, the percentage of female-headed households (father/husband absent) in the black community was about 30 percent. Today, consistent with the continued disastrous levels of high unemployment, the percentage is nearer to 70 percent. This means that black families (mainly women and children) are much more dependent on government welfare programs than are whites. This is because white women are much more likely to find employed men to help support them and their children.

Persistently high unemployment is one important cause, if not the principal cause, of the high rate of divorce, separation, and out-of-wedlock births in the black community, a phenomenon traceable at least in part, as Senator Moynihan pointed out a generation ago, to the disastrously high levels of black male joblessness.[21] Black male unemployment is also one reason why African American families are so heavily dependent on welfare— Aid to Families with Dependent Children (AFDC)—and why the decision by President Clinton and the Congress to abolish AFDC as a universal (federal) benefit threatens to do such harm to the black community.

The disastrous level of African American unemployment got worse during the George W. Bush administration. From 2001 to 2003 more than 2.5 million jobs were lost by the U.S. economy. Ninety percent of these jobs were in the manufacturing sector, where blacks are disproportionately employed and where benefits (particularly health insurance) are relatively good. Overall, between 2001 and 2003 black unemployment grew at a rate twice as fast as the white rate; indeed, black unemployment in this period grew at a faster rate than anytime since the 1970s.[22] Thus, in 2000 there were 2 million blacks employed in manufacturing jobs—10.1 percent of the total manufacturing employment—but by 2003 the number was down to 1.7 million. This represented a 15 percent job loss among blacks (compared to 10 percent among whites), reducing the total share of black manufacturing employment to 9.6 percent in 2003.[23]

The overall adult black unemployment rate was 10.5 percent in April 2003, compared to 7.5 percent three years earlier. And in New York and other northern and midwestern cities researchers found that almost half of black men were unemployed (48.2 percent of black men aged 16–64 in New York City).[24] Some of this joblessness was due to the loss of jobs during the recession, but it is also partly attributable to continuing racism on the part of employers (see Box 15.1).

Ending Welfare as We Know It

In his 1992 campaign, President Clinton pledged two major reforms in domestic social welfare policies: national health insurance and an "end to welfare as we know it." The president's complicated plan to provide health insurance for all Americans was not enacted by the Congress (on the impact of national health insurance on black Americans, see Box 15.2). However, he was able to keep his promise and end the 60-year-old federal guarantee of aid to poor families with dependent children.

"Ending Welfare as We Know It" as Election Strategy

Historically, Americans have been reluctant to provide assistance to the poor, believing that it is up to individuals to provide (through hard work) for their own income and family welfare. Government "handouts" or the "dole" therefore are not generally

---

BOX 15.2   AFRICAN AMERICAN HEALTH AND NATIONAL HEALTH INSURANCE

African Americans are not as healthy as whites. Two measures that frequently serve as summary measures of a people's health—the infant mortality rate and life expectancy—may be used to establish this point. The black infant mortality rate (the number of deaths per 1,000 live births before a child reaches one year of age) is 19.6, nearly twice that of whites, which is 10.1. The black life expectancy rate is 69.2 compared to 75.6 for whites. Why this enormous gap between the races in health? The most basic explanation is the lack of adequate care and health insurance among African Americans.[a]

Roughly 20 percent of African Americans lack health insurance compared to 12 percent of whites. Studies have shown that this lack of health insurance is directly related to their health and life expectancy. For example, Eugene Schwarz and his colleagues examined the records of Americans age 15–54 who died between 1980 and 1986 from 12 illnesses that normally are curable if treated: pneumonia, hernia, gallbladder, and influenza, among others. Between 1980 and 1986, nearly 18,000 persons died of these illnesses. More than 80 percent of the people who died in what Schwarz and his colleagues call "excess deaths" were black. The study concludes that blacks died of the diseases four times more frequently than whites because they did not receive adequate, routine health care. They did not receive health care, in large part, because they did not have health insurance.[b]

In the post–civil rights era, universal health insurance—after full employment—has been the major item on the African American leadership agenda. African American Congress members and interest groups were strong supporters of President Clinton's national health care legislation. The reason is obvious: for blacks, its defeat in the Congress is literally a matter of life and death.

[a]Brigid Schulte, "Americans Face Separate and Unequal Health," *West County Times*, August 21, 1998.

[b]Eugene Schwarz et al., "Black/White Comparisons of Deaths Preventable by Medical Intervention: United States and District of Columbia, 1980–86," *International Journal of Epidemiology* 19 (1970): 591–98.

Table 15.2 Attitudes Concerning the Government's Responsibility to Take Care of the Poor: Selected Countries, 1991

	PERCENTAGE AGREEING THAT GOVERNMENT HAS RESPONSIBILITY TO CARE FOR POOR
Spain	70
Russia	70
Italy	66
France	62
Great Britain	61
Poland	56
East Germany[a]	64
West Germany	45
United States	23

[a]The poll was conducted prior to the formal unification of the two Germanies.

Source: Times Mirror Center for the People and the Press. We are grateful to Professor David Tabb of San Francisco State University for making this data available to us.

acceptable because they contribute to laziness and individual irresponsibility. As shown by the data reported in Table 15.2, Americans are dead last among major nations of the world in believing it is the responsibility of the government to take care of the poor. Nearly two-thirds of the French, British, Spanish, Italians, and Russians believe that the government has such a role, compared to only 23 percent of Americans. In addition to these negative attitudes toward government help for the poor in general, most Americans are specifically hostile to welfare because they believe that most people on welfare are black and that blacks are lazy and prefer welfare over work. Although at any given time there are usually more whites on welfare than blacks, blacks are disproportionately more likely to be receiving welfare (roughly a third of black families compared to about 10 percent of white families were receiving welfare prior to the 1996 reforms). Thus, the *perception* among whites that welfare is a black program is not wholly off the mark. And this perception profoundly affects attitudes about welfare.

According to the 1992 General Social Survey, 47 percent of whites believe that African Americans as a people are lazy, and 59 percent believe that blacks would prefer to live on welfare rather than work.[25] And these beliefs—that the majority of people on welfare are black and that blacks are lazy—profoundly affect how the public views welfare. Table 15.3 shows that those who believe most welfare recipients are white (18 percent) are more likely to think people on welfare want to work, that they are on welfare because of circumstances beyond their control, and that they really need help. On the other hand, those who think most recipients are black (44 percent) believe the opposite.

It is out of this historical and cultural context of individualism and white supremacist thinking that President Clinton developed his "end welfare as we know it" strategy. In 1992 President Clinton's strategist told him that to win back the so-called Reagan Democrats in the key battleground states of the Midwest (Pennsylvania, Ohio, Illinois, and Michigan),

Table 15.3 Attitudes of Americans Toward Welfare According to Whether Respondent Believes Most Recipients Are Black, 1994

	RESPONDENT BELIEVES MOST ON WELFARE ARE:	
	BLACK (44%)	WHITE (18%)
Why are people on welfare?	61%	38%
Lack of effort	25	48
Circumstances beyond control		
Do most people on welfare want to work?		
Yes	29	51
No	65	43
Do most people on welfare really need it?		
Yes	34	48
No	60	49

Source: 1994 *New York Times* poll. We are again grateful to Professor David Tabb at San Francisco State University for sharing this data.

he would have to take a tough antiwelfare stance. For example, a 1984 Democratic Party poll concluded that the Democrats had lost the support of many whites because the party was viewed as the "giveaway party, giving white tax money to blacks and poor people."[26]

"Ending Welfare as We Know It" as Public Policy

In 1996 as his campaign for reelection was getting under way, Clinton signed legislation passed by the Republican Congress that ended the 60-year-old federal, universal program of welfare for poor women and their children who did not have employed husbands and fathers and who themselves could not find work at living wages. Specifically, welfare in the form of cash allowances was limited to five years; most adults were required to work within two years and states were given the authority to design their own programs. At the time, opponents of the legislation worried that the reforms would throw millions of women and children into destitution once the time limits expired. However, during the prosperous 1990s, welfare recipients were able to find jobs, and studies indicate they were able to keep those jobs during the high unemployment period of 2000–2003.[27] However, critics continued to express concern that many former recipients had not found work, and that many of those employed were working at jobs with wages and benefits too low to support families.[28] Rebecca Blank, dean of the University of Michigan's Gerald Ford School of Public Policy, summarizes what we know about the effects of the legislation as follows:

> While there is a lot of evidence that work has increased and that earning on average rose more than benefits fell, the translation of these facts into a definitive statement about well-being is hard to make. More women are working and poor, rather than nonworking and poor [but] we do not . . . have enough data on the long-term effects of these behavioral changes on children or families to yet make definitive pronouncements on the long-term successes and failure of welfare reform.[29]

African Americans and the HIV/AIDS Epidemic

When acquired immune deficiency syndrome (AIDS) and human immunodeficiency virus (HIV) first received national attention in 1981, it was generally regarded as a "gay disease" found almost exclusively among white homosexuals. Therefore, it received little attention from the African American media, from the black church, or civil rights or political leaders. Even when it became clear that AIDS was not confined to white homosexuals, the black media and black leaders were reluctant to acknowledge its prevalence among blacks. This reluctance may be attributed to the strong taboo against homosexuality in African American culture generally, and to the power of African American religiosity that strongly condemns homosexuality as sinful. Similarly, because the disease is also disproportionately transmitted among blacks through illegal, intravenous drug use and "promiscuous" sexual activity, there was also a religious and cultural reluctance to acknowledge the existence of AIDS or to develop programs to deals with its causes and consequences.[30]

By the early 1990s, however, this pattern of denial and neglect could not be continued as the disease began to disproportionately impact the black community. By the late 1990s it was undeniable that AIDS was an epidemic among blacks, with federal health agencies reporting that while blacks were only 12 percent of the population they constituted 40 percent of those with AIDS. Among women, 56 percent were black and among children 58 percent. (By the late 1990s AIDS also had reached epidemic proportions in Africa. Although representing only 13 percent of the world's population, it was estimated that perhaps as much as 70 percent of AIDS cases in the world were African.) In 1996 the Harvard University AIDS Institute reported that more African Americans were infected with HIV than all other racial and ethnic groups combined. In other words, AIDS was fast becoming the leading cause of death of blacks in the United States.

The epidemic proportions of the disease (and the fact black celebrities such as basketball's Ervin "Magic" Johnson had become infected) finally led the black media, black church, and political and civil rights leaders to start paying attention to it and to push for development of targeted educational and health policies and programs that would address its causes and consequences in both the United States and Africa.[31]

African Americans and Same-Sex Marriage: A Cross-Cutting Issue

Same-sex marriage is a cross-cutting public policy issue in African American politics. Generally, the policy is supported by liberals and opposed by conservatives. Yet African Americans—the most liberal group in the electorate—are strongly opposed to same-sex marriage. The issue, however, divides African American leadership, which tends to be somewhat more liberal on the issue than ordinary blacks.

When the Massachusetts Supreme Court legalized same-sex marriages, it choose May 17 as the effective date of its ruling. May 17 was the date of the historic *Brown* v. *Board of Education* decision, and the justices probably deliberately selected it in order to link the struggle for same-sex marriage to the African American civil rights struggle. Some black leaders accept this linkage between gay rights and civil rights, including, among others, Coretta Scott King (the late widow of Martin Luther King Jr.); Al Sharpton and Carol Mosley Braun, candidates for the 2004 Democratic presidential nomination (Mosley Braun and Sharpton were the only candidates for the nomination to support same-sex marriage; the remaining candidates supported civil unions, which provide some marital rights and benefits to homosexual couples); Julian Bond, chair of the NAACP board; and Congressman John Lewis of Georgia. Lewis, the last surviving organizer and speaker at the 1963 March on Washington, said, "I have fought too hard and too long against discrimination based on race and color not to stand against discrimination based on sexual orientation."[32] Although he rejects the comparison to the civil rights struggle, Jesse Jackson also supports same-sex marriage.

However, Colin Powell, Louis Farrakahan, and most black clergy oppose same-sex marriage, and argue that there this is no relationship between the civil rights and gay rights struggles. The National Baptist Convention, the largest black church organization, unequivocally condemns same-sex marriage but also homosexuality itself as morally wrong and sinful. When Democratic presidential nominee John Kerry compared the struggle for civil rights with same-sex marriage, the chairman of the Congressional Black Caucus rebuked him.[33] And former District of Columbia Congressman Rev. Walter Fauntroy, Dr. King's principal assistant in Washington during the civil rights movement, is a founder and leader of the Alliance for Marriage, the organization that helped the Bush administration draft a constitutional amendment defining marriage as a union between a woman and man. Using the biblical word "abomination," Fauntroy claims that same-sex marriage could destroy the family, society, and the government.[34]

African American public opinion is also strongly opposed to same-sex marriage. Indeed, to illustrate the cross-cutting nature of the issue, opposition to same-sex marriage is concentrated among the most conservative and Republican group in the electorate—white evangelical Christians—and African Americans, the electorate's most liberal and Democratic group. A 2003 Pew poll found that 83 percent of white evangelicals were opposed to same-sex marriage, followed by 64 percent of blacks.[35] Among all ethnic groups, support for same-sex marriage increased dramatically between 1996 and 2003 except among blacks and white evangelicals, where it increased only 1 percent.[36] And in 2008 blacks in California voted overwhelmingly for Proposition 8, which the repealed the State's same-sex marriage law.

African American opinion, however, does bring cross-pressures on black leaders inclined to support same-sex marriage. For example, although the NAACP board chair supports same-sex marriage, the organization itself has not taken a position on the issue although its magazine has run articles sympathetic to same-sex couples.[37] The Congressional Black Caucus is described by Congressman Barney Franks, one of two openly gay House members, as "the most supportive elected officials in the country on gay issues."[38]

Race, Concentrated Poverty, Black Politics, and Katrina

Many Americans were surprised at the concentrated poverty among African Americans in New Orleans revealed by the televised images of individuals and families unable to evacuate. However, this kind of poverty can be found in most large American cities, as well as throughout the rural South, where about 20 percent of the black population resides. Poverty among African Americans is especially concentrated in what political scientists refer to as "black regime cities," cities with majority or near-majority black populations and where blacks control the government—the mayor's office, the city council, the school board, and most of the senior positions in the bureaucracy.[39]

There were nine such cities in the 1970s (Atlanta; Baltimore; Detroit; Gary, Indiana; Newark, New Jersey; Richmond, Virginia; Washington, D.C.; Birmingham, Alabama; and New Orleans). At the time of the election of these regimes the poverty rate in these cities averaged 16 percent, ranging from 12.3 percent in Gary to 22 percent in New Orleans. By 1990 the average poverty rate had increased to 28 percent, ranging from 16.9 percent in Washington to 32.4 percent in Detroit (New Orleans had the second highest poverty rate at 31.6 percent).[40] The concentration of poverty among African Americans results in social isolation, crime, welfare dependency, single-parent households, inadequate schooling and health services, and relatively low levels of political participation.[41] And in three decades of black regime cities, the problem of concentrated poverty has only gotten worse.

A similar situation exists in the rural South. Sharon Wright Austin writes, "In rural towns and counties and to some extent urban cities, African American politicians have found it impossible to reduce economic disparities among the privileged and the powerful . . . . The poverty rates in all the Delta's predominantly African American communities, however, including those with high amounts of black political power, usually doubled and tripled state and national averages."[42]

The problem of concentrated poverty—whether urban or rural—is beyond the resources and legal authority of local governments to address.[43] And at least since the 1980s the federal government has abandoned attempts to develop universal programs and policies to eradicate poverty, leaving cities and towns to cope alone with near insurmountable problems.[44]

This is not just a black problem. Concentrated poverty is increasingly found among Latino immigrants in towns and cities. Although largely ignored by the media, in New Orleans, nearly 40,000 Latinos (living largely in trailers) were displaced by Katrina.[45] These undocumented immigrants worked in a variety of occupations that paid poverty-level or below-poverty-level wages. In the aftermath of Katrina the *New York Times* reported that about a quarter of the construction workers rebuilding New Orleans were illegal immigrants who were getting lower pay and working in less safe conditions than legal workers.[46]

FACES AND VOICES IN THE STRUGGLE FOR UNIVERSAL FREEDOM

JOHNNIE TILLMON (1926–1995)

Johnnie Tillmon contributed to universal freedom and equality by attempting to make the welfare of *all* children a universally accepted right in the United States. In contrast to the United States where welfare polices stigmatize children born out of wedlock and are used to encourage marriage, in much of Western Europe welfare polices are designed to support all children equally, whatever the marital status of their parents. As founding chair and later executive director of the National Welfare Rights Organization (NWRO), Tillmon worked to achieve these kinds of reforms for American children. Born in Scott, Arkansas, to impoverished sharecroppers, Tillmon moved to Los Angeles to escape Jim Crow segregation and poverty. The mother of six children, she was disabled as a result of diabetes and other illnesses and began to receive welfare assistance. While living in a Los Angeles housing project, Tillmon—after a series of degrading encounters with welfare officials in 1962—organized Aid to Needy Children and Mothers Anonymously. This support network for women on welfare eventually led to her leadership of NWRO, the first national organization in African American politics devoted exclusively to the interests of poor black women and their children.

Between 1967 and 1975 (when NWRO ceased operations), NWRO under Tillmon's leadership mobilized a national grassroots network of over 100 local chapters and more than 10,000 members who filed lawsuits and engaged in numerous protest demonstrations at welfare offices, state legislatures, and in Washington. Although NWRO did not achieve its ultimate objective of transforming welfare polices in the United States, it was effective in increasing the number of children receiving assistance and in expanding benefits. It also enhanced the image of welfare mothers among themselves and was responsible for helping to establish a right of privacy for welfare recipients. NWRO also helped to eliminate state residency requirements and establish due process procedures for the termination of benefits. Ironically, perhaps its greatest achievement was its role in the defeat of the Nixon administration's Family Assistance Plan, which would have established universal assistance for all children. NWRO opposed the plan because it believed the benefit levels were to low and the work requirements for mothers too harsh and punitive.

Although Tillmon had little formal education, her 1972 *Ms.* magazine essay "Welfare Is a Women's Issue" is a sharp analysis of the intersection between gender, race, and poverty in the United States and is widely read in women's studies courses.

Summary

Since the federal government assumed responsibility for management of the economy, to assure economic growth, employment, and price stability, full employment has been the top priority of African Americans and their leaders. It appears, however, that the American economy cannot be made to operate at full employment (without risking high inflation) except in times of war. Rather, today most economists seem to assume that an unemployment rate of 5–5.5 percent is the "natural rate" of unemployment. This rate translates into an ongoing recession in black America. Generations of recession-level unemployment of 10 percent or more have had devastating consequences for the African American family and community, and this unemployment is related to crime, disparities in health, inequalities in the criminal justice system, the AIDS/HIV epidemic, and other social problems. Beginning in 1935 the federal government maintained AFDC as a federal, universal program of welfare for poor women and children who did not have employed husbands and who themselves could not find work at living wages. In 1996, the Republican Congress passed and President Clinton signed into law a bill abolishing this 60-year-old universal safety net, returning responsibility for welfare of poor children and women to the states.

This chapter has focused on the African American quest for universal freedom in terms of access to material-based benefits. This quest has met with limited success. African Americans are not likely to be satisfied with this limited success. How the African American community and its leaders and white society will deal with this dissatisfaction is one of the more fascinating and puzzling questions for the future of the African American freedom struggle.

Selected Bibliography

Bailey, Stephen. *Congress Makes a Law.* New York: Vintage Books, 1964. A classic legislative case study, focusing on the Congress's first attempt to enact full employment legislation.

Cohen, Kathy. *Beyond the Boundaries: AIDS and the Breakdown of Black Politics.* Chicago: University of Chicago Press, 1997. A comprehensive study of the cultural, social, and political impact of AIDS on the African American community.

Cole, David. *No Equal Justice: Race and Class in the American Criminal Justice System.* New York: Free Press, 1999. The most recent study documenting the systematic nature of racism in the criminal justice system.

Edelman, Peter. "Clinton's Worst Mistake." *Atlantic Monthly* (May 1997). An incisive critique of the welfare reform bill signed by President Clinton.

Ellwood, David. *Poor Support: Poverty in the American Family.* New York: Basic Books, 1988. A detailed discussion of humane reforms in welfare by a Harvard professor and former Clinton administration welfare official.

Frendreis, John, and Raymond Tatalovich. *The Modern Presidency and Economic Policy.* Itasca, IL: F. E. Peacock, 1994. A descriptive analysis of how economic policy is made.

Harvey, Phillip. *Securing the Right to Employment: Social Welfare Policy and the Unemployed in the United States.* Princeton, NJ: Princeton University Press, 1989. An analysis with recommendations on how to achieve full employment.

Kirshernman, J., and K. Neckerman. "We'd Love to Hire Them But . . . The Meaning of Race for Employers." In C. Jencks, ed., *The Urban Underclass.* Washington, DC: Brookings Institution, 1992. A study of the role of race and racism in the employment decisions of white employers.

Moynihan, Daniel P. *The Politics of a Guaranteed Income.* New York: Vintage Books, 1973. A study of the Nixon administration's failed attempt to enact a universal family assistance plan to replace AFDC.

Piven, Frances, and Richard Cloward. *Regulating the Poor: The Functions of Public Welfare.* New York: Vintage Books, 1971. A provocative analysis of how welfare is used as a mechanism to control the political behavior of the poor.

Smith, Robert C. "The Humphrey-Hawkins Act as Symbolic Politics." In Robert C. Smith, *We Have No Leaders: African Americans in the Post–Civil Rights Era* (chap. 7). Albany: SUNY Press, 1996. A case study of Congress's second attempt to enact full employment legislation.

Williams, Linda. *The Constraint of Race: Legacies of White Skin Privilege and Politics of American Social Policy.* College Park: Pennsylvania State University Press, 2003. An illuminating study of racism's impact on the development of social welfare policies from Reconstruction to the Clinton administration.

Wilson, William. *The Truly Disadvantaged: The Inner City, the Underclass and Public Policy.* Chicago: University of Chicago Press, 1987. A very influential study that focuses on the loss of industrial jobs as the key factor in the rise and growth of the underclass.

Notes

1. See Arthur Schlesinger, Jr., *The Coming of the New Deal* (New York: Houghton Mifflin, 1959).
2. For a history of the 1946 act's adoption, see Stephen Bailey, *Congress Makes a Law* (New York: Vintage Books, 1964).
3. For a discussion of the economic policy-making apparatus, including the work of the president and his budget and economic advisors, the Congress, and the Federal Reserve Board, see John Frendreis and Raymond Tatalovich, *The Modern Presidency and Economic Policy* (Itasia, IL: F. E. Peacock, 1994).
4. Phillip Harvey, *Securing the Right to Employment: Social Welfare Policy and the Unemployed in the United States* (Princeton, NJ: Princeton University Press, 1989); and Richard Gill, *Economics and the Public Interest* (Pacific Palisades: Goodyear, 1968).
5. Committee on Labor and Public Welfare, Subcommittee on Employment, Poverty and Migratory Labor, Senate, *Hearings on S. 50 and S. 472* (May 14, 17, 18, 19, 1976): p. 141.
6. Quoted in the *Congressional Record—House* (March 8, 1978): 6122.
7. Augustus Hawkins, "Whatever Happened to Full Employment," *Urban League Review* 10 (1986): 11.
8. F. Thayer, "A Bipartisan Fear of Full Employment," *New York Times*, October 12, 1988.
9. Testimony of Secretary Cuomo, House Appropriations Subcommittee on VA, HUD, and Independent Agencies broadcast on C-Span, March 25, 1998.
10. Harvey M. Brenner, "Estimating the Effects of Economic Change on National Health and Social Well-Being," paper prepared for the Subcommittee on Economic Goals and Intergovernmental Policy, Joint Economic Committee, July 15, 1984.
11. Jeanne Prial Gordus and Sean McAliden, "Economic Change, Physical Illness and Social Deviance," paper prepared for the Subcommittee on Economic Goals and Intergovernmental Relations, Joint Economic Committee, July 14, 1994.
12. "Justice System Holds About 3 percent of the U.S.," *New York Times,* July 2, 1996; p. A9.
13. Marc Mauer, *Young Black Americans and the Criminal Justice System* (Washington, DC: The Sentencing Project, 1995).
14. Laura Frank, "U.S. Courts Give Blacks Longer Terms," *West County Times*, September 24, 1995, p. B1.
15. Quoted in Charles Ogletree, "Blind Justice?: The Constitution and the Justice System," in John Hope Franklin and Genna Rae MacNeil, eds., *African Americans and the Constitution* (Washington, DC: Smithsonian Institution, 1995): 261.
16. See Ronald Walters, *White Nationalism in the United States* (Washington, DC: Eadford, 1987); and Kim Lersch, "Current Trends in Police Brutality: An Analysis of Recent Newspaper Accounts," master's thesis, University of Florida, Gainesville, 1993.
17. Jonah Goldberg, "The Color of Suspicion," *New York Times Magazine*, June 20, 1996.
18. Quoted in Robert C. Smith and Richard Seltzer, *Contemporary Controversies and the American Racial Divide* (Boulder, CO: Rowman & Littlefield, 2000): 104.
19. William Lester, "Many Think Police Have Racial Bias," *West County Times*, December 11, 1999.
20. Daniel Patrick Moynihan, "The Negro Family: A Case for National Action," in Lee Rainwater and William Yancey, eds., *The Moynihan Report and the Politics of Controversy* (Cambridge, MA: MIT Press, 1967): 369, 375.
21. M. Belinda Tucker and Claudia Mitchell-Kernon, eds., *The Decline in Marriage Among African Americans* (New York: Russell Sage, 1995). We should note that divorce rates and the rate of out-of-wedlock births have gone up sharply among whites in the United States and throughout the Western industrial world. See Tamar Lewin, "The Decay of Families Is Global, Study Says," *New York Times,* May 30, 1995.
22. Louis Uchitele, "Blacks Lose Jobs Faster as Middle Class Drops," *New York Times,* July 12, 2003.

23. Ibid.

24. Janny Scott, "Nearly Half of Black Men Found Jobless," *New York Times*, February 28, 2004.

25. These data are reported in Robert C. Smith, *Racism in the Post–Civil Rights Era: Now You See It, Now You Don't* (Albany: SUNY Press, 1995): 39. See also Martin Gilens, *Why Americans Hate Welfare* (Chicago: University of Chicago Press, 1999). Although most whites view blacks as lazy and not willing to work, blacks have historically constituted a large proportion of the nation's working poor, doing much of America's "dirty" work as housecleaners, janitors, and hospital orderlies. See U.S. Department of Labor, *A Profile of the Working Poor* (Washington, DC: Government Printing Office, 1983): Tables 3, 13.

26. Million Kolter and Nelson Rosenbaum, "Strengthening the Democratic Party Through Strategic Marketing: Voters and Donors," a confidential report for the Democratic National Committee, Washington, DC. On the background of the strategic approach followed by Clinton, see his campaign "bible" by Thomas Edsal and Mary Edsal, *Chain Reaction: The Impact of Race, Rights and Taxes on American Politics* (New York: W.W. Norton, 1992). See also Smith, *We Have No Leaders*, chap. 10.

27. Elizabeth Shogren, "New Welfare System Seen as Recession Proof," *Los Angeles Times*, April 24, 2003.

28. Ibid.

29. Rebecca Blank, "Was Welfare Reform Successful?" *Economist's Voice* (March 2006): 4–5.

30. Kathy Cohen, *Beyond the Boundaries: AIDS and the Breakdown of Black Politics* (Chicago: University of Chicago Press, 1997).

31. Ibid.

32. Phuong Ly and Hamil Harris, "Blacks, Gays in Struggle of Values," *Washington Post*, March 15, 2004.

33. Brian Debose, "Black Caucus Resists Comparison to Gay Marriage," *Washington Times*, March 15, 2004.

34. Ly and Harris, "Blacks, Gays in Struggle of Values."

35. "The Pew Forum on Religion and Public Life," "Longitudinal U.S. Public Opinion Pollson Same-Sex Marriage and Civil Unions," www.religioustolerance.org/hom_poll5.htm, February 18, 2004.

36. Ibid.

37. Keith Baykin, "Your Blues Ain't Like Mine: Blacks and Gay Marriage," *The Crisis* (January/February 2004): 23–24.

38. Ibid. The Caucus, for example, overwhelmingly opposed the ban on gays serving in the military.

39. Adolph Reed, "The Black Urban Regime: Structural Origins and Constraint," in Peter Orleans, ed., *Power, Community and the City: Comparative Urban Research* (New Brunswick, NJ: Transaction Publishers, 1988).

40. Robert C. Smith, "Urban Politics," *Encyclopedia of African American Politics* (New York: Facts on File, 2003): 367–63.

41. Yvette Alex-Assensoh, "Race, Concentrated Poverty, Social Isolation and Political Behavior," *Urban Affairs Quarterly* 33 (1997): 209–27.

42. Sharon Wright Austin, *The Transformation of Plantation Politics: Black Politics, Concentrated Poverty, and Social Capital in the Mississippi Delta* (Albany: SUNY Press, 2006): 173.

43. Paul Peterson, *City Limits* (Chicago: University of Chicago Press, 1981).

44. Demetrious Caraley, "Washington Abandons the Cities," *Political Science Quarterly* 107 (1992): 431–43.

45. Michael Eric Dyson, *Come Hell or High Water: Hurricane Katrina and the Color of Disaster* (New York: Basic Civitas, 2006): 142.

46. Leslie Eaton, "Study Sees Increase in Illegal Hispanic Workers in New Orleans," *New York Times*, June 8, 2006.

CHAPTER 16

The African American Quest for Universal Freedom and U.S. Foreign Policy

In the 1940s, Edith Sampson, Chicago attorney, was appointed by President Truman as a delegate to the United Nations General Assembly. Over the years she has been followed by Pearl Bailey, Zelma George, Marian Anderson, Coretta Scott King, and a host of others. Sampson became the first African American, male or female, to represent the United States at the United Nations.[1]

African Americans have served as consuls, ministers, and ambassadors to foreign capitals as well as to the United Nations. African Americans have been employed as foreign service officers and career officials at the Department of State. Outside the bureaucracy, African Americans have served the nation in an ad hoc fashion. For example, in 1889, upon learning that historian-lawyer George Washington Williams would be making a visit to the Congo, President Benjamin Harrison asked him to gather information and submit a report on his return, which could be used in determining the nation's policy toward the Congo.[2] President Jimmy Carter sent Muhammad Ali on a goodwill tour of Africa, and President Clinton, during his first term, sent Jesse Jackson as a special representative to Nigeria and William Gray, a former congressman, as special envoy to Haiti. In addition to performing these brief diplomatic functions, African Americans have been selected to serve and represent the nation on international commissions and tribunals. Fisk University president and sociologist Charles S. Johnson was appointed by President Herbert Hoover in 1929 to serve on the International Commission to Investigate Slavery and Forced Labor in Liberia.[3]

There is one other role that African Americans have played in implementing U.S. foreign policy: as participants in most of the nation's wars. Whether it was as buffalo soldiers in the Indian wars or as troops in the Spanish–American War, both world wars, the Korean conflict, Vietnam, the invasion of Grenada, Panama, or the Iraq War, African Americans have carried the sword.

Although they have played numerous roles in implementing and managing American foreign policies, African Americans have also served as *creators* in foreign matters, particularly as America's policy has related to the Third World and Africa. In fact, in their role as creators, African Americans have been critics, as was the NAACP after its investigation of the U.S. Marine occupation of Haiti (1915–1934). African Americans have been innovators, as were Sylvester Williams and W. E. B. Du Bois in organizing the Pan-African Congresses; or William Monroe Trotter and Du Bois at the Paris Peace Conference in 1919; or Mary McCleod Bethune, Walter White, and Du Bois at the founding conference of the United Nations. William Patterson and Malcolm X presented petitions to the United Nations on human rights.

Thus, in their quest for universal freedom, African Americans, who were born in foreign affairs through African slavery and the slave trade, have turned to America's foreign policy to support ideals of human rights and humanitarianism. Any appreciation of the universal freedom thrust of African American politics must include an understanding of African Americans' role in foreign affairs.

African Americans as Foreign Policy Implementors/Managers: The Search for "Black Nationality"

In his study of African Americans in the foreign policy apparatus, Jake Miller made the following comments: "When one considers the input of Blacks into the foreign policy-making machinery, the State Department immediately becomes the major part of the focus, since it is in this governmental department that foreign policy is traditionally formulated."[4] But looking at the State Department as late as 1998, only 2.7 percent of the entire Foreign Service Corps was African American.

Given this basic reality, Miller concluded that decision-making powers in the State Department reside in a very limited number of officers, few of whom are blacks.[5] African Americans have not had the key positions in the bureaucracy, yet as an interest group they have had a recognizable and continuing role throughout their sojourn in America. And they have had to fashion this role inside the bureaucracy in a different manner from that used by other pressure groups.

Inside the bureaucracy, African Americans had to fashion their role from positions as ministers and ambassadors to small African nations. To locate and extrapolate this role, it is useful to analyze the diplomatic correspondence of these individuals as well as their symbolic actions to protest and advance the cause of "a black nationality, both on the continent of Africa and in the diaspora."[6] Elliot P. Skinner, African American scholar, former ambassador to the Republic of Upper Volta, and student of these early African American diplomats, notes that this collective role could be encapsulated in the concept of *black nationality*.[7] Skinner writes, "Diplomats such as J. Milton Turner, Henry H. Smyth and Ernest Lyon were openly confrontational with the State Department to achieve their objectives. They endeavored to prove that they could serve faithfully as American foreign service officers even while protecting the black nationality."[8] Many of these African American implementors of American foreign policy believed that by helping to create a strong and developed Africa, they would contribute to the solution of its people's problems the world over. They would also be helping to preserve the already existing nation-states of Liberia and Haiti. This was their expression of "black nationality," which they would leave as a legacy to future African Americans coming into the foreign policy bureaucracy.

One of the roots of black nationality began in Abraham Lincoln's annual message to Congress in December, 1861. President Lincoln announced, "If any good reason exists why we should persevere longer in withholding our recognition of the independence and sovereignty of Haiti and Liberia, I am unable to discern it."[9] At a National Convention meeting in Syracuse, New York, African Americans passed a resolution praising Congress for honoring Lincoln's request.[10] Senator Charles Summer of Massachusetts introduced the bill, which authorized the president to appoint diplomatic representatives to Haiti and Liberia. The bill was attacked but eventually passed by 32 to 7 in the Senate and 86 to 37 in the House. For decades Southerners had blocked the formal recognition of Haiti and Liberia, but even with this action the United States was the last Western nation to open normal diplomatic relations with Haiti and Liberia.[11]

After recognition of the two countries, the first African American diplomats to these nations began to use their influence in the State Department on their behalf. Miller writes that an analysis of the diplomatic correspondence of the black ministers accredited to Port-au-Prince revealed that no issue tended to be more dominant than those involving the granting of asylum to Haitians and the protection of Americans and their interest in the "black republic."[12] Clearly related to this issue was the question of political instability in the country.[13]

In Liberia, black ministers were preoccupied with the attempts by European powers to encroach on the territorial sovereignty of the young black republic. Their notes to the State Department reflected their concern with such matters as Liberian border frictions with England and France.

In pressing the concerns of Haiti and Liberia, diplomats in both these nations found themselves in conflictual and confrontational stances with the State Department. Here is an example of bureaucrats opposing their own bureaucracy. As Miller writes: "The structural challenge for African Americans chosen as envoys (diplomats) was that they also had to serve a nation that denigrated them and Africa itself."[14] The first African American diplomat to Liberia, J. Milton Turner (1871–1878) realized that these black diplomats had to use "extreme prudence"; he designed his dispatches "as much . . . to educate the officials in the State Department about the realities of Liberia as to enlist the help of his government for the Liberians."[15]

However, not all the black diplomats took such a frontal and conflictual approach with the State Department. Some moved in fugitive, back-channel, and secretive manners, acting on their own beyond the normal diplomatic channels. Of this tactic Miller writes that while most black ministers participated in the drive for greater Liberian security in a noncontroversial manner, the State Department has felt compelled to chastise some for overstepping guidelines.

An example was diplomat Ernest Lyon. Lyon, a protégé of Booker T. Washington, who became adept at "back-channel" manipulation, establishing important contacts outside the State Department in order to effect policy. Lyon knew how to exploit Booker T. Washington's strong support among both northern and southern African Americans and his accommodationist attitude toward the white power structure to accomplish his goals.[16] To achieve their aims and objectives, these back-channel diplomats used symbolic structures as a means of seeking to influence U.S. policy toward Africa and its people. These "symbolic structures" were conferences and hortatory rhetoric, newspaper coverage, lectures, letters, and contact with interested and powerful white individuals and groups.[17] Symbolic structures were devices to mobilize public opinion and mass interest in both African American and white communities.

In sum, African American ministers, envoys, and ambassadors found in their own individual manner three discernible ways to articulate their concern for universal freedom and respect. First, they could be conflictual and confrontational with the State Department. This tactic was an effort to move the department toward a more positive policy in maintaining and enhancing the independence of these new black republics. The second technique was individual initiatives. Here, they took matters in their own hands, devising solutions independent of the State Department. The third and final tactic was the back-channel technique. Here insiders passed vital information to elites inside the black community. This procedure, unlike the others, forged a link between the diplomats and the African American community, as well as with key individuals in the white community.

These strategies may not have been influential, but they perpetuated a legacy for the future. For instance, when African Americans served as delegates to the United Nations General Assembly, they continued the tradition taken by the early diplomats. In 1960 alternate delegate Zelma George displayed contempt for the position taken by the United States when she stood and joined African and Asian representatives in applauding the adoption of the resolution calling for an end of colonialism—a resolution on which the United States had abstained.[18]

In 1971, UN delegate Congressman Charles Diggs of Michigan sent a telegram to Secretary of State William Rogers expressing his opposition to the U.S. position on apartheid and resigned from the delegation. In its response to Congressman Diggs, "the State Department noted that while it recognized the value of consultation, there was a need for the United States to speak with one voice in the United Nations General Assembly."[19]

African Americans as Foreign Policy Dissenters

Black diplomats were not solely concerned with black nations. Because of their posting to these nations, they could speak to only this one aspect. But the limitations of federal bureaucrats are not the limitations of the entire black community. Elites, organizations, and institutions inside the community also helped shape responses to a wider array of issues and concerns.

Paul Cuffe began an aspect of black nationality when in 1815 he took 38 blacks to Africa at a personal expense of $3,000 or $4,000.[20] His African colonization plan was a critique of the possibilities of African American universal freedom in the United States. His critique was a harbinger of a new American policy of colonization, as well as an African American policy of emigration.

Cuffe's initial articulation through activism was taken up by Martin Delany and Robert Campbell when they launched a trip to explore the Niger River area as a site for emigration. On their return to America, Delany and Campbell had to face the reality that it was not easy for African Americans to go to Africa.[21] After the Berlin Conference of 1884–1885, colonialism arrived full force in Africa and the visions created by Cuffe, Delany, and Campbell went sour under the terror brought on by some of the colonial powers. At the 1884–1885 Berlin Conference, the Congo was given to King Leopold of Belgium and he "instituted one of the harshest, cruelest and most violent systems of colonialism in Africa."[22] American foreign policy stood silent as the atrocities of King Leopold occurred on a daily basis.[23] George Washington Williams—historian, politician, and Ohio legislator—bitterly criticized King Leopold's policies in the Congo.[24] African American dissenters to American foreign policy now began to fashion a role in line with specific events and places. The actions by Williams were more specific and more focused than had been the work of Cuffe, Delany, and Campbell.

Many African American leaders were vigorous opponents of the Mexican–American War. Frederick Douglass, for example, was scathing in his criticism, writing in his newspaper *North Star,* that the U.S. government had

> succeeded in robbing Mexico of her territory, and are rejoicing over their success under the hypocritical pretense of a regard for peace. Had they not succeeded in robbing Mexico of the most important and most valuable of her territory, many of those now loudest in their professions of favor for peace would be loudest and wildest for war.[25]

Following in the path blazed by Williams and Douglass was Bishop Alexander Walters of the National African American Council, who was strongly critical when the United States annexed the Philippines during the Spanish–American War.[26] There, in the cause of white supremacy, the United States turned from a policy of cooperating with Tagalog insurgents against the Spanish colonial authorities to one of joining with the defeated Spaniards against the Filipinos.[27] Therefore, as a foreign policy dissenter, Walters noted that "had the Filipino been white and fought as brave as they have, the war would have been ended and their independence granted a long time ago."[28] But those in the Walters-led group were not the only dissenters. One of the African American troops sent the following letter to an African American newspaper, the *Wisconsin Weekly Advocate,* in Milwaukee, May 17, 1900:

> I have mingled freely with the natives and have had talks with American colored men here in business and who have lived here for years, in order to learn of them the cause of their (Filipino) dissatisfaction and the reason for this insurrection, and I must confess they have a just grievance. All this never would have occurred if the army of occupation would have treated them as people. The Spaniards, even if their laws were hard, were polite and treated them with some consideration; but the Americans, as soon as they saw that the native troops were desirous of sharing in the glories as well as the hardships of the hard-won battles with the Americans, began to apply home treatment for colored peoples: cursed them as damned niggers, steal [from] and ravish them, rob them on the street of their small change, take from the fruit vendors whatever suited their fancy, and kick the poor unfortunate if he complained, desecrate their church property, and after fighting began, looted everything in sight, burning, robbing. . . . Heaven's sake, put the party [Democratic] in power that pledged itself against this highway robbery. Expansion is too clean a name for it.[29]

After analyzing the entire conflict, one historian noted:

> By the time the black troops departed from the Philippines, it was generally agreed that their relationships with the natives were more cordial than those of white soldiers.

When the Negro soldiers first arrived in the islands, Filipinos viewed them with awe and fear as an "American species of bete noir." A typical reaction was: "These are not Americans; they are Negritoes." But their fear quickly turned into friendliness and their awe into admiration. Filipinos came to accept black Americans as "very much like ourselves only larger" and gave them the affectionate appellation, "Negritos Americanos." Negro soldiers generally reciprocated the good will of peaceful natives and treated them with consideration and respect. In letters home they often referred to the contempt which white soldiers displayed toward all Filipinos and insisted that such an attitude underlay much of the natives' hostility to American rule.[30]

In the Boer War, where the British fought the white South Africans, and American foreign policy was one of solidarity with the British, African Americans spoke out, denouncing the war as aggression.[31] At first blacks viewed the struggle as between whites with little interest to them. As they learned more of the racism in Afrikaner society, they became increasingly hostile to the Boers.[32]

With the coming of World War I, African American socialists A. Philip Randolph and Chandler Owens demanded a change in America's foreign policy. They published a newspaper, *The Messenger*, in New York, and because of an article they wrote, "Pro-Germanism Among Negroes," Randolph and Owens were sentenced to jail and their second-class mailing privileges were revoked.[33]

The Paris Peace Conference, the Treaty of Versailles, and the founding of the League of Nations all gave African American leaders an opportunity to further express their foreign policy concerns. Both W. E. B. Du Bois and William Monroe Trotter attended the Paris Peace Conference. While Du Bois was able to influence the creation of the League of Nation's mandate system for the colonial-held Third World nations,[34] Trotter found that the State Department denied him a passport and thereby an official presence at the Conference.[35] Yet Trotter attended and wrote his critical observations in his newspaper, the *Boston Guardian*.[36]

The Italian invasion of Ethiopia mobilized the African American community to action on foreign policy like no other event. Mussolini had come to power in Italy in 1922 and by 1935 he was seeking to restore the Roman Empire by overrunning Ethiopia.[37] In the face of such naked imperialism, it could be expected that a few lonely voices and organizations might have spoken out. However, Franklin and Moss write, "When Italy invaded Ethiopia African Americans protested with all the means at their command. Almost overnight even the most provincial among black Americans became international-minded. Ethiopia was a black nation, and its destruction would symbolize the final victory of white over blacks."[38] In opposition, "African-Americans held pro-Ethiopian demonstrations in Harlem, Chicago, Miami, Washington, and elsewhere; they sent money and medical supplies to Addis Ababa and boycotted Italian-made goods. They saw race as central to the dispute."[39] Ethiopia was also a major concern of the black press in the 1930s, with most of the black media criticizing the Italian invasion of Ethiopia.[40] The *Pittsburgh Courier* assigned J. A. Rogers as a war correspondent to send the news on the war front back to the United States; and there were pleas made both to the U.S. government and the League of Nations. For instance, the NAACP telegraphed the League of Nations on behalf of 12,000,000 American Negroes, demanding action to restrain dictator Benito Mussolini.[41]

All this frenzied lobbying set the African Americans against outspoken Italian American groups that, as a matter of ethnic pride, supported their ancestral homeland. In some eastern cities where Italian and black neighborhoods adjoined, riots erupted.[42] In this intense and rising competition between the two groups to affect policy toward the war, the African Americans were more successful than the Italian Americans because the Roosevelt administration imposed an arms embargo on Italy.[43] The intensity as well as the strength of the African American reaction to the Italian invasion helped considerably in arousing a general American sympathy for Ethiopia.[44] This time the outcry came from all quarters and sectors of African American society. Indeed, the demand for help for Ethiopia was so systematic and comprehensive this time that in the midst of the conflict, in January 1937, African American leaders founded the Council on African Affairs, a national organization to lobby for Africa—a forerunner of Trans Africa.

During World War II the global nature of the struggle and the indeterminate post–world war realities forced African Americans to wage a "Double V" campaign, victory at home as well as abroad.[45] In World War II, African Americans were willing to do their part and to make necessary sacrifice to ensure victory, but they constantly reminded the people of the United States that they resented all forms of discrimination.[46] In addition to the Double V, the African American press simultaneously called for a new and more progressive approach to colonialism and the problems of Third World nations.[47]

African American leaders supported an independent Israel, but after the 1973 Yom Kippur War, increasing numbers of African Americans began to speak for the cause of Palestinian independence as well.

During 1946–1947, leading black newspapers were opposed to the cold war policies of the United States. At the same time, these papers reminded Americans that the best defense against communism was universal freedom, at home and abroad.[48]

When the Korean conflict made the cold war a hot war, white American soldiers, De Conde writes, "disparaged their opponents in racial terms, dismissing the North Koreans and the Chinese—even their own South Korean allies—with epithets such as 'barbarians,' 'beasts,' and 'gooks'. . . . [Being] aware of this attitude most African Americans analyzed the conflict from their own racial perspective. Many of them and their organization opposed it."[49] And during this conflict, African American dissenters had to fight the army to integrate its units, as stipulated in President Harry Truman's executive order in 1949. In the midst of the war, General Matthew Ridgeway received permission to integrate African Americans throughout his command. Between May and August 1951, the extent of troop integration in Korea increased from 9 to 30 percent.[50]

One of the crisis events of the cold war that U.S. policy makers had to cope with was the Nigerian civil war, better known as the Biafran secession, which emerged during the Nixon administration. President Nixon supported the Biafran secession, a position that put him at odds with the African American community.[51] From the outset, African Americans put their support behind the Nigerian federal government. Thus, when the Biafra secessionists surrendered in January 1970, the Nigerians expressed gratitude toward African Americans who helped to keep Washington committed to the one-Nigeria policy.[52] Like the situation in Ethiopia some three-and-a-half decades earlier, blacks had helped to shape events in Nigeria in a way supportive of African nationality.

Muhammad Ali, Martin Luther King Jr., and many other prominent blacks also voiced opposition to the Vietnam War. When Martin Luther King Jr. dissented from the rising American consensus about the war, it divided the civil rights movement and angered liberals and President Johnson. Several African American leaders, notably Whitney Young of the Urban League, denounced King and supported President Johnson. But King's prestige made him a major voice in the antiwar movement.[53]

Inside the military, African American troops spoke out against both the racial epithets and some of the inhumane policies of American troops fighting in Vietnam.

> Replacing the careerists were black draftees, many just steps removed from marching in the Civil Rights Movement or rioting in the rebellions that swept the urban ghettos from Harlem to Watts. All were filled with a new sense of black pride and purpose. They spoke loudest against the discrimination they encountered on the battlefield to protest these indignities and provide mutual support. And they called themselves "Bloods."[54]

When President Reagan ordered an invasion of the Caribbean island nation of Grenada in October 1984, five members of the Congressional Black Caucus moved to impeach the president while the entire Caucus condemned the invasion as being nurtured essentially by white racism. African Americans also opposed George Bush's Persian Gulf War.[55] Finally, African Americans lobbied the Clinton administration to send troops to Haiti to restore President Jean Bertrand Aristide to power after his ouster in a military coup.

African Americans have not had a commanding influence in American foreign policy, but they have had a continuing presence. On several occasions, that presence has had a decided impact on the outcome of American foreign policy, such as the Ethiopian War. African Americans were successful in changing the Nixon administration policy during the Nigerian civil war and in pressuring President Clinton to intervene in the Haitian situation. These are *direct* linkages between the expressed desires of black Americans and American foreign policy. However, there is a very important, indirect link. For example, King's outspoken stance against the Vietnam War led to a larger, much more powerful and vocal antiwar and peace movement, and it contributed to the eventual withdrawal of the United States from Vietnam.

Trans Africa: African Americans as Foreign Policy Lobbyists

Figure 16.1 reveals the rise, fall, and evolution of African American organized interest and pressure group activity up to the founding of Trans Africa. In 1976 Congressmen Charles Diggs of Michigan (chair of the House Foreign Affairs Subcommittee on Africa) and Andrew Young convened 30 black leaders to challenge the Ford administration policy toward white-ruled Rhodesia. Little changed during the Ford administration. The incoming Carter administration, however, was concerned with human rights, and its leaders were willing to listen to Congressman and later UN Ambassador Young. As a result, the political context changed significantly. In May 1978, Young and his colleagues organized Trans Africa, the first mass-based African American lobby.

Figure 16.1   Sources and Outcomes of African American Foreign Policy-Making Initiatives

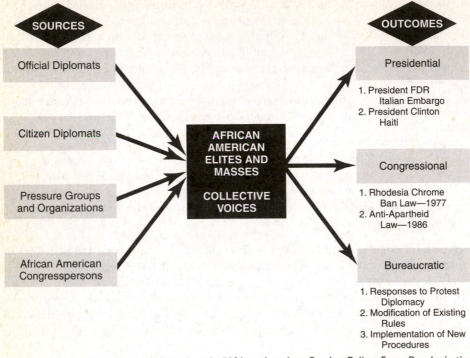

Sources: Adapted from Hanes Walton, Jr., ed., "African American Foreign Policy: From Decolonization to Democracy," in, *African American Power and Politics: The Political Context Variable* (New York: Columbia University Press, 1997), chap. 18; and Jake Miller, *The Black Presence in American Foreign Affairs* (Washington, DC: University Press of America, 1978).

To carry out its lobbying, Trans Africa—the "Black American Lobby for Africa and the Caribbean"—sends out "Issue Briefs" and a newsletter to alert its membership and individuals in the Congress to matters on which its leaders want action. It holds news conferences, public demonstrations, and annual dinners and symposiums to keep its constituency informed. To involve as well as mobilize people, Trans Africa has engaged in boycotts, marches, mass demonstrations, letter writing, and a hunger strike by its former director, Randall Robinson. Out of these different tactics and strategies, the organization has met with considerable success.

Outstanding among its efforts was its protests against South Africa, which began on Thanksgiving eve, 1984, as a sit-in at the South African Embassy in Washington. These protests eventually led to the Comprehensive Anti-Apartheid Act. Introduced by Congressman William Gray of Pennsylvania, this act passed both houses of Congress but was vetoed by President Reagan. However, the veto was overridden when Republicans joined with African American and white Democrats to impose sanctions on the South African regime.

During the Clinton administration, Trans Africa's executive director, Randall Robinson, used a hunger strike to force the president to change his policy toward

Haiti.[56] Initially, Clinton had essentially followed the more restricted Bush immigration policy and had successfully defended that policy in the Supreme Court.[57] Trans Africa, under Robinson's leadership, helped to reverse that policy.

Trans Africa has also embarked on a program of action designed to influence some of the African and other Third World dictatorships (especially Nigeria) to pursue, with America's help, democratic elections and governance.[58] With colonialism as a political system disappearing from African and Third World countries, this new course may yet help to achieve democracy in the countries of Africa.

Thus, this organizational presence of African Americans, through interest group lobbying, like its counterparts in other parts of the foreign policy process, has had both successes and failures in changing America's foreign policies toward Africa and the Third World.

African Americans and Citizen Diplomacy: Historical Background and Context

African American foreign policy leaders have a long history of creating new strategies and tactics to influence and shift the State Department's direction of foreign policy.[59] One of these strategies for articulating the African American position is *citizen diplomacy*.

Professor Karin Stanford has defined citizen diplomacy "as the diplomatic efforts of private citizens in the international arena for the purpose of achieving a specific objective or accomplishing constituency goals."[60] This particular technique for influencing foreign policy arose when George Logan, a white private citizen, decided on his own to intervene when the United States ratified the Jay Treaty with Great Britain in 1798. The French responded negatively, and with military force seized U.S. ships on the high seas. Logan went to Paris and asked the French to avoid a military crisis and defuse the situation by releasing the hostages and expressing goodwill. The government responded to Logan's efforts by passing the Logan Act on January 30, 1799, an act that prohibited individual citizens from trying to conduct official diplomatic endeavors.[61] But the government did not prosecute Logan then, and it has never prosecuted anyone for violating this law. The truth is that throughout America's history, numerous individuals have engaged in citizen diplomacy. During the Vietnam War, scores of individual citizens journeyed to Hanoi to participate and engage in citizen diplomacy. Among them were former Attorney General Ramsey Clark, movie stars Jane Fonda and Clint Eastwood, and the 1996 Reform Party presidential candidate H. Ross Perot.

African American Citizen Diplomats

From the time of slavery, African Americans have consistently engaged in citizen diplomacy, for example Frederick Douglass and many others traveled to Europe in efforts to universalize the struggle against slavery.[62]

As mentioned earlier, in the post-Reconstruction Era there were forays by George Washington Williams and Booker T. Washington into the Congo.[63] At the turn of the century, Sylvester Williams and W. E. B. Du Bois launched the Pan-African Congresses. The NAACP sent an observer to Haiti when American occupation began. Black journalist George Schuyler went to Liberia in 1931 for three months to investigate slavery there, and on his return used the data he had amassed on forced labor and slavery to write a novel, *Slaves Today: A Story of Liberia*.[64] In the preface to the novel he stated his objective:

> If this novel can help arouse enlightened world opinion against this brutalizing of the native population in a Negro republic, perhaps the conscience of civilized people will stop similar atrocities in native lands ruled by proud white nations that boast of their superior culture.[65]

The 1930s were a period of great activity. Colonel Hubert Julian, a fighter pilot, fought for Ethiopia in that conflict and tried to serve as a diplomatic negotiator,[66] while numerous African Americans did the same in the Spanish civil war.[67] African American historian Robin Kelly tells us of these citizen diplomats:

> When the Communist International asked for volunteers to come to Spain in the fall of 1936, African Americans who joined the Abraham Lincoln Brigade regarded the Civil War as an extension of the Italo-Ethiopian conflict . . . Oscar Hunter . . . explained, "I wanted to go to Ethiopia and fight Mussolini . . . This ain't Ethiopia, but it'll do." . . . Black volunteers linked the struggles of the Iberian peninsula to racism and poverty in America; for them Spain had become the battle field to revenge the attack of Ethiopia and part of a larger fight for justice and equality that would inevitably take place on U.S. soil.[68]

There were also African Americans who advocated the Soviet point of view about the communist system and its vision of universal freedom and global peace. Chief among them were W. E. B. Du Bois and entertainer-scholar Paul Robeson in the 1950s and early 1960s.[69]

Malcolm X made numerous pilgrimages to Africa and the Middle East, where he met with the heads of state of such nations as Egypt, Ghana, and Tanzania. The purpose of these missions was to universalize the African freedom struggle by developing linkages between the African and African American leadership communities. At the time of his murder, Malcolm X was attempting to develop support among African and other Third World nations for a UN resolution condemning the United States for violating the human rights of its African American citizens. Another example of a citizen diplomat was the Reverend Leon Sullivan and his articulation of the Sullivan principles (requiring equality in employment and working conditions) in regard to American corporations doing business in South Africa.

Reverend Jesse Jackson was continuing the long history of African American citizen diplomats when he went to Syria on December 31, 1983, to secure the release of Lieutenant Robert O. Goodman, Jr. Lieutenant Goodman was an African American pilot who had been shot down in an air raid over Syria earlier in the month.[70] Out of this history of black citizen diplomats there is a fairly discernible model and pattern.

On the whole, African American citizen diplomats have been (1) well-known domestic leaders, (2) spokespersons for a specific issue, (3) persons wanting to activate world public opinion, and (4) citizens who want to reshape American foreign policy. However, the Jackson forays depart significantly from the models of the past. They differed from past efforts because Jackson was an announced Democratic presidential candidate in the midst of the presidential primary season and had a long history of international human rights missions. Jackson also had significant personal relations and friendships with many world leaders. These domestic and global characteristics significantly distance the

President Bush in a meeting with Colin Powell and Condoleezza Rice.   *Source:* Scott Applewhite/AP Images

Jackson model of citizen diplomat from many of his African American predecessors. Jackson's model was different because of his credentials—personal and political.

Moreover, because of the political context of the Democratic presidential primaries, Jackson's citizen diplomat model was ensured of wide media coverage. Hence, successes like attaining the release of Lieutenant Goodman ensured a stepping-stone pattern and greater potential for success in other foreign policy initiatives.[71] Such a linkage enriched the Jackson model and further distanced it from the citizen diplomat models of earlier times. In 1997 President Clinton appointed Jackson as a special unpaid envoy to Africa, thus formally recognizing his citizen diplomacy. During the 1999 NATO air war on Yugoslavia, Jackson led an interfaith delegation to Belgrade and successfully negotiated the release of three American soldiers held captive. The Clinton administration had discouraged Jackson's mission, but congratulated him on its success.

African Americans and the Iraq War

Since the Vietnam War, most African Americans have opposed every U.S. war. Early during the Johnson administration most blacks supported the Vietnam War, but partly as a result of the opposition of Malcolm X, Muhammad Ali, Stokely Carmichael, and Martin Luther King Jr., they turned against the war so that by 1967 "a higher percentage of black Americans felt the war was a mistake and favored quick disengagement than any other group."[72] Since then, from the invasions of Grenada and Panama to the first Iraq War in 1991, blacks have been at the forefront of antiwar sentiments.[73] Such was the case with President Bush's invasion of Iraq in 2003.

Although it is not clear, President Bush apparently decided to invade and occupy Iraq sometime after the 9/11 terrorist attack.[74] Although the record is somewhat ambiguous, Secretary of State Powell was apparently opposed to the war or was at least skeptical, but once Bush took the decision, Powell—"forever the good soldier"—decided to support his commander in chief.[75] Powell did, however, persuade President Bush to seek authority for the war from the Congress and the UN (the UN refused, however, to authorize the war). Condoleezza Rice, on the other hand, was by all accounts an advocate of the war, coordinator of the decision making, and a vigorous public spokesperson.[76]

Powell and Rice's roles in the war led Harry Belafonte, African American entertainer and human rights advocate, to attack them as "house slaves" doing the work of their white master.[77] Although most black leaders and commentators criticized Belafonte for his attack,[78] his sentiments probably resonated well with African American mass opinion. Surveys conducted in the weeks leading up to the war showed, as one headline read: "Blacks Least Likely to Support War."[79] For example, an April 2003 poll found that 81 percent of whites, 61 percent of Hispanics, but only 39 percent of blacks supported the war.[80]

The opposition to the war among African Americans was reflected in the positions of black leaders. The NAACP and other civil rights organizations expressed opposition, the National Baptist Convention adopted a resolution "prayerful opposed to our country

The Reverend Jesse Jackson on one of his many exercises in citizen diplomacy. Here he is with Cuban leader Fidel Castro. On this mission, Jackson secured the release of scores of political prisoners. *Source:* Jacques M. Chenet/Corbis

going to war against Iraq," and the National Conference of Black Political Scientists adopted a resolution condemning the war as immoral, illegal, and as the "twenty-first century's first imperialist war." Jesse Jackson and Al Sharpton opposed the war, and the Nation of Islam's Louis Farrakhan several months before the war went to Baghdad to hold talks with Saddam Hussein, the Iraqi president. While in Iraq, he denounced the U.S. policy as "wicked" and said it was leading to the "mass murder" of the Iraqi people.[81] And of the 37 black voting members of the House, only five supported the Iraq War resolution (Republican J. C. Watts of Oklahoma, and Democrats Sanford Bishop of Georgia, Albert Wynn of Maryland, William Jefferson of Louisiana, and Harold Ford of Tennessee), about 13 percent of the black delegation compared to more than 70 percent of the nonblack House members (the resolution passed 296-133).

African American opposition comes as no surprise to students of U.S. foreign policy. In some ways it is as old as black opposition to the 1848 Mexican–American War and the 1890s war against the Filipino insurgency. Since Vietnam this opposition has come earlier and been more intense and widespread. Scholars trace the sources of this antiwar sentiment in black America to a kind of Third World solidarity with the world's people of color; what one scholar calls an "Afro-Centric" foreign policy perspective.[82] Also, many blacks feel that racism and poverty force many young blacks into the military because they cannot find educational and economic opportunities in the civilian economy. Thus, it is argued that blacks will suffer disproportionate casualties in what some refer to as the "white man's wars." Of the 130,000 troops dispatched to Iraq, 28 percent were black, and as of September 2004, blacks were 13 percent of the 980 killed.[83] Finally, African Americans view U.S. policy toward Iraq with a high degree of skepticism, viewing its war aims as having less to do with freedom and democracy and more to do with oil and economics.[84]

FACES AND VOICES IN THE STRUGGLE FOR UNIVERSAL FREEDOM

RALPH BUNCHE (1904–1971)

Ralph Bunche contributed to the idea of universal freedom in international politics through his work as a founding diplomat at the United Nations. The first African American to be awarded the Nobel Peace Prize (in 1950 for his work in negotiating peace between Arabs and Israelis in 1948), Bunche viewed the UN as indispensable in the maintenance of world peace and the establishment of a rule of law that would respect the human rights and aspirations for freedom of all the world's peoples. Although President Truman in 1949 offered him an appointment that would have made him the first African American assistant secretary of state, Bunche declined, preferring to work as an international rather than an American diplomat. In 1954 he was named UN under secretary general for political affairs, a position he held until his death.

Source: AP Images

Born in Detroit, the son of a barber, Bunche was graduated summa cum laude from UCLA and in 1934 became the first African American to earn a Ph.D. in political science from Harvard. While a professor at Howard University, he wrote a series of monographs on black politics and leadership for the landmark work *An American Dilemma. The Negro Problem and Modern Democracy.* While at the UN he advocated for civil rights in the United States and marched with Martin Luther King Jr. in the famous Selma-to-Montgomery voting rights protest. Throughout, however, he remained committed to the UN as mankind's last best hope for peace, freedom, and equality.*

---

*Charles Henry, *Ralph Bunche: Model Negro or American Other* (New York: New York University Press, 1999).

Apparently this skeptical view of the war and perhaps the daily casualties in Iraq have taken a toll on the enlistment of blacks in the army. According to army data, the percentage of blacks among those enlisting for active duty service fell from 24 percent in 2000 to 14 percent in 2005. This is the lowest percentage for blacks since the all-volunteer service was created in 1973.[85] According to a 2004 report "The U.S. Military Image Study," the percentage of blacks who viewed the military favorably declined from 22 percent in 2003 to 11 percent a year later. And compared with other ethnic groups, black youth are the least supportive of the war, the least likely to believe the war is justified, and the most disapproving of U.S. foreign policy.[86] Accordingly, the army shifted its focus to recruiting Latinos and Asian Americans, whose enlistment percentages between 2000 and 2005 rose from 10.5 to 13.2 percent and 2.6 to 4.1 percent, respectively.[87]

Summary

As with most areas of American life, African Americans have had to struggle to become participants in the making of U.S. foreign policy. But since historically foreign policy in the United States has been the almost exclusive preserve of the white Anglo-Saxon establishment, the black struggle for inclusion here has required innovative and creative strategies involving service in the nation's wars, as diplomats and consuls in official positions, as foreign policy dissenters (from the Mexican–American War to the Vietnam War to the Iraq War), as lobbyists through interest groups such as Trans Africa, and as "citizen-diplomats." In all of these strategies and approaches, African Americans have consistently pursued universal freedom, opposing the international slave trade, imperialist wars, colonialism, and wars of aggression—whether by Italy in Ethiopia or the United States in Vietnam. And in their efforts to influence and shape U.S. foreign policy, the African American minority—sometimes alone and sometimes in coalitions with whites—has produced results that occasionally have directed and reshaped the nation's foreign policy in the direction of its ideal of freedom, universal freedom.

Selected Bibliography

Challenor, Herschell. "The Influence of Black America on U.S. Foreign Policy Toward Africa." In A. A. Said, ed., *Ethnicity and U.S. Foreign Policy.* New York: Praeger, 1981. A good, brief overview of the subject.

DeConde, Alexander. *Ethnicity, Race and American Foreign Policy: A History.* Boston: Northeastern University Press, 1992. An excellent comparative history, covering all major ethnic groups over the course of American history.

Dudziak, Mary. *Cold War Civil Rights* (Princeton. Princeton University Press, 2000). A study of how the international struggle against communism influenced the domestic struggle for civil rights.

Henderson, Errol. *AfroCentrism and World Politics: Toward a New Paradigm.* Westport, CT: Praeger, 1995. An important work that suggests and details a new "Afrocentric" approach to U.S. foreign policy.

Kegley, Charles, and Eugene Wittkopf. *American Foreign Policy: Pattern and Process,* 3rd ed. New York: St. Martin's Press, 1987. A good introduction to the structures and processes of U.S. foreign policy making.

Krenn, Michael. *Black Diplomacy: African Americans and the State Department, 1945–1969.* Amonk, NY: M. E. Sharpe, 1998. A study of the integration of the State Department after 1945 and the appointment of black ambassadors to Africa and other Third World nations.

Krenn, Michael, ed. *The African American Voice in U.S. Foreign Policy Since World War II.* New York: Garland Publishing, 1999. A collection of articles that demonstrates how the fight for civil rights in the United States spilled over into concerns about the cold war and race and foreign policy.

Lusanne, Clarence. *Colin Powell and Condoleezza Rice: Foreign Policy, Race and the New American Century* (Westport, Ct: Praeger, 2006). This first book length study of the role of Powell and Rice in the formulation of US foreign policy is critical of the two diplomats for their failure to embrace their racial identities and stress global equality.

Miller, Jake. *The Black Presence in American Foreign Affairs.* Washington: Howard University Press, 1978. The standard work on the subject, with an excellent summary and overview from a historical perspective.

Skinner, Elliot. *African Americans and U.S. Policy Toward Africa, 1850–1924,* vol. 1. Washington: Howard University Press, 1992. The definitive work by the African American historian and diplomat, with detailed and comprehensive treatment through 1924. Unsurpassed as a source.

Skinner, Elliot, and Pearl Robinson, eds. *Transformation and Resiliency on Africa.* Washington, DC: Howard University Press, 1983. A good collection of case studies and a wonderful essay on the African American intelligentsia and Africa.

Stanford, Karin. *Beyond the Boundaries: Reverend Jesse Jackson in International Affairs.* Albany: State University of New York Press, 1997. A pioneering exploration of the concept of citizen diplomacy, African American citizen diplomats, and Jesse Jackson's role in foreign affairs.

Notes

1. Hanes Walton, Jr., *Black Women at the United Nations* (Irvine, CA: Borgo Press, 1995): chap. 2.
2. John Hope Franklin and Alfred Moss, Jr., *From Slavery to Freedom,* 7th ed. (New York: McGraw-Hill, 1994): 391.
3. John Stanfield, II, "Preface," in Charles Johnson, ed., *Bitter Canaan: The Story of the Negro Republic* (New Brunswick, NJ: Transaction Books, 1987): vii.
4. Jake Miller, *The Black Presence in American Foreign Affairs* (Washington, DC: University Press of America, 1978): 1.
5. Ibid.
6. Elliott P. Skinner, *African Americans and U.S. Policy Toward Africa, 1850–1924: In Defense of Black Nationality,* vol. 1 (Washington, DC: Howard University Press, 1992): 526.
7. Ibid., pp. 515–25. Black nationality is the idea that American blacks should encourage the U.S. government to help create, protect, and defend black nation-states in Africa and the Caribbean, as well as oppose European colonialization and conquest of Africa.
8. Ibid., p. 517.
9. Quoted in Skinner, *African Americans and U.S. Policy,* vol. 1, p. 53.
10. Ibid.
11. Alexander DeConde, *Ethnicity, Race and American Foreign Policy: A History* (Boston: Northeastern University Press, 1992): 39.
12. Miller, *The Black Presence in American Foreign Affairs,* p. 18.
13. Ibid., pp. 23–32. See also Norma Brown, ed., *A Black Diplomat in Haiti: The Diplomatic Correspondence of U.S. Minister Frederick Douglass from Haiti, 1889–1891* (Salisbury, NC: Documentary Publications, 1977).
14. Ibid., p. 32.
15. Skinner, *African Americans and U.S. Policy,* p. 519.
16. Ibid., p. 517.
17. Ibid., pp. 520–21.
18. Miller, *The Black Presence in American Foreign Affairs,* p. 99.
19. Ibid., p. 100.
20. Franklin and Moss, *From Slavery to Freedom,* p. 98. See also Lamont Thomas, *Rise to Be a People: A Biography of Paul Cuffe* (Urbana: University of Illinois Press, 1986).
21. Skinner, *African Americans and U.S. Policy,* p. 52.
22. Booker T. Washington, "Cruelty in the Congo Country," *Outlook* 78 (October 8, 1904): 375–77.
23. Ibid.
24. Franklin and Moss, *From Slavery to Freedom,* p. 296. See also John Hope Franklin, *George Washington William* (Chicago: University of Chicago Press, 1985).
25. "Frederick Douglass on the Mexican American War," in Herbert Aptheker, ed., *A Documentary History of the Negro People,* vol. 1 (New York: Citadel Press, 1967): 267.

26. DeConde, *Ethnicity, Race and American Foreign Policy*, p. 64.
27. Ibid., p. 63.
28. Ibid., p. 65.
29. Reprinted in Willard Gatewood, *Smoked Yankee and the Struggle for Empire: Letters from Negro Soldiers, 1898–1902* (Urbana: University of Illinois, 1975): 279.
30. Willard Gatewood, *Black Americans and the White Man's Burden 1898–1903* (Urbana: University of Illinois Press, 1975): 279.
31. DeConde, *Ethnicity, Race and American Foreign Policy*, p. 66. See also Willard B. Gatewood, Jr., "Black Americans and the Boer War, 1899–1902," *South Atlanta Quarterly* 75 (Spring, 1976): 234.
32. Ibid.
33. Franklin and Moss, *From Slavery to Freedom*, p. 345.
34. Hanes Walton, Jr., "The Southwest Africa Mandate," *Faculty Research Bulletin* 26 (December 1972): 94–98.
35. William Monroe Trotter, "How I Managed to Reach the Peace Conference," in Phillip Foner, ed., *The Voice of Black America* (New York: Simon & Schuster, 1972): 740–42.
36. See Stephen Fox, *Guardian of Boston: William Monroe Trotter* (New York: Atheneum, 1971); George Padmore, "Review of the Paris Peace Conference," *Crisis* (November 1946): 331–33, 347–48; and George Padmore, "Trusteeship: The New Imperialism," *Crisis* (October 1946): 302–9.
37. Franklin and Moss, *From Slavery to Freedom*, p. 433.
38. Ibid.
39. DeConde, *Ethnicity, Race and American Foreign Policy*, p. 107.
40. Miller, *The Black Presence in American Foreign Affairs*, p. 235. See also J. R. Hooker, "The Negro American Press and Africa in the 1930s," *Canadian Journal of African Studies* (March 1967): 43–50; and W. E. B. Du Bois, "Interracial Implications of the Ethiopian Crisis," *Foreign Affairs* 14 (October 1935): 1982–92.
41. DeConde, *Ethnicity, Race and American Foreign Policy*, p. 107.
42. Ibid.
43. Ibid.
44. Ibid., p. 108.
45. Franklin and Moss, *From Slavery to Freedom*, p. 454.
46. Ibid., p. 453.
47. Ibid., p. 236.
48. Ibid., p. 237. See also Mark Solomon, "Black Critics of Colonialism and the Cold War," in T. Patterson, ed., *Cold War Critics* (Chicago: Quadrangle Books, 1971): 205–39. For a comprehensive study of the relationship between the international struggle against communism and the struggle for civil rights see Mary Dudziak, *Cold War Civil Rights* (Princeton: Princeton University Press, 2000).
49. DeConde, *Ethnicity, Race and American Foreign Policy*, p. 149.
50. Franklin and Moss, *From Slavery to Freedom*, p. 462.
51. Deconde, *Ethnicity, Race and American Foreign Policy*, p. 148.
52. Ibid.
53. For a discussion of King's anti-Vietnam remarks, see Martin Luther King Jr., *The Trumpet of Conscience* (New York: Harper & Row, 1968). The first African American civil rights group to oppose the Vietnam War was the SNCC, which did so in 1966, two years before King.
54. Wallace Terry, *Bloods: An Oral History of the Vietnam War* (New York: Random House, 1984): xvi.
55. Lynne Duke, "Emerging Black Anti-War Movement Rooted in Domestic Issues," *Washington Post* (February 8, 1991).

56. Hanes Walton, Jr., "African American Foreign Policy: From Decolonization to Democracy," in Walton, *African American Power and Politics: The Political Context Variable* (New York: Columbia University Press, 1997): chap. 18.

57. Ibid.

58. Ibid.

59. Miller, *The Black Presence in American Foreign Affairs*, pp. 127–242.

60. Karen Stanford, *Beyond the Boundaries: Reverend Jesse Jackson in International Affairs* (Albany: SUNY Press, 1997): 9.

61. Ibid., p. 19.

62. Hanes Walton, Jr., *Invisible Politics: Black Political Behavior* (Albany: SUNY Press, 1985): 294.

63. Elliott P. Skinner, "Booker T. Washington: Diplomatic Initiatives," in Skinner, *African Americans and U.S. Policy*, pp. 291–348.

64. George Schuyler, *Slaves Today: A Story of Liberia* (Baltimore: McGrath, 1931): 5.

65. Ibid., p. 6.

66. Robin Kelley, "This Ain't Ethiopia but It'll Do: African Americans and the Spanish Civil War," in Robin Kelley, *Race Rebels* (New York: Free Press, 1994): 130.

67. Ibid., pp. 123–60.

68. Ibid., pp. 123–24.

69. See Gerald Horne, *Black and Red: W. E. B. Du Bois and the Afro-American Response to the Cold War* (Albany: SUNY Press, 1986).

70. For a short account of that rescue mission, see Wyatt Tee Walker, *The Road to Damascus* (New York: Martin Luther King, Jr. Fellows Press, 1985).

71. Stanford, *Beyond the Boundaries*, pp. 1–4.

72. Peter Levy, "Blacks and the Vietnam War," in Michael Krenn, ed., *The African American Voice in U.S. Foreign Policy Since World War II* (New York: Garland Publishing, 1999): 214.

73. For detailed analysis of survey data on black opposition to the first Iraq War, see Robert C. Smith and Richard Seltzer, *Contemporary Controversies and the American Racial Divide* (Lanham, MD: Rowman & Littlefield, 2000): chap. 3.

74. Todd Purdum, *A Time of Our Choosing: America's War in Iraq* (New York: Times Books, 2004); and Bob Woodward, *Plan of Attack* (New York: Simon & Schuster, 2004).

75. James Mann, "Colin Powell, Forever the 'Good Soldier' " *Los Angeles Times*, March 28, 2004.

76. For a critique from an Afro-Centric perspective of the role of Powell and Rice in the formulation of US foreign policy see Clarence Lusanne, *Colin Powell and Condoleezza Rice Foreign Policy, Race and the New American Century* (Westport, CT: Praeger, 2006).

77. Colbert King, "Belafonte vs. Powell Revisited," *Washington Post*, March 6, 2004.

78. Steven Miller, "Black Leaders Hit Belafonte for Slur," *Washington Times*, November 6, 2002.

79. Chaka Ferguson, "Blacks Least Likely to Support War in Iraq," *West County Times*, February 25, 2003.

80. Darryl Fears, "Hispanics Split Over Iraq War," *Washington Post*, April 9, 2003.

81. "Farrakhan in Iraq Hopes to Stave off U.S. Strike," tehrantimes.com, July 8, 2002.

82. Errol Henderson, *Afrocentrism and World Politics: Toward a New Paradigm* (Westport, CT: Praeger, 1995).

83. "A Portrait of the U.S. Dead," *USA Today*, September 8, 2004.

84. Smith and Seltzer, *Contemporary Controversies and the American Racial Divide*, pp. 52–54.

85. Drew Brown, "Enlistment of Blacks in US Army Declines," *West County Times*, December 21, 2005.

86. Ibid.

87. Ibid.

The Declaration of Independence

In Congress, July 4, 1776
The Unanimous Declaration of the Thirteen United States of America

When in the course of human events it becomes necessary for one people to dissolve the political bands which have connected them with another, and to assume, among the powers of the earth, the separate and equal station to which the Laws of Nature and of Nature's God entitle them, a decent respect to the opinions of mankind requires that they should declare the causes which impel them to the separation.

We hold these truths to be self-evident, that all men are created equal, that they are endowed by their Creator with certain unalienable Rights, that among these are Life, Liberty and the pursuit of Happiness. That to secure these rights, Governments are instituted among Men, deriving their just powers from the consent of the governed. That whenever any Form of Government becomes destructive of these ends, it is the Right of the People to alter or to abolish it, and to institute new Government, laying its foundation on such principles and organizing its powers in such form, as to them shall seem most likely to effect their Safety and Happiness. Prudence, indeed, will dictate that Governments long established should not be changed for light and transient causes; and accordingly all experience hath shewn that mankind are more disposed to suffer, while evils are sufferable, than to right themselves by abolishing the forms to which they are accustomed. But when a long train of abuses and usurpations, pursuing invariably the same Object evinces a design to reduce them under absolute Despotism, it is their right, it is their duty, to throw off such Government, and to provide new Guards for their future security.—Such has been the patient sufferance of these Colonies; and such is now the necessity which constrains them to alter their former Systems of Government. The history of the present King of Great Britain is a history of repeated injuries and usurpations, all having in direct object the establishment of an absolute Tyranny over these States. To prove this, let Facts be submitted to a candid world.

He has refused his Assent to Laws, the most wholesome and necessary for the public good.

He has forbidden his Governors to pass Laws of immediate and pressing importance, unless suspended in their operation till his Assent should be obtained; and when so suspended, he has utterly neglected to attend to them.

He has refused to pass other Laws for the accommodation of large districts of people, unless those people would relinquish the right of Representation in the Legislature, a right inestimable to them and formidable to tyrants only.

He has called together legislative bodies at places unusual, uncomfortable, and distant from the depository of their Public Records, for the sole purpose of fatiguing them into compliance with his measures.

He has dissolved Representative Houses repeatedly, for opposing with manly firmness his invasions on the rights of the people.

He has refused for a long time, after such dissolutions, to cause others to be elected; whereby the Legislative Powers, incapable of Annihilation, have returned to the People at large for their exercise, the State remaining in the mean time exposed to all the dangers of invasion from without, and convulsions within.

He has endeavored to prevent the population of these States; for that purpose obstructing the Laws of Naturalization of Foreigners; refusing to pass others to encourage their migration hither, and raising the conditions of new Appropriations of Lands.

He has obstructed the Administration of Justice, by refusing his Assent to Laws for establishing Judiciary powers.

He has made Judges dependent on his Will alone, for the tenure of their offices, and the amount and payment of their salaries.

He has erected a multitude of New Offices, and sent hither swarms of Officers to harass our people, and eat out their substance.

He has kept among us, in times of peace, Standing Armies without the Consent of our legislatures.

He has affected to render the Military independent of and superior to the Civil power.

He has combined with others to subject us to a jurisdiction foreign to our constitution, and unacknowledged by our laws, giving his Assent to their Acts of pretended Legislation:

For quartering large bodies of armed troops among us:

For protecting them, by a mock Trial, from punishment for any Murders which they should commit on the Inhabitants of these States:

For cutting off our Trade with all parts of the world:

For imposing Taxes on us without our Consent:

For depriving us in many cases, of the benefits of Trial by Jury:

For transporting us beyond Seas to be tried for pretended offences:

For abolishing the free System of English Laws in a neighboring Province, establishing therein an Arbitrary government, and enlarging its Boundaries so as to render it at once an example and fit instrument for introducing the same absolute rule into these Colonies:

For taking away our Charters, abolishing our most valuable Laws, and altering fundamentally the Forms of our Governments:

For suspending our own Legislatures, and declaring themselves invested with power to legislate for us in all cases whatsoever.

He has abdicated Government here, by declaring us out of his Protection and waging War against us.

He has plundered our seas, ravaged out Coasts, burnt out towns, and destroyed the lives of our people.

He is at this time transporting large Armies of foreign Mercenaries to compleat the works of death, desolation and tyranny, already begun with circumstances of Cruelty and perfidy scarcely paralleled in the most barbarous ages, and totally unworthy the Head of a civilized nation.

He has constrained our fellow Citizens taken Captive on the high Seas to bear Arms against their Country, to become the executioners of their friends and Brethren, or to fall themselves by their Hands.

He has excited domestic insurrections amongst us, and has endeavored to bring on the inhabitants of our frontiers, the merciless Indian Savages, whose known rule of warfare, is an undistinguished destruction of all ages, sexes and conditions.

In every stage of these Oppressions We have Petitioned for Redress in the most humble terms: Our repeated Petitions have been answered only by repeated injury: A Prince, whose character is thus marked by every act which may define a Tyrant, is unfit to be the ruler of a free people.

Nor have We been wanting in attention to our British brethren. We have warned them from time to time of attempts by their legislature to extend an unwarrantable jurisdiction over us. We have reminded them of the circumstances of our emigration and settlement here. We have appealed to their native justice and magnanimity; and we have conjured them by the ties of our common kindred to disavow these usurpations, which would inevitably interrupt our connections and correspondence. They too have been deaf to the voice of justice and consanguinity. We must, therefore, acquiesce in the necessity, which denounces our Separation, and hold them, as we hold the rest of mankind, Enemies in War, in Peace Friends.

We, therefore, the Representatives of the United States of America, in General Congress, Assembled, appealing to the Supreme Judge of the world for the rectitude of our intentions, do, in the Name, and by Authority of the good People of these Colonies, solemnly publish and declare, That these United Colonies are, and of Right ought to be Free and Independent States; that they are Absolved from all Allegiance to the British Crown, and that all political connection between them and the State of Great Britain, is and ought to be totally dissolved: and that as Free and Independent States, they have full power to levy War, conclude Peace, contract Alliances, establish Commerce, and to do all other Acts and Things which Independent States may of right do. And for the support of this Declaration, with a firm reliance on the protection of divine Providence, we mutually pledge to each other our Lives, our Fortunes and our sacred Honor.

JOHN HANCOCK

NEW HAMPSHIRE
Josiah Bartlett,
Wm. Whipple,
Matthew Thornton.

MASSACHUSETTS BAY
Saml. Adams,
John Adams,
Robt. Treat Paine,
Elbridge Gerry.

RHODE ISLAND
Step. Hopkins,
William Ellery.

CONNECTICUT
Roger Sherman,
Saml. Huntington,
Wm. Williams,
Oliver Wolcott.

NEW YORK
Wm. Floyd,
Phil. Livingston,
Frans. Lewis,
Lewis Morris.

NEW JERSEY
Richd. Stockton,
Jn. Witherspoon,
Fras. Hopkinson,
John Hart,
Abra. Clark.

PENNSYLVANIA
Robt. Morris,
Benjamin Rush,
Benj. Franklin,
John Morton,
Geo. Clymer,
Jas. Smith,
Geo. Taylor,
James Wilson,
Geo. Ross.

DELAWARE
Caesar Rodney,
Geo. Read,
Tho. M'kean.

MARYLAND
Samuel Chase,
Wm. Paca,
Thos. Stone,
Charles Caroll of
Carrollton.

VIRGINIA
George Wythe,
Richard Henry Lee,
Th. Jefferson,
Benj. Harrison,
Thos. Nelson, jr.,
Francis Lightfoot Lee,
Carter Braxton.

NORTH CAROLINA
Wm. Hooper,
Joseph Hewes,
John Penn.

SOUTH CAROLINA
Edward Rutledge,
Thos. Heyward, Junr.,
Thomas Lynch, Junr.,
Arthur Middleton.

GEORGIA
Button Gwinnett,
Lyman Hall,
Geo. Walton.

Parts of the Constitution Relating to the Presence of Africans in America

ARTICLE I

SECTION 2.   Representatives and direct Taxes shall be apportioned among the several States which may be included within this Union, according to their respective Numbers which shall be determined by adding to the whole Number of free Persons, including those bound to Service for a Term of Years, and excluding Indians not taxed, three fifths of all other Persons.

SECTION 9.   The Migration or Importation of such Persons as any of the States now existing shall think proper to admit, shall not be prohibited by the Congress prior to the Year one thousand eight hundred and eight, but a Tax or duty may be imposed on such Importation, not exceeding ten dollars for each Person.

ARTICLE IV

SECTION 2.   No Person held to Service or Labour in one State under the Laws thereof, escaping into another, shall, in Consequence of any Law or Regulation therein, be discharged from such Service or Labour, but shall be delivered up on Claim of the Party to whom such Service or Labour may be due.

ARTICLE V

Provided that no Amendment which may be made prior to the Year One thousand eight hundred and eight shall in any Manner affect the first and fourth Clauses in the Ninth Section of the first Article;

AMENDMENT XIII

[RATIFIED ON DECEMBER 6, 1865]

SECTION 1.   Neither slavery nor involuntary servitude, except as a punishment for crime whereof the party shall have been duly convicted, shall exist within the United States, or any place subject to their jurisdiction.

SECTION 2.   Congress shall have power to enforce this article by appropriate legislation.

Amendment XIV

[Ratified on July 9, 1868]

Section 1.   All persons born or naturalized in the United States, and subject to the jurisdiction thereof, are citizens of the United States and of the State wherein they reside. No State shall make or enforce any law which shall abridge the privileges or immunities of citizens of the United States; nor shall any State deprive any person of life, liberty, or property, without due process of law; nor deny to any person within its jurisdiction the equal protection of the laws.

Section 2.   Representatives shall be apportioned among the several States according to their respective numbers, counting the whole number of persons in each State, excluding Indians not taxed. But when the right to vote at any election for the choice of electors for President and Vice President of the United States, Representatives in Congress, the Executive and Judicial officers of a State, or the members of the Legislature thereof is denied to any of the male inhabitants of such State, being twenty-one years of age, and citizens of the United States or in any way abridged, except for participation in rebellion, or other crime, the basis of representation therein shall be reduced in the proportion which the number of such male citizens shall bear to the whole number of male citizens twenty-one years of age in such State.

Section 3.   No person shall be a Senator or Representative in Congress, or elector of President and Vice President, or hold any office, civil or military, under the United States, or under any State, who, having previously taken an oath, as a member of Congress, or as an officer of the United States, or as a member of any State legislature, or as an executive or judicial officer of any State, to support the Constitution of the United States, shall have engaged in insurrection or rebellion against the same, or given aid or comfort to the enemies thereof. But Congress may by a vote of two-thirds of each House, remove such disability.

Section 4.   The validity of the public debt of the United States, authorized by law, including debts incurred for payment of pensions and bounties for services in suppressing insurrection or rebellion, shall not be questioned. But neither the United States nor any State shall assume or pay any debt or obligation incurred in aid of insurrection or rebellion against the United States, or any claim for the loss or emancipation of any slave, but all such debts, obligations and claims shall be held illegal and void.

Section 5.   The Congress shall have power to enforce, by appropriate legislation, the provisions of this article.

Amendment XV

[Ratified on February 3, 1870]

Section 1.   The right of citizens of the United States to vote shall not be denied or abridged by the United States or by any State on account of race, color, or previous condition of servitude.

Section 2.   The Congress shall have power to enforce this article by appropriate legislation. . . .

Martin Luther King Jr.'s "I Have a Dream" Speech

I am happy to join with you today in what will go down in history as the greatest demonstration for freedom in the history of our nation.

Fivescore years ago, a great American, in whose symbolic shadow we stand today, signed the Emancipation Proclamation. This momentous decree came as a great beacon light of hope to millions of Negro slaves who had been seared in the flames of withering injustice. It came as a joyous daybreak to end the long night of their captivity.

But one hundred years later, the Negro still is not free; one hundred years later, the life of the Negro is still sadly crippled by the manacles of segregation and the chains of discrimination; one hundred years later, the Negro lives on a lonely island of poverty in the midst of a vast ocean of material prosperity; one hundred years later, the Negro is still languished in the corners of American society and finds himself in exile in his own land.

So we've come here today to dramatize a shameful condition. In a sense we've come to our nation's capital to cash a check. When the architects of our republic wrote the magnificent words of the Constitution and the Declaration of Independence, they were signing a promissory note to which every American was to fall heir. This note was the promise that all men, yes, black men as well as white men, would be guaranteed the unalienable rights of life, liberty, and the pursuit of happiness.

It is obvious today that America has defaulted on this promissory note in so far as her citizens of color are concerned. Instead of honoring this sacred obligation, America has given the Negro people a bad check; a check which has come back marked "insufficient funds." We refuse to believe that there are insufficient funds in the great vaults of opportunity of this nation. And so we've come to cash this check, a check that will give us upon demand the riches of freedom and the security of justice.

We have also come to this hallowed spot to remind America of the fierce urgency of now. This is no time to engage in the luxury of cooling off or to take the tranquilizing drug of gradualism. Now is the time to make real the promises of democracy; now is the time to rise from the dark and desolate valley of segregation to the sunlit path of racial justice; now is the time to lift our nation from the quicksands of racial injustice to the solid rock of brotherhood; now is the time to make justice a reality for all God's children. It would be fatal for the nation to overlook the urgency of the moment. This sweltering summer of the Negro's legitimate discontent will not pass until there is an invigorating autumn of freedom and equality.

Nineteen sixty-three is not an end, but a beginning. And those who hope that the Negro needed to blow off steam and will now be content, will have a rude awakening if the nation returns to business as usual.

There will be neither rest nor tranquility in America until the Negro is granted his citizenship rights. The whirlwinds of revolt will continue to shake the foundations of our nation until the bright day of justice emerges.

But there is something that I must say to my people who stand on the warm threshold which leads into the palace of justice. In the process of gaining our rightful place we must not be guilty of wrongful deeds.

Let us not seek to satisfy our thirst for freedom by drinking from the cup of bitterness and hatred. We must forever conduct our struggle on the high plane of dignity and discipline. We must not allow our creative protest to degenerate into physical violence. Again and again we must rise to the majestic heights of meeting physical force with soul force.

The marvelous new militancy which has engulfed the Negro community must not lead us to a distrust of all white people, for many of our white brothers, as evidenced by their presence here today, have come to realize that their destiny is tied up with our destiny and they have come to realize that their freedom is inextricably bound to our freedom. This offense we share mounted to storm the battlements of injustice must be carried forth by a biracial army. We cannot walk alone.

And as we walk, we must make the pledge that we shall always march ahead. We cannot turn back. There are those who are asking the devotees of civil rights, "When will you be satisfied?" We can never be satisfied as long as the Negro is the victim of the unspeakable horrors of police brutality.

We can never be satisfied as long as our bodies, heavy with fatigue of travel, cannot gain lodging in the motels of the highways and the hotels of the cities. We cannot be satisfied as long as the Negro's basic mobility is from a smaller ghetto to a larger one.

We can never be satisfied as long as our children are stripped of their selfhood and robbed of their dignity by signs stating "for whites only." We cannot be satisfied as long as a Negro in Mississippi cannot vote and a Negro in New York believes he has nothing for which to vote. No, we are not satisfied, and we will not be satisfied until justice rolls down like waters and righteousness like a mighty stream.

I am not unmindful that some of you have come here out of excessive trials and tribulation. Some of you have come fresh from narrow jail cells. Some of you have come from areas where your quest for freedom left you battered by the storms of persecution and staggered by the winds of police brutality. You have been the veterans of creative suffering. Continue to work with the faith that unearned suffering is redemptive.

Go back to Mississippi; go back to Alabama; go back to South Carolina; go back to Georgia; go back to Louisiana; go back to the slums and ghettos of the northern cities, knowing that somehow this situation can, and will be changed. Let us not wallow in the valley of despair.

So I say to you, my friends, that even though we must face the difficulties of today and tomorrow, I still have a dream. It is a dream deeply rooted in the American dream that one day this nation will rise up and live out the true meaning of its creed—we hold these truths to be self-evident, that all men are created equal.

I have a dream that one day on the red hills of Georgia, sons of former slaves and sons of former slave-owners will be able to sit down together at the table of brotherhood.

I have a dream that one day, even the state of Mississippi, a state sweltering with the heat of injustice, sweltering with the heat of oppression, will be transformed into an oasis of freedom and justice.

I have a dream my four little children will one day live in a nation where they will not be judged by the color of their skin but by the content of their character. I have a dream today!

I have a dream that one day, down in Alabama, with its vicious racists, with its governor having his lips dripping with the words of interposition and nullification, that one day, right there in Alabama, little black boys and black girls will be able to join hands with little white boys and white girls as sisters and brothers. I have a dream today!

I have a dream that one day every valley shall be exalted, every hill and mountain shall be made low, the rough places shall be made plain, and the crooked places shall be made straight and the glory of the Lord will be revealed and all flesh shall see it together.

This is our hope. This is the faith that I go back to the South with.

With this faith we will be able to hear out of the mountain of despair a stone of hope. With this faith we will be able to transform the jangling discords of our nation into a beautiful symphony of brotherhood.

With this faith we will be able to work together, to pray together, to struggle together, to go to jail together, to stand up for freedom together, knowing that we will be free one day. This will be the day when all of God's children will be able to sing with new meaning—"my country 'tis of thee; sweet land of liberty; of thee I sing; land where my fathers died, land of the pilgrim's pride; from every mountain side, let freedom ring"—and if America is to be a great nation, this must become true.

So let freedom ring from the prodigious hilltops of New Hampshire.

Let freedom ring from the mighty mountains of New York.

Let freedom ring from the heightening Alleghenies of Pennsylvania.

Let freedom ring from the snow-capped Rockies of Colorado.

Let freedom ring from the curvaceous slopes of California.

But not only that.

Let freedom ring from Stone Mountain of Georgia.

Let freedom ring from Lookout Mountain of Tennessee.

Let freedom ring from every hill and molehill of Mississippi, from every mountainside, let freedom ring.

And when we allow freedom to ring, when we let it ring from every village and hamlet, from every state and city, we will be able to speed up that day when all of God's children—black men and white men, Jews and Gentiles, Catholics and Protestants—will be able to join hands and to sing in the words of the old Negro spiritual, "Free at last, free at last; thank God Almighty, we are free at last."

Washington, D.C.
August 28, 1963